Defining Rape

Defining Rape

Linda Brookover Bourque

Duke University Press   Durham and London 1989

© 1989 Duke University Press
All rights reserved
Printed in the United States of America
on acid-free paper ∞
Library of Congress Cataloging-in-Publication Data
Bourque, Linda Brookover, 1941–
Defining rape / Linda Brookover Bourque.
p.   cm.
Bibliography: p.
Includes index.
ISBN 0-8223-0901-7
1. Rape—United States.   2. Rape—California—Los Angeles—Case
studies.   3. Rape—United States—Public opinion.   4. Public
opinion—United States.   5. Rape—Research—United States.
I. Title.
HV6561.B68   1989
364.1'532'0973—dc1988-30764

For my parents and Lisa, Amy, Eliza, Jacob, and Sam

Contents

Tables

Figures

Preface

When I have told friends that I am writing a book on how people define rape, I have often been met with puzzled responses and comments that say, in effect, "What's to define? Everyone knows what rape is." Not so. Except at the extremes, there is much disagreement in evaluating a particular instance as a rape or not a rape.

The topic itself is an emotionally loaded one; many prefer to deny its existence or at least to avoid dealing with it. As a result, definitional consensus is difficult to attain. Scholars, clinicians, community members, jurors, and legislators disagree on what constitutes a rape and what may be the line between assertive persuasion and impermissible force or assault. Frequently the perpetrators and even the victims of what is legally rape do not themselves define the encounter as a rape. Such confusion and lack of consensus make intervention and legal protections difficult to enforce.

This book aims to provide a comprehensive review of the research on rape, with particular emphasis on why people differ in their recognition of sexual violence. A second aim is to present a comparison of some major community studies of rape attitudes and judgments. Studies of victims, perpetrators, the judicial system and the law, and the many studies done under the rubric of attribution theory are reviewed.

Another objective of the book is to examine the research methodologies used in rape research. Vignettes, widely used in rape research, are of particular interest. The relative strengths and weaknesses of research designs used in various studies, several of which are summarized in some detail, are examined.

It is the author's hope that this book will be useful and of interest to sociologists, clinical and social psychologists, criminologists, lawyers, public health and social welfare professionals, and also to methodologists interested in cross-disciplinary research and the use of vignettes.

Acknowledgments

Many people have contributed to this book and the study reported as part of it. The research proposal for the study was written in collaboration with Josiah Golden, Howard Freeman, and Linda Nilson. Funding for the research was provided under National Institute of Mental Health Grant R01 MH30720. Richard Berk, Rita Engelhardt, Miles Rogers, Peter Rossi, Tom Smith, and Don Witzke provided consultation on the design of vignettes at different times during the proposal writing and study periods. A Community Advisory Committee met during the design of the study to insure that the final questionnaire and vignettes profited from the advice and counsel of nonacademic practitioners familiar with the problem of rape. Serving on the committee were George Dell, then judge of the Superior Court, Connie Guerrero, Jean Holtz, Jean Matusinka, then of the Domestic Violence Unit, Terri Price, then a doctoral student in clinical psychology at UCLA, and Regina Pally, a psychiatrist in private practice.

Eve Fielder, director of the Survey Research Center, Institute for Social Science Research (ISSR), University of California, Los Angeles, supervised data-gathering and data-reduction operations and provided helpful suggestions throughout the course of the study period. Vi Dorfman assisted in the design and formatting of the questionnaires and questionnaire specifications. As field supervisor, Ms. Dorfman took charge of the actual interviewing and, with the help of Kathy Thompson and Jean Mielke, supervised the seventeen interviewers who worked on the project at different times. Geri Greenberg, Betty Gould, Winifred Henke, and Rosellen Welle served as interviewers throughout the project and provided particularly helpful suggestions while the questionnaire was being developed and pretested.

Rita Engelhardt, head of statistical services for the ISSR, developed the sample plan, provided consultation on blocked designs, and wrote the programs that created the vignettes used in the study. Rita also suggested the use of contrast matrices to summarize vignette rating patterns and, with the assistance of Beverly Cosand, devised the vignette-collapsing procedures described in appendix 2. Cheryl Groves and Kathleen O'Kane supervised the coding of the questionnaires, and Madeleine De Maria, assistant director of the Institute, assisted in budget preparation and monitoring and handled various administrative problems over the course of the study.

Larry Landers served as research assistant during the first part of the study and devised the procedures used for the data processing and documentation of the vignettes. Collier Butler Kaler devised procedures for obtaining the neighborhood crime rates used in part III and made numerous other contributions during the middle stages of data collection and analysis. Magda Stayton provided bibliographic and clerical assistance during the second year of the data collection.

Of greatest importance were the contributions of Beverly Cosand who was with the study from its inception through much of the final analysis. Ms. Cosand coordinated activities with the Survey Research Center, developed protocols for data processing, and assisted in data analysis and interpretation throughout the study period.

At different stages in the writing process, a number of people read and made helpful comments on drafts or portions of the manuscript. These included Carol Aneshensel, Ralph Dunlap, Jeanne Giovannoni, Jacqueline Goodchilds, Wyatt Jones, and Susan Sorenson. The thorough and constructive suggestions of the two anonymous reviewers for Duke University Press were particularly helpful and, along with the careful editing provided at different times by Jody Jenkins, Margaret Norman, Elizabeth Tornquist, and Patience Vanderbush, significantly improved the final product. Thyne Sieber provided badly needed bibliographic assistance while part II was being written. My brothers, George and Tom Brookover, helped explain some of the judicial terms described and were particularly helpful in critiquing some of the footnotes. Carey Reid and Shirley Yuen provided clerical assistance, and Jennifer Bhattacharya and Heather Leicester taught me how to make the figures. Nonie Holz, Ralph Dunlap, and Gloria Krauss assisted with proofreading and construction of the index.

Finally, I must recognize the important but intangible contributions of Kurt Back, Ralph Dunlap, and Jeanne Giovannoni, who really believed that this book would be completed and provided psychological support and understanding throughout the sometimes frustrating process of its completion.

Part I Introduction

1 Rape and Society

Over the last twenty years the visibility of rape and society's response to it have increased dramatically. Police departments and hospitals have developed special programs to increase the sensitivity of their personnel to rape victims; twenty-four-hour hotlines have been installed across the United States; self-help and other counseling groups have been developed to assist victims, families, and friends in coping with the aftermath of rape. Old laws have been changed and new ones enacted to ensure that victims of rape obtain a fair hearing and rapists are punished. Research and popular literature on rape have increased dramatically.

As a result of society's concern, there has been a vast increase in the number of persons involved in defining rape and deciding, in any given instance, whether rape has occurred. In the past it was primarily the police who made such decisions. Now family, friends, anonymous counselors on hot lines, emergency room personnel, mental health therapists, social workers, and victims themselves actively participate in deciding whether a rape has occurred, should be reported, prosecution sought, and compensation obtained. As the number and diversity of reported sexual assaults increase and the array of persons involved in defining and responding broadens, so do definitions of rape and conflict about which cases are worthy of attention and scarce resources. A recent case in Pasadena, California highlights the confusion that sometimes results from diverse perceptions of rape.

Pasadena Superior Court, May 1986

The Case

In the Spring of 1986, Pasadena Superior Court Judge Gilbert C. Alston dismissed charges of rape and sodomy brought by Rhonda DaCosta, a thirty-year-old Hispanic prostitute, against Daniel Zabuski, a white male in his mid-twenties. After dismissing the suit, Judge Alston commented, "A whore is a whore is a whore!"

According to court transcripts, Zabuski picked up the alleged victim, Rhonda DaCosta, on the evening of July 10, 1985. DaCosta testified she agreed to perform oral copulation for $30, but said Zabuski was not satisfied, became "extremely violent," and forced her to engage in sexual intercourse and sodomy (Arax, 1986). Judge Alston said in court that a working prostitute could not be the victim of a rape, even if she was forced to engage in sexual intercourse.

After granting his own motion for dismissal of the case, Alston told jurors, "I have never seen a case like this before. And I would like to apologize for having you spend your time doing what essentially was trying to reform or decide a breach of contract between a whore and trick" (Arax, 1986). During a subsequent interview Alston elaborated, saying, "A woman who goes out on the street and makes a whore out of herself opens herself up to anybody. She steps outside the protection of the law. That's a basic and fundamental legal concept . . ." (Arax, 1986). Deputy District Attorney JoAnne Barton, attorney Gloria Allred, Sandy Buttitta, head of the district attorney's sex crimes unit, and a majority of the jury disagreed with Judge Alston's characterization of the case.

Deputy District Attorney Barton objected strongly to Alston's dismissal of the case, saying that Alston had displayed bias against the alleged victim throughout the proceedings, constantly referring to her in private deliberations as a "whore," and allowing Zabuski's attorney to ask questions about Ms. DaCosta's personal life. When asked by Mark Arax of the *Los Angeles Times* to comment on the case, Professor John Kaplan of Stanford University Law School agreed with the prosecutor, saying, "The Legislature has decided very clearly that rape is sexual intercourse without the consent of a woman to sexual intercourse. The judge's decision strikes me as insupportable. It's wrong" (Arax, 1986).

Attorney Allred filed a complaint against Judge Alston with the State Commission on Judicial Performance, which subsequently reported that "appropriate corrective action" had been taken. Consistent with commission policy and the level of sanction imposed, the nature of the "corrective action" was not made public. Allred also asked Los Angeles County prosecutors to boycott Judge Alston's court when victims of any crime were female and initiated a civil suit against Mr. Zabuski on Ms. DaCosta's behalf.

Sandy Buttitta, head of the sex crimes unit, who said she routinely processed rape cases in which the victim was a prostitute, was quoted by the *Los Angeles Times* as saying, "They are difficult cases because people in the community hold certain prejudices. But a prostitute can be raped. Just because you agree to one form of sex doesn't necessarily mean you agree to everything" (Arax, 1986).

What is unusual about this case is not the action of Judge Alston. Numerous cases have come to public attention in the last decade in which judicial behaviors clearly were determined by personal definitions of rape rather than by judicial precedent or existent legislation. What is unique is the willingness of a sex crimes unit to take rape of prostitutes seriously, a district attorney's office to prosecute such cases, and lawyers unassociated with the case to publicly condemn the decision of one of their colleagues. Of even greater interest is the media's continued attention to the case and jury members' obvious irritation with Judge Alston's behavior.

Because the case was dismissed before going to the jury, we will never know what the jury would have decided. Many members of the jury, however, publicly criticized Judge Alston's dismissal. Juror Sunnie Linscott said, "I was just thunderstruck at his whole statement . . . the whole idea of what he was saying. I interpreted it as meaning, 'We don't give rights to prostitutes.'" Juror Mary Ann Clayton said, "The consensus among us was that a prostitute could be raped and that this prostitute was a credible witness. We were all frustrated that the judge didn't allow us to decide the case" (Arax, 1986).

Although members of the jury (which included men and women; whites, blacks, and Hispanics; persons from thirty to sixty years old most of whom had at least some post-high school education) thought the prosecution's case was weak and coming to a unanimous guilty verdict would have been improbable, they were united in their belief that Zabuski was guilty and that Alston's reasons for dismissing the charges were out of line.

Implications

The Zabuski case emphasizes the wide diversity of opinions on what constitutes a rape. At the conservative extreme, rape remains a charge "easily made and difficult to defend against." Only vaginal penetration by the penis with evidence of ejaculation counts as a rape. The victim must be above reproach, the perpetrator a psychopathic stranger, and the man must have forced the woman, preferably with a weapon, to have intercourse. The woman must not have consented and must have actively resisted the attack, preferably to the point of injury. The act must have been witnessed, and the victim must have reported the assault immediately to the police.

At the liberal extreme, any sexual behavior, even off-color jokes at work, unsolicited use of diminutives, or a hand on the arm, constitutes rape if a woman indicates by word or deed that such actions impinge on her personal space. Here context—be it inside marriage, on a date, or with a stranger—is irrelevant. Between these conservative and liberal views lie countless other perceptions about what constitutes rape.

Social Perceptions of Rape

Discussions and research on the causes, prevention, and treatment of rape tend to dichotomize the issue: this is a rape; that is not a rape. Each individual has a conscious or unconscious image or definition of rape and makes assumptions about other persons' perceptions. If I am talking about rape with another woman, because she is a woman I might assume that she defines it as I do. Or I might assume that my brothers and I use the same definition, because we were raised in the same household. I might assume that a colleague involved in similar kinds of research has the same definition, because as members of the same professional discipline we have similar training and interests.

Both personal experience and research findings show my assumptions would be wrong. My definition of rape is not necessarily identical to that held by other women, by my siblings, or by my colleagues. Some dimensions I bring to bear in defining a sexual encounter as rape may be similar to those they use, but the worth I attach to a particular dimension may differ radically.

At one end of the continuum is a set of narrowly defined acts unequivocally judged to be rape. At the opposite end are acts judged not to be rape. It is difficult to reach consensus between the two extremes regarding parameters describing rape. For some, passive acquiescence to sex under all circumstances is rape; others may consider it wrong, but will disagree with the view that it is rape. Even less consensus exists in the literature regarding aggressive sexual acts by males against females and how such acts are interpreted.

Furthermore, studies suggest that there is little consensus regarding the kind and amount of information used to decide whether a rape occurred or how various subgroups in contemporary Western society arrive at definitions of rape. Some evidence suggests that women, whites, younger persons, more highly educated persons, and those with nontraditional sex roles define a wider range of sexual encounters as rape (e.g., Williams and Holmes, 1981; Feild, 1978; Klemmack and Klemmack, 1976). More liberal attitudes toward feminism and sexuality also correlate with defining rape more broadly. However, other studies, particularly those conducted within attribution theory,[1] do not replicate these general findings. For example, Alexander (1980) found that persons with more exposure to victims of rape and/or those who perceive themselves as more likely to be victims are more likely to perceive the victim in a simulated rape as responsible for the rape.

Ageton (1983), Koss (1985), Goodchilds (1983), Malamuth (1985), and their colleagues reported that adolescent and college-age males and females differ in their exposure to violence in dating relationships, their acceptance of the appropriateness of such violence, and their perceptions about circumstances that elicit or exacerbate such violence. Williams and Holmes (1981), Feild and Bienen (1980), and Burt (1980) found that community members differ in attitudes about rape and in their perceptions of when a rape has occurred. Burt (1983), Feild (1978), and Scully and Marolla (1984) reported that convicted rapists are more likely than other men in the community to think women do not really mean it when they say "No." Such men believe that these women really are saying they want to be raped. Ageton, Malamuth, Koss, Kanin (1984), and their colleagues found similar differences between males who admit instances of sexual aggression and those who do not. Aggressors said women did not really mean it when they said "No," that such women had engaged in provocative behavior and deserved to be raped.

Both Ageton and Goodchilds and colleagues found that what adolescent boys judge to be provocative behavior or appearance differs substantially from what girls think. Boys are much more likely to equate certain kinds of dress, acts of friendliness, social reputation, agreement to attend certain kinds of events or to go to certain kinds of places as an invitation to or consent to sex. Ageton also reports, however, that participating in aggressive sex either as perpetrator or victim does not correlate with ethnicity, socioeconomic status, or other demographic indicators.

Ageton's findings are consistent with the feminist contention that rapists are no different from other men and are sprinkled evenly throughout society. Her findings, however, are not consistent with studies of judicial records by LaFree and others in which young, lower socioeconomic status blacks are more often found to be both victims and offenders in rape cases. Neither Ageton's nor LaFree's findings concur with recent surveys of victims in which white females are found to be most frequently victimized (e.g., Russell, 1984; Sorensen et al., 1987; Koss and Gidycz, 1987). At the same time some evidence suggests that white females report rapes less frequently than other women, and that black males more often than other men are charged and convicted of rape rather than lesser offenses.

Bohmer (1974), Deming (1984), LaFree (1982), and others have shown that the process by which a rape case enters and proceeds through the judicial system is complex and subject to idiosyncrasies of both the legal system and the persons who serve as gatekeepers at various stages. Numerous writers have documented the extent to which such gatekeepers in the social, medical, and judicial systems fail to take complaints of rape victims seriously, treat them with disdain, and subject them to further pain and suffering if they insist on prosecuting their cases. Feminist writers in particular argue that such treatment is an inherent part of the sexist, male-dominated society in which we live. They believe that because major social institutions such as legislatures, medical establishments, and the judiciary are dominated by males, their official actions and decisions are simply an extension of their conscious and unconscious need to protect their power against encroachment by women.

Galvin and Polk (1984) suggest that research over the last decade attempting to describe, define, and understand rape has been done from the perspective of the victim. If we are to understand where rape falls in the range of human actions, however, we must build our theoretical models from studies of a much broader population including legal, medical, and social helpers as well as incarcerated rapists, self-defined rapists, and so-called normal men.

This Book

This book and the study it reports document the remarkable diversity of opinion that exists within the research literature and within one Southern California community about what constitutes rape, what causes it, and what should be done about it. It examines the influence of social structure on personality and how the two in combination determine behavior we call rape. It assesses society's influence on sexual and violent behavior and looks at the correlation between an individual's position within society and the sexual encounters she or he labels as rape.

The book's focus is on how social roles influence definitions of rape rather than on how or why that influence occurs.[2] Because remarkable diversity exists within every socially definable subgroup regarding almost any behavior or attitude, I do not expect to find that social structures, situations, roles, environments, and/or life-styles completely predict or determine an individual's attitudes toward and perceptions of rape. At the same time I believe that a person's place in society is of much greater import than is generally recognized in the literature in understanding the sexual scripts or norms under which rape is tolerated.

Rape Becomes an Issue

As crime rates began rising in the early and mid-1960s the women's movement was forming and gaining strength. The description below explains how these two events focused attention on rape as a subject of inquiry and legitimate social concern.

Rising Rates of Crime

Between 1933 and 1960 figures compiled by the Federal Bureau of Investigation showed that rates of reported violent crimes compared to other crimes remained constant, declined, or, in the case of rape and aggravated assault, increased at a steady but unremarkable rate (see figure 2.1). Around 1960 a sudden surge in crime occurred. Rates for rape, robbery, and aggravated assault climbed most dramatically. Between 1960 and 1970 the number of reported rapes and aggravated assaults doubled in the United States, while the number of reported robberies nearly tripled. Between 1970 and 1980 reported rapes again doubled, increasing from 18.7 to 36.4 per 100,000 population. Because under the traditional legal definition of rape the victims are always women, this meant that about 70 of every 100,000 females reported rapes in 1980. Because a large proportion of crimes are unreported, these Federal Bureau of Investigation figures present only a partial picture of the incidence of rape.

In a 1972 victimization survey conducted by the Law Enforcement Assistance Administration (LEAA), 315 of every 100,000 females aged 12 or over reported that they had been victims of completed or attempted rape within the past year. Approximately one fourth (6,738) reported completed rapes while the remaining three fourths (20,885) reported attempted rapes (Hindelang and Davis, 1977). Working with the same data, Johnson (1980) estimated that 20–30 percent of women 12 and over would be victims of one or more attempted or completed rapes during their lifetimes.

Estimates of the prevalence of rape from the 1972 victimization survey contrast sharply with those obtained from *Uniform Crime Reports* data for the same year. According to the *Uniform Crime Reports*, 22 rapes and attempted rapes were reported for every 100,000 persons in 1972, or approximately 45 for every 100,000 females. Furthermore, the ratio of completed to attempted rapes reported in official police statistics during the early 1970s is exactly opposite from that obtained in the national victimization surveys. In official statistics 75 percent of reported rapes are completed and 25 percent are attempted; in victimization surveys 25 percent are completed and 75 percent are attempted.

Rape and the Women's Movement

Law-and-order groups and victims' rights groups were the first to incorporate data on rising crime rates into lobbying efforts supportive of capital punishment and greater services for victims. But the value of such data, particularly data on rape, was not lost on members of the women's movement who quickly saw its potential as a rallying point for organizing.[1] Under traditional, common-law definitions of rape, only women are its victims and only men are its perpetrators. Its symbolic value in a movement whose primary objective is to enhance the concerns and status of women was and is enormous.

Publication of Betty Friedan's *The Feminine Mystique* in 1963 and the formation of the National Organization for Women (NOW) in 1966 marked the beginning of the contemporary women's movement. The movement's basic objectives were to obtain equal opportunity and pay for women. But, like any social movement, it needed issues to catalyze consciousness-raising and act as rallying points for organization. Ideally such issues would both provoke the attention of the media and be uniquely relevant to women. During the late 1960s abortion was the primary issue for some; others focused on prostitution. Only in 1970, when it was clear that prostitution had failed as a mobilizing issue, did Susan Griffin and others concentrate their full attention on rape.

The pivotal year for rape as an issue was 1971 when both Kate Millett and Susan Griffin published essays on the topic and the New York Radical Feminists sponsored a "Speak-Out on Rape," providing a forum for women to discuss insensitive treatment by police, doctors, lawyers, and courts and the ways in which fear of rape had restricted their lives. NOW's fourth annual conference formed a task force on the "masculine mystique," focusing on men's apparent acceptance of violence as an appropriate problem-solving mechanism. A major objective of all antirape activities of the 1970s was to point out the similarity of rape to other violent personal crimes and its dissimilarity to other sex crimes.[2]

In 1972 the first rape crisis centers, funded by the National Institute of Justice's Law Enforcement Assistance Administration, opened in Ann Arbor, Michigan, Los Angeles, California, and Washington, D.C. In 1973 Senator Charles Mathias of Maryland introduced the original bill to establish a National Center for the Prevention and Control of Rape in the National Institute of Mental Health. Vetoed by President Ford, the bill was subsequently passed in 1975. The National Center for the Prevention and Control of Rape became a major source of funds for both treatment programs and research (including funding the study reported in this book and many of the studies referenced herein, e.g., Kilpatrick, Veronen, and Best, 1985; Koss and Oros, 1982; Russell, 1984; and Goodchilds and Zellmann, 1984). Also in 1973, by acclamation at its sixth annual conference, NOW established a National Task Force on Rape. In 1974 Michigan became the first state to adopt a completely revised sexual assault statute.

Throughout the early and mid-1970s, feminists developed consciousness-raising groups and rape crisis hotlines. The number of NOW chapters actively engaged in rape-related activities increased from 13 in 1973 to 200 in 1975. Rape cases were publicized through demonstrations and the media. Community services proliferated. By 1977, due primarily to the work of feminists, people had become aware of the antirape movement and were gradually accepting its perception of rape as a serious social problem (Rose, 1977, p. 86).

2 Feminist Theory and Victims of Rape

With few exceptions the first publications in what ultimately became a flood of new research on rape assumed a feminist perspective in which social structure and social context played a dominant role in explaining and describing rape. More specifically, it was with the publication in 1975 of Susan Brownmiller's book, *Against Our Will: Men, Women and Rape,* that feminist psycho-social-cultural theories of rape were first set forth.

As applied to rape, feminist theory is essentially a theory of stratification, social control, and implied social conflict. Its major tenet is that power is unequally distributed by sex: Men have power; women do not. Power is inherent in being male and is enhanced by physical attributes and control over access to education, jobs, and money. Men deny women equal access to social and economic power structures and apply physical, social, and economic pressure to keep them in dependent roles. Society portrays women as passive, expressive, and emotional, characteristics that are viewed negatively. Men are portrayed as aggressive, dominant, and virile, characteristics that are viewed positively.

Gender Roles

Feminists' use of sex or gender as a stratifying social variable is not new. Sex, like race, age, and socioeconomic status, has long been recognized as an important determinant of social stratification. In contemporary Western societies, the social position of the family has traditionally been determined by the male head. Thus, the status of females is determined by males—either husbands or fathers. Females acquire their own status only when they are not attached to males. Within the family, males and females learn appropriate behaviors to maintain the family and society. In the United States, until recently, normative roles limited women to positions in the household sustaining familial needs and concerns, while men performed extrahousehold functions sustaining instrumental familial needs. Although few families ever have been perfectly representative of this societal norm, definitions of rape reflect this idealized social structure.

As males and females out of necessity or choice deviate from traditional social roles, the system by which society stratifies and organizes its members begins to shift. Expectations and behaviors connected with social roles, whether defined by gender, occupation, or class, begin to change. Boundaries between roles become unclear, and individuals fulfilling certain roles become uncertain as to what is expected of them. As individuals adopt new roles and adapt to changing expectations, role strain increases. Persons who continue to conform with traditional roles come into conflict with those who have adopted new roles. Some rape researchers suggest that changes in behaviors and expectations that occur as women move out of traditional roles increase their vulnerability to rape (e.g., Russell, 1975).

Research on the sociology of sex roles (e.g., Huber, 1973; Hochschild, 1973) has led to the application of role and stratification theory to rape. In contrast to prior social science research focusing primarily on male subjects and perspectives, feminist research emphasizes women as study subjects (e.g., Hansen and O'Leary, 1985). Sometimes the major objective is to document women's experiences and feelings; other times the objective is to focus on similarities existing between men and women and to challenge traditional perceptions of differences between the sexes.

The major component of role theory relevant to rape research is that gender roles are learned. While feminist writers acknowledge that innate physiological differences exist between men and women, they argue that most of what we label as feminine or masculine behavior is learned during early socialization and is reinforced by society's normative, institutional, and legal structures. It is their view that what is learned can be unlearned. If society assumes that interactions between males and females are highly differentiated based upon learned gender roles, societies can change their expectations.

Rape and Sex Roles

UNLIKE HOMICIDE

Feminist theorists view rape as extreme sexual exploitation, a violent method for keeping women in their place. Rape, they argue, is a product of a patriarchal society in which rape-supportive beliefs are reinforced by institutions that preserve men's dominance over women. These beliefs are transmitted across generations during sex-role socialization.

According to this perspective, rape is not an isolated act of a sick, *UNLIKE HOMICIDE* sexually deprived, or inadequately developed male; it is aggressive behavior that is an inevitable part of the social milieu. Males are socialized into the role of aggressive seducer while females are socialized into the role of passive prey. Although society limits the amount of aggression it tolerates, permitted aggression also varies with social roles and tolerance increases when actors deviate from expected and socially prescribed behavior. In the case of rape, male aggression is tolerated as appropriate sex-role behavior, particularly when women engage in what is perceived to be sex-inappropriate behavior. Rape is seen, therefore, as a variant or slight extension of socially condoned, normal sexual relations. From this perspective, normal sex is often coercive or nonconsensual sex.[1]

Feminist Contributions to Rape Research

Feminist contributions to rape research are twofold. First and foremost, the women's movement and feminist theory brought rape out of the closet and into mainstream research as a topic of serious study. Second, to increase social awareness of sexual inequities feminist writers eloquently identified prevalent sexual stereotypes pervading the mythology surrounding rape. Griffin (1971) coined the term "rape myths" to refer to assumptions commonly held about rapists, their victims, and the act itself. The term was quickly adopted, and a number of investigators developed indexes to measure the prevalence of rape myths in community studies (e.g., Burt, 1980; Feild and Bienen, 1981; Williams and Holmes, 1981; Schwartz, Williams, and Pepitone-Rockwell, 1981). Results of some of these studies are discussed in chapter 6.

Rape myths include assumptions that women secretly want to be raped, that women cannot be raped against their will, that women provoke rape by leading men on, that rapists are abnormal, that rape is rare, that all rape victims are prostitutes, and that rapes occur because men have uncontrollable sexual needs. Underlying rape myths are assumptions about the sexuality of males and females.

Early feminist writers argued that rape myths underlie the public's conscious opinions about the men and women involved in rape and the circumstances surrounding it. Consistent with such attitudes is the belief that nonconsensual or coercive sex is unremarkable and undeserving of social sanction. These authors hypothesized that wide acceptance of and adherence to such attitudes helped explain judicial attitudes and behaviors brought to bear in processing rape cases. By focusing public attention on rape myths and challenging their accuracy, feminists hoped to initiate social change among both individuals and institutions.

As a result of the publicity and research generated, feminist activists, theorists, and researchers hoped to demonstrate that rape was far more widespread than official statistics revealed. They were also concerned about elucidating the consequences of rape for victims and documenting the fact that rapists often were unexceptional members of the community. Finally, they wished to demonstrate the extent to which attitudes supportive of rape permeated communities and institutions.

Attempts at Specifying and Testing Theory

Curtis (1976), Dietz (1978), and Deming and Eppy (1980) are among the few researchers who have attempted to evaluate research on rape to suggest how rape or feminist hypotheses about it are related to other, more established sociological and psychological theories. Ageton (1982) and Williams and Holmes (1981) were among the first to explicitly test hypotheses derived from feminist theory.

To explain high rates of rape within the black community, while adhering to the early feminist position that all men are socialized in such a way as to promote the potential for committing rape, Curtis adapted Yinger's (1960) concept of subcultures and contracultures. Curtis suggested that black society is a subculture within the dominant culture of white American society with which it shares some values and rejects others. His premise was that a black minority contraculture exists in which violence is a way of expression and a process for obtaining desired objectives. Rape, he hypothesized, is largely a product of this violently oriented contraculture inhabited primarily by young black males. Since rape researchers have generally avoided the issue of race in their research, few explicit tests of Curtis's hypotheses have been made. The exceptions are works by Williams and Holmes (1981) and LaFree (1982).

Williams and Holmes believe rape is an expression against white patriarchy. Rape, or the threat of it, is an important tool of social control in a complex system of racial-sexual stratification. The researchers conducted a study in San Antonio to test the extent to which perceptions of rape differed with ethnicity and gender, and found that perceived risk of rape and attitudes toward it varied with ethnicity and gender in complex ways.

LaFree used hypotheses partially generated from Curtis's findings to test whether differential rates of black/white interracial rape resulted from the breaking down of ethnic barriers leading to greater opportunities for heterosexual interaction or from increased conflict between racial groups. He concluded that data pointed to increased racial conflict, but findings were mixed and suggested that both perspectives needed significant modification.

Without explicit reference to feminist theory, Dietz (1978) looked at how established social and psychological theories explained the behavior of rapists. He suggested that "rape is best understood as an example of violence in male-female relations" (p. 69) and said that existing theories did not account adequately for the *intersection* within rape of sex, violence, and male-female relationships. Among the theories Dietz examined were crime (e.g., rape) as normative (e.g., Durkheim, 1964) or anomic (e.g., Merton, 1968), subcultural theories of crime (e.g., Cohen, 1955), crime as a product of differential opportunity (e.g., Cloward, 1959), crime as a subculture of violence (e.g., Wolfgang and Ferracuti, 1967), crime as having instrumental utility to the social structure (e.g., Dietz, p. 66), crime in relation to role theory (e.g., Gibbons, 1973), and social learning (e.g., Newcomb, 1966). Dietz concluded that none of the eight theories reviewed explained rape adequately, and suggested that an inductive theory of rape should be developed emphasizing its relationship to sexual behavior, violence, and male-female relations.

Using a procedure similar to Dietz's, Deming and Eppy (1980) sorted research on rape into theoretical categories based on the sociological or social psychological perspective(s) the research most explicitly or implicitly resembled. Here the objective was more to identify the variety of theories represented than to develop a new theoretical perspective. Areas considered were ecological and subcultural theories, feminist and conflict theories, sexual access theories, criminal justice system variations, classification of rapists, attribution theory, and victim precipitation.[2] Most studies contained elements of multiple perspectives and the boundaries between perspectives were not easily specified.

Ageton (1983) is one of the few researchers who has considered the relative usefulness of feminist theories in explaining rape. She tested hypotheses generated from feminist theory against those derived from delinquency theory. Of particular interest was the extent to which adolescents involved in sexual assault would hold more traditional views of women and sexuality. She found that delinquency theory (which predicts that rape is committed by adolescents who also have been involved in other delinquent behavior) more adequately explained adolescent participation in assaultive sex.

Theoretical Limitations

Although the women's movement and feminist theory form the backdrop against which most contemporary research on sexual assault and rape has been conducted, a feminist theory of rape has yet to be formulated, and few explicit tests of hypotheses reflecting a feminist perspective have been made. A number of writers have included lengthy summaries of the feminist perspective of rape and sexuality within their works without making explicit efforts to test the propositions put forth (e.g., Russell, 1975). Others simply assume the perspective as given and proceed with their own findings (e.g., Bart and O'Brien, 1985). Still other researchers avoid conflicts between feminist theory and other social and psychological theories by adopting an atheoretical stance or by emphasizing personality and attitudinal variables while ignoring social structural variables in their analyses (e.g., Burt, 1980; Feild and Bienen, 1980).

Researchers are reluctant to confront feminist theory because of its limited and cross-disciplinary history, its tendency implicitly or explicitly to challenge traditional research areas such as criminology, the difficulty of developing appropriate tests, and flaws in the theory itself. A major early flaw leading to difficulties in testing was its tendency to oversimplify the relative social positions of males and females and the nature of their interactions.[3] Although it was never explicitly stated, feminist theorists often implied that traditional indicators of status (e.g., education, income, occupation, race, ethnicity, etc.) are irrelevant to discussions of heterosexual interactions and that only gender matters. Feminist theory failed to account for marked similarities and differences between males and females of the same ethnic communities, social classes, and educational levels.

Research on Women and Rape

Research findings reported during the last ten years challenge many rape myths and provide new information about the extent and diversity of rape.[4] The primary objective has been to broaden knowledge about rape while simultaneously emphasizing the woman's perspective as a victim or as a person vulnerable to rape. To that end, many studies have concentrated on obtaining prevalence rates, challenging available official statistics, and sympathetically documenting the victim's experience. In this chapter and the next, by comparing findings from studies conducted in response to feminist pressure to statistical data on rape, I examine the extent to which feminist objectives have been realized.

Incidence and Prevalence of Rape:
Official Statistics

Figure 2.1 summarizes the rapid rise in reported rapes per 100,000 population between 1933 and 1984. In 1980, 69 attempted or completed forcible rapes were reported to the police for every 100,000 women in the United States (*Uniform Crime Reports*, 1981). National victimization data for 1980 show a rate of 40 completed and 120 attempted rapes per 100,000 females. Table 2.1 shows that similar differences exist between official police reports and data obtained from the National Crime Survey for all years between 1978 and 1983: The number of rapes reported to police represents no more than 50 percent of those reported in the National Crime Survey.[5] Both sources of data suggest that the number of completed and attempted rapes per 100,000 females has reached a plateau or declined slightly in the last

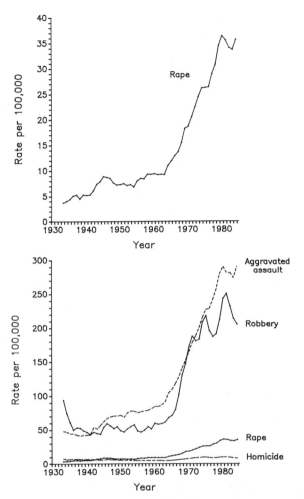

Figure 2.1 Rapes, homicides, robberies, and aggravated assaults reported to police per 100,000 population, United States, 1933–84. Data from *Uniform Crime Reports*, 1979–84, and Hindelang and Davis (1977).

decade. In contrast, the ratio of completed to attempted rapes reported by National Crime Survey respondents appears to have increased, with completed rapes representing a greater proportion of the total reported. Reasons for the apparent stabilizing of overall rates or the changing distribution of completed to attempted rapes are not clear, but both changing attitudes about rape and well-documented inadequacies in official statistics may explain recent shifts (e.g., O'Brien, 1985; Skogan, 1986; Reiss, 1986).

Table 2.1 Estimated incidence and prevalence of completed rapes, attempted rapes, and more inclusive categories of sexual assault as reported in official police reports, National Crime Surveys, and community surveys

Source of data	Year data collected	Sources of data	Response rate for surveys (in percent)	Time period over which data were collected	Denominator data
Official national crime statistics					
Uniform Crime Reports	1978	Official police reports	—	12 months	Rate per 100,000 females
	1979				
	1980				
	1981				
	1982				
	1983				
	1984				
National Crime Survey	1972	10,000 house-holds in 26 cities; persons over 11	95	6 months	Rate per 100,000 females
Johnson, 1982	1972	250,000 persons over 11 in 13 cities	95	6 months	Rate per 100,000 females
Johnson, 1982	1972	Same	Same	Estimate of lifetime prevalence	Rate per 100 females over 11
National Crime Survey	1978	National sample of 116,000 persons in 53,000 households by telephone and face-to-face interview	96	6 months	Rate per 100,000 same sex
National Crime Survey	1979	National sample of 111,000 persons in 51,000 households by telephone and face-to-face interview	96	6 months	Rate per 100,000 of same sex over 11

Women			Men		
Completed rape	Attempted rape	Sexual assault broadly defined	Completed rape	Attempted rape	Sexual assault broadly defined
	60				
	67				
	71				
	69				
	65				
	66				
	69				
77	238				
77					
4–20 percent	4–22 percent				
50	120		#	20	
70	120		#	20	

Table 2.1   (continued)

Source of data	Year data collected	Sources of data	Response rate for surveys (in percent)	Time period over which data were collected	Denominator data
National Crime Survey	1980	National sample of 123,000 persons in 57,000 households by telephone and face-to-face interview	96	6 months	Rate per 100,000 of same sex over 11
National Crime Survey	1981	National sample of 126,000 persons in 59,000 households by telephone and face-to-face interview	96	6 months	Rate per 100,000 of same sex over 11
National Crime Survey	1982	National sample of 127,000 persons in 60,000 households by telephone and face-to-face interview	97	6 months	Rate per 100,000 of same sex over 11
National Crime Survey	1983	National sample of 127,000 persons in 60,000 households by telephone and face-to-face interview	96	6 months	Rate per 100,000 females

Women			Men		
Completed rape	Attempted rape	Sexual assault broadly defined	Completed rape	Attempted rape	Sexual assault broadly defined
40	120		#	20	
50	120		#	10	
50	100		0#	10	
50	90		10#	10#	

Table 2.1   (continued)

Source of data	Year data collected	Sources of data	Response rate for surveys (in percent)	Time period over which data were collected	Denominator data
National Crime Survey	1984	Not available	NA	6 months	Rate per 100,000 persons same sex
National Crime Survey	1985	102,000 persons over 11 in 49,000 households	96	6 months	Rate per 100,000 persons same sex over 11
National Crime Survey	1986	100,000 persons over 11 in 47,000 households	96	6 months	Rate per 100,000 persons same sex over 11
Community surveys of adults					
Russell, 1984	1978	Face-to-face interviews with San Francisco females over 17	67	12 months	930 females
Burt, 1979	1977	Face-to-face interviews with Minnesota residents over 17	Not reported	Lifetime prevalence Lifetime prevalence	328 females & 258 males

Women			Men		
Completed rape	Attempted rape	Sexual assault broadly defined	Completed rape	Attempted rape	Sexual assault broadly defined
52	113			15	
70	60		10#	10#	
40	70		0#	10#	
	2.7 percent				
24 percent a. 8.4 percent "forced sex against your will" b. 3.2 percent "had sex only because afraid of physical force"	41 percent (with marital = 44 percent) c. 26.6 percent	26.4 percent = a and/or b and/or c	1.7 percent	9.6 percent	10.6 percent

Table 2.1 (continued)

Source of data	Year data collected	Sources of data	Response rate for surveys (in percent)	Time period over which data were collected	Denominator data
Kilpatrick et al., 1985	1983	Telephone interviews with 2,004 Charleston County, South Carolina, females over 17	84	Lifetime prevalence	1,985 females
Brickman & Briere, 1984	Not reported	Self-administered questionnaires to 551 Winnipeg females	46.2	Lifetime prevalence	551 females
DiVasto et al., 1984	Not reported	Self-administered questionnaires to convenience sample of 500 females	97	Lifetime prevalence	500 females
George & Winfield-Laird, 1986	Not reported	Face-to-face interviews with 3,981 community & 502 institutionalized black and white residents of Durham, Vance, Franklin, Granville, & Warren Counties in North Carolina. Includes oversampling of 1,000 residents over age 60.	70	Lifetime prevalence	

Women			Men		
Completed rape	Attempted rape	Sexual assault broadly defined	Completed rape	Attempted rape	Sexual assault broadly defined
5.0 percent	4.0 percent	14.5 percent			
6.0 percent	21.0 percent				
14 percent	10 percent				
		4.82 percent			0.66 percent

Table 2.1   (continued)

Source of data	Year data collected	Sources of data	Response rate for surveys (in percent)	Time period over which data were collected	Denominator data
		Weighted for analysis.			
Los Angeles studies					
Sorenson et al., 1987	1983–84	Face-to-face interviews with Hispanic & non-Hispanic whites in two mental health catchment areas of L.A. County	68	Prevalence since age 16	1,444 females & 1,290 males
Essock-Vitale & McGuire, 1985	Not reported	300 non-Hispanic white middle class women, 35–45 in greater Los Angeles	66	Lifetime prevalence	300 females
Wyatt, 1985; and as reported in Sorenson et al., 1987	Not reported	First 248 of 709 females, 18–36, who agreed to be interviewed by telephone in multistage, stratified, quota sample	54	Lifetime prevalence	126 black and 122 white females
Adolescents or young adults					
Kirkpatrick & Kanin, 1957	1955	Self-administered questionnaires to 291 female college students	99	1954–55 academic year	291 females
Kanin & Parcell, 1977	1972	Self-administered questionnaires to 282	78.8	1971–72 academic year	282 females

Women			Men		
Completed rape	Attempted rape	Sexual assault broadly defined	Completed rape	Attempted rape	Sexual assault broadly defined
		13.5 percent			7.2 percent
8 percent		25 percent "ever raped or molested"			
20 percent					
28.5 percent	55.7 percent				
26.5 percent	50.7 percent				

Table 2.1 (continued)

Source of data	Year data collected	Sources of data	Response rate for surveys (in percent)	Time period over which data were collected	Denominator data
		female college students			
Herold, Mantle, Zemitis, 1979	Not reported	Questionnaires to 103 Ontario females enrolled in two college social science classes	100	Lifetime prevalence since age 14	103 females
Koss, 1985	Not reported	Questionnaires to representative sample of 3,862 college students	Not reported	Lifetime prevalence	2,016 females
Koss, Gidycz, Wisniewski, 1987	Not reported	Questionnaire to national sample of 6,159 students enrolled in 32 institutions	98.5	Lifetime prevalence	3,187 females
Belcastro, 1982	Not reported	Self-administered questionnaires to 1,090 students enrolled in health education classes	Not reported	Lifetime prevalence	442 females
Sigelman, Berry, Wiles, 1984	Not reported	Self-administered questionnaires to 504 students enrolled in psychology, sociology, & nursing classes	94	Lifetime prevalence	388 females & 116 males

Women			Men		
Completed rape	Attempted rape	Sexual assault broadly defined	Completed rape	Attempted rape	Sexual assault broadly defined
1 percent	16 percent	44 percent sexually molested			
12.7 percent	24 percent				
15.8 percent	12.1 percent				
10.2 percent					
		34.5 percent			20.9 percent

Table 2.1 (continued)

Source of data	Year data collected	Sources of data	Response rate for surveys (in percent)	Time period over which data were collected	Denominator data
Hall & Flannery, 1984	Not reported	Telephone interviews followed by mail questionnaires to 497 Milwaukee residents, 14–17	54	Lifetime prevalence	Sex ratio of sample not reported
Ageton, 1983	1977–80	1,725 youth, 11–17 in 1976 interviewed nationwide	73	12 months for 1978, 1979, & 1980	Sex ratio of of sample not reported

\# Estimate, based on zero or less than 10 cases, is statistically unreliable.

The number of reported rapes varies with location. Approximately one in four reported rapes occurs in the Western region of the United States (although that proportion has apparently dropped in the last five years). Nationally, each year between 1979 and 1986, 65–71 women in every 100,000 were raped, but rates were substantially higher in metropolitan areas (76–85 per 100,000) and in the West (86–101 per 100,000).

Not surprisingly, given the geographic location and predominance of urban areas in the state, rates of all crimes in California are substantially higher than the national average (figure 2.2 and table 2.2). The number of rapes per 100,000 Californians peaked at 58.2 in 1980 and has declined steadily since then, with 45.7 rapes per 100,000 reported in 1984. Similar declines have been noted, however, in all Part One Crimes in California during the 1980s.[6]

Between 48 percent and 54 percent of rapes reported nationally were cleared by arrest or exceptional means[7] between 1979 and 1984, with the

Women			Men		
Completed rape	Attempted rape	Sexual assault broadly defined	Completed rape	Attempted rape	Sexual assault broadly defined
		12 percent "a guy ever used physical force or threatened you to make you have sex when you didn't want to"			2.0 percent
		9.2 percent (1978)			
		6.8 percent (1979)			
		12.7 percent (1980)			

trend being gradually upward. Between 1976 and 1980 the number of rapes cleared by arrest increased by 18 percent (*Uniform Crime Reports*, 1980). Of those arrested, approximately half were under the age of 25, and 25–30 percent were between the ages of 18 and 22. When identified by ethnicity, 50–53 percent of men arrested for rape were white including Hispanic (until 1984 Hispanic males were not differentiated from non-Hispanic white males in rape statistics) while 46–49 percent were black. In 1984, 11 percent of the total or 20 percent of the white males arrested were identified as Hispanics.

Incidence and Prevalence of Rape:
Research Studies

National estimates of the incidence of rape are not the only ones that differ significantly across time and by data source. Nine community stud-

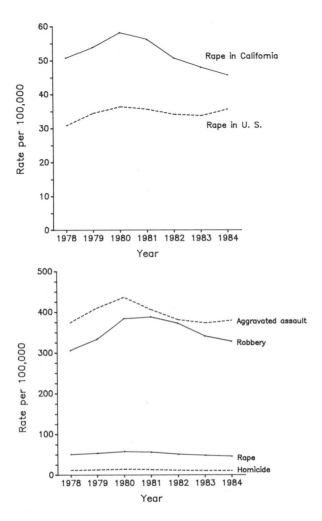

Figure 2.2 Rapes, homicides, robberies, and aggravated assaults reported to police per 100,000 population, 1978–84. Data from *Uniform Crime Reports*, 1979–85.

ies report incidence rates as high as 2,688 per 100,000 females (for attempted and completed rape combined) and lifetime prevalence rates ranging from 5 percent to 44 percent (see table 2.1). Data for these studies were elicited in a variety of ways using a range of definitions of rape and sexual assault. Comparisons of the few studies using representative samples are hindered by differing definitions of rape and sexual assault,

Table 2.2 Rates per 100,000 population for Part One Crimes, California, 1978–84[a]

| Year | Rate per 100,000 population | | | | | | |
	Murder rate	Rape rate	Robbery rate	Aggravated assault rate	Burglary rate	Larceny/ grand theft rate	Motor vehicle theft rate
1978	11.7	50.8	306.1	374.4	2,193.3	3,488.0	691.3
1979	13.0	53.9	333.8	410.3	2,186.8	3,732.6	738.3
1980	14.5	58.2	384.2	436.7	2,316.5	3,880.0	742.9
1981	13.0	56.2	388.2	405.6	2,238.5	3,816.1	672.9
1982	11.2	50.7	372.1	380.7	2,020.2	3,785.1	665.5
1983	10.5	48.0	340.9	373.1	1,829.1	3,444.5	631.2
1984	10.6	45.7	327.5	379.5	1,729.3	3,346.1	629.6

a *Source: Uniform Crime Reports*, 1979–84.

differing sampling strategies, differing response rates, and differing data collection procedures (e.g., Sorenson et al., 1987; Koss, 1988). Nonetheless, prevalence and incidence rates obtained in community studies do more nearly resemble those reported by National Crime Surveys than those reported by the *Uniform Crime Reports*.

In a sample of 930 San Francisco women interviewed in 1978, 2.6 percent reported an attempted or completed rape during the previous twelve months. This would translate into a rate of 2,688 per 100,000 females (Russell, 1982). Forty-one percent reported one or more completed or attempted extramarital rapes during their lifetimes, and an additional 3 percent reported marital rapes.

Kilpatrick, Veronen, and Best (1985) found that 14.5 percent of 2,004 women interviewed in Charleston County, South Carolina, reported one or more attempted or completed sexual assaults during their lifetimes; 5.0 percent said they had been raped and 4.0 percent reported attempted rape. In contrast, in George and Winfield-Laird's study (1986) of women aged 18 to 64 in the Piedmont area of North Carolina, the lifetime prevalence of sexual assault was 4.86 percent in the total sample and 5.92 percent in a subsample of noninstitutionalized women. Approximately 82 percent of the sexual assaults were reported to have resulted in intercourse.

In a 1977 survey conducted by Burt (1979), in which 328 female and 258 male adult residents of Minnesota were interviewed, 26.4 percent of

Table 2.3 Characteristics of rapes, United States, 1979–84[a]

Year	Number reported to police	Percentage change in reports	Percentage of total crimes	Percentage of violent crimes	Percentage in West	Number of women per 100,000		
						Total	Urban areas	West
1978	67,131							
1979	75,989	13.2	1.0	6.0	27.0	67	80	96
1980	82,088	8.0	1.0	6.0	27.0	71	85	101
1981	81,536	− 0.7	1.0	6.0	27.0	69	81	98
1982	78,898	− 3.3	1.0	6.0	27.0	65	76	89
1983	78,918	0.0	1.0	6.0	26.0	66	76	86
1984	84,233	6.7	1.0	7.0	24.0	69	79	87

a *Source: Uniform Crime Reports*, 1979–84.

the women and 10.6 percent of the men reported one or more incidents of completed or attempted forced sex during their lifetimes. In their nonrandom study of 516 women, DiVasto and colleagues (1984) reported that 8 percent had experienced a rape and 59.9 percent had experienced other stressful sexual events including exhibitionism and voyeurism. Brickman and Briere (1984) report lifetime sexual assault rates of 6 percent for rape and 21 percent for contact abuse. Both Wyatt (1987) and Essock-Vitale and McGuire (1985) report rates of 20–25 percent for lifetime sexual assault among Los Angeles County females.

In a stratified sample of black and white females aged 18–36, Wyatt reported that 20 percent had experienced a rape or attempted rape. Within a sample of 300 white, middle-class women aged 35–45, 8 percent reported having been raped since the age of 17, and 25 percent reported "ever being raped or molested" (Essock-Vitale and McGuire, 1985). As part of the Los Angeles Epidemiologic Catchment Area Study fielded in 1983–84, Sorenson et al. (1987) reported a lifetime prevalence of 10.5 percent for "forced or pressured sexual contact" in a probability sample of 3,125 males and females from two census tracts. Rates for Hispanic and non-Hispanic white females (13.5 percent) were almost twice that of males (7.2 percent).

Studies restricted to young adults or adolescents reported similar or even higher estimates of the incidence and prevalence of attempted or completed sexual assaults. Using convenience samples, Kirkpatrick and Kanin (1957) found that 55.7 percent of college females surveyed reported

Percentage cleared by arrest	Percentage increase in arrests	Characteristics of males arrested (in percentage)				
		<25	18–22	White	Hispanic	Black
48	14	57	30	50		48
49	1	54	29	51		48
48	2	52	27	50		48
51	6	52	27	50		49
52	1	50	25	50		49
54	8	47	31	53	11[b]	46

b Percent Hispanic first reported in 1984.

one or more offensive sexual episodes during the 1954–55 academic year; 28.5 percent reported attempted or completed rapes. In a subsequent study of sexual assaults during the senior year of high school, again using a convenience sample, 8.6 percent of 262 college freshmen women surveyed reported one or more rapes while 20.9 percent reported attempted rapes. Kanin and Parcell (1977) replicated these studies in the 1971–72 academic year and found that 50.7 percent of 282 women surveyed reported being sexually offended during the year. Although procedures used in reporting make it difficult to determine how many were actually raped, it appears that 26.5 percent reported an attempted or completed rape during the 1971–72 academic year.

Koss and Oros (1982) administered a twelve-item, yes/no sexual experiences survey to 3,863 college students and reported a lifetime prevalence of 12.7 percent for completed rape and 24 percent for attempted rape among the 2,016 respondents (Koss, 1985). In a second national survey of 6,159 students enrolled in thirty-two institutions, 15.8 percent of the women reported ever experiencing a completed rape and 12.1 percent an attempted rape. Thirty-eight of every 1,000 women surveyed reported an actual or attempted vaginal rape within the previous six months (Koss, Gidycz, Wisniewski, 1987).

In a Milwaukee telephone survey (obtained by random digit dialing) of men and women aged 14 to 17, 12 percent of the females reported having been sexually assaulted (Hall and Flannery, 1984). In comparison, 35 percent of the women in a convenience sample of Eastern Kentucky students reported having been victims of sexual aggression (Sigelman, Berry, Wiles, 1984).

Lifetime prevalence (since age 14) reported by 103 Ontario college females was 1 percent for completed rape, 16 percent for attempted rape, and 44 percent for attempted molestation (Herold, Mantle, Zemitis, 1979). Defining rape as forcible penetration, Belcastro (1982) reported a prevalence of 9.0 percent (40) in a sample of 442 female students at Southern Illinois University at Carbondale. An additional five women (1.1 percent) reported multiple incidents of rape and/or homosexual rape. Over half (57.5 percent) the reported rapes occurred before the woman had entered college.

Using data collected as part of the 1976 National Youth Survey (a national sample of youths aged 13 to 17) Ageton (1983) found that 7 to 10 percent of the females had experienced one or more sexual assaults in each of the years 1978, 1979, and 1980. To compare these data with National Crime Survey data for the same years, incidents involving violent force and/or use of a weapon were extracted. Rates of 3.5 and 4.2 rapes and sexual assaults for every 1,000 females were reported respectively for 1978 and 1979 by the National Crime Survey. These are much lower than the rates reported by Ageton of 9.2 for 1978, 6.8 for 1979, and 12.7 for 1980 (Ageton, table 3.3, p. 31).

Demographic Characteristics of Rape and
Sexual Assault Victims

Both the *Uniform Crime Reports* and the National Crime Surveys consistently find non-Anglo, lower socioeconomic status women under thirty years old at greatest risk of being victims of rape. In 1983, 1.3 attempted rapes were reported for every 1,000 white females and 1.7 for every 1,000 black females. Women aged 12 to 34 were at greatest risk regardless of race (Bureau of Justice Statistics, 1985). Rates were six to seven times higher for never-married and separated or divorced women and for women in urban areas (table 2.3).

Although studies generally find higher rates of rape among younger women, community studies as well as recent National Crime Survey data challenge the finding that lower-class minority women are heavily overrepresented in rape statistics. When stratified by age, place of residence, and race, National Crime Panel data showed that young (<24) white women in urban areas were at higher risk of rape than young urban black women. However, when stratified by age, race, and ethnicity, data showed that rates for blacks are highly unstable (Bureau of Justice Statistics, 1985). Russell's (1984) survey of women in San Francisco found that Anglo women, who were more highly educated than minority women, were at greater risk of rape than minority women. In Burt's (1980) study, reports of completed sexual victimization showed a modest negative association with years of completed education ($r = -.18$) and occupational status ($r = -.13$) for the entire population, while reports of attempted rape showed a mild positive association with socioeconomic status (education $= .17$; occupation $= .07$). Burt's survey did not include minority respondents.

Kilpatrick, Veronen, Best, et al. (1985) reported that in Clarkston County, South Carolina, whites are at higher risk than blacks for attempted rape and attempted and completed molestation, but at comparable risk for completed rape. They also found that younger women and women with higher incomes were at greater risk of sexual assault. In the Piedmont area of North Carolina, highly educated urban women under 44 were at greatest risk of sexual assault (George and Winfield-Laird, 1986). Non-whites were at slightly greater risk (6.1 percent) than whites (5.6 percent). Unique to the North Carolina study was the collection of data from institutionalized persons. Inmates of prisons and psychiatric hospitals were at particularly high risk for sexual assault.

In a study by Williams and Holmes (1981) using a disproportionately stratified sample of 335 Anglos, 336 blacks, and 340 Mexican-Americans, more Anglos (5 percent) reported being victims of sexual assault than did either blacks (2 percent) or Mexican-Americans (3 percent). This pattern of victimization by race is consistent with, but significantly lower than, that found by Russell in San Francisco. Since 4 of the 34 rapes were reported by males, exact prevalence rates for females cannot be computed, but are assumed to approximate 10.2 percent for Anglos, 3.5 percent for blacks, and 6.4 percent for Mexican-Americans. Sexual victimization is not reported by socioeconomic status.

Sorenson et al. (1987) found that rates of sexual assault in Los Angeles differed by gender, age, ethnicity, and educational status. More highly educated (15+ years), younger (<40), non-Hispanic white females had the highest lifetime prevalence of sexual assault (28.3 percent), while

RESEARCH

older (>39) Hispanic women with low education (<11 years) had the lowest prevalence (4.4 percent). Wyatt, in contrast, found no differences in Los Angeles between non-Hispanic white and black women aged 18–36.

In studies restricted to adolescents or college students, rapes and attempted rapes appear to be evenly distributed across ethnic and socio-economic groups. Hall and Flannery (1984) found no relationship between reports of rape and either race/ethnicity or socioeconomic status. Kanin and colleagues found some evidence in 1957 that lower-status women were victimized by higher-status men, but no evidence in 1972 that offensive sexual episodes varied with age, social class, or intelligence (Kanin and Parcell, 1977). Ageton (1983) found no significant differences in prevalence of sexual assault among college students by either social class or race, but did find that a higher proportion of urban as compared to rural females had been victimized. When the number of incidents reported is examined, however, working-class females reported higher numbers of sexual assaults than either lower- or middle-class females. Rural females reported more incidents than urban or suburban residents.

Koss and colleagues (1982, 1985, 1987) report differences among college students by ethnicity: Rape was reported by 16 percent of white women, 10 percent of black women, 12 percent of Hispanic women, 7 percent of Asian women, and 40 percent of Native American women. Rates did not differ by income, religion, size of the institution, size of the city where the college was located, or by the proportion of minority enrollment. Rates of sexual victimization did differ by geographic region and type of institution: Women in private colleges (14 percent) and major universities (17 percent) reported higher rates of rape than those in religiously affiliated colleges (7 percent).

Characteristics of the Sexual Assault

According to the National Crime Survey, the 61,000 completed and 119,000 attempted rapes reported in 1984 represent 3.0 percent of all violent crimes attempted or committed that year. Although attempted rapes (as opposed to completed rapes) represent a large proportion (66 percent) of rapes reported to interviewers, completed rapes represented a larger proportion of the total in 1984 than in previous years.

Of completed rapes reported between 1973 and 1982, 62 percent involved strangers while 38 percent involved nonstrangers, whereas 71 percent of attempted rapes involved strangers and 29 percent or 299,280 involved nonstrangers (Bureau of Justice Statistics, 1985). Over the same ten-year period most attempted and completed rapes occurred at home (27 percent), near home (7 percent), at a vacation home (2 percent) or on the street, in a park, playground, parking lot, or parking garage (39 percent). Completed rapes were reported to occur at night (79 percent) more often than attempted rapes (59 percent).

Women between 16 and 24 were most likely (52 percent) to be victims with black women aged 20–24 at greatest risk. Rapes reported to National Crime Survey interviewers were generally intraracial, but white victims more frequently reported rapes by black males (23 percent) than did black victims by white males (8 percent). Most victimizations involved a single victim and a single offender (77 percent) and the majority of offenders were reported to be over 21 years of age.

Over the ten-year period, weapons were used in only 25 percent of completed and attempted rapes, but were used more frequently in completed (34 percent) rapes, with guns and knives being the weapons used most commonly. In 1984 weapons were much more frequently used by strangers (28.1 percent) than nonstrangers (7.7 percent), but risk of being raped in one's own home was approximately equal whether the assailant was a stranger (35 percent) or a nonstranger (39 percent).

Over the ten-year period, 68 percent of the victims reported some resistance, with self-protection more often reported by victims of attempts (73 percent) than victims of completed rapes (27 percent). The 872,000 victims who resisted were more likely (57 percent) to report injuries beyond the rape itself than were the 171,000 nonresisting victims (47 percent). Victims of completed rapes also reported more injuries (58 percent) than did victims of attempted rapes (29 percent). Injuries generally involved bruises, black eyes, and cuts. In 1984, 85 percent of the women resisted by using physical force (25.3 percent), trying to frighten the assailant or calling for help (30.4 percent), threatening or reasoning with the assailant (18.5 percent), or various nonviolent means (20.2 percent). The propensity to resist or the type of resistance did not differ with the identity of the assailant, but whites (89.2 percent) were more likely than blacks (71.3 percent) to resist. Approximately 75 percent of offenders were under thirty years of age. Sixty-one percent were white.

When asked to describe their most recent sexual assault, over 75 percent of Los Angeles Hispanic and non-Hispanic whites reported that the assailant was an acquaintance, friend, relative, or intimate. No differences were found by gender, age, ethnicity, or education (Sorenson et al. 1987). With regard to force used, pressure alone was reported in 37.9 percent of the assaults, threats or actual physical harm in 28.4 percent, and a combination of pressure and physical harm in 33.7 percent. Here differences did exist by gender, with females more frequently reporting use of physical threats or force (63.4 percent) than males (38.2 percent). Reported force did not differ by age, ethnicity, or educational level. Brickman and Briere (1984) reported that 91 percent of those raped (*N* = 33) and 52 percent of those assaulted (*N* = 117) reported they were physically restrained, and 70 percent and 23 percent respectively reported that verbal threats were used against them. Women reported a number of different responses to attackers, including trying to reason (52 percent), screaming (18 percent), entreating (begging, pleading, crying) (46 percent), kicking, hitting, scratching (36 percent), remaining quiet or motionless (24 percent), and passing out (12 percent).

Reporting Rapes

In 1970, 18.7 rapes per 100,000 persons were reported to law enforcement agencies (table 2.1). By 1980 the number had nearly doubled to 36.4 rapes per 100,000. Many people have attempted to explain the dramatic rise. Some believe that the absolute number of rapes has actually increased while others suggest that only the propensity to report has increased. Factors that have encouraged women to report include: the availability of rape crisis centers and the support system they represent, better investigation and more sensitive response by police and medical personnel, changing laws, changing attitudes toward and respect for women, demographic changes including a decrease in the proportion of the population that is between 18 and 25, and society's greater appreciation of the nature of the crime.

Yet researchers and commentators repeatedly maintain that rapes are

WHY RAPES WERE NOT REPORTED

substantially underreported, and that victims of rape are still more likely than victims of other crimes to fail to report. Between 1973 and 1982, 52 percent of the victimizations were reported to the police, with completed rapes (58 percent) more frequently reported than attempted rapes (50 percent). Reasons given for not reporting included "nothing could be done" (24 percent), "didn't think it was important" (7 percent), "police would not want to be bothered" (9 percent), "didn't want to take the time" (2 percent), "private or personal matter" (29 percent), "didn't want to get involved" (6 percent), "afraid of reprisal" (16 percent), "reported to someone else" (12 percent), and other (36 percent) (Bureau of Justice Statistics, 1985).

In 1984, 53 percent of the completed rapes and 46.5 percent of the attempted rapes reported by respondents in the National Crime Survey were reported to the police. In comparison, 56.5 percent of the attempted aggravated assaults and 40.6 percent of attempted simple assaults were reported to police. Attempted rapes by strangers were only slightly more likely to be reported (46.9 percent) than those committed by nonstrangers (45.9 percent), but black females were more likely (68.2 percent) than white females (47.7 percent) to report attempted rapes by strangers while white females were more likely (60 percent) than black females (31 percent) to report completed rapes. Reasons for not reporting included "not important enough" (10 percent), "private, personal matter" (21.8 percent), "lack of proof" (11.1 percent), "police inefficient, insensitive, etc." (10.1 percent), and "fear of reprisal" (8.3 percent). Two reasons —that it was a private, personal matter and that the woman feared reprisal —were identified somewhat more often when the assailant was a nonstranger. White females assaulted by strangers were somewhat more likely than blacks to say that they had not reported the assault because of police inefficiency or insensitivity.

Other surveys confirm and emphasize the low propensity to report rapes to officials, and the extent to which reporting varies with characteristics of the assault and the woman. Brickman and Briere (1984) found that only 12 percent of women who were raped and 7 percent of those who were sexually assaulted reported the crimes to police. Those raped at night by a stranger were most likely to report, and those who had had a prior sexual relationship with the assailant were *least likely* to report the rape or assault. Of the one rape and 16 attempted rapes reported to Herold,

Mantle, and Zematis (1979), ten were by a stranger, three by an acquaintance, and one by a casual date. Although sixteen discussed the incident with someone, usually a friend, only three reported the incident to the police and one sought professional help. In spite of the low number reporting, ten reported being extremely upset by the assault. DiVasto et al. (1984) studied the victims of sexual assaults and found no differences between reporters and nonreporters, but they also discovered that a high proportion of assaults was committed by nonstrangers (71 percent), relatives (14.6 percent), and current or ex-spouses (9.6 percent) and that there was a low propensity of victims to report such assaults to police or other authorities (22 percent). Of the forty raped women studied by Belcastro (1982), 30 percent were raped by a stranger and 70 percent by an acquaintance.

Koss (1985) studied victims who label their assault a rape (acknowledged victims) and those who do not (unacknowledged victims), and found that more than half failed to discuss their rape with anyone. Among acknowledged victims, 8 percent reported their experience to the police while 13 percent went to a rape crisis center or hospital emergency room. Koss also reported that most of the victims knew their offender: Fifty-nine percent of acknowledged victims and 100 percent of unacknowledged victims said that they at least recognized the man. Thirty-one percent of acknowledged rape victims and 76 percent of unacknowledged rape victims were romantically involved with the offender.

Attitudes of Police and Prosecutors

Numerous researchers have demonstrated the large number of rape cases that never reach the courtroom (e.g. Chappell & Singer, 1973; Hindelang and Davis, 1977; Galvin and Polk, 1983; LaFree, 1980; Lizotte, 1985; National Institute of Law Enforcement and Criminal Justice, Volume III, 1978; Loh, 1980). They also believe that the proportion of rapes reported is significantly lower than the proportion of other crimes reported, and blame the discrepancy on sexist attitudes of police and others (Feldman-Summers and Ashworth, 1981). Indeed, these perceptions may be justified. LeDoux and Hazelwood (1985) in a national study of 2,170 county and municipal law officers, concluded that police were insensitive to rape victims and were suspicious of victims who had had previous and willing sex with the assailant or who "provoked" rape through their appearance or behavior. They also found that a small subset of police officers agreed strongly with statements such as "Nice women do not get raped," or "Most charges of rape are unfounded" (LeDoux and Hazelwood, 1985, p. 219).

Feldman-Summers and Ashworth (1981), in a study of 150 Seattle women presented with a hypothetical rape, found that white women were more likely than minority women to say that they would report the rape, but propensity to report also varied with perceptions that such behavior is socially desirable and will lead to recovering feelings of well-being. In a later study of 179 rape victims, Feldman-Summers and Norris (1984) found that the decision to report ($N = 48$) was unrelated to demographic characteristics, attitudes about self and others, or attitudes and beliefs about rape. But reporting was related to perceived results of reporting and to situational variables. Reporters indicated greater social pressure to report, experienced greater physical injuries, and were less likely to know their assailant. Reporters also thought police would treat them in a positive way while nonreporters expressed concerns about testifying in a trial. Williams (1984) reports similar findings in a study of 246 victims. The 146 victims who reported the assault more often indicated that the rape occurred in public or as part of a break-in and that the rapist was a stranger who used or threatened force resulting in injuries necessitating medical treatment. Kidd and Chayet (1984), in a review of the literature on victims of various crimes, suggested that persons do not report crimes because they are afraid, feel helpless, perceive the police to be powerless, or fear further victimization from authorities.

Using data from the National Crime Surveys of 1972–75, Lizotte compared factors associated with reporting among 650 women who experienced attempted or completed rapes with indicators influencing reporting among 5,850 women who had experienced attempted or completed assaults and 8,250 men who had experienced attempted or completed assaults. He explained his findings as follows:

In general, factors that make a strong case for prosecution are more powerful predictors for reporting rape than for reporting assault. That is, victims report rape to the police in response to factors that make the incident more serious and, hence, easier to prosecute. For example, the more property a rapist steals, the more likely the victim is to report a rape to the police. The more familiar the offender is to the victim, the less likely she is to report a sexual assault to the police. Highly educated women are less likely to report to the police than those with less education . . . . This research suggests [that] differences between reporting rape and assault may be qualitative. This in turn implies that researchers should be careful when comparing rape to other offenses at later points in the criminal justice processing, because qualitative differences may continue to exist. (Lizotte, 1985, pp. 183–85.)

Correlates of Victimization

Although few studies of sexually victimized women have collected data comparing them to women who have not been victimized, evidence suggests that they may differ from other women in their attitudes toward sexuality, women's roles, and violence, and in reported current and past levels of violent, deviant, and sexual behaviors. A number of studies have found that women who report victimizations often report multiple incidents. Of the 407 women in Russell's (1982) sample who reported attempted or completed rapes, nearly half (49.6 percent) reported two or more rapes. Of both males and females reporting sexual assaults in the Los Angeles Catchment Area Study, two-thirds reported two or more assaults (Sorenson et al., 1987). In another study, five of sixteen Ontario, Canada, females reported multiple attempted rapes (Herold, Mantle, and Zemitis, 1979).

In 1978, 1979, and 1980 respectively, Ageton found an average of 1.7, 2.8, and 2.9 incidents reported for each woman assaulted. Furthermore, women reporting assaults in 1978 were likely to report assaults in subsequent years. Once a woman has been sexually assaulted, the risk of another assault in the following year is three to four times greater than the risk for nonvictimized female adolescents (Ageton, 1983). Victimized women were also more likely to have engaged in delinquent behaviors or to be part of a delinquent network. While attitudes toward sex roles did not differ between victimized and nonvictimized women, relations with family and attitudes toward deviance did.

Ellis, Atkeson, and Calhoun (1982) compared 25 victims of multiple

Victims & THEIR LIFE

rapes in Atlanta with 92 victims of a single rape. Multiple-incident victims were younger, more frequently white, of lower socioeconomic status, and more transient than single-incident victims. Multiple-incident victims had had fewer and less satisfying social and sexual relationships, more problems with depression, and a history of suicide attempts. They also reported more victimizations of other kinds, including violent crime and physical abuse as a child or adult.

Hall and Flannery (1984) found that victimized females were more likely than other women to live apart from their biological fathers, to be unaffiliated with religious institutions, and to be active in peer groups in which sexual victimization was high. Kanin and colleagues (1957) also reported that women who had been assaulted were less likely to attend church or to have older brothers. In 1957, Kanin and colleagues found that assaults were more likely to occur in long-term relationships in which prior consensual sex play had occurred. In contrast, data from studies of students in the 1970s showed that offensive acts were "concentrated among the less involved and less durable pairings" (Kanin and Parcell, 1977, p. 73), and were not preceded by consensual sex play. The 143 females who reported assaults averaged 5.1 episodes during the academic year. "The currently offended female demonstrates an overall history of being sexually victimized. She is victimized more frequently and more seriously in both her high school and college years" (Kanin and Parcell, 1983, p. 75). Kanin's finding, that women involved in casual dating with multiple men are more vulnerable to assault than those involved in monogamous dating relationships, and the implication that this pattern has shifted over the last few decades, provide some support for hypotheses that sexual victimization increases with liberalization of sex roles (cf. the introduction to part II, note 1).

In a convenience sample of 504 students at Eastern Kentucky University, Sigelman, Berry, and Wiles (1984) found that women who had been physically abused by a man in a dating relationship were more likely to have been sexually abused as adults, to have witnessed and/or been the victim of parental abuse, and to have inflicted physical abuse themselves within a dating relationship. Experiencing physical or sexual assault was not related to attitudes about sex roles. Belcastro (1982) reported that females who have been raped are more likely to have had more heterosexual partners than females who have never been raped, to have had more heterosexual partners they dated exclusively for six months or more, to have lived with a heterosexual partner, and to have engaged in homosexual behaviors.

Students raped by acquaintances did not differ on these parameters from those raped by strangers. Women raped by strangers, however, reported having had sex at an earlier age and sexual intercourse more frequently than women raped by acquaintances. In addition, they were registered for fewer credits, were more religious, and experienced fewer multiple orgasms via masturbation. Essock-Vitale and McGuire (1985) also reported a relationship between sexual assault and sexual partners. Women who reported being raped or molested reported having almost twice as many sexual partners (14.2) as those who were not raped or molested (7.2).

Koss (1985) examined differences between women who reported being raped, women who reported experiences equivalent to rape but did not admit to rape (unacknowledged rape victims), women who suffered moderate sexual victimization, women who suffered low sexual victimization, and nonsexually victimized women. The study concluded that the five groups differed significantly in values regarding premarital sexual intercourse, number of previous sexual partners, age at first sexual intercourse, and situational variables specific to the assault. Women in the acknowledged rape group were significantly more likely to have been victimized in inappropriate social relationships, but were also more likely to have more liberal sexual values and to report a greater number of sexual partners. Women in the unacknowledged rape group were more likely to know their assailant well and to have engaged in prior sexual intimacy with him. As the level of reported victimization increased, age at first intercourse decreased and the total number of sexual partners increased. Consistent with Ageton's (1986) findings, personality characteristics and attitudes about such things as rape myths, women, and aggression did not differ across the five groups.

Victims of Rape

The aftermath of rape as experienced by self-identified victims is the aspect of rape that has been studied most thoroughly. Initial investigations in the early and mid-1970s were largely anecdotal reports or case histories.

Today research often involves a prospective design (e.g., Kilpatrick, Veronen, and Best, 1985), is theoretically grounded in more broadly defined victimization literature (e.g., Sales, Baum, and Shore, 1984), and utilizes control groups of nonvictims (e.g., Belcastro, 1982; Myers, Templer, and Brown, 1984) and multivariate analyses (e.g., Ruch and Chandler, 1983). Major objectives of current research on rape victims are to ascertain the extent to which a rape leads to temporary or extended stress and/or trauma and its duration, to identify factors that ameliorate and intensify negative postrape experiences, to identify ways to resist or minimize injury and reduce the probability of completed rape, and to identify factors differentiating women who report rapes from those who do not.

The traumatizing effect of rape has been widely documented. Burgess and Holmstrom (1974) referred to post-assault reactions as the "rape trauma syndrome," a phrase now widely used. Many writers argue that the trauma suffered by rape victims is severe enough to qualify as "post-traumatic stress disorder" or PTSD (e.g., Kilpatrick, Veronen, and Best, 1985; Burgess and Holmstrom, 1985; American Psychiatric Association, 1980). Acceptance of trauma resulting from rape as a type of PTSD might enhance and legitimize rape victims' status in courts and other social institutions.

Postrape trauma has at least two stages: an immediate, acute stage during which feelings such as shock, fear, humiliation, and vulnerability are experienced, and a second stage of reorganization characterized frequently by a strong need to avoid situations or people reminiscent of the rape experience. Sexual dysfunction and changes in life-style, job, residence, and relationships frequently occur. Veronen and Kilpatrick (1983) found that rape victims were more likely to suffer from fear and anxiety than were control subjects; victims were also more likely to be sensitive to situations that signaled vulnerability to attack and to experience low self-esteem for as long as one year after the rape.

Although findings are mixed, both the intensity and duration of trauma may vary with characteristics of the rape itself, with pre-rape characteristics of the victim, and with postrape events. Ethnicity and marital status have been found to be associated with rape trauma: Nonblack minorities (e.g., Japanese, Chinese, Hawaiian, Mexican-American) and married victims experience the most trauma (e.g., Ruch and Chandler, 1983; Williams and Holmes, 1981). Both youngest and oldest victims have been found to be at greater risk of intense or extended trauma. Young women are particularly vulnerable to long-term sexual dysfunction (e.g., Bart, 1975). Belcastro (1982) reports an association between rape and increased homosexual experiences.

Women living alone who are raped, particularly those who are isolated from social support networks, may experience higher levels of trauma than other women, as may women who experienced significant life crises before the assault (e.g., Ruch and Chandler, 1983; Kilpatrick, Veronen, and Best, 1985). On the other hand women who have recently experienced major life crises before the rape may experience a numbing effect after the rape that can actually ease recovery (Sales, Baum, and Shore, 1984). Moreover, women with modest and temporary stress in their lives prior to the assault may experience less trauma after being raped than do women who lived relatively stress-free lives, because the former have developed better coping skills. Myers, Templer, and Brown (1984) reported evidence that rape victims, when compared to controls, exhibited lower coping skills, lower self-acceptance, lower self-esteem, and external locus of control,[8] as well as higher rates of pre-rape alcohol and drug abuse, suicidal thoughts, and prior psychiatric hospitalization. Kilpatrick, Best, Veronen, et al. (1985) found higher retrospectively reported rates of nervous breakdowns, suicidal ideation, and suicide attempts among victims of completed and attempted rape, sexual molestation, robbery, and aggravated assault than among women who had not been assaulted. Although all such victims reported higher levels of psychiatric disorder after the assault, disorders were most pronounced among victims of completed rape. Incidence of psychiatric disorder was not appreciably mediated or differentially distributed by race, age, or income of victims. Social support may ameliorate trauma following rape (e.g, Popiel and Susskind, 1985), and women with better past and current heterosexual relationships may recover more quickly (Kilpatrick, Veronen, and Best, 1985).

Although early studies found evidence that postrape trauma was associated with certain characteristics of the rape including the number of assailants, the amount of force used, whether a weapon was used, the amount of injury suffered, and the degree of prior intimacy between the victim and perpetrator, recent studies are more equivocal. When researchers compared trauma experienced by women who were raped to that experienced by those who avoided it, they found that both acute and long-term responses were similar even though women who were raped were more likely to have been attacked by multiple rapists or by a single assailant using a weapon or physical force.

Resisting Rape

Studies show consistently that women who successfully avoid being raped during an attempt resist in a greater variety of ways than those who do not. Conclusions as to the relative merit of verbal or physical resistance, however, vary (e.g., Sanders, 1980; Furby and Fischhoff, 1986). Cohen (1984) found multiple verbal strategies more effective than physical resistance both in preventing rape and reducing injury. The relative effectiveness of various types of resistance may, however, depend on where the attack occurs. Women who successfully resist are more likely to have been attacked outside their homes by strangers, while unsuccessful resisters are more likely to have been attacked at home by acquaintances. Physical force and use of a weapon by the attacker is less frequently reported by successful resisters (Becker et al., 1982; Bart, 1981; Quinsey and Upfold, 1985).

Some researchers have examined interactions among resistance and other factors. In two quite different studies, Griffin and Griffin (1981) and Quinsey and Upfold (1985) found complex relationships among threats of the attacker, resistance tactics of the intended victim, and the amount of physical and sexual injury suffered. Using National Crime Survey data, Griffin and Griffin concluded that the greater the threat (e.g., use of weapons, physical force), the greater the likelihood the woman would increase her resistance to the attack. High threat, however, was more likely than high resistance to result in sexual injury (a completed rape) and physical injury. Quinsey and Upfold, using information obtained from convicted rapists, also concluded that level of threat is more predictive of physical injury than is type and amount of resistance. Yet the amount of resistance did reduce the likelihood that an attempted rape would be completed.

In a meta-analysis of research on the effectiveness of various resistance strategies, Furby and Fischhoff (1986) concluded that using assertive self-defense strategies is more effective than using nonforceful strategies such as crying or pleading. Although more assertive strategies are associated with increased risk of nonsexual physical injury, the researchers found that using assertive strategies does not increase the likelihood that the rape will be completed or the severity of sexual injury.

The element of surprise, which is usually involved in rape and rape attempts (e.g., Sanders, 1980; Bart, 1981; Selkin, 1981), may also be relevant to evaluating various methods of resistance. Women often do not resist or resist ineffectively because they are surprised by the attack. In at least some instances males do not resort to high levels of force because the element of surprise is sufficient to overcome the victim. Surprise is particularly relevant in two situations. First there is the surprise of being attacked in one's own home (common in rapes by both strangers and acquaintances), an environment where one feels "safe" and is not on guard. Second (most applicable in acquaintance rapes) is the surprise of being attacked by someone who is known to the victim and is not perceived as dangerous.

Researchers and practitioners disagree as to the value of resistance. Many who argue that women should not resist believe that physical resistance increases the likelihood of serious physical injury. Studies by Griffin and Griffin (1981) and Quinsey and Upfold (1985), which show injury being preceded by the man's acts of force rather than by the woman's acts of resistance, suggest that such arguments are too simplistic. Studies of unreported acquaintance rape (e.g., Kanin, 1984; Ageton, 1983) and incarcerated rapists (e.g., Marolla and Scully, 1984) suggest that many rapes are completed with little use of overt force by the male or overt resistance by the female. Using data reported to San Diego police, Sanders (1980) made a persuasive argument for substantial resistance. His data show that the greater the level of resistance, the less the likelihood of being raped. If surprise is a potent weapon for an assailant, even mild resistance may turn the tables on the attacker by surprising him. No studies have systematically examined how surprise works as a form of force or resistance or as a deterrent to effective resistance, but its presence is repeatedly noted in both research and media reports.

Summary and Implications

Data summarized in this chapter clearly show that sexual assault is not the rare event it was once thought to be. But evidence concerning who is at greatest risk and the process by which an individual decides she has been raped is unclear. Where official sources continue to present rape victims as primarily black and lower class, research studies suggest that white females are victims more frequently than was previously thought. But findings are inconsistent regarding which white women are most at risk, and it is unclear whether they are more often or as often victims as blacks and other minority women. Some evidence suggests that young women of all social classes, both black and white, are equally victimized. Information on nonblack minorities, when available, suggests that they are rarely victimized. Should these rates be believed? Or does other information about male-female interactions within nonblack minorities suggest that women within these groups do not see nonconsensual, coercive, or even assaultive sex as unusual or worthy of comment? Research shows rape to be more prevalent in the North and West than in the South. While surveys have uncovered unreported assaults primarily among young middle-class white women, differences in these rates also exist by geographic area. However, conflicting results are obtained in studies conducted within a single state. Explanations for these differences are not readily available. Although differences may be real, lack of stability across studies suggests that they may also result from methodological problems and conceptual differences between researchers and respondents and within groups of respondents.

Comparisons of data across studies and between research and official statistics is difficult for several reasons. One clear source of difficulty is the method by which samples are selected. Convenience sampling and other nonprobabilistic procedures have been particularly prominent in studies of college students and victims. Often social science classes are used as the sample source. These students are likely to be more knowledgeable about sexuality and violence and more sensitive to sexual assault than students in, for example, math classes. Their propensity to self-report sexual victimizations may, therefore, be higher than the norm.

Such samples clearly bias studies and lead them to focus on the experiences of more highly educated young white women who are overrepresented relative to minority women in such locations. The similarity of prevalence rates between racial groups observed within such samples may simply represent the experiences of certain social classes while seriously under-representing effects of ethnicity. For representative samples, rape research-ers are still largely dependent on government statistics which are not very detailed regarding the experience of rape. To assess the situation better researchers might want to lobby for the inclusion of more extensive ques-tions on sexual assaults within a subsample of subjects in the National Crime Panel.

Differential response rates across studies may contribute to observed differences, with responders being either more likely or less likely to be interested in sexual assault or to be victims of assaults. Sorenson et al. (1987) point out that as response rates decline, prevalence rates increase. This suggests that high rates are found within less representative and less generalizable samples.

The content and number of questions asked in surveys and the adminis-trative procedures used undoubtedly influence study results. Russell (1982) documents inadequacies of questions in the National Crime Survey and suggests that the high prevalence of rape found in her study of San Fran-cisco women resulted from careful questionnaire design and two weeks of interviewer training including education about rape and incestuous abuse. Sorenson et al. (1987) point out that rates vary according to the adminis-trative technique used. Although the trend is inconsistent, higher preva-lence rates are more often obtained when face-to-face interviews are con-ducted, while lowest rates are obtained in self-administered questionnaires.

Problems in the design of questionnaires also confound comparison across studies and make it difficult to arrive at any generalizations. Ques-tions often are phrased in a way that makes it impossible to separate rape from other types of sexual assault, and, although rape has a formal his-torical definition, definitions adopted within a given study often deviate from it. As a result, attempted rape is often combined with completed rape and molestations that occurred in childhood often cannot be sepa-rated from coercive heavy petting that occurred during adolescence or in early adulthood. To help clear up the confusion, researchers need to develop and validate a concise set of questions that will accurately and compre-hensively assess the entire range of sexual assaults. Only when we have such an instrument can we accurately compare findings across studies.

Certainly methodological differences and inadequacies explain some differences in prevalence rates among studies, but it is also possible that people differ in their definition and sensitivity to rape. Here data on reporting rape, on postrape reactions, and Koss's distinction between unacknowledged and acknowledged rape victims all provide helpful insights. As reviewed in this chapter, this research clearly demonstrates that on occasion women who are victims of coercive intercourse do not label the assault as rape; that many never seek services to ameliorate resultant emotional distress; that the threshold at which a normal sexual act becomes a tabooed violent act is not strictly determined by the presence or extent of force or the amount and kind of resistance; that women's decisions are influenced by the type of relationship they have with men who rape them and by their own prior sexual experiences; and that some women react severely to rape while others appear to react minimally.

Regardless of the true relationship between rape acknowledgment and help-seeking behavior, it seems likely that variations in postrape reactions, like reporting behavior, vary with the woman's perception of the sexual encounter as violent and abnormal. To the extent that she thinks normal sex includes coercive behaviors, she will probably exhibit less post-assault distress. Even within the highly selective samples studied, the amount of emotional distress experienced and its duration apparently vary greatly, suggesting that a woman's perceptions of rape may influence her reactions and recovery.

For many, rape is the most extreme sexual assault. For others, it probably is not. The number of sexual behaviors recognized by a woman as assaultive will influence her reports of rape. We need to learn why many women apparently tolerate quite violent sexual encounters without calling them rapes, and discover whether activities exist that these women would call rapes. Does increased education and exposure to nontraditional women's roles decrease tolerance of sexual assault? Does tolerance decline with increased sexual sophistication or with economic independence? Are sexual behaviors and attitudes impervious to change?

Definitions of rape tend to be dichotomous and simplistic, reflecting researchers' perceptions rather than those of society as a whole. While most researchers are convinced that rape is a violent act, it is not clear that respondents agree with our perceptions. The violence seen by an observer may be judged normal sexual behavior by the participant. Many respondents think that actions that meet our definitions of rape are within the range of acceptable sexual behaviors. These questions and areas need to be probed to map the universe of behaviors that differentiate consensual sex, nonconsensual sex, coercive sex, and rape.

③ Men Who Rape: Psychodynamic and Sociocultural Evidence

ntil recently, most information about rapists came from official government statistics or studies of incarcerated rapists. Both sources have obvious biases (e.g., Koss and Leonard, 1984; Albin, 1977; O'Brien, 1983). While official statistics portray rapists as overwhelmingly young, black, and poor (e.g., Hindelang, 1981; Hindelang and Davis, 1977), psychodynamic studies portray them as mentally diseased men with uncontrollable sexual impulses. From the traditional psychodynamic viewpoint, few men are defined as rapists. Those who do commit rape are thought to have experienced problems during childhood and adolescence that result in their being "over- or undersocialized" into the biologically determined male sex role. In contrast, contemporary psychodynamic research emphasizes overcompensation by males who have low sex drives or inadequate self-esteem. Here rape is characterized as an expression of violent behavior, and research is aimed at discerning why rape is used as an avenue of aggression.

Regardless of the emphasis, psychologists link so many different mental and emotional abnormalities to rapists that it is difficult to distinguish between offenders and nonoffenders. Psychological explanations of rape also do not adequately account for substantial differences among groups in numbers of offenders and victims (Smith and Bennett, 1985, p. 296).

Psychodynamic Theory and Research

Prior to 1970, most research on rape adopted a psychoanalytic orientation that assumed that sexual dysfunctions originate during infancy and childhood and result from inappropriate integration of id, ego, and superego. Often the resulting sexual deviance was blamed on inappropriate child-rearing behaviors of mothers or sexual inadequacies of wives. Much contemporary clinical work still adopts this psychoanalytic perspective.

Most early research on rape was conducted by psychiatrists or clinical psychologists who studied offenders. Their subjects were men who had been incarcerated for sexual offenses. The men were studied alone or compared to men who had been incarcerated for other offenses. Often the sexual offenders included pedophiles and homosexuals as well as rapists. Frequently, the objective of the research was to develop early identification procedures and methods to prevent rape or treat offenders.

Researchers looked at variables such as age, education, employment history and status, marital history and status, intelligence, use of intoxicants, and personality measures. More recent studies of incarcerated rapists have examined offense history and social functioning particularly in relation to women. The general conclusion of these studies has been that rapists are not easily distinguished from other violent criminals. In general, they resemble violent criminals more closely than they resemble other sexual offenders or than other sexual offenders resemble violent criminals. Ironically, these findings lend more support to the feminist view that rape is a violent rather than a sexual crime and that rapists are distributed throughout the society than they do to the psychodynamic view that rape is rare and rapists are sexual deviants.[1]

The earliest studies were conducted under a distinctly Freudian psychoanalytic orientation with its heavy emphasis on early childhood experiences and sexual development. Later studies adopted the perspective of rape as a learned personality disorder (e.g., Cohen et al., 1971; Prentky and Knight, 1986), and learning theory (e.g., Abel and Blanchard, 1974; Abel et al., 1977). Clinical studies of incarcerated offenders categorized rapists by motivation (Guttmacher, 1951; Kopp, 1962; Gebhard, Gagnon, and Pomeroy, 1965), sexual and aggressive impulses (Cohen et al., 1971), and descriptive features of the rape itself (Cohen et al., 1971; Amir, 1971; Groth and Burgess, 1977).

Psychodynamic Typologies

Many writers have developed typologies to differentiate incarcerated rapists from other groups of violent and sexual offenders and normal controls and to differentiate among subgroups of rapists. One of the earliest typologies was proposed by Guttmacher (1951). Based on psychoanalytic theory, they differentiated three types of rapists determined by what was thought to motivate their behavior. True sex offenders had predominantly sexual aims, and the offense was hypothesized to result from latent homosexual tendencies or pent-up sexual impulses. Aggressive rather than sexual objectives dominated the motivations of sadistic rapists, while rape was just one of a series of antisocial acts in which aggressive offenders engaged.

Kopp (1962) divided rapists into two types. Type I rapists were offenders for whom rape was not a characteristic behavior. Such rapists were described as compliant, often feeling guilty after the fact. These men, it was believed, were more amenable to treatment. Type II rapists were antisocial, psychotic men who were unconcerned about consequences of their behavior. These men, it was thought, were difficult to treat because rape was just one of a number of violent behaviors in which they engaged.

Gebhard et al. (1965) created 17 categories of possible sexual offenders using information about presence/absence of sexual contact, presence/absence of a family relationship to the victim, presence/absence of force, sex of the victim, and age of the victim. Within the taxonomy obtained, rapists were categorized into six types roughly differentiated by age, assumptions about motivation, and correlates of the rape. The six types identified were assaultive, amoral, drunken, explosive, and double-standard, and a residual category was used for men who could not be fitted into one of the other categories.

Rada (1977) differentiated five types of rapists labeled psychotic rapists, situational stress rapists, masculine identity conflict rapists, sadistic rapists, and sociopathic rapists. The study showed that 30–40 percent of incarcerated rapists were sociopathic rapists who did not demonstrate marked psychopathology other than the rape behavior. More than his predecessors, Rada clearly appreciated the confusion about the roles violence and sexuality play in rape, and its close proximity to normal, or culturally defined, sexuality. Ultimately, however, he defined rape as abnor-

DEFINITION OF RAPE

mal behavior, combining sexual and aggressive behaviors. Normal adult sexuality also combines sexual and aggressive components, but allows for mutually enjoyable sexual relationships.

Groth (1979) also identified the intermingling of violence and sexuality in rape. "In every act of rape, both aggression and sexuality are involved, but it is clear that sexuality becomes the means of expressing the aggressive needs and feelings that operate in the offender and underlie his assault" (p. 13). His threefold typology of rapists is premised on aggressive expression and differentiates anger rape from power rape and sadistic rape. Like feminist theorists he believes that rape is "a pattern of sexual behavior that is concerned much more with status, hostility, control, and dominance than with sensual pleasure or sexual satisfaction" (p. 22). While Groth agrees with feminist theories regarding the role of violence in rape, he apparently rejects feminist notions that rape is an extension of socially condoned coercive norms of sexual interaction between men and women and, in contrast, considers rapists mentally ill deviants.

According to Cohen and colleagues (1971), rape is correlated with personality. Their typology associates three types of rape with personality disorders. Rape with an aggressive aim is an expression of an explosive personality; with a sexual aim the expression of an inadequate personality; and with a combination of sexual and aggressive aims an expression of an antisocial personality.

Physiological and Behavioral Studies of Rape

Behaviorally oriented experimental psychopathologists have conducted a series of behavioral and physiological studies of rapists. Abel, Quinsey, Marshal, Barbaree, and colleagues have applied social learning theory and behavior-modification techniques to the study of rape. Their studies emphasize the objective assessment of sexual preference and social incompetence. Their primary aim is to modify the antisocial behavior of rapists. Their major tool is the use of penile tumescence measures to evaluate physiological responses to written, oral, or visual portrayals of rape or mutually consenting sex. A rape index score is created by computing the ratio of penile responses to rape stimuli versus responses to stimuli depicting mutually consenting sex. Although considered a more "objective" measure of sexual excitement or response than self-report, the validity of the rape index is still open to discussion (Keltner and Doyle, 1986; Davidson and Malcolm, 1985).

Two types of studies have been done using penile tumescence. The efficacy of treatments to modify incarcerated rapists' inappropriate sexual behaviors has been evaluated (Abel and Blanchard, 1974; Abel et al., 1979), and the sexual responses of rapists have been compared to nonrapist criminal and/or normal groups (Quinsey, Chaplin, and Upfold, 1984).

Findings from Clinical Research

Within the psychodynamic research, several variables are studied most frequently and are found to consistently differentiate sexual offenders from nonsexual offenders and rapists from other sexual offenders. These variables are: the kinds of sexual acts engaged in by the offender, social skills and alcohol abuse by the offender, the age and sex of the victim, the relationship between victim and offender, and the offender's age, heterosexual adaptation, intelligence, sexual arousal, and antisocial personality. Rapists are consistently younger than other sexual offenders, but not necessarily younger than other nonsexual offenders. Generally rapists seek adult women rather than children or men as their victims, and incarcerated rapists who have been studied generally prey on strangers rather than relatives or acquaintances. Clinicians have found some evidence that rapists are less competent in social relationships and heterosexual interactions and they often become aggressive while under the influence of alcohol or drugs.

Knight, Rosenberg, and Schneider (1985) reviewed the various typologies of rapists and found remarkable consistency in the theoretically derived types, identifying four well-distinguished groupings. One type is aggressive during the offense either to enhance his sense of power or masculinity or to express feelings of mastery and conquest. Another type commits rape out of anger toward women and seeks to hurt, humiliate, and degrade his victim. He becomes sexually aroused in response to violence and commits brutal, sometimes bizarre assaults. A final type is the rapist with an extensive criminal history whose sexual offenses are only one component of an impulsive, antisocial life-style (p. 253).

Rapists in the Community

Knight, Rosenberg, and Schneider (1985) neglected to consider findings from studies of self-reported rapists in community and college populations in their review of rape typologies. Malamuth and colleagues have done innovative contemporary research that broadens the learning theory tradition to include nonincarcerated community members (e.g., Malamuth, 1983; Malamuth and Donnerstein, 1984; Malamuth and Check, 1985; Malamuth, Check, and Briere, 1986; Malamuth, 1986). Using primarily convenience samples of college undergraduates, Malamuth and colleagues used penile tumescence, self-reported propensity to rape, and self-reports of aggressive sex (Koss and Oros, 1983) to document the extent to which undetected rapists are found in normal male populations and to investigate the extent to which the propensity to rape correlates with a wide range of personality, attitudinal, and behavioral measures.

Malamuth and colleagues have repeatedly found that as many as 50 percent of their male subjects would consider raping if they knew they could get away with it. Propensity to rape has, in turn, been shown to correlate with belief in rape myths, with perceptions that women experience pleasure in simulated rapes, and with sexual experience. Men with a high propensity to rape reacted positively to simulations of forced sex in which the woman was depicted as being sexually aroused, whereas men with low rape propensities did not. Self-reported aggression reportedly is associated with hostility toward women, sexual experience, antisocial characteristics, psychoticism, acceptance of interpersonal violence, dominance motive, and interactions between these measures.

Although the ability to generalize from these findings is limited by the nature of the samples and high correlations between variables that have not been shown to represent independent constructs,[2] this group of studies represents one of the first attempts to bridge the gap between traditional psychodynamic and psychophysiological perspectives of rapists and the feminist perspective. In their effort to reconcile their research with feminist theories of rape, however, Malamuth and colleagues sometimes overinterpret their research and generalize it to groups of males not represented in the samples. Although prior sexual experience consistently correlates with indicators of sexual aggression in these studies, these researchers seem reluctant to acknowledge the role of sexuality in sexual aggression.

Kanin (1984, 1985), in contrast, focuses on the role of erotically oriented peer groups in facilitating sexually aggressive behavior. Seventy-one self-reported rapists in a college population were compared to a similar group of 227 males from the same population. All rapes occurred on dates and involved women who were classified as occasional dates. Unlike the convicted rapists, none of the men showed pronounced evidence of criminal or impulsive behavior. All rapes reported were preceded by some consensual sexual activity similar to what had occurred on prior dates. Although no explicit promises of coitus had been made by the women (68 percent had, in fact, stated that they did not wish to go further) 90 percent of the men felt that an implicit agreement to continue had been made. The men rationalized their behavior by saying that because the woman was sexually aroused, they ignored any other signs of resistance. In other words, if a man perceived a woman to be sexually aroused then he perceived a woman's "no" to really mean "yes." Other reasons given for the completion of the rape were use of alcohol and the man's ability to physically overpower the woman. Kanin concluded that "a substantial number of these rapes occurred because the 'right man' (sexually aggressive and determined) did the 'right thing' (presented a level of force not usually encountered in dating) to the 'right girl' (easily frightened or inebriated)" (Kanin, 1984, p. 102).

Kanin (1985) reports that date rape does not occur because of lack of sexual outlets. Self-identified rapists reported an average of 1.5 orgasms per week compared to 0.8 per month reported by nonrapists. Yet rapists were more likely (79 percent) than controls (32 percent) to express dissatisfaction with their sexual activities. Sixty-two percent of the rapists said they would try to seduce a new date most of the time and 86 percent felt that rape is justifiable under certain conditions. When asked about the behavior of peers, rapists reported a much higher prevalence of participation in gang rapes and sexual sharing (41 percent) than did nonrapists (13 percent). Pressure from peers to be heterosexually active was reported to be "great" or "considerable" by 85 percent of rapists and 95 percent said that best friends would "definitely approve" of using exploitative tactics to seduce certain women. Tactics reported used by rapists in seduction efforts included alcohol (76 percent), false professions of love (86 per-

Table 3.1 Comparison of data reported by Kanin (1985) with data reported by Giarrusso et al. (1979) (in percentage)

	Source of data			
	Kanin (1985)[a]		Giarrusso et al. (1979)[b]	
Items used	Rapists	Controls	Males	Females
Aggressive sex is OK when:				
The woman is a bar "pick-up"	54	16		
The woman has a "loose" reputation	27	10		
She's had sexual intercourse with other guys			29	18
She's a known "teaser"	81	40		
She gets him sexually excited			51	42
He's so turned on he can't stop			26	21
She's led him on			54	27
She says she's going to have sex with him, then changes her mind			54	31
She lets him touch her above the waist			39	28
She's an economic exploiter	73	39		
He spends a lot of money on her			29	12
She is stoned or drunk			29	18
She's a more or less regular date	9	7		
They have dated a long time			43	32
Total N	71	227	72	72

a From table II in E. J. Kanin, "Date Rapists: Differential Sexual Socialization and Relative Deprivation." *Archives of Sexual Behavior* 1985; 14(3):219–31. Rapists were self-reported to the author during the 1970s; comparison group was solicited from 15 undergraduate university classes. All respondents were Anglo. Respondents were asked what they thought the reputational consequences would be if their best friends found out "you offended a woman by trying to force her to have sexual intercourse, during the course of which you used physical force and/or threats."

b From table 3 in R. Giarrusso, P. Johnson, J. Goodchilds, G. Zellman, "Adolescents' Cues and Signals: Sex and Assault." Paper presented at the Western Psychological Association Meeting, San Diego, April 1979. Respondents are 144 Anglo adolescents, 14 to 18 years, interviewed in Los Angeles in 1978. Although black and Hispanic teenagers were interviewed, their responses were not reported. Responses are to the question "Under what circumstances is it OK for a guy to hold a girl down and force her to have sexual intercourse?"

cent), false promises of future commitment (46 percent), and threats to end an ongoing relationship (31 percent).

Table 3.1 compares data reported by Kanin (1985) with that obtained by Giarrusso et al. (1979) from a sample of 14- to 17-year-old Anglos living in Los Angeles in 1979. Interestingly, women with a "loose" reputation or who are known to have had sex with other guys are less likely to be viewed as legitimate victims by the teenagers in Los Angeles than are women who participate in active consensual sex short of coitus. In the Los Angeles sample of high school age males, 51 percent thought aggressive sex was justifiable if the "girl" got the "guy" sexually excited and 54 percent if she had led him on. Of further interest is the substantial number of high school women (42 percent) who said aggressive sex is justified when "she gets him excited" but not when "leading him on." While boys apparently equate "getting him excited" with "leading him on," adolescent girls do not. Adolescent girls are only slightly more likely to say aggressive sex is permissible when the woman "leads the man on" than when "he's so turned on he can't stop," while adolescent boys are almost twice as likely to say it is justified.

Although the underlying reasons for these responses are unclear, it may be that boys are differentiating between situations they perceive to be their responsibility and those they perceive to be the girl's responsibility. They accept more responsibility when the situation is one in which they allow themselves to become excited by the girl, but perceive "leading him on" and "she gets him excited" to be intentional behaviors on the part of the girl. Girls, in contrast, seem to think that the balance of responsibility for assaultive sex only increases for girls when the girl actively excites the boy. Leading him on does not, apparently, have an explicit sexual referent for girls.

For the Los Angeles boys, sexual aggression is justified primarily when it occurs in the context of an ongoing relationship or when the woman participated in prior, explicitly sexual behavior with him. Los Angeles girls are less likely to approve of aggressive sexual behavior under any circumstances. Some agree with male perceptions some of the time, but they make distinctions that males apparently ignore. Los Angeles girls are much less likely than boys to justify the legitimacy of aggressive sex when a girl "leads him on" or when she changes her mind. But, like their male peers, they believe that sexual aggression, when it occurs, is made legitimate by the nature, past history, or context of the relationship between the male and female involved.

In contrast, Midwest college men perceive aggressive behavior to be justified by other than explicitly sexual events, e.g., economic exploitation

(Kanin, 1985). Since these studies differ in design or objective, similarities and differences in findings can only be considered suggestive. It seems clear, however, that variations exist among self-defined predatory males, nonpredatory males, and females in the extent to which and the circumstances under which such behavior is deemed appropriate. Differences also seem to exist across geographic, urban-rural, age, and socioeconomic status boundaries.

Goodchilds, Kanin, and colleagues' findings are not unlike those reported by Green (1943) and Whyte (1941) 45 years ago. "Cornerville" men, as reported by Whyte, differentiated between "good girls" and "lays." Casual sex with "lays" yielded personal prestige with male peers as well as physical satisfaction. While generally protected from sexual confrontations, "good girls" must not be teasers. "The virginity of a teaser is thought to be only a technicality and if she is raped it serves her right" (Green, 1943, p. 25). In the Polish-American community studied by Green, sexual exploitation was common and sexual success was a sure road to status for boys (p. 347).

Sociological Studies of Rapists

The use of excuses and justifications by men and women in the general population (including self-identified nonincarcerated rapists) to explain aggressive sex was also found by Scully and Marolla (1984, 1985) in their study of 114 convicted male rapists in Virginia. Scully and Marolla were among the first researchers to apply feminist and social psychological theory to the study of incarcerated rapists. They divided rapists into categories of "admitters" and "deniers" in accordance with the "vocabulary of motive" that is used by the rapists. Admitters agree that they committed rape, say it was a horrible thing to do, but feel it only happened because of some external facilitator (e.g., drugs, alcohol, or emotional problems) or that it was an aberrant act (e.g., "I'm really a nice guy!"). Deniers justify their behavior with one of five themes: the woman was the victim of her own seduction, women mean "yes" when they say "no," most women eventually relax and enjoy it, nice girls don't get raped, or it was only a minor wrongdoing.

At least three of the themes identified as "justifications" by Scully and

Marolla resemble the sexual themes used by Kanin's self-reported rapists and by many of the adolescents in Los Angeles. Similar among rapists in the three studies are references to women as seducers, the belief that women really mean "yes" when they say "no," and the labeling of certain kinds of women, "bad girls," as appropriate rape objects. These same three themes are among the rape myths identified by feminists in the early 1970s.

Many researchers have reported data that complement, replicate, or extend findings of Malamuth and colleagues, Goodchilds and colleagues, Scully and Marolla, and Kanin. Burt (1983) compared perceptions of violence of thirty-six men participating in two treatment programs for sex offenders with those of 598 Minnesota adults. Vignettes depicting interactions between a man and a woman were read to respondents. Both intimacy (stranger, acquaintance, married) between the man and woman and three levels of force were varied across nine vignettes. Each respondent was read only one vignette. Respondents were asked how violent the simulated situation was, their perceptions of the man portrayed, and their perceptions of what the woman portrayed might have done to deserve what happened. The level of force portrayed within the vignette was the strongest predictor of judgments in both the rapist and community samples. Additionally, within the community respondents with higher levels of acceptance and personal experience with violence were both *more* tolerant of violent behavior and more willing to go easy on the perpetrator in terms of moral judgment and sympathy (p. 141). Among rapists who reported much higher past exposure to intrafamilial violence, acceptance of rape myths predicted greater tendencies to exonerate the man.

Of perhaps greater interest was the rapists' somewhat greater tendency (67 percent) than that of community members (55 percent) to provide one or more justifications for the man's violence. When high force resulting in injury was portrayed, differences between community members and rapists were particularly pronounced: Forty-six percent of community members suggested that a behavior by the woman might have elicited the violence while 73 percent of the rapists suggested such a possibility. Burt's findings are consistent with Scully and Marolla's suggestion that rapists reject responsibility for their behavior and use "excuses" and "justifications" to explain it. Burt's findings further suggest that rape and other sexual assaults may be simultaneously more prevalent and less subject to comment within social subgroups that condone and/or engage in greater amounts of violence on a daily basis.

In their study of Eastern Kentucky University students, Sigelman, Berry, and Wiles (1984) asked both males and females whether they had been victims or perpetrators of both sexual and physical abuse. Males who reported sexual aggression (1.8 percent) also reported physical aggression against women. Unusual in this sample is the 20.9 percent of males who reported being victims of sexual abuse. Male reports of sexual abuse did not correlate with reports of being physically abused. Although the source of the sexual and physical abuse reported by males is not stated, it is implied it was perpetrated by women. Male sexual aggressors tended to hold traditional attitudes toward women.

In Tieger's (1981) convenience sample of 179 males, 37 percent, or 64, responded that they might rape. Propensity to rape correlated with perceptions that a simulated rape was a sexual rather than a violent crime and that women, particularly unattractive women, contribute to their own victimization. Males who said they would be likely to rape were more likely to say that the woman in the simulated rape was acting seductively, that victims enjoy the thrill of rape, that substantial numbers of women enjoy rape, that substantial numbers of males would rape, and that regardless of the victim's attractiveness the assailant was sexually attracted to her.

Alder (1985) used one of Kanin's questions in collecting data from 212 male participants in the Marian County (Oregon) Youth Study. Originally enrolled in the study as high school sophomores in 1964, the respondents were again interviewed in 1976 at age 31. The question asked "It has been noted that in the course of men's and women's sexual lives together, some men on occasion make physically forceful attempts at sexual activity which are disagreeable and offensive enough that the woman responds in an offended manner such as crying, fighting, screaming, pleading, etc. Have you ever engaged in such behavior?" Of the 212 men responding, 11.4 percent admitted one or two episodes of such behavior, 2.1 percent "a few" episodes, and the remaining 86.5 percent admitted no episodes. No differences were found across the three groups in education, family social class, occupational status, alienation and power, sex role beliefs, or sex role behaviors. The lack of differences in traditional indicators of social status are reported to be ". . . consistent with the feminist position and contrary to what is suggested by studies of official rapists . . ." (p. 318). The primary difference between men who forced sex and men who did not was their having sexually aggressive friends (r = +.58): Men reporting episodes of sexual aggression were much more likely to say that they had close friends who were sexually aggressive. Two other variables contributed to distinctions between the groups. Among men who had sexually aggressive friends, the likelihood of reporting episodes of sexual aggression was further increased if the respondents had been in Vietnam or if they held attitudes conducive to sexual victimization. Although sexual aggression was not directly influenced by demographic characteristics of the men surveyed, education was an indirect predictor. Men with lower educations were more likely to have conservative attitudes about sex which, in turn, predicted attitudes conducive to sexual victimization.

Smithyman (1979) conducted telephone interviews with fifty rapists who responded to newspaper advertisements. While demographic characteristics of his convenience sample were not unusual and did not resemble rapists portrayed by official statistics, the number of men who had experienced heterosexual contact with a family member (usually a sister) seemed surprisingly high (38 percent). Moreover, 34 percent reported having had some form of homosexual relationship. Seventy-four percent had raped more than once, 40 percent had raped within the last year, and an additional 40 percent had raped within the last four years. Taking the most conservative estimate, these fifty men had raped 252 women. Most of the rapes (78 percent) occurred when the men were less than 30 years old. Like Kanin's date rapists, Smithyman's self-identified rapists did not have a history of sexual deprivation. If anything, his data support Kanin's observation that rapists are somewhat more heterosexually active and begin having sex at a younger age than other men.

In their first report of the Sexual Experiences Survey data, Koss and Oros (1983) reported the following prevalences in aggressive sexual behavior by men: 2.4 percent reported physically forcing women to participate in anal or oral intercourse; 2.7 percent reported physically forced intercourse; 1.9 percent reported verbally forced intercourse; 2.4 percent reported a physical attempt at rape; 2.0 percent reported a verbal attempt at rape; 6.4 percent reported physically forced kissing and petting; 19.5

percent reported the use of deception to get intercourse; 15.0 percent reported the use of constant argument to get intercourse; and 23 percent reported being so aroused that they couldn't stop themselves.⟩

In a later study (Koss et al., 1985) the responses in the first study were used to assign 1,846 men to one of five levels of sexual aggression: assaultive (4.3 percent), abusive (4.9 percent), coercive (22.4 percent), nonaggressive (59.0 percent), and no reported heterosexual activity (9.4 percent). A subsample of men in the first four categories who agreed to participate was then interviewed to find out whether men representing different levels of nonstranger sexual aggression differed on the basis of psychological characteristics (p. 983). Factor analysis of adapted measures of adversarial sex roles, sexual conservatism, belief in rape myths, acceptance of interpersonal violence (Burt, 1980), women's responsibility for rape (Feild, 1980), attitudes toward women (Spence et al., 1973), and number of heterosexual partners revealed two factors that significantly discriminated between the four groups: a measure of sexually aggressive attitudes and behaviors and sexual experience; and a measure of attitudes toward women and sexual experience. Measures of psychopathy did not contribute to the discrimination.

> The more sexually aggressive a man had been, the more likely he was to attribute adversarial qualities to interpersonal relationships, to accept sex-role stereotypes, to believe myths about rape, to feel rape prevention is the woman's responsibility, and to view as normal an intermingling of aggression and sexuality. While men who were most verbally or physically coercive tended to have large numbers of sexual partners, physically aggressive men saw women as significantly more sexually free than verbally coercive men did (pp. 989–90).

In a later survey of 3,187 women and 2,972 men enrolled in 32 colleges, 25.1 percent of the men said they had been sexually aggressive. Of those men, 4.4 percent reported that they had committed a rape and an additional 3.3 percent reported an attempted rape (Koss, Gidycz, and Wisniewski, 1987). Reports did not differ with religion or family income but did differ by ethnic group. Black males were most likely to admit acts of sexual aggression (10 percent), followed by Hispanics (7 percent), whites (4 percent), Asians (2 percent), and Native Americans (0 percent). Twenty men reported 36 incidents of forced, nonconsensual intercourse within the twelve-month period preceding the survey, 57 men reported 103 incidents of obtaining intercourse through intentional intoxication, and 19 men reported 48 incidents of nonconsensual forced oral or anal penetration. The researchers considered all unwanted oral, anal, and vaginal intercourse attempts and completions in determining a perpetration rate of 34 per 1,000 men. Restriction to the FBI definition of rape resulted in a perpetration rate of 9 per 1,000 men during a six-month period. Consistent with Kanin's and others' findings, men who admit to sexual aggression frequently report multiple aggressions within a brief period of time.

As in many other studies of nonincarcerated rapists, Ageton's (1983) sample is restricted to adolescents (those aged 13 to 19 in 1978). It has the advantage, however, of being a national rather than a geographically restricted or college student sample. The proportion of males reporting sexual assaults in each of the three years of the National Youth Survey (1978, 1979, 1980) were respectively 3.8 percent or 33, 2.9 percent or 24, and 2.2 percent or 25. No consistent differences were found in either prevalence or incidence by race, social class, or place of residence. Over the course of the study 68 interviews were conducted with 51 offenders. Lack of significant differences in this instance may, however, result from small numbers. Assaults were reported to be spontaneous (70 percent), usually involving acquaintances (85 percent). The most common form of force reported was verbal persuasion. Consistently cited precipitating factors were the victim's physical build, the victim's teasing and flirting, and the offender's being sexually excited. In contrast, victims cited the time of day and the fact that the offender was sexually excited as major causes of the rape.

Ageton proposed a theoretical model derived from delinquency theory and modified by feminist theory to predict participation in sexual assault. The model was tested using discriminant analysis. Male offenders differed significantly from peers in their involvement with delinquent peers, in committing crimes against persons, in attitudes toward rape and sexual assault, and in family normlessness. But a single variable—involvement with delinquent peers—sufficiently differentiated the two groups. Sexually assaulted females also differed from peers primarily in their involvement with delinquent peers. Offenders and the peer groups to which they belong do not have more traditional attitudes about sex roles, nor do they hold more liberal attitudes about use of violence than other men. Ageton concludes that attitudes supportive of rape myths and peer group behaviors supportive of sexual aggression explain sexual aggression offenses only to the extent that they characterize peer groups to which offending males and victimized females belong.

Summary and Implications

Recent findings suggest that males who are incarcerated for rape almost surely represent a minority of rapists. They probably are "hard-core" rapists who commit sexual acts most closely resembling "classic" rapes. They attack women they do not know; they use physical violence or force; victims resist in ways universally judged to indicate they do not consent to intercourse; the women come from backgrounds indicating they are socially respectable and sexually chaste; and the circumstances under which assaults take place do not compromise the women's respectability. Therefore, it is not surprising that early research on rape, coming from research on incarcerated rapists, reinforced the theory that few men rape and that those who do are psychological deviants.

Recent studies of both incarcerated and nonincarcerated rapists confirm this bias and highlight characteristics and attitudes that distinguish incarcerated rapists from other men. Convicted rapists and men with self-identified proclivities towards rape are more likely than other men to define rape as a sexual act with which the victim acquiesces. Men who do not rape define rape as a violent act. Men who engage in sexual aggression apparently become sexually active earlier and maintain a higher level of sexual activity than do other men.

Like studies of rape victims reviewed in chapter 2, recent research confirms feminist suspicions that many men rape and that rapists are not inherently different from other men. But there tends to be a pattern to their attitudes, beliefs, and learned social behavior. Research consistently shows that rapists have conservative attitudes and beliefs about sex, women, and sex roles, and have learned to behave in similar ways. They are more likely than other men to have been exposed to violence but not necessarily to pornography, and are more likely to have attitudes supportive of violence. Whereas women, if assaulted, are likely to call it rape, men who assault women are less likely to call the assault a rape. The attitudes and behaviors of peers seem particularly important in understanding the assaultive behavior of men.

The Role Peer Groups Play for Men and Women

Although a few studies of women victims have examined the role of social networks in the recovery process and in encouraging or discouraging their reporting of assaults to police, little attention has been paid to the role peer groups play as agents of socialization for women victims. Studies available on men, however, consistently find peer groups to be significant reinforcers and, possibly, initiators of sexually aggressive behavior.

Hall and Flannery (1984) reported that adolescent rape victims (14–17 years old) were somewhat more likely to have sexually active friends who had been raped, and Ageton's (1983) findings, while not addressing the issue directly, suggest that peer groups influence the sexual and delinquent behaviors of both males and females. Using data from college students, Reed and Weinberg (1984) found that peers influenced coital behavior of both males and females, but under different circumstances. Males dating *serially* were more likely to have intercourse if they perceived that their friends did. In contrast, females dating *steadily* were more likely to have intercourse if they perceived that their friends did. Acceptance of assaultive sex seems to differ in similar circumstances. As reported in chapter 2, females involved in ongoing relationships were less likely than women dating serially to label forced intercourse (usually with a steady boyfriend) generally but not exclusively rape. In contrast, findings from this chapter suggest that men involved in past and current serial relationships are more likely to think that forced sex is acceptable. What these men do when they start dating steadily is not clear, but their tendency to justify rape when it occurs with a previous sexual partner or when they perceive the woman to be sexually excited suggests that they would continue to be sexually coercive and assaultive in stable relationships. Reed and Weinberg (1984) suggest that men in permanent relationships defer to women rather than peers in deciding whether or not to have intercourse. If it is the woman's first experience with extensive sexual intimacy, however, and/or her peers consider coercive sex permissible in ongoing relationships, a combination of both the man's and woman's past and present experiences and interactions will influence whether sexual assault occurs and whether it is called rape.

Research taken as a whole seems to support Dietz's (1978) contention that rape combines sexuality, violence, and the interactions of men and women. Men's tolerance for and definitions of rape vary, as do women's. They vary with sexual experience, peer group attitudes and behaviors, exposure to violence, and certain attitudes. Tolerance for rape, however, seems to be greater among men than women, and it is easier to differentiate rape-tolerant males from rape-intolerant males than to differentiate between less tolerant or more tolerant females. Appearances may be deceiving, however, given the small number of studies that have been conducted and their almost exclusive use of college students as subjects.

Only a few researchers have studied both men and women (e.g., Ageton, 1983; Kanin, 1985; Koss, 1985; Sorenson et al., 1987), and only Ageton's study had identical data available on assaulted women, unassaulted women, male assaulters, and male nonassaulters. No one has studied both members of the dyad involved in sexual assaults. To better understand the similarities and differences in men's and women's definitions of rape, more research with more representative samples needs to be conducted in which both men and women are studied. Methods need to be devised to study the interactions occurring within the dyad and between each member and his or her best friends and peers.

4 Individual Definitions of Rape: Perspectives from Attribution Theory

Since 1973, interest in attribution theory has stimulated a great deal of research on how individuals arrive at conclusive judgments. In spite of the fact that much of this work has focused on social perceptions of rape, only recently have these studies been integrated with rape research conducted from other theoretical perspectives. While researchers have reviewed rape studies based upon attribution theory (e.g., Feild and Bienen, 1980; Borgida and Brekke, 1985), they have not reviewed the theory underlying the research. Thus my first task will be to summarize key characteristics of attribution theory.

Attribution Theory

Attribution theory evolved during the late 1960s as a logical extension of Heider's theory of balance and "naïve psychology" (Kelley, 1973; Jones et al., 1972). Whereas balance theory is concerned with consistency in cognition and naïve psychology with cognitive behaviors of the "man in the street," attribution theorists focus on how the "average person" explains behavior and makes judgments. Drawing upon naïve psychology, attribution theorists recognize "everyman's" need to impose structure on the environment and to have consistent, rational meanings for the "whys" and "hows" of behavior even when aspects of an event appear contradictory.

The theory recognizes discrepancies in perception, cognition, and evaluation that can occur among persons participating in or observing the same event, between similar events, and over time. When an act occurs, e.g., a sexual assault, attribution theorists are interested in how the perpetrator, the victim, and observers explain the event. What caused it? Who or what is responsible? Responsibility can be assigned to the actor(s), to the environment or context in which the act took place, or to chance, or it can be divided in some way among these components. In a sexual assault, for example, is it the man's responsibility, the woman's responsibility, the environment, or a chance occurrence that caused the assault to occur? Or was it some combination of factors? Attribution theorists also are interested in finding out what type and amount of information is used in making such judgments.

Attribution theory has three interrelated emphases. First, theorists want to find out what motivates a person to decide that it is important to know the cause of an event and to seek relevant information. Second, they seek to discover which environmental and personal characteristics determine the cause or causes that will be assigned to a given event. And third, they want to understand the consequences of making one causal attribution rather than another. Focusing on these three goals, theorists make four assumptions about people's cognitive behaviors. First, they assume that persons seek causes to explain both their own behavior and the behavior of others. Second, they assume that, when necessary, persons seek information to help them decide what caused the behavior. Third, they assume information is sought in systematic ways. And fourth, they assume that the causes given for a particular event have important consequences for a person's subsequent feelings and behavior.

In the case of a sexual assault, it is assumed that both the man and woman involved and relevant observers such as family, friends, and police will systematically evaluate the event to decide whether a rape occurred and who was responsible. It is also assumed that conclusions reached will affect future behavior, future feelings about oneself, and future judgments of other similar situations and people. Thus, if the woman concludes that a rape did occur and that she was largely responsible for it, the theory predicts that her behavior will change in ways she thinks will prevent future rapes. It is also assumed that she will feel that women who are raped under similar circumstances are similarly responsible for their assaults. Conversely, if she concludes that she was not responsible for the rape, her behavior will be less likely to change and her judgments of other similar rapes will absolve the woman of responsibility. /

To determine causality and assign responsibility, an actor evaluates information about the nature of the act itself (what was done and how), the environmental outcomes of the act (e.g., success or failure and reaction of the victim), and the actor's experience (pleasure, anger, embarrassment). Kelley proposes two models by which "attributions" are made: a covariance model and a configuration model. Both are based on a multidimensional matrix that in the simplest form has three dimensions—the actor(s), the event(s), and time. In a covariance model, the person making the attribution has a complete matrix of information available. For example, the observer knows how a lot of people react to a specific event; how each person reacts to many similar events; and how each individual reacts to each event over time or repeated exposures.

In reality, complete data are rarely available. Yet we all attempt to make "sense" out of an action despite the absence of complete information. Kelley's (1973) configuration model applies to these common situations where actors or observers try to "fill in" the matrix to understand how the event or behavior "fits in" or relates to a larger environment or context. To do this, prior information about the person, the situation, or the act is used. Lacking information about *this* person, *this* act, or *this* situation, normative information about similar persons, acts, and situations is used. An observer might, for example, reason that this cannot possibly be rape because these two people are engaged, because the man is a close friend whom he/she has never seen hurt anyone, or because the woman is known to be an "easy lay." Conversely, an opposite conclusion might be reached if it is known that the man beat up his ex-wife and this is a first date.

Discrepancies can occur among observers and actors regarding single or multiple events under both models. However, the possibilities for discrepancy in the configurational situation are infinitely greater. Yet even with a great deal of information, well-meaning, knowledgeable persons can arrive at different conclusions about what happened and explain the occurrence quite differently. Moreover, they evaluate the "worth" of the outcome differently even more often. While they may agree on what happened, they may disagree on the value of the resources invested or the meaning of the conclusions reached. Take, for example, the influence researchers attribute to a defendant's and/or victim's race in the study of crime. In some instances they conclude that race has no impact on arrest or conviction, while in others they conclude that blacks receive differentially negative treatment. Both conceptual and methodological differences have been proposed to explain what must be assumed to be honest disagreement among honorable researchers.[1]

In configurational situations the selection of events, persons, and temporal sequences to put in the matrix is open to misinterpretation and dispute. So also is the process by which the matrix is filled and the relative weights given to the data. In judging a sexual act as rape, the amount of force used and whether the woman consented are legally pertinent pieces of information. For some, persistent verbal harassment by the man constitutes sufficient force and is seen as proof that a rape has occurred. Others might only conclude that a rape has occurred if a weapon was used *and* the woman resisted the attack. For still others, historical information about the man and woman involved, such as knowledge that the man is a burglar or the woman is a nun, can modify how the reported force and resistance is perceived.

Although attribution theory intends to deal in large part with the actors in a social interaction, much of the relevant literature involves simple situations in which a third party observes one or two actors (Kelley, 1972). Many conclusions about how someone in a situation will actually behave are thus extrapolated from studies in which the research subject takes the role of the observer in a simulated situation. This may have some drawbacks, because other research suggests that there are major and consistent discrepancies in how actors and observers perceive situations. Actors or participants in an event often perceive themselves to be at the mercy of an unchanging environment, while observers often think the actor is able to control or change the environment or has a responsibility to change the event. These different views might pertain to sexual assault wherein the woman in an isolated environment who perceives herself to be at the mercy of her date's greater physical size fails to resist. An observer hearing the assault described, however, may wonder why the woman allowed herself to get into the isolated location, why she accepted a date with that particular man, or why she did not at least verbally challenge the man.

Attribution and Locus of Control

Weiner et al. (1972) combine Rotter's concept of locus of control (1966) with the concept of stability to explain discrepancies that can occur in perceptions of actors and observers. Locus of control differentiates between beliefs about internal and external control of events. Events that are internally controlled are those the actor is able to control, avoid, or master through his or her abilities or behaviors. Events that are externally controlled are those in which the actor perceives the environment to be out of his or her control or influence. The concept of "locus of control" has been used both to describe "states" and "traits." In other words, it can refer to an individual's perception of his or her ability to control events in a single discrete instance, or it can be used to describe the person's general personality structure. Weiner et al. add the dimension of "stability" to the model suggesting that a judgment must be made as to the extent to which the situation is unchangeable, either in the immediate instance or over time.

To explain behavior, actors more often perceive events to be outside their control, whereas observers perceive events to be subject to the actor's control. A wide variety of studies suggest that this discrepancy varies with the extent to which the actor is naturally externally oriented and the observer is naturally internally oriented. An actor who is usually internally oriented but is in a situation in which he or she has little or no control may exhibit extreme "cognitive dissonance" because he or she knows that a behavior normally used successfully will not influence the outcome in this instance (e.g., Festinger, 1967).[2]

There is some evidence that locus of control varies with sex-role attitudes and that it influences perceptions of rape and sexual harassment and victims' self-perceptions of responsibility. Women who score high on internal control also score high on nontraditional feminism, viewing women as less passive and more aggressive. Women who score high on external control also score high on traditional feminism, accepting socially defined, normative roles for women. Krulewitz and Payne (1978) found that sex-role attitudes correlated with some aspects of how a rape is perceived. Women with nontraditional sex-role attitudes did not evaluate rape on the basis of the amount of force used, while traditionally oriented females and males did. Women with traditional sex-role attitudes were more likely to blame themselves and other women for being sexually harassed (Jensen and Gutek, 1982). Coates, Wortman, and Abbey (1979) and Calhoun, Cann, Selby, and Magee (1981) found that how victims react to a rape influences observers' judgments of the victim's responsibility for the rape. Victims who displayed more emotion were seen as more credible and less responsible than controlled victims.

Janoff-Bulman (1979) differentiates between the postrape coping of women who use characterological self-blame and those who use behavioral self-blame. Women who cite their own character flaws as a reason for the rape cope less well than those who cite their behaviors. The latter believe that behaviors can be changed, allowing such women to feel they can control future threats of rape.

Configurational Model

Since a full matrix of information is rarely available, attributional studies of sexual assault most often use Kelley's configurational model in which actor-perpetrator, actor-victim, and observers—whether friends, officials, or disinterested third parties—infer much of the information that is used in deciding whether a rape occurred, why it happened, how it happened, and what or who is responsible for it. In filling in the covariance matrix neither actors nor observers obtain information systematically. Usually an evaluative judgment will be made without conscious, deliberate consideration of what is being evaluated and why. Kanouse (1972) argues that linguistic forms and ways in which they are used to arrive at inductive and deductive conclusions are keys to the process of attaching labels to behaviors and in making generalizations about behaviors. Kanouse points out that people tend to use different attributional rules to explain positive and negative feelings. He identifies two criteria that must be satisfied for an object to be considered likeable: it must not have negative qualities of any importance, and its positive and negative attributes must combine into a positive totality. He also points out that once an individual has formed an attribution that s/he deems sufficient to account for a given piece of information, s/he is unlikely to give other potentially satisfactory alternatives much consideration.

In evaluating sexual assaults, Kanouse's theory predicts that judgments will be made most easily if all the information about the man, the woman, and the assault is consistent. Thus the assault would most easily be labeled rape if all the available information resulted in the observer liking and respecting the woman, hating the man, and being sure that the man forced the intercourse and the woman made every effort to resist. To the extent that information is contradictory, decisions are more difficult. Kanouse suggests that a single important piece of negative information about the woman, e.g., she willingly accompanied the man, may nullify other overwhelming evidence in her favor.

Kanouse's summary of psycholinguistic labeling can be applied to observers' assignment of responsibility for a rape. If the observer has decided that the level of force used determines whether an assault is a rape, but that resistance is a key component of responsibility, s/he may decide that a rape occurred, but attribute responsibility to the woman as well as or instead of the man, the circumstances, or chance. Both Feild (1978) and Borgida and White (1978) concluded in their studies using jury simulations that negative information about the woman increased the likelihood that mock jurors would think she was responsible for her rape. Kanouse and others argue that evaluative judgments such as assignment of responsibility may be made completely by inference and with little appreciation of the events or actors that are being judged.

Early Attribution Theory Studies

The first studies in attribution theory preceded detailed formulation of the theoretical model. Early studies focused on how physical characteristics and other potentially nonrelevant characteristics of a situation affected judgments about who or what was responsible and how rewards should be allocated (e.g., Lerner, 1965). Two situational contexts, the accident and the simulated jury, were studied. A frequently cited early study is Walster's (1966) study of how responsibility is assigned in accidents. Highly innovative at the time, Walster's objective was to test whether ". . . the worse the consequences of an accidental occurrence, the greater the tendency of subjects to assign responsibility for the catastrophe to some appropriate person . . ." (p. 73). Forty-four males and 44 females from an introductory psychology class were asked to give "research input" for what was described as a different study. Respondents were presented with taped vignettes in which the mother of the owner of a car that rolled down a hill described the accident. Four "outcome" conditions were specified varying damage to the car and the extent to which uninvolved bystanders were injured. Walster found that the greater the consequences, the greater the tendency to assign responsibility for the accident to the car owner.

A point that is often missed in later references to the study is that the author did not find that the greater the consequences the greater the tendency to blame the victim(s). In contrast to later studies that used rape simulations and that frequently cite this classic study, Walster carefully points out in her discussion that the "perpetrator" in her taped vignettes of an accident is also one of the "victims." Thus, conclusions about victims versus perpetrators cannot be made in the Walster study.

Landy and Aronson's 1969 study of how the character of a criminal and victim affect jurors' decisions is a good example of early work in jury simulations. Citing Walster's study and sociological studies (e.g., Kalven and Zeisal, 1966; Strodbeck, 1962; James and Strodbeck, 1957), Landy and Aronson wished to find out whether criminals were more harshly judged if the victim was an "attractive individual." They did two experiments using male and female undergraduates. In the first, each subject was given a single long vignette in which the victim's attractiveness or unattractiveness was varied. No differences were found by sex of subject, but longer sentences were given when the victim was more attractive. In the second experiment, the attractiveness of the defendant was also varied among attractive, neutral, and unattractive. The researchers concluded that the "attractiveness" of both victim and defendant had some bearing on the punishment prescribed.

Studies on Rape from Attribution Theory Perspective

Jones and Aronson (1973) designed the first attribution study in which rape was simulated. Citing earlier studies of Landy and Aronson (1969) and Walster (1966), the objective was to find out how the social respectability of victims affects perceptions of their responsibility for a crime. They found that victims who were more attractive were perceived as being more "responsible" for their victimization. The seeming discrepancy between this finding and their expectations was explained using Lerner's (1965) "just world" concept in which victims of bad events always deserve their bad end. The "just world" concept is an outgrowth or resolution of Festinger's theory of cognitive dissonance (Festinger, 1967).

Jones and Aronson argue that observers experience cognitive dissonance when bad things happen to attractive people. Unable to assign the event to chance or to the general situation, they resolve the dissonance by rationalizing that the victim, attractive as she may appear, did something to invite the bad event. Although rarely acknowledged, this strain of theoretical reasoning fits neatly with the concept of "victim precipitation" that has evolved in the sociological and criminological literature.[3] In this study, as in earlier studies, male and female undergraduates were used as subjects and lengthy vignettes were used to operationalize the variables.

Jones and Aronson's study (1973) proved pivotal in that numerous studies adopting its general design, a simulated rape event, have tried to replicate, modify, or expand their findings.[4] In general, their findings have not been replicated. Borgida and Brekke (1985) provided a detailed summary of many of the attempts and possible reasons for their failure. Some suggest that rapid change in attitudes about rape caused Jones and Aronson's findings to rapidly become obsolete, while others suggest that the results were simply a statistical artifact. More likely explanations are methodological in nature, suggesting that concepts such as "blame" and "respectability" are multidimensional and not easily captured in a single, unidimensional measure. Borgida and Brekke (1985) suggest, for example, that use of marital status as the indicator of victim respectability may confound the effects of the perceived severity of the consequences of rape for the victim, the victim's prior sexual experience, and perhaps the victim's presumed physical appearance (p. 317).[5]

An "act of rape" can be set up as a perfect model for testing a wide variety of hypotheses about how attributions are made. In rapes there are an action, a victim, and an attacker. Of more relevance for attribution theorists is the wide variety of characteristics that can be varied to test hypotheses about the victim and the attacker while holding the basic identity of the two actors constant. The potential victim is by definition always a female and the alleged attacker is always a male. The age, race, and sociostructural characteristics of the male and female as well as the situation or context in which the act takes place can be varied in an infinite number of ways.

A recurrent theme in attribution research has been the extent to which observers identify with actors and the extent to which this identification correlates with assigning greater or less responsibility to the person with whom they identify. Of interest in studying rape is the extent to which women identify with the alleged victim and men identify with the alleged rapist. Do gender identifications or normative identifications of right and wrong take precedence? Of further interest is the extent to which "same sex" identification is (or can be) modified by changing various characteristics of the two actors. For example, if the woman is portrayed as being of lesser social status than the male, sexually chaste, or as the former wife of the assaulter, will attributions of responsibility for the rape change?

While much of the attribution research, the variables defined, and the findings obtained parallel research done within the sociocultural paradigm, attribution studies represent a more self-contained set of literature. Crossover citations can be found between the two areas (e.g., L'Armand and Pepitone, 1982; Shotland and Goodstein, 1983; Pugh, 1983; Alexander, 1980), but usually are made by nonattribution researchers citing attribution studies rather than the reverse (e.g., Feild, 1978; Williams and Holmes, 1981).

Most attribution studies of rape replicate, with slight variations, earlier research. Most can be traced to Jones and Aronson's original study of 1973. The driving force behind this work is to test attribution theory, rather than to better understand rape. This is evident in the general failure of attribution studies to develop and test measures or indicators of "force" and "resistance," two key legal concepts, in rape simulations, or to test directly various issues of direct relevance to defendant and victim credibility. Borgida and Brekke (1985) point out that even though many of the studies are presented as simulations of juror behavior, few have tested cognitive processes that would be of interest and importance to lawyers prosecuting rape cases.

Only Krulewitz and colleagues (1978, 1979) and Shotland and Goodstein (1983) have investigated directly the effects of the assailant's use of force on attributions about rape. They found that the more physical force a rapist was portrayed as using and the more the victim was portrayed as resisting, the more certain most subjects were that a rape had occurred. Perceptions differ, however, by sex and feminist orientation. Feminists consider the simulated incident a rape at all levels of force. Resistance in the absence of force has been manipulated by Scroggs (1976) and Yarmey (1985) with similar effects on decisions about sentencing. The more the woman was portrayed as resistive, the lengthier the sentence recommended.

While recent studies of rape grounded in other than attribution theory increasingly cite work by researchers in other disciplines, it is ironic that recent attribution researchers are less and less likely to cite the theorists or theory in which the studies originated (e.g., L'Armand and Pepitone, 1982; Shotland and Goodstein, 1983). Thus not only are simulation studies of rape more often tests of principles of attribution theory than inquiries into rape, but many recent studies in the genre are remarkably divorced from their theoretical origins.

Methodology in Studies of Rape Using Attribution Theory

Most studies of rape within the attribution tradition have been laboratory-based experiments using college students as subjects and vignettes written to manipulate independent variables. Generally vignettes are quite long and the portion representing manipulated, independent variables is relatively small. Almost without exception each subject receives a single vignette about which he or she is asked to make a series of judgments. Most common are requests to judge the extent to which the portrayed victim is "responsible for" or "to blame for" the victimization or to indicate the kind or extent of punishment that should be meted out to the male perpetrator.

Usually two to four variables or types of information are varied across vignettes, and each variable is dichotomized or trichotomized. Within the vignettes three kinds of information are usually manipulated: characteristics of the victim, characteristics of the perpetrator, and characteristics of the context or environment in which the encounter takes place. Sex of subjects reading and rating the vignettes is an independent variable that often has been incorporated into analysis of the data. With very few exceptions, analysis of variance[6] has been the preferred and often single analytical procedure used.

Findings

Victim Characteristics

The victim's sexual experience is the variable that has been studied most thoroughly. The earliest studies (e.g., Jones and Aronson, 1970) implied in vignettes how much sexual experience a woman had had by describing her marital, sexual, or occupational status. For example, they described whether the woman was married, a divorcée, virgin, nonvirgin, prostitute, or nun. More recent studies sometimes make explicit statements about the woman's sexual history or reputation, e.g., she is "easy" (e.g., L'Armand and Pepitone, 1982; Borgida and White, 1978; Burt and Albin, 1981).[7] Jones and Aronson found in their original study that women of high respectability were perceived to be more "at fault" for their rape, but men accused of raping such women were judged to deserve more punishment (Jones and Aronson, 1970). Later studies obtained conflicting results (e.g., Feldman-Summers and Lindner, 1976; Kahn et al., 1977; Kanekar and Kolsawalla, 1977; Kerr and Kurtz, 1977), some reporting no differences with sexual experience or "respectability" and others finding inverse relationships between sexual respectability and judgments of victim responsibility. Other researchers find that decisions about responsibility and punishment vary with characteristics of the victim such as attractiveness, dress, prior acquaintance with the defendant, or that such characteristics interact in complex ways with information about the victim's sexual respectability (e.g., Seligman et al., 1977; Thornton, 1977; Kanekar and Kolsawalla, 1980; Kanekar et al., 1981; Scroggs, 1976; Smith et al., 1976; Feild, 1978; Yarmey, 1985).[8]

Defendant Characteristics

Significantly fewer studies have examined the impact of defendant characteristics on judgments about responsibility and punishment. Those that do report similarly contradictory and inconclusive results. Kahn et al. (1977), for example, reported no differences in sentence recommendations or attributions of fault by occupation of the portrayed man, while Deitz and Byrnes (1981) reported differences both by occupation and physical attractiveness. Yarmey (1985) found that the demeanor and appearance of the man affects judgments. Better-dressed men were judged less likely to be rapists. Varying the race of the man yields similarly contradictory results. Both Feild (1978) and Ugweugbu (1979) reported an interaction between the race of the portrayed male and the race of the subject making the judgment. Whites judged black males more harshly. In contrast, Oros and Elman (1979) reported no differences by race of the defendant.

Contextual Characteristics

Few attributional studies have systematically included information about the context or situation in which the rape occurred. Greater levels of force increase a subject's perception that a rape occurred (Krulewitz and Payne, 1978; Shotland and Goodstein, 1983) and the amount of victim resistance affects perceptions (Krulewitz and Nash, 1979; Scroggs, 1976; Yarmey, 1985). Consistent with information from other kinds of studies, rape by a stranger is judged to be more serious (L'Armand and Pepitone, 1982), while provocation is perceived to be a factor in rapes between acquaintances (Smith et al., 1976). Time and place of the rape and information about prior rapes in the area affect perceptions, but in general attempts have not been made to replicate the few studies that include such variables (Bolt and Caswell, 1981; Calhoun et al., 1976).

Subject Characteristics

Subject's sex as a determinant of judgments of responsibility and punishment has been studied frequently. In the absence of any evidence, lawyers, judges, and prosecuting attorneys have long believed that women jurors are biased against defendants in rape cases. Psychologists, on the other hand, suggest just the opposite on the grounds that women want to put psychological distance between themselves and the female victim. Both sexes have been reported to identify more strongly with the victim than the rapist, but the tendency is more pronounced for women. Consistent with this and with research reported in chapters 2 and 3 are reports that men are more likely to identify with the male defendant and to judge the woman as responsible for the rape due to her carelessness, seductive behavior, or unconscious desire (e.g., Kahn et al., 1977; Krulewitz and Nash, 1979; Calhoun et al., 1976; Cann et al., 1979; Selby et al., 1977; Smith et al., 1976). In contrast, women attribute more responsibility to chance or to the rapist and are more likely to perceive the woman to be psychologically affected by the rape.

Other researchers find females more likely than males to assign responsibility for a rape to females who are depicted as meeting traditional social criteria of innocence or sexual inexperience (e.g., Jones and Aronson, 1973; Smith et al., 1976; Calhoun et al., 1976; Rumsey and Rumsey, 1977; Luginbuhl and Mullin, 1974). Within the attribution model, the explanation for this is that persons perceive actors as responsible for their own fate; therefore, to the extent that a victim's innocence appears greater there must then be unknown factors that help explain the series of unfortunate circumstances that occurred. Furthermore, to the extent that the observer perceives himself to be vulnerable to the same fate (e.g., rape), and to the extent that he perceives himself as being able to control his own fate rather than becoming a victim of circumstances, he is more likely to attribute responsibility or "blame" for the rape to the female victim.

To the extent that the concepts of locus of control, sex-role attitudes, and perceptions of rape are correlated, women with a high internal locus of control may be more likely to resist rape if attacked, but if raped may have more emotional difficulty after the rape. A woman's ability to avoid rape may correlate with her self-perception that women have some control over their lives and, therefore, can effectively resist situations that might lead to rape. If she perceives herself as "in control," but "loses" control, no matter how great the external forces, greater cognitive dissonance may result. "If the person explains a bad event by an internal factor, then he/she loses self-esteem. If a person explains the event by an external factor, then self-esteem is not reduced" (Peterson and Seligman, 1983, p. 108). The danger of persistent loss of self-esteem would be particularly potent if the internally oriented woman feels that she did not try hard enough to resist or escape the attack. Dissonance results from the woman's inability to avoid rape when she perceives herself to be a person who is in control of her life. In order to lessen the dissonance, internally oriented women may be more likely to blame themselves or assume responsibility for the rape's occurrence, thereby continuing to maintain a self-image of control.

As noted earlier, Janoff-Bulman (1979) suggests that self-blame takes two forms with characterological self-blame being more destructive than behavioral self-blame. To the extent that changeable behaviors rather than immutable character traits are the focus of self-blame, internally oriented

WHAT IS IT & WHY

female victims are thought to cope better and recover more quickly after rape. To the extent that third parties doubt the rape's occurrence, imply the woman's culpability, or blame her character, cognitive dissonance will increase for all female victims and coping ability will decline.

Differing perceptions of what rape is and what motivates it may explain some of these differences between men and women. As noted in chapters 2 and 3, some evidence from nonattribution studies suggests that males more frequently than females think rape is a sexually motivated act. While some females appear to share this perception (or at least accept its viability for male peers), generally women condemn the violent aspects of rape. Although never explicitly tested, even when females forgive or condone sexual assaults by male dates or friends and accept the male's explanation that the assault was sexually motivated and within the bounds of normal sexual behaviors, there is no evidence to suggest that they think they were participating in a sexual act. On the other hand, although evidence suggests that women are more likely to perceive rape to be a violent rather than sexual act, explicit testing might reveal that some females think some rapes and sexual assaults are primarily sexual or some mixture of sex and violence. Thus perceptual differences found between men and women in attribution studies may suggest that similar gender-determined differences exist in men's and women's perceptions of sexual assaults in which they are involved either as participants or observers (e.g., Heilbrun, 1980).

Men and women differ in their perceptions of the effectiveness of resistance to assaults. Such differences affect judgments of the women portrayed in simulations. There is much confusion and controversy regarding what constitutes effective resistance. These differences exist among actual and potential rape victims, and also among college students who participate in attribution studies. Males think rape is more likely if the woman does not resist, while females think it is more likely if she does resist (Krulewitz, 1981). Furthermore, men think that the more a woman resists, the less she is at fault and the more intelligent she is. Women, on the other hand, attribute more fault and less intelligence to women who resist (e.g., Krulewitz and Nash, 1979). Given some male students' apparent inability to perceive verbal protests as real resistance, particularly when they think the woman is sexually excited, results from these attribution studies are consistent with findings reported by Kanin and colleagues in chapter 3.

Relevance to Judicial Processing

While many attribution studies suggest that men and women perceive rape differently, "the nature of sex differences on some of the more legally pertinent dimensions is less clear . . ." (Borgida and Brekke, 1985, p. 319). Decisions about the guilt or sentencing of defendants have been reported to: differ with sex (Thornton, 1977; Feldman-Summers and Lindner, 1976; L'Armand and Pepitone, 1982); not differ with sex (Kaplan and Miller, 1978; Lenehan and O'Neal, 1981; Jones and Aronson, 1973; Kahn et al., 1977; Oros and Elman, 1979); and interact with beliefs about victim respectability (Feldman-Summers and Lindner, 1976; Luginbuhl and Mullin, 1981), victim attractiveness (Kanekar and Kolsawalla, 1980; Seligman et al., 1977; Thornton, 1977), and characteristics of the case under review (Borgida and White, 1978). Similarly, consistent associations between the subject's sex and the portrayed victim's responsibility for her own rape have not been found.

Borgida and Brekke (1985) suggest that a ". . . promising explanation for the inconsistencies in this research area may lie in the failure of most researchers to control for other subject characteristics which may be less than perfectly correlated with gender and differentially distributed across subject populations" (p. 320). They argue that certain attitudinal and experiential variables, but not personality variables, have been found to be associated with rape attributions. As examples they point to Kaplan and Miller's (1978) report that parents of daughters differed in their perceptions of rapes from parents who had only sons, and to the conclusion of Deitz et al. (1982) that empathy with the victim predicts decisions about guilt and sentencing. Further, victims in rape simulations are seen as responsible for the rape more often by persons who see themselves as likely victims and by those with more actual exposure to victims (Alexander, 1980; Prytula et al., 1975).

Implications and Cautions

The strength of the attribution research literature, which shows perceptions of rape clearly varying with characteristics of the man, the woman, and the situation and the observer, is its development of models through a series of replications that have been done with slight variations on large numbers of similar respondents. This is also a major weakness, because the entire body of literature has been defined by the parameters of the first few studies, and almost all of the investigations use college undergraduates as subjects. We must, therefore, be cautious about generalizing results beyond this narrow, homogeneous group of educated young adults. We simply do not know how other convenience samples or representative samples might react to the same set of stimuli.[9] We also do not know whether we can assume that what is learned in the laboratory will pertain in real life (e.g., Feild and Barnett, 1978; Pugh, 1983). Although these studies can provide valuable insights into how individuals make judgments about relative responsibility, guilt, and sentencing in rapes, it is a long way from the university classroom to the courtroom where actual judgments of guilt and innocence are made.

Indications that caution should be used come from within the attribution literature itself where we find that subjects frequently change judgments when allowed to discuss simulated cases in a way analogous to jury deliberations (e.g., Rumsey, 1976; Izzett and Leginski, 1974; Rumsey and Rumsey, 1977). It is also probable that the actual context or environment or normative assumptions about the environment all affect the process by which attributions are made (e.g., Borgida and Brekke, 1985). Although little systematic research exists, it is probable that the attributions arrived at within a courtroom—as part of a real trial or even a mock trial—differ from those arrived at in a college classroom or psychology laboratory (e.g., Myers, 1980; Bermant et al., 1974).

The potential to generalize is further restricted by researchers' failure to include social structural variables in their analyses. Sex of the subject is the only macrostructural variable consistently analyzed in attribution studies. Thus, no descriptions of ethnic composition, socioeconomic status of the family of origin, religious affiliation, or education are provided or used as predictor or control variables. As a result, no statements can be made regarding how one's place in the social structure or how forces in the larger society may affect perceptions of rape or the attribution process surrounding it.

Moreover, because most studies present respondents with a single vignette, we do not know how a given respondent might respond to slight but systematically controlled changes in the description of the stimulus action. Since the rationale by which vignettes are designed is rarely described or pretested, we also have no information about the relative power of the manipulated versus the nonmanipulated variables in determining judgments. Most studies present data in verbal or written form *in spite of evidence from attribution research itself* that perceptions of linguistic material vary widely with order of presentation, mode of presentation, and presenter (e.g., Chaikin and Darley, 1973; Juhnke et al., 1979).

Furthermore, studies are designed with actors (the male and female in the situation) and observers (subjects/respondents) clearly differentiated and distanced from one another in spite of the fact that both attribution theory and research argue that the role assumed—whether by actor or observer—is a potent determinant of how an event is perceived and evaluated (e.g., Storms, 1973; McArthur, 1972; Nisbett, 1973). In many studies said to be replications (or slight revisions of earlier work) careful reading reveals that the replication differs from the original in numerous respects. Modifications and their ramifications are explored in greater detail in appendix 2.

Almost without exception, variables within the simulations are dichotomized or trichotomized (e.g., Alexander, 1980). Thus, the victim or perpetrator is either attractive or unattractive; the action is rape or assault; either the victim is responsible or the perpetrator is responsible. Dichotomizing the variables restricts the situations portrayed and forces subjects to choose between unrealistic extremes. When multidimensional data are collected, rarely are they analyzed or presented in a way that explores the relative weight of the various pieces of information used by the subject in coming to a conclusion.

Attribution researchers themselves have identified limitations of their studies. Fishbein and Ajzen (1973) point out that inconsistent results occur across studies when theoretical concepts intrinsic to attribution theory are inappropriately operationalized. Responsibility, for example, may be interpreted in a number of ways. In asking whether a woman is responsible for a rape, the real question might be any of the following: Was she associated with the rape? Did her behavior directly result in the rape? Is she responsible in the sense that she could have foreseen its possibility? Did she consciously intend for it to happen? To what extent can her behavior be justified? Subjects are usually not told at what level they are to respond. After reviewing studies of accidents, Fishbein and Ajzen concluded that because there is no uniform way to interpret responses, conflicting findings are hardly surprising (pp. 149–53).

Another limitation of attribution studies of rape is that in most studies the simulation is presented in such a way that it is assumed the rape occurred. The subject is then asked to determine responsibility for the rape. To the extent that variation occurs, it is variation between rape and some other crime such as assault or robbery. No studies so far have asked the subject whether he or she thinks the event portrayed was rape (e.g., Smith et al., 1976). Nor are subjects asked whether or not they think the simulated event is realistic, representative, or appropriate to their own frame of reference and experience.

Further complicating any attempt to generalize the results of attribution studies is the tendency to design studies so that they focus only on the male or the female portrayed. Often the subject is asked about only one of the actors, either the male or the female, rather than about both. The focus is on the subjects' or observers' reaction to that single individual. Subjects have not been asked to judge male-female interactions for the amount of intimacy, sexuality, or violence presented. Nor have they been asked to compare male-female interactions to male-male and female-female inter-actions. Such studies might help researchers determine the threshold at which a sexual encounter becomes a violent encounter, the extent to which the two characteristics intertwine in sexually assaultive and coercive behavior, and the extent to which male-female interactions differ from same-sex interactions.

Finally, with few exceptions (e.g., Shotland and Goodstein, 1983; Pugh, 1983) data are analyzed using analysis of variance as the only analytical tool. Thus the impact of multiple variables or the development of staged causal models has rarely been attempted.

In summary, although attribution studies provide information about how individuals define a sexual encounter as rape, limitations in samples and methodology produce conflicting findings from which it is difficult to generalize. This is not to say that we cannot learn from such studies. But it does say that readers must be cautious about generalizing from results of a single study or basing policy recommendations on a single study. Insight into the multifaceted dimensions of rape as a social act can be obtained only by cautiously combining results across attribution studies and comparing them to results obtained with other methodologies.

5 Institutional Definitions of Rape: The Judiciary

N umerous researchers have demonstrated that many rape cases never reach the courtroom (e.g., Chappell and Singer, 1973; Hindelang and Davis, 1977; Galvin and Polk, 1983; LaFree, 1980; Lizotte, 1985; Loh, 1980; National Institute of Law Enforcement and Criminal Justice, volume III, 1978). Most that do are tried in state courts under procedures determined by a combination of state-generated statutory and case law, with precedents established over time and from numerous individual trials.[1] Before 1974, case law governed most of what occurred in state courtrooms during a rape trial. Between 1974 and 1980, however, most state legislatures, in response to lobbying by the women's movement, rewrote rape statutes. Often both a substantive statute defining rape and evidentiary statutes are relevant in trying a rape case.[2]

Although irrelevant for the majority of rape cases, federal regulations apply or take precedence in three instances: when the rape occurs in a federal jurisdiction (e.g., on federal property such as an Indian reservation, or on a ship flying the American flag), when the accused is employed by the United States government (e.g., military personnel), and when a case originally tried in a state court is appealed to a federal court on the grounds that some aspect of the procedures under which the trial was conducted violates federal procedures. In the vast majority of constitutional challenges, the issue for appeal is a claim that some constitutionally guaranteed right of the defendant has been violated. Prior to 1978, cases tried under federal jurisdiction followed procedures generated by federal case law or specified by the Code of Military Justice. In 1978, Congress passed new evidence legislation, Rule 412, under which such trials are now held.

English Common Law and Case Law

Prior to 1974, most state laws defining rape were recodifications of the narrow definition of rape that had evolved under English Common Law.[3] Under common law, rape was defined as ". . . the carnal knowledge of a female, not one's wife, forcibly and against her will . . ." (Bienen, 1976). Carnal knowledge was defined as penetration of the vagina by the penis. In many jurisdictions, penetration had to be proved by physical evidence around and within the woman's vagina or on the male's penis. Under many evidence statutes, emission of semen had to be demonstrated.

The state had to offer evidence that the act was done forcibly and against a woman's will. In other words, it had to prove that she did not consent. Over the years state case law and state statutes have included numerous mechanisms to differentiate consent from nonconsent. These included requirements for corroboration by witnesses and physical evidence, mandatory cautionary instructions to the jury as derived from Lord Hale, and introduction of a woman's prior sexual history either as part of a "consent defense" or to impeach the woman's credibility as a witness.

It is through case law that Lord Hale's cautionary instruction to the jury that "a charge of rape is easily to be made and hard to be proved and even harder to be defended" became part of the evidentiary code in most states (Hale, 1778). (Sir Matthew Hale was Lord Chief Justice of the king's bench from 1671 to 1676 and author of the posthumously published *History of the Pleas of the Crown,* which was among the earliest compilations of English Common Law.)

In an attempt to differentiate consensual from nonconsensual sex through case law, the judicial system essentially institutionalized a decriminalized view of rape. Before trying the accused, the state had to "prove" the chastity of the complainant and her credibility. Many of the resulting procedures reflected a biased, inaccurate, and prejudiced view of both women and rape.[4] Defendants were allowed to bring evidence into court about the victim's character, her prior sexual history, her propensity to consent, and her reputation for chastity in an effort to prove that she consented to the rape or was lying when she said she did not. As case law developed, particularly during the mid-twentieth century, consent to rape came to include sexual intercourse under circumstances of force, brutality, humiliation, and degradation (Bienen, 1981). Justification for this view included the belief that women were essentially vindictive in nature and that they fantasized and fabricated rapes (Marsh, Geist, and Caplan, 1982; Simpson, 1986).

It was from this area of the law—the introduction of past sexual conduct as evidence of a woman's character—that feminists and others, seeking to overturn traditional rape and evidence statutes, collected their most powerful ammunition. Even after rape laws were revised, this area remained most controversial. Rights of the victim to privacy and freedom from unnecessary harassment and humiliation conflicted with the defendant's constitutional right to a fair trial (e.g., Hermann, 1977; Tanford and Bocchino, 1980; Galvin, 1986). Under the sixth amendment a defendant is guaranteed the right to confront hostile witnesses through cross examination and to call witnesses favorable to his presentation of events. Debate focuses on just when demands for fairness and due process justify introducing evidence on the victim's sexual history (Tanford and Bocchino, 1980). To deny such demands may afford special protections for rape victims that are not available to most prosecution witnesses.

Tanford and Bocchino (1980) argue that evidentiary rules should focus on issues common to all trials and should not develop differently for each substantive crime and civil cause of action. Yet within the still largely male-dominated court system, it is still difficult to separate historical and contemporary sexism from legitimate concerns about the defendant's rights.

Even in revised statutes the line between "consent" and "nonconsent" remains murky. They use such phrases as "by force," "against her will," and "without her consent," sometimes synonymously and sometimes as distinct elements to define nonconsent. The difference between "without her consent" and "against her will" has actually worked against the prosecution by leading courts to consider "resistance" as an element of nonconsent. Legal commentators are repeatedly calling for a clear standard of consent or nonconsent (e.g., Harris, 1976; Loh, 1980; Estrich, 1987).

To better understand the legal context in which rape cases are tried, we must understand the meaning of "character evidence" and the relative roles and rights of the various actors involved in a trial.

The Victim Complainant as a Witness

As with other criminal offenses, the victim or complainant in a rape case has no party status. Rape is a crime against the state and it is the state represented by the prosecuting attorney that files charges against the accused. It is the state, not the victim, that calls witnesses, introduces evidence, cross-examines defendants' witnesses, plea bargains prior to trial, or appeals an unsatisfactory outcome to a higher court. It is the defendant, not the victim, who decides whether to go to trial or to negotiate a plea bargain and, if a trial is sought, whether evidence will be heard by a jury or a judge. Revisions in rape statutes affect only those trials that are heard before a jury. In cases that never reach trial the victim frequently is not told the disposition. Even under reform statutes only the State of Indiana has institutionalized a procedure by which the victim is informed of results of a plea bargain.

Police and Prosecution

If a complaint is ever to result in a trial, the police must formally accept the complaint and investigate it consistent with ways of obtaining evidence that can be used in court. Not all complaints are accepted (University of Pennsylvania Law Review, 1968), and, as was dramatically pointed out by the LEAA-sponsored Battelle study, the conduct of police investigations varies widely across jurisdictions in both thoroughness and timeliness (National Institute of Law Enforcement and Criminal Justice, Police Volume I, 1978). If the investigation is to progress, the victim must be willing to cooperate with police even if that necessitates medical, psychiatric, or polygraphic (lie-detector) examinations she finds traumatic or with which she philosophically disagrees. Cluss et al. (1983), in a study of 77 victims, found that women who prosecuted their cases had higher overall self-esteem, but participating in the trial disrupted their recovery from rape.

Once an investigation concludes, police must decide whether to take the case to the district attorney's office or declare it "unfounded."[5] Reasons for declaring a rape unfounded include a delayed report on the part of the victim, lack of physical evidence, the victim's refusal to submit to a medical examination, the victim's refusal to prosecute, failure to apprehend the offender, evidence of a prior relationship between the victim and the offender, or judgments about the victim's character.

Rape cases formally enter the criminal justice system when the prosecutor or district attorney issues a warrant. To issue a warrant the prosecutor must have confidence in the investigation conducted by the police. In some cases the prosecutor will reinvestigate all or part of the evidence. Thus, judgments about the victim's character can again informally influence the progress of the case.

Marsh, Geist, and Caplan (1982) found that prosecutors are much less likely to say they would issue warrants for arrest of an accused rapist than police are to say they would seek an arrest, regardless of the circumstances surrounding the rape. The researchers asked 39 police officers and 40 prosecutors how they would react to two hypothetical rape scenarios, one portrayed in the context of a date and the other in the context of work. In each instance, four versions of the scenario were presented, differing according to whether there was a prior sexual history between the male and female, whether they had been drinking prior to the assault, and whether physical or job-related threats were made. Differences between police and prosecutors were particularly pronounced when couples portrayed had been drinking or had previously engaged in consensual sex. Prosecutors, in particular, thought such portrayals were not rapes.

To the extent that the police department and the district attorney's or prosecutor's office historically have had a good working relationship, the prosecutor is more likely to accept the case as presented and less likely to duplicate or extend investigations conducted by the police. If, on the other hand, the police have often urged prosecution of cases that the prosecuting attorney has subsequently lost in court or on appeal, the prosecuting attorney will be more skeptical. Even after a warrant has been issued, a case may fail to come to trial. The accused may plea bargain the charge down to a lesser charge to which he pleads guilty, thus negating the need for a trial, or the case may be dismissed, usually because the complainant refuses to prosecute or fails to show up at the trial.

Although some persons assume that the outcome for the victim is better when the case is heard by a judge rather than a jury, this is not necessarily so. Bohmer (1974) demonstrated through interviews with 38 judges that many held highly stereotypical views of rape, believing that evidence of third-party sexual behavior, prior consensual sex with the defendant, and delayed reporting by the woman are proof that the woman was not raped or that she deserved it.

The U.S. legal system emphasizes protection of the accused and seeks to ensure the defendant's right to present witnesses and to confront and cross-examine all hostile witnesses. Given the orientation of the U.S. judicial system, cross-examination of a prosecution witness by the defense in any criminal trial is likely to be unpleasant as is cross-examination of a defense witness by the prosecution. Although boundaries exist and judges can, at their discretion, rule that a particular tactic is unnecessarily harassing the witness or not relevant to the defendant's guilt or innocence, such discretionary decisions more often benefit a defendant than a victim.

Data on Judicial Processing

It is debatable whether the rate at which rape cases pass through the judicial system is substantially different from that for other crimes. Feminists argue that rapes are processed at significantly lower rates than all other crimes. LaFree (1980) found that of 881 sexual assaults reported to police from 1970 through 1975 in a Midwestern city, only 37 percent resulted in arrests. Prosecutors filed charges against 47 percent ($N = 153$) of those arrested. Of those convicted, either through trial ($N = 30$) or a guilty plea ($N = 74$), 80 percent were incarcerated, half in state prison and half in some other institutional setting. Results differed, however, with the racial composition of the victim-defendant dyad. Blacks who assaulted white women received more serious charges and sentences.

Myers and LaFree (1982) compared data on 176 of these same forcible sexual offenses to 373 property offenses and 396 other violent crimes. They found striking differences between sexual assaults and other crimes in terms of the characteristics of victims, defendants, and evidence. However, differences did not consistently result in changes in the way officials reacted to and dealt with sexual assaults, nor were markedly different criteria used to evaluate and determine the outcome of such cases.

Galvin and Polk (1983), using California data for 1974–77, found that the pattern of processing of rape complaints in California approximated that found by LaFree in Indiana and Chandler and Torney in Hawaii. Galvin and Polk then compared processing of rape complaints in California to those of homicide, robbery, assault, and burglary. They reached the conclusion, based on the probability of a rape charge being processed further into the criminal justice system, that both police and prosecution treat rape similarly to other crimes of violence.

2 While police are unlikely to make an arrest in response to a rape offense report, reported rapes are cleared by arrest less frequently than homicide or assault but more frequently than robbery or burglary.

3 . . . prosecutors file felonies on rape arrests at about the same rate as they file felonies on robbery, but at a much higher rate than either assault or burglary and at a lower rate than homicide; felony filings for rape lead to a lower level of felony conviction than is true for homicide, a slightly lower rate than for robbery, but a higher rate than assault and burglary.

4 While judges are unlikely to sentence a rapist to a prison term, felony convictions lead to imprisonment for rape at a lower rate than homicide, a slightly lower rate than robbery, but at a higher rate than assault and burglary. . . . (Galvin and Polk, 1983, pp. 135, 146)

Debate also persists concerning whether recently revised rape statutes have led to differences in the processing of rape and other violent crimes. To evaluate the impact of changes in Michigan's sexual assault statutes, Carignella-McDonald (1985) examined all 1981–82 sexual and nonsexual assault cases in the Kalamazoo County (Michigan) prosecutors' files. She extracted information relating to corroboration, precipitation, credibility, character, and decisions regarding the issuance of warrants, plea bargaining, nolle dismissal,[6] or acquittal. Her findings were mixed. Arrest warrants were issued more often in sexual assault (67 percent) than nonsexual assault (54 percent) cases, yet reduction of charges through authorization,[7] dismissal, and acquittal was similar between the two types of offenses. Nevertheless, sexual assault cases were reduced to a greater extent than other assaults when plea bargaining occurred.

Complicating the interpretation of these differences were differences in evidence between the two types of cases. In cases of nonsexual assault witnesses were more often available, victims were older, and assailants were more often strangers whom victims had physically resisted and who had inflicted injury. It appears that sexual assaults in Kalamazoo County were as likely to be prosecuted as nonsexual assaults, and that differences result from differences in the amount and quality of available evidence. On the other hand, since prosecutors' files provided the data it is possible that they differentially recorded information in ways that discriminate against the successful prosecution of some kinds of sexual assault cases, resulting in increased rates of plea bargaining.

Past Sexual Conduct as Evidence of Character and Credibility

The past sexual conduct of a victim has been brought into rape trials either as character evidence to be used to prove consent or to impeach the witness-victim's credibility. Galvin (1986) suggests that admission of such evidence in court was often justified by traditional notions of women and sexuality and rules pertaining to character evidence.[8]

Character Evidence

Character evidence is ". . . a form of circumstantial evidence offered at trial to prove [that] a person possessing a particular character trait acted in conformity with that trait on the occasion in question" (Galvin, 1986, p. 777). Much of the case law relevant to character evidence has developed in murder cases where, for instance, by entering evidence that the victim had a violent "character," a defendant may try to prove that the murder occurred in self-defense. The use of character to infer or prove conduct is circumscribed by archaic, paradoxical rules (Galvin, 1986). In rape cases, the conduct generally being disputed when sexual history evidence is presented is whether the woman consented to intercourse.

Character evidence generally is excluded from the courtroom for two reasons. First, it is thought to be of low probative value: It adds little firm evidence that a jury can use to decide what actually happened. And second, it is thought to have a high potential for prejudice. Concerns about prejudice relate to the moral connotations surrounding judgments about a person's character. Potentially prejudicial use of character evidence evolves in four ways. First, character evidence, because of its flamboyance, may divert the jury from other more relevant and factually based evidence. Second, it may introduce side paths of investigation not relevant to the issue. Third, the length of time needed to establish character evidence may be excessive relative to its value. And fourth, the jury may base decisions to award or punish the defendant on perceptions of the good or bad character of the defendant or witnesses, instead of on more pertinent evidence.

Although generally inadmissible, character evidence can get into the courtroom via one of three routes: The defendant can introduce evidence about his own good character; the defendant can attempt to establish the fact that a hostile witness, namely the victim, has a bad character and that on the occasion under scrutiny her behavior conformed with her bad character; and, finally, character evidence can be used to establish whether a witness is truthful or untruthful. Notice that in the first two instances, the emphasis is on protecting the defendant and guaranteeing him every opportunity to establish his innocence.

Sexual Conduct as Character

Evidence about past sexual conduct was brought into court by the defendant as part of a common law "consent defense." This defense was admitted on the grounds that lack of chastity is a character flaw that could suggest consent in the present situation (Davis, 1984). If the man could establish that the woman consented, then he could not be convicted of rape. The problem was the breadth of information that could be presented as evidence of consent and the extent to which such evidence overshadowed other, more substantial factual evidence. Women were either good or bad. Good women confined their sexual activities to a marital relationship and bad women deviated to any degree from this idealistic norm.

Over the years, sexual history became the *only* evidence used to establish the character of the victim in a rape trial. If the victim was unmarried and not a virgin (unchaste) then she was a bad woman whose claims of rape were either fantasized or the product of spite. The idiosyncratic way in which character evidence was allowed to be used becomes even clearer when one considers that similar sexual information about men was never used to establish character and that a woman's sexual history could not be used as evidence of her character in any other kind of case (e.g., a robbery).

Sexism and social attitudes toward women can be blamed for allowing prior sexual conduct to be the criterion for judgments about whether a woman consented and whether she was credible, but the legal basis for that criterion can be traced to three specific sources: Lord Hale, Wigmore, and early case law focusing on the relatively rare "rapes by fraud." In addition to warning that rape was an accusation that was easy to make but hard to prove, Hale warned of false or malicious rape accusations.

Wigmore issued a similar warning in his definitive treatise *On Evidence*.

Modern psychiatrists have amply studied the behavior of errant young girls and women coming before the courts in all sorts of cases. Their psychic complexes are multifarious, distorted partly by inherent defects, partly by diseased derangements or abnormal instincts, partly by bad social environment, partly by temporary physiological or emotional conditions. One form taken by these complexes is that of contriving false charges of sexual offenses by men. The unchaste (let us call it) mentality finds incidental but direct expression in the narration of imaginary sex incidents of which the narrator is straightforward and convincing. The real victim, however, too often is the innocent man; for the respect and sympathy naturally felt by any tribunal for a wronged female helps to give easy credit to such a plausible tale. (As quoted in Galvin, 1986, p. 788)

The "ample psychiatric evidence" cited by Wigmore consisted of five case studies from a 1915 textbook in which women under psychiatric care filed rape charges, and a variety of letters and monographs written by four psychiatrists prior to 1933 (see Berger, 1977; Galvin, 1986; Harris, 1976). Three of the five cited cases never went to trial. It is from this never-updated "evidence" that Wigmore concluded that women have a propensity for falsifying charges of sexual offenses by men. Believing that juries would be more sympathetic to the victim, Wigmore recommended that a conviction for rape never be based solely on the testimony of the complaining witness, and that the complainant's social history and mental makeup be examined and attested to by a qualified physician before the case was presented to a jury (Sasko and Sesek, 1975). Berger (1977) suggests that Wigmore's ideas on proper proof in rape proceedings have carried disproportionate weight because of his stature as an authority on evidence and his position as dean of a major law school.[9]

Harris (1976), in arguing for a legal standard of consent, reviewed early rape case law and suggested that early legal commentators' emphasis on cases of fraud simply exacerbated an already bad situation. "Scholarly discussion on consent in rape jelled in an era when legal thinkers were emotionally distrustful of rape complaints in general, but were fascinated by cases where consent was allegedly induced by subterfuge" (Harris, 1976, p. 628). The subterfuge under consideration was of two kinds: impersonation of the woman's husband or a doctor's assurance that the act was a medical treatment. In 1925, Puttkammer applied a strict "nature of the act" test to rape concluding that a virgin could be raped because she did not know what intercourse was and thus could not consent to it. In contrast, for all practical purposes, nonvirgins could not be raped because they knew the "nature of the act." Married nonvirgins could not be raped not only because they knew the "nature of the act" but because they would never let it occur because they knew the penalties of being judged unchaste. Unmarried nonvirgins were by definition unchaste because they must have consented at least once without bringing charges of rape. Exactly how a raped virgin was supposed to know she had been raped and could bring charges if she could not recognize the "nature of the act" was never clarified.

Types of Character Evidence

Three kinds of character evidence are used in all trials: reputation evidence (the aggregate community view of a person), opinion evidence (a given witness's personal opinion of a person's character), and specific instances of a person's conduct that demonstrate a particular character trait. Under common law, reputation evidence, although generally agreed to be least useful and least dependable, was the preferred method of presenting evidence about a person's character. Under modern statutory law opinion evidence is also generally permitted, but evidence of previous conduct is generally allowed only on cross-examination.

In nonrape cases only general statements can be made about a victim-witness's community reputation as having a violent or nonviolent character, and sexual reputation is not a relevant part of his or her character under any circumstances. In contrast, in rape cases prior to revision of the law, many states allowed both the victim-witness's general sexual reputation in the community and specific instances of her sexual behavior (including such irrelevancies as whether she used an IUD for birth control or slept nude) to be entered as evidence of whether she was chaste or unchaste, and hence whether she consented to the intercourse.

The Movement for Legislative and Court Reform

Between 1974 and 1980 all state legislatures considered and most passed some change in statutes governing rape. This fact alone is remarkable. Although rape laws were studied systematically in only Michigan, California, Washington, New Jersey, and Pennsylvania, similar forces seem to have coalesced in all states to enact these changes. Forces influencing reform included active lobbying by the women's movement, the existence of and lobbying by the law-and-order movement, the residual impact of the Model Penal Code developed during the 1950s, and the rapid increase in rape complaints between 1960 and 1975 (Marsh, Geist, and Caplan, 1982; Geis, 1977; Bienen, 1981). The extent of revisions and the success of reforms in a given state apparently depended on the extent to which feminists were able to gain legitimacy and to form successful coalitions with law-and-order forces.

One of the earliest and most extensive reforms was passed in Michigan in 1974 and took effect in 1975. Successful enactment of the law depended on an active women's movement strategically located in Ann Arbor close to major media outlets in Detroit and to the state's major law school at the University of Michigan. The Supreme Court ruling that legalized abortion in January 1973 allowed women's groups nationally to give primary consideration to rape, an area of feminist concern previously overshadowed by efforts to obtain safe abortions. A series of brutal rapes in Ann Arbor rallied the local women's movement and led to research to augment the scarce statistics collected by law enforcement agencies. Bipartisan coalitions were developed, and as a result, a white Republican, Gary Byker, sponsored the bill in the State Senate, and a black Democrat, Earl Nelson, sponsored the bill in the State House. Virginia Nordby, a lecturer at the University of Michigan Law School, participated in drawing up the proposed statute.

A key explanation of the differences in state statutes, such as those in New Jersey and Pennsylvania, is the extent to which a state had previously adopted sections of the Model Penal Code developed in the 1950s (Bienen, 1976). Bienen argues convincingly that states that had previously adopted all or part of the Model Penal Code enacted only minor or conservative changes in rape statutes between 1974 and 1980. Bienen further points out that the Model Penal Code's Criminal Law Advisory Committee was basically conservative and had only one female member. The Model Penal Code required corroboration and prompt complaint of rapes. More radical reform statutes did not include such requirements. Furthermore, the Model Penal Code gave no protection to spouses or to women judged "sexually promiscuous complainants."

Changes in Legal Commentary

Evidence of increased attention to rape and changing focuses of attention within rape law can be seen in the legal literature itself. A search of two indices, the *Index of Legal Periodicals* and *Current Law Index*, quickly reveals three things. First, prior to 1971, rape trials and statutes were of little concern to the U.S. legal establishment. Prior to 1926 only scattered references to case notes or comments on rape are listed. The scarce case law available on rape prior to 1900 concentrates on exceptional minutiae rather than typical rapes and its writers are predominantly concerned with the rights of the male.[10]

Beginning in 1916 and continuing through 1970 the average number of citations to rape was two per year. In many years there were no references. Starting with 1971, references to judicial concerns regarding rape escalate. Between 1971 and 1979, 135 articles are listed, and research articles and legal commentary are increasingly referenced. Between 1980 and mid-1986, 382 comments, notes, and research articles on the subject were listed in *Current Law Index*, and female authors were increasingly prevalent.[11]

Much of the pre-1973 commentary focused on protecting males against false accusations of rape. Other topics receiving significant attention were statutory rape (21 comments and notes), prior sexual history as evidence of character (4 comments and notes), consent as a defense (3 articles), and the need for corroborating evidence (8 articles).

During the 1970s legal commentary was characterized by calls for reform of existing case and statutory law, and subsequent description of the various new statutes as they were passed (20 articles). With the exception of 17 articles on capital punishment that generally called for its abolition in cases of rape, the focus of most articles was on the role of the victim-witness (33 articles) rather than on the defendant. Written primarily toward the end of the 1970s, nine articles focused on conflict between roles of the victim-witness and the defendant, paying particular attention to how rape shield[12] provisions conflicted with constitutionally guaranteed rights of the defendant. A few articles focused on issues related to statutory rape (4 articles), marital rape (7 articles), and the application of civil law to rape cases.

During the 1980s legal commentary continues to focus on the description and evaluation of new statutes (49 articles), but the number of articles devoted to marital rape in particular has increased dramatically (34 articles). Statutory rape also has drawn much attention (27 articles), but many of the articles focus on a single prominent case. Increasingly prevalent are articles that investigate the courtroom status of rape crisis center counselors as expert witnesses, and the legitimacy of the rape trauma syndrome.

Objectives and Accomplishments of Reform Statutes

The advisability of focusing reform efforts on changing legal statutes was debated during the 1970s. Results of reform are also a topic for debate (e.g., Bienen, 1981; Marsh, Geist, and Caplan, 1982). The consensus of the coalition of reform groups prior to revision is summarized by Sasko and Sesek (1975) as follows:

> Despite the fact that rape reform legislation does not provide a total solution to the problem, it should be enacted since it will, at the very least, establish a strong policy in support of the rape victim. Such a policy should counteract the historical bias against rape victims by giving notice that the rights of the rape victim will no longer be subordinated to those of the accused. (Sasko and Sesek, 1975, pp. 502–3)

Among the more knowledgeable reformers were some cynics who considered the adoption of reform statutes a symbolic act with the actual benefits of such statutes being largely unknown.

The overriding objective of reform was to move the burden of proof from the victim to the offender by: (1) redefining and recriminalizing rape and other forms of sexual assault and extending equal protection to excluded groups, (2) bringing legal standards for rape cases in line with those used in other violent crimes by normalizing requirements for evidence, and (3) exercising control over decisions made in the criminal justice system (Marsh, Geist, and Caplan, 1982, p. 4). Bienen identified five specific aspects of rape laws that were targeted for revision, namely redefinition of the offense, protection of the victim in trials, repeal of the spousal exemption, changes in the penalty system, and changes in the statutory age.

Expanding somewhat on Bienen, Galvin (1986) listed four specific aspects of revised laws that were introduced as part of the overall objective of protecting the victim: elimination of the resistance standard and the mandatory cautionary instructions, modification of corroboration requirements, and addition of rape shield provisions. She identified other major objectives of the reform movement to be the establishment of innovative programs such as rape crisis counseling centers, mandatory emergency treatment in hospitals, reimbursement for medical treatment, and consciousness-raising programs for police and prosecutors in some state statutes. The increased attention to civil procedures in rape cases has certainly been an innovative outgrowth of the movement, even if it was not an original objective of the legal reformers (LeGrand and Leonard, 1979; Hanks and Zimet, 1981).

One of the most important changes sought by reformers, the exclusion of irrelevant sexual history evidence, could have been made by the judicial branch through case law (Galvin, 1986). In fact, however, all the major revisions in rape laws were initiated by the legislative branch following pressure from lobbyists.

Redefinition of the Offense

In rewriting rape statutes, many states replaced the common-law term "rape" with the terms "sexual assault" and "sexual abuse." The objective was threefold: (1) to emphasize the violent, nonsexual aspects of the offense, (2) to broaden the acts covered by the statutes, and (3) to allow for a sex-neutral definition of the crime. New statutes replaced and/or consolidated laws on rape, attempted rape, sodomy, deviant sexual intercourse, molestation of a child, statutory rape (corruption of minors and seduction), fornication, incest, and sexual assault. Both men and women were defined as possible victims of the consolidated crimes as well as possible perpetrators. A graduated statute often resulted with the gradations differentiated by one or more of the following: degree of force used, nature of the sexual acts committed, age differential between victim and offender, or relationship between victim and offender.

Protection of the Victim at Trial

A major objective of reformers was to shift the burden of proof in rape cases from victim to accused. They sought to minimize harassment and humiliation of victims during trials by changing the kinds of evidence and the ways in which evidence could be brought into a trial. Such changes could be instituted as part of a substantive sexual assault statute or could be incorporated into new evidence statutes.

In rewriting legislation, three overlapping changes in evidence requirements were attempted. The first attempted to eliminate mandatory cautionary instructions to the jury. The second attempted to reduce the kinds and amounts of corroboration required to proceed to trial. Whereas in other kinds of assaults victims' statements are accepted as true, in rape cases evidence that assaults occurred without consent had to be corroborated through physical evidence or third-party testimony. In many instances, every essential fact of the victim's testimony had to be corroborated. In New York prior to 1972, for example, that required corroboration that penetration of the vagina and emission had occurred. Not surprisingly, in New York courts one year only 18 rape convictions were obtained despite thousands of complaints (Bienen, 1977).

Although the corroboration rule has been dropped in most states, current efforts to insist on psychiatric or polygraphic (lie detector) validation of the victim's testimony, often during pretrial investigations, suggest that there still are males in the judicial system who insist that the veracity of women cannot be trusted (Bienen, 1981).

The third and most debated change attempted was to partially or completely eliminate evidence of a woman's prior sexual conduct from the courtroom. This introduced so-called "rape shield laws." Courts had admitted evidence of the victim's prior sexual history generally either to impeach her credibility as a prosecuting witness or to show the likelihood that she consented to the act. Thus one assumption behind admitting evidence of past sexual history is that a woman's sexual behavior is directly related to her credibility. Another assumption is that a woman who has consented to sexual advances in the past is more likely to have consented to the encounter in question than is a chaste woman (Borgida, 1980). The logic behind both assumptions has been widely criticized in recent years (e.g., Berger, 1977; Letwin, 1980; Note, Valparaiso Law Review, 1976; LeGrand, 1973).

The most significant continuing debate, however, juxtaposes the defendant's sixth-amendment rights with the prejudicial nature of testimony about the plaintiff's sexual history (e.g., Berger, 1977; Tanford and Bocchino, 1980; Galvin, 1986.[13] On the one hand, the prejudicial nature of such testimony on jurors is argued to outweigh its minimum value as evidence of consent. It is argued that it is illogical to suggest that past consensual sexual behavior with a man other than the defendant increases the likelihood that a woman consented to be raped. Yet it has been argued that jurors' attitudes toward sex prohibit them from appropriately minimizing such illogical evidence, allowing it instead to deflect them from the task at hand. The other side argues that no matter how tangential the evidence, if there is any chance that past third-party sexual behavior has relevance, it is the defendant's right under the Sixth Amendment to present such evidence to the jury. Galvin (1986) proposes evaluating evolving case law in seven areas in which prior sexual history evidence might legitimately be admitted: when it applies to a relationship between victim and defendant; when it is used to demonstrate the source of physical consequences such as trauma, pregnancy, or disease; to prove complainant bias or motive to fabricate; to show a pattern of behavior so similar as to prove consent; to prove a mistaken belief in consent; to rebut the state's proof; and to show the complainant's prior false allegations of rape.

Thus far forty-eight states (all but Arizona and Utah) and the federal government have passed some form of rape shield provision. Galvin (1986) divides current statutes into four categories according to the extent to which and procedures by which prior sexual history evidence can be offered on the issue of consent. The first category comprises twenty-five states that exclude virtually all evidence of third-party sexual conduct. Prior sexual conduct is admitted only under highly specific, statutory exceptions. The exceptions most widely allowed are when the prior sex involves the defendant (e.g., cases of date, acquaintance, or spousal rape) or when it is necessary to prove the source of pregnancy or disease.

The eleven states in the second category do not restrict the use of third-party sexual conduct as evidence of consent. An *in camera* hearing to establish the relevance of the evidence is required, but the decision as to what is admitted depends entirely on the discretion of the judge.[14] Interestingly, most of these states continue to use the common-law definition of rape.

The seven states in the third category model their laws on the federal statute, which combines features of both restrictive and discretionary approaches. These laws generally exclude sexual conduct evidence while allowing for certain exceptions. They do, however, include a provision for introducing evidence of unexcepted sexual conduct if such evidence is, for example, "constitutionally required to be admitted" or "relevant and admissible in the interests of justice" (Galvin, 1986, p. 775). Sexual conduct evidence is separated into two categories determined by whether it will be used to prove consent or to attack credibility. Five states (California, Delaware, Mississippi, North Dakota, and Oklahoma) exclude the use of sexual conduct, except with the accused, to prove consent. Inexplicably, the other two states allow its use to prove consent, but do not allow it to be used to attack the complainant's credibility. Galvin (1986) says "the primary flaw in this legislation is that sexual conduct evidence does not neatly break down into 'consent' or 'credibility' uses" (p. 775). In the last two groups of states, judicial screening generally takes the form of an *in camera* hearing in the judge's chambers. For the evidence to be admissible, the judge must agree with the defense that it has some relevance to the case.

Changes in Penalty Systems

Most states have enacted statutes that simultaneously reduce extreme penalties for rape and establish mandatory minimum penalties. In 1965, eighteen Southern and border states imposed the death penalty for rape (e.g.,

Partington, 1965; Wolfgang and Riedel, 1975). In 1977, seven states mandated the death penalty for certain types of rape convictions. Ironically, in five of the jurisdictions there are situations in which the death penalty imposed for rape would not be applicable if the offender instead murdered his victim under the same circumstances (White, 1976). Reformers argue that extreme mandatory sentences reduce the number of convictions because both judges and juries are unwilling to impose the mandatory sentence. Furthermore, researchers have demonstrated that extreme sentences, when permitted, are differentially applied to blacks convicted of raping white women (e.g., Partington, 1965; Wolfgang and Riedel, 1975; White, 1976; LaFree, 1980).

Prior to reform, many men accused of rape chose to plea bargain the charge. Such cases never went to trial, and the defendant often pled guilty to a lesser, nonsexual offense. These defendants were often released on probation. In states where mandatory minimum penalties were not defined, men convicted in trials presided over by judges as well as in jury trials often received light sentences at the judge's discretion. Passage of graduated statutes with minimum, mandatory penalties was designed, in part, to reverse this trend.

Following the Michigan example, many states have enacted laws in which there are degrees of criminal sexual assault. Thus, an offender originally accused of first-degree criminal sexual assault may plea bargain to second-, third-, or fourth-degree sexual assault, but not to a nonsexual assault charge. Minimal penalties are attached to each degree of criminal sexual assault. The intent of the revised penalty provisions is to gain more convictions, to identify offenders as sex offenders rather than other kinds of felons, and to obtain a higher rate of incarceration upon conviction.

Repeal of Spousal Exemption

Under English Common Law a man could not be charged with raping his wife. As Bienen (1981) points out in the following passage, this was consistent with societal views of women and marriage.

. . . the notion that a woman had the right to deny her husband sexual access to her body would have been inconsistent with the social expectations regarding married women which were embodied in the legal institution of coverture, the laws of inheritance, primogeniture, spousal immunity for torts, and other doctrines which demonstrated that women were considered the physical property of their husbands, as children were the property of their fathers. The purpose of marriage was procreation, and the wife's promise to obey meant that the husband had a right to sexual intercourse with the wife upon all occasions. Her personal consent was irrelevant; the woman's subjective feelings on a particular occasion were not important. A wife's refusal to have sexual intercourse was a ground for divorce. (Bienen, 1981, p. 184)

Efforts to reform rape statutes in the early 1970s and later concern about battered women motivated the first attempts to reconsider the spousal exemption.[15]

The earliest revised statutes did little to change the status of married women who were raped by their husbands. To the extent that a statute was modeled on the Model Penal Code, a statute may have even extended the marital exemption to include women in nonmarital, cohabiting consensual sexual relationships. But the Model Penal Code also recommended that the marital exemption should not apply to women who lived physically apart from their husbands and who had filed (or whose husbands had filed) for divorce or separate maintenance.

Oregon was the first state to rewrite its statute to allow a woman living with her husband to bring charges of sexual assault against her husband. While many other states have considered the issue, the status of sexual assault within marriages or cohabiting relationships with a history of consensual sex remains controversial. Traditionalists argue that expanding coverage by sexual assault (rape) statutes to include such relationships will result in a sharp increase in frivolous and vindictive charges. Nontraditionalists argue that sexual assault clearly occurs within such relationships and it is a woman's right under equal protection to protect herself against nonconsensual sexual assault.

Changes in Statutory Rape

Definitions of statutory rape and penalties that should be attached to it are among the most troublesome and unresolved areas of revised sexual assault statutes. Much of the controversy involves the extent to which girls and women should be protected against sex of any kind, and at what age and with whom they can consent to sex. Existing laws differ significantly on these issues, indicating that a high level of uncertainty exists on the part of legislators.

Most people agree that children must be protected from sexual assault regardless of who or how old the perpetrator is. On the other hand many people are reluctant to legally prohibit consensual sexual activity between unrelated adolescents. But when does a child become an adolescent? And when does an adolescent become an adult? Some states, in an effort to decriminalize consensual sex between teenagers, have drafted laws making it virtually impossible for a female under the age of eighteen to bring sexual assault charges against a nonrelated male in the same age group. Yet young women are the most common victims of sexual assault, and young men the most frequent perpetrators (e.g., *Uniform Crime Reports*, 1979–85).

Innovative Changes in Criminal and Civil Law

With the revision of state statutes, two innovative and somewhat unusual changes should be noted. First, some states (e.g., Nevada, Ohio, Michigan) now mandate minimal treatment for victims of sexual assault and provide payment out of state funds for treatment or ensure that victims have access to care. Hospital emergency rooms must accept sexual assault victims, and in Nevada the state is also required to pay for the emotional injury of victims and their spouses. In some instances a victim must file charges in order to be eligible for treatment.

Secondly, cooperation between authorities and the victim/complainant is now encouraged. Indiana ensures the victim the right to know the outcome of any plea bargaining that takes place before a case comes to trial. Thus the victim/complainant is ensured a judicial status somewhat greater than that normally accorded witnesses in criminal cases. Consciousness-raising programs for police and prosecutors have been encouraged by statutes in some jurisdictions, and evaluations of such programs suggest a positive effect on police attitudes (e.g., Gottesman, 1977).

An innovative change resulting from efforts of law-and-order and victims' rights movements as well as feminist lobbying is the increasing tendency to bring civil suits for damages against sexual assault offenders or third parties. Victims have been compensated for treatment costs and injuries, have been awarded punitive damages, and have successfully brought suit against schools, landlords, motels, public transit companies, and employers of both the victim and the accused (Hanks and Zimit, 1984). Eventually institutional defendants might be compelled by the threat of suits to provide more effective safety measures to prevent sexual assault. This will shift the burden of protection from the victim to larger entities or institutions (Hanks and Zimit, 1981).

Effectiveness and Limitations of Legislative Changes

The extent to which revised statutes have actually effected change in the judicial system is unknown. Short-term evaluations of judicial processing conducted in California, Michigan, and Washington, as well as evolving case law, have been assessed across all jurisdictions (e.g., Deming, Landry, and McFarland, 1984; Marsh, Geist, and Caplan, 1982; Loh, 1981; Davis, 1984; Polk, 1985; Galvin, 1986). Some argue that changes observed result from societal changes as much as from legislative changes. Those who minimize the impact of revised statutes cite the influence of society's greater recognition of rights of women, the development of effective support networks for rape victims, and the increased incidence of rape in changing the judicial system's procedures for handling rape. Skeptics point out that legal statutes only affect what happens during a trial and thus may have little or no impact on receptivity of police to accept complaints, decisions to recommend cases to the prosecutor, or the prosecutor's decision to plea bargain.

Skeptics may be wrong. In Michigan a greater percentage of rape cases has resulted in convictions since reform, while the number of cases plea bargained or not prosecuted has not increased. According to Marsh, Geist, and Caplan (1982), changes in the definition of rape and loosening of evidence requirements led police to investigate more cases and arrest more suspects. In contrast, judges and defense attorneys less frequently perceived laws to have effected change; further, judges and defense attorneys were more often perceived by police and prosecuting attorneys to have allowed clearly prohibited sexual evidence to be presented to juries without appropriate judicial screening. The use of *in camera* hearings in Michigan and other states is still rare. Likewise, the incidence of nontraditional (e.g. date or acquaintance rape) cases, which under the new graduated statute would be brought to trial as criminal sexual conduct in the third or fourth degree, remains low in Michigan.

Deming, Landry, and McFarland (1984) paint a more discouraging picture in California. After elimination of the mandatory cautionary instruction and passage of the Robbins Rape Evidence Law, law enforcement agents released a greater percentage of rape suspects and district attorneys filed a smaller percentage of cases in lower courts. Using available data on four Southern California counties from the California Offender-Based Transaction Statistics, 1974–77, Deming et al. compared statistics on rapes and other sexual crimes to statistics on assault and robbery. During the period studied, arrests reaching the district attorney's office declined from 88 percent to 83 percent, and the proportion of cases sent by the district attorney's office declined from 74 percent to 69 percent. However, the percentage of men convicted of rape in Superior Court who were sentenced to state institutions increased from 49 percent to 61 percent, and the percentage of men who pled guilty in Superior Court and received sentences to state institutions increased from 29 percent to 37 percent. To explain the decrease in the percentage of cases handled by the system, Deming et al. speculate that increased reporting of rape may lead to weaker cases getting into the system in the first place.

Using data produced by the California Bureau of Criminal Statistics for 1975 through 1982, Polk (1985) compared trends in rape processing to those for homicide, robbery, assault, and burglary. Reforms with direct and indirect relevance for the processing of both rape cases and other violent crimes were instituted in 1975, 1976, 1978, and 1979. Thus, Polk's comparison across type of crime is particularly pertinent. He found that the clearance rate for rape remained stable at just under 50 percent over the eight years.[16] This rate was consistently lower than those reported for homicide or assault, but higher than those for robbery and burglary. The percentage of arrests for rape that resulted in filing felony complaints was slightly higher in 1982 than in 1975. He found that the most dramatic change occurred in sentencing. Those convicted of rape were much more likely to be sentenced to a state institution in 1982 (81 percent) than in 1975 (58 percent) (Polk, 1985).

Loh (1981) examined the effect of reforms, similar to those in California, on charging and disposition of 445 rape complaints filed in King County, Washington, from 1972 to 1977. His sample included 208 cases filed before reform (July 1, 1975) and 237 cases filed after reform. He found no differences in overall conviction rates (which remained slightly over 60 percent, excluding statutory rape cases). However, reform did reduce, from 35 percent to 15 percent, the percentage of plea bargainings resulting in convictions for nonrape offenses.

After reform, convicted rapists were far more likely to be incarcerated in state institutions (83 percent versus 58 percent), but sentences to prison declined (35 percent to 27 percent) while sentences to inpatient treatment facilities increased sharply (22 percent to 55 percent). Although the number of complaints filed increased steadily, the proportion of cases prosecuted remained constant, and factors differentiating prosecuted from unprosecuted cases remained the same. These factors included evidence of force, social interaction between suspect and victim prior to the offense, corroborative evidence, victim credibility, and race. Loh concluded that certain factors must be present in order to win at trial, and that these remained the same despite reforms in the legal elements of rape.

Galvin (1986) evaluated four different rape shield statutes to examine their effect on the use of prior sexual history under nine specific situations or exceptions. She examined approximately 370 cases conducted under the fifty new statutes, grouping states according to whether their rape shield statutes resembled those in Michigan (the most restrictive), Texas (the least restrictive), California (which only allows evidence of sexual conduct to be used to prove either consent or credibility), or the Federal Statute. She concluded that the restrictive approach errs by excluding an entire category of factual evidence without regard to the particular facts of a case. As a result, the courts have either ruled the statute unconstitutional in particular cases or more often reclaimed the use of their own discretion in deciding relevancy of evidence. Courts using the least restrictive approach, on the other hand, have determined the relevancy of sexual conduct history on a case-by-case basis in a manner consistent with the intent of rape shield legislation. Although there was little case law under the federal statute approach, Galvin predicted that these courts too would act in a manner consistent with legislative purposes. She concluded that courts under the California approach also were avoiding sexist assump-

ir scrutiny of sexual conduct evidence. She did, however,
cern about the lack of restrictions under this approach.

n she concluded after her review of case law that the four types
are working according to legislative intent, she said that all
statutes are inadequate. She advocated adoption of new legislation allowing sexual conduct to be entered as evidence under certain exceptions and
after showing cause. Davis (1984) also studied revised rape laws, and
similarly concluded that many rape shield statutes as currently written are
unduly restrictive.

Not addressed by the reform of rape statutes, but contributing to the
differential treatment of rape complainants in the judicial system, is the
increased use of nonsexual history evidence to establish credibility and
nonconsent. Marsh, Geist, and Caplan (1982) report that widespread use
of polygraphs (lie-detector tests), particularly by police, establishes the
credibility of the victim's story. The extensive use of polygraph tests on
victims was first and most completely documented by the Battelle Institute studies in the mid-1970s. They reported that 27 percent of police
departments surveyed used polygraph testing frequently while another 56
percent used it occasionally. A majority of those surveyed felt that polygraph tests were either very (48 percent) or somewhat (41 percent) effective (Battelle Institute, Police Volume I, March 1977, table 42, p. 36).
Even when such evidence is not or cannot be brought into court, it may
persuade police to pursue an investigation or recommend prosecution to
the district attorney's office. Of further concern is the fact that victims do
not have recourse against requests for polygraph testing: Refusal to submit
to testing, like refusal to submit to medical examination, is often interpreted to be evidence of consent or fabrication. Although psychiatric examination is not used as frequently as in the past, it has also been used by the
prosecution to establish the victim's credibility and by the defense to dis-
credit the victim's credibility (Nemeth, 1984). The admissibility and
appropriateness of polygraph and psychiatric examination has not been
addressed in revised sexual assault statutes.

The Behavior of Juries

Although only a minority of rape cases ever reaches a jury trial, only jury
trials are directly affected by revised rape statutes. Fair treatment of the

complainant depends on the extent to which juries base decisions on prejudicial evidence, particularly the characteristics of the woman's sexual history and her credibility as a witness. Two kinds of jury research have been conducted: studies that indirectly study the behavior of actual juries and studies using simulations of jury behavior. Because most contemporary jury simulations have been conducted within the context of attribution theory, the design of and findings from many jury simulations were discussed in chapter 4.[17] Five studies of the behavior of impaneled jury members and one community-based jury simulation are discussed here.

As part of the Chicago Jury Project, Kalven and Zeisel (1966) sampled juries in 3,576 trials at two times during the 1950s. Questionnaires were sent to each presiding judge inquiring about the general pattern of facts that had been presented, the jury's verdict, and conclusions the judge would have reached had it not been a jury trial. The study's results have been widely cited as evidence that juries are prejudiced against the prosecution in rape trials (e.g., Geis, 1977; Harris, 1976; Berger, 1977; Hans and Vidmar, 1986).

To test whether contributory or precipitative behavior of complainants affects jury behavior, trials were divided according to whether a simple or aggravated rape was at issue. Simple rapes were defined as those with a single assailant, where victim and assailant knew each other, and in which there was no evidence of extrinsic violence. Juries acquitted the defendant or reduced the charge in simple rapes far more frequently than judges claimed they would have. Kalven and Zeisel (1966) and Berger (1977) conclude that the tendency of juries to dismiss charges in simple rapes demonstrates that the concept of contributory negligence on the part of the victim, common in civil cases, was being applied inappropriately in criminal rape cases.

Tanford and Bocchino (1980) argue that most commentators have cited Kalven and Zeisel out of context, making assumptions about the extent to which sexual history evidence was brought into the trials under review. They argue that the most frequently cited table shows that juries tend to be lenient with defendants under very narrow circumstances. They concluded that when all rape cases are considered, juries treat rape defendants similarly to defendants tried for other crimes.

Borgida (1980) administered simulated rape cases to 180 jurors on the last day of their duty in Minneapolis and asked them to judge the extent to which they were certain that the victim consented to the intercourse and whether the defendant was guilty. Results from this study confirm fears that juries would find sexual behavior information prejudicial.

Lengthy vignettes were used to present the case with two variables presented at each of three levels to create a 3 × 3 design. Each unique vignette was administered to 20 jurors.[18] Consent conditions varied were: a low probability that the woman consented, an ambiguous probability that the woman consented, and a high probability that the woman consented. In an effort to vary the extent to which a victim's prior sexual history with third parties is brought into court under the variety of new rape shield laws, the following three conditions of sexual history evidence were operationalized:

Common law: high admissibility. A witness for the defense who had known the accusing party since college and had the opportunity to learn her reputation for chastity testified that it was generally known that the accusing party had sex frequently with many different men, some of whom were strangers, and that once during a college fraternity party she had sex with several men on the same evening.

Moderate reform: low admissibility. A witness for the defense who had known the accusing party for several years and had the opportunity to learn her reputation for chastity testified that it was generally known among her friends and acquaintances that she had frequently had sexual relations with men who had picked her up at a bar.

Radical reform: low admissibility. No third-party sexual history presented in the vignette.

Probability of consent affected jury members' perceptions of both defendant guilt and victim consent. The types of exclusionary rule were related only to jury members' perceptions of whether the vignette victim consented to intercourse and were not significant for perceptions of guilt. Interactions were not significant with either dependent variable. Jurors perceived as much victim consent in the moderate-reform conditions as in the common-law conditions, and the proportion of guilty verdicts was 33 percent for both common-law and moderate-reform conditions. The proportion of guilty verdicts increased to 53 percent under the radical-reform exclusionary rule (Borgida, p. 22).

Unfortunately, Borgida's attempt to test differences between what he labels a common-law exclusionary rule and a moderate-reform statute was confounded with the type of sexual evidence presented in the vignettes. Even though the first condition was intended to represent states in which no statute is in force, and the second condition states that allow evidence to be admitted only after an *in camera* hearing, jurors obviously reacted identically to the two third-party sexual scenarios. Rather than simultaneously changing the type of sexual evidence presented to respondents and the legal admissibility of evidence, Borgida and colleagues might have created two variables. The first would have presented withheld third-party sexual evidence, while the second would vary judicial instructions to the jurors.

There is no ideal way to simulate an *in camera* hearing. Borgida and colleagues tried to do so by creating a sexual scenario they thought resembled the kind of evidence a judge would allow a jury to hear. The reason for the lack of differences between the two groups is that this particular operationalization failed to capture all the necessary variables. Varying both a judge's instructions to the jury and the sexual evidence as two independent variables within the simulation would allow study of the extent to which jurors are able to evaluate and ignore evidence deemed prejudicial or of little probative value in proving innocence or guilt. Although such a simulation would not fully represent the intent of statutory reform in states with inclusive rape shield laws, it would replicate what often happens during a trial (e.g., LaFree, Reskin, and Visher, 1985; Hans and Vidmar, 1986).

Borgida and colleagues reported that male jurors more frequently than female jurors perceive the victim as consenting to intercourse. Jurors in the radical-reform condition were more likely (47 percent) than jurors in the common-law condition (26 percent) to want more information. The most frequently requested information across all conditions was for a more detailed account of the interaction between the victim and the defendant on the night in question. The next most frequent request was for character and sexual-history information. The latter requests were more frequently for evidence about the defendant than about the victim (Borgida, 1980).

Perceptions of the defendant's guilt were related to juror age, income, education, scores on the Just World Scale of Rubin and Peplau, Burt's Rape Belief Scale, and their perception of the victim's consent. The selection of stepwise regression and the existence of a high correlation ($r = .77$) between perceived victim consent and perceived defendant guilt obscures the usefulness of the results ($R^2 = .51$). Staged regressions in which demographic variables preceded personality and experimental manipulations might have provided more insight into the data. Elimination of sex from the regression equations is not explained.

In an earlier study using 348 jurors as subjects (Borgida and White, 1978), two-hour videotaped simulations were presented in which likelihood of consent was varied between low probability of consent and high probability of consent. The exclusionary rule was varied between common law, moderate reform, and radical reform. Included as information about the likelihood of consent were the nature of the relationship between the man and woman, the extent of her resistance, and the location of the meeting. Jurors were asked to judge the credibility of the man and the woman and the probability of the man's guilt. Consistent with expectations, the manipulated information more strongly influenced jurors' perceptions of the woman's credibility than the man's. As in the later study, however, jurors did not differentiate between common-law and moderate reforms when the victim was portrayed as probably consenting to the rape. Although the process by which manipulations were conducted is much more difficult for the reader to comprehend in this study, it seems likely that, as in the earlier study, the volume of information contained within a single manipulation influences the findings.

LaFree, Reskin, and Visher (1985) interviewed jurors who served in thirty-eight trials concerning forcible sexual assault; these trials were held in Marion County, Indiana, between July 1978 and September 1980. were also observed. Of interest was the jurors' perception of the defendant's guilt or innocence at the conclusion of the trial but prior to jury deliberations. Trials were divided into two groups: (1) cases in which the defense claimed that the victim had either consented to intercourse or had not been sexually assaulted, and (2) those in which the defense acknowledged that the victim had been sexually assaulted, but claimed that the wrong man was being accused or there was diminished responsibility for his behavior (e.g., he had taken drugs, alcohol). Although the latter two defenses are valid in nonsexual cases, use of the former two defenses is restricted to rape cases. In such cases the issue is more the complainant's status as victim than the defendant's status as accused.

Of further interest to the researchers was the extent to which information of concern to feminists affects jurors' reactions in the first group of cases where a "no-sex" or "consent" defense is used. Researchers examined the following parameters on jurors' perceptions of defendant guilt prior to jury deliberations: (1) effects of victims', defendants', and jurors' characteristics, (2) information about prior intimacy between the male and female, (3) force used, and (4) resistance attempted.

Jurors' predeliberation perceptions of defendant guilt in consent and no-sex cases were affected by victim characteristics, defendant characteristics, whether the victim and defendant were acquainted, jurors' attitudes toward crime, the interaction between jurors' sex-role attitudes, and the victim's use of alcohol or drugs. Victim characteristics to which jurors responded were race, whether or not the victim was portrayed as currently sexually active, and her use of alcohol or drugs. Defendant characteristics to which jurors responded were the extent to which the defendant was perceived to be a "loser" and his prior criminal record. Perceptions of cases in which a consent defense was used did not differ significantly from those in which a no-sex defense was used.

Among identification and diminished-responsibility cases the same variables and interactions predicted juror judgments with three exceptions and the addition of four evidence variables and an interaction. Neither the race of the victim nor evidence that she was sexually active affected perceptions of guilt in these cases. A prior criminal record by the defendant actually reduced the possibility that he would be considered guilty. The four new variables affecting guilt were the number of charges filed, whether there was an eyewitness, whether a weapon was used, and whether injury occurred. Finally, an interaction between jurors' attitudes toward sexual-social freedom and use of drugs and/or alcohol by the victim influenced judgments.

Interpretation of findings within this group of cases and comparison of these results to findings from the first group of cases is complex. Unlike consent and no-sex cases, perceptions of guilt differed between the two kinds of defenses with defendants in diminished-responsibility cases being more likely to be judged guilty. Thus, other variables found to differentiate guilty from not guilty defendants may simply be differentiating defendants who used a diminished-responsibility defense from defendants who used a mistaken-identity defense. The investigators found that defendants' characteristics and behavior predicted jurors' perceptions of guilt for each kind of trial. Defendants' criminal records, lack of social ties, and negative courtroom appearances increased the likelihood that they would be found guilty. Victim characteristics influenced juror perceptions in the consent and no-sexual-contact cases: Evidence that the victim did not engage in extramarital sex, did not use drugs or alcohol, was not acquainted with the defendant, or was white increased the likelihood that the defendant would be found guilty. Whereas most demographic and attitudinal characteristics of jurors were reported to have no influence, jurors' belief in the importance of being tough on crime did increase the likelihood that the defendant would be found guilty. The number of jurors participating in each type of trial and the extent to which jurors' characteristics are similar across the two types of trials is not reported.

On the face of it, it appears that the effect of information about the victim is greatest when a consent defense is used, leading the authors to conclude that the variables affecting rape processing may depend on legal issues disputed. Some variables (e.g., victim sexually active or black) affected jurors' judgments only when the rape was disputed, some when the rape was not disputed (e.g., number of charges, whether or not there was a weapon), and others regardless of whether the rape was disputed (e.g., the victim drank or used drugs, victim and defendant acquainted). The authors concluded that when the victim's word was of primary rele- to a consent, jurors were influenced more by her character than by hard evidence, even corroborative evidence.

Although results suggest the importance of examining legal characteristics of cases as well as victim and defendant characteristics when predicting juror verdicts, analytic problems complicate interpretation. In evaluating the results of the study it must be assumed that insufficient cases were available to allow the researchers to stratify jurors into four groups by type of defense used and then examine regressions within strata or use discriminant analysis. Although bivariate correlations suggest that the two groups differ in demographic and attitudinal characteristics, the authors fail to report whether these differences were significant and might have influenced the outcomes. Specifically, and a possible result of voir dire,[19] socioeconomic status appears to be differentially distributed across the two groups of jurors leading to substantial differences in the distribution of attitudes about sex and victims and defendants.

To simulate juror behavior in a rape trial, Feild (1978) administered descriptions of rape cases to 1,056 residents of a Southeastern community. Six variables were manipulated within each description or vignette: race of the victim (black or white), attractiveness of the victim, sexual experience of the victim, race of the defendant (black or white), type of rape, and amount of evidence.[20] The length of sentence recommended differed significantly for white "jurors" according to the race of the victim, the race of the defendant, the type of rape described, and the amount of evidence reported. Black males who raped white females in nonprecipitory rapes with a great deal of evidence were given the longest sentences.

The length of sentence prescribed by white "jurors" was affected by their age and education, the belief that it is a woman's responsibility to prevent rape, the belief in severe punishment, the belief in victim-precipitated rape, and the belief in the normality of rapists. Sentences prescribed by black respondents were affected by education, prior jury service, and the beliefs that women are responsible for rape prevention, that sex motivates rape, and that rapists should be severely punished. Feild and Bienen (1980) conclude that attitudinal variables account for more of the differences among jurors' decisions than do jurors' background characteristics. To some extent, however, the role of background may have been obscured by stratification in the analysis.

Summary and Implications

If changes in statutory law constitute evidence of an effective social movement, rape reformers' efforts to change legal institutions were an unqualified success. Nevertheless, while undoubtedly rape victims were poorly treated by the judicial system prior to rape reform, whether that reform has effectively removed the unequal treatment of rape victims relative to victims of other crimes has yet to be determined. Changes enacted in statutory law primarily affected the disposition of rape cases once they reached jury trial. Reform had no direct effect on precourt judicial processing. Even within courtrooms the effect of reform in some jurisdictions may be more show than substance. The few evaluations conducted demonstrate that although the conviction rate has increased and plea bargaining has been restricted, judges still are remarkably unable to define rape as a violent rather than a sexual act. New statutes often demand that convicted rapists be incarcerated, but they are often sent to hospitals rather than prisons. Apparently treatment is thought to be of greater benefit to rapists than to other felons.

In spite of restrictions placed on judges and attorneys, judges in particular retain enormous power in the courtroom and if so disposed can selectively apply criminal sanctions to male assailants of women. Even in states with restrictive rape shield laws, a judge with a conservative definition of rape can, through the use of instructions and *in camera* hearings, allow into the courtroom technically inadmissible evidence such as that related to prior sexual history. Moreover, the significant discretion they retain can be exploited by clever defense attorneys. Whereas Galvin (1986) concludes from case law that judges generally have respected the intent of statutory reforms, Marsh, Geist, and Caplan's (1982) findings regarding the attitudes of Michigan judges suggest that further study is needed. It must be remembered that most reforms enacted by legislatures could have evolved through case law rather than legislation and that, consciously or unconsciously, judges and attorneys chose not to make those changes. Because historically change and evolution in the U.S. judicial system has depended heavily on precedents derived from case law, we cannot assume that the judiciary fully accepts statutory rape reforms until such statutes are firmly incorporated into that case law.

Available data indicate that jurors are clearly influenced by the amount and type of legally irrelevant information presented to them. While juries appear to be more heavily influenced by information about the victim than the defendant, this may simply reflect the fact that more irrelevant information about victims has been included in studies. With the exception of research conducted by LaFree, Reskin, and Visher (1985), in which actual case data were studied, most studies using jury simulations have included only one or two pieces of irrelevant information about the defendant (usually concerned with race). Whether information about the defendant's past sexual experiences would influence judgments (as it does with victims) is unknown. While study of the defendant's past sexual history is irrelevant in the courtroom, it is not irrelevant to assessing perceptions about what constitutes rape earlier in judicial processing and informally in the courtroom. Judges, attorneys, and jurors are not immune to the attributional processes and needs discussed in chapter 4.

Even more worrisome is the influence that legal maneuvers of attorneys and judges may have on jurors' perceptions. In the three studies in which clear attempts were made to determine the impact of legal characteristics on juror behavior, findings suggest such information to be as important as or more important than jurors' preconceived biases about rape in determining the jury's verdict (Borgida and White, 1978; Borgida, 1981; LaFree, Reskin, and Visher, 1985). Attorneys are clever manipulators of truth. It is not just the existence of evidence that influences a jury; often it is what the prosecuting attorney, defense attorney, and judge make of the evidence that makes it important to a juror. It seems likely that jurors respond as much to the perceptions of the players directing the case as to the information provided. The process of voir dire, dismissal of juries for *in camera* hearings, the judge's instructions and interactions with the attorneys, and jurors' perceptions of the judge and attorneys can all influence a jury's later deliberations and the subsequent verdict.

Although some statutes instituted programs to educate police and others about rape, it is not clear that processes by which cases of rape enter the judicial system and proceed to trial have changed significantly. To become a court case or obtain a conviction, a rape complaint must first be accepted for investigation, undergo investigation, and then be reported to prosecutors for acceptance or rejection. The extent to which reforms changed this process is unknown.

The few available studies suggest that police and prosecutors are more conservative than community members in attitudes about rape, but that attitudes among police who have been exposed to educational programs do change, at least in the short term. To the extent that attitudes about rape have liberalized within the broader community, however, police attitudes would also be expected to liberalize even without educational programs targeted specifically at them. Unfortunately, no studies have been conducted to measure either community or police attitudes over time; thus, the extent and direction of attitude change among police, other judicial personnel, and the community at large are unknown.

No research compares the acceptance and early investigation of rapes to those of other violent crimes. We need to learn how police decide to initiate an investigation, carry out the investigation, and then either drop it or take it to the district attorney. Such studies should be conducted across crimes and across jurisdictions, both within a state and across states with different types of reform statutes. How police handle victims and the relative importance of different types of evidence would be of particular interest. Comparisons between rape cases and nonrape cases regarding the use of lie detectors, psychiatric examinations, and the relative treatment of male and female victims would help determine whether rape reforms have, in fact, influenced early judicial processing of rape complaints.

Definitions of rape differ within and between judicial jurisdictions just as they do in the community at large. These differences undoubtedly influence adherence to the intent and letter of rape reform statutes by police, prosecutors, defense attorneys, and judges.

⑥ Community Definitions of Rape

C ommunity surveys provide the best information about what ordinary people think about rape. Six community studies in particular enhance our knowledge of how people define rape and the extent to which definitions vary with life-style, place in the larger society, personality, and attitudes: Ageton, 1983; Goodchilds et al., 1983; Klemmack and Klemmack, 1976; Burt, 1980; Feild and Bienen, 1980; and Williams and Holmes, 1981. To assist the reader in making comparisons and contrasts among these six studies and the Los Angeles study, both methodology and findings are abstracted in detail.

National Youth Survey

Ageton concluded that an integrated theory of delinquency better predicts who will become the victim or offender in a sexual assault than do feminist theories about pervasive socialization to sexual passivity and coercive sex.[1] Her conclusion rests on her finding that sexually assaulted females and assaultive males do not differ from their age peers in their attitudes about rape, sexuality, or women, but do differ in their affiliation to delinquent peers and in their participation in delinquent behaviors. Ageton concluded that the demographic characteristics of such subgroups are not distinctive but, as noted earlier, her choice of analytical procedures may have obscured such differences. Although victims and offenders are never directly compared, Ageton implies that similar socialization and peer group forces combine to affect both males and females involved in sexual assaults.

Ageton's (1983) study of victims and perpetrators of sexual assault developed out of the National Youth Survey (NYS), which had a longitudinal, sequential design with multiple birth cohorts. Selected in 1976, the sample was a national probability sample of youths aged 11 through 17 years. Respondents were surveyed five times over a five-year period between 1976 and 1981. Of 2,360 eligible youths, 1,725 (73 percent) agreed to participate; 231 youths (13.4 percent) failed to complete all five years of the study. Ageton's study concentrates on those 135 females and 51 males who reported participation in one or more sexual assaults as victims or perpetrators in one of three years, 1978–80. Questions used to generate the sample read as follows:

How many times in the last year have you:
1 Had or tried to have sexual relations with someone against their will?
2 Pressured or pushed someone such as a date or friend to do more sexually than they wanted to do?
3 Physically hurt or threatened to hurt someone to get them to have sex with you?
4 Been sexually attacked or raped or an attempt made to do so?
5 Been pressured or pushed by someone such as a date or friend to do more sexually than you wanted to do?

Data used in analyses included sociodemographic information (age, race, social class, and place of residence), general attitudinal and behavioral scales, and specific information about the sexual assault(s). General attitudinal and behavioral scales measured were: attitudes toward sex roles; attitudes toward interpersonal violence; attitudes toward rape and sexual assault; perceptions of negative labeling, social isolation, and normlessness from family, peers, and teachers; attitudes toward deviance; exposure to delinquent peers; perceived disapproval of delinquent behavior by parents and peers; involvement with family, peers, and school; aspirations; achievement relative to aspirations; peer pressure in support of drinking and drug use; and trouble resulting from drinking and drug use. Incidence and prevalence estimates were calculated, sexual assaults were described, and youths reporting assaultive episodes were compared to randomly generated female and male comparison groups from the larger study. This latter set of analyses is particularly relevant here.

T-tests and discriminant analyses were used to test propositions generated from an integrated theory of delinquent behavior and from feminist conflict theory. Sexual assault victims did not differ from nonvictims in demographic characteristics, sex-role attitudes, or deviant life-style. Victims had engaged significantly more often in delinquency that was supported by peers, and had experienced more nonsexual victimization. Peer group and delinquency patterns of sexually assaulted females resembled those of female participants in delinquency who had not experienced sexual victimization. Involvement in peer-supported delinquent activities preceded occurrence of the sexual assault by as much as two years.

Offenders, likewise, reported higher rates of involvement in delinquent behavior supported by peers and did not differ from a comparison group of nonoffenders in demographic characteristics or attitudes about sex roles, rape, and sexual assaults. Offenders, however, had experienced more disruptions in their home life than had same-aged peers. Ageton's conclusion that sociodemographic variables do not distinguish sexual assault victims or offenders from their age peers must be viewed with caution. For purposes of some comparisons, groups apparently were stratified by race and social class (Ageton, 1983, p. 106). With stratification the effect of race and social class would be largely controlled and thus would obscure meaningful comparative statements.

Although a great deal of descriptive information is reported about both victims' and offenders' perceptions of the sexual assault(s) in which they were participants, neither t-tests nor discriminant analyses were used systematically to compare these perceptions. Only information on the amount of force used in the assault is presented in tables. While comparison of the adolescent victims to the adolescent offenders would be only suggestive (since the male offenders and female victims are not reporting participation in the same sexual assaults), to do so would highlight existing perceptual differences and similarities between victims and offenders. As currently presented, the burden is on the reader to infer such information.

Table 6.1 shows the extent to which reports of force differ between the sexually assaulted females and the assaultive males. While both report verbal persuasion or threats of blackmail to be the major form of force,

Table 6.1 Comparison of female victims' and male offenders' reports of force used in sexual assaults by year of assault (Ageton, 1983) (in percentage)

Type of force reported	Year of assault and sex of reporter					
	1978		1979		1980	
	Males	Females	Males	Females	Males	Females
Verbal persuasion or threats of blackmail	50	39	44	21	47	17
Victim drugged, drunk, or taken by surprise	21	10	22	10	24	11
Threats: verbal threats of injury; size and strength of offender; number of offenders; display of weapon	18	23	22	29	6	28
Physical force: pushing, slapping, roughness; physical beating or choking; injured by weapon	7	23	13	29	12	43
Missing data	4				12	

female victims report being recipients of higher levels of force than male offenders admit to. Both males and females reported that the majority of sexual assaults occurred within the context of a date, and both tended to say that the offender's sexual excitement was a precipitating factor. A general tendency to blame the assault on the behavior of the other person was evident for both participants. Over 40 percent of the males said that the woman's sexual excitement, teasing, and/or flirting behaviors were instrumental in the assault. In contrast, over 75 percent of the females did not attribute the assault to their behavior, dress, or physical appearance, and a substantial proportion of the women attributed at least partial responsibility to the offender's use of alcohol. No information about sex-role attitudes or attitudes supportive of rape were reported for the two groups or for males and females in the larger sample except to say that the offender-victim groups do not differ from peers of the same sex.

Los Angeles Adolescents

Goodchilds and colleagues (1983) interviewed a tri-ethnic sample of 432 volunteer high school students recruited through the summer job office of the Youth Employment Service of the California State Department of Employment during 1978. Equal numbers of black, Anglo, and Hispanic males and females between 14 and 18 years of age were interviewed. Over 98 percent reported living with the family of origin and, of those, 49 percent were living with a single parent. Two thirds reported plans to go to college or other post-high school training. Seven in 10 (71 percent) males and half (51 percent) of the females reported having engaged in sexual intercourse. Data from four items were used to place respondents into one of three sexual-experience groups: high (34 percent), average (40 percent), and low (26 percent). Sexual experience did not correlate with respondent age.

The study's objective was to find out what attitudes and expectations adolescents bring to heterosexual dating and sexual relationships, with particular attention paid to the extent to which adolescents read sexual cues into various situations and behaviors. Data were collected using both vignettes and traditional questions.

Thirty-two unique vignettes—27 portraying rape scenarios—were designed. Each subject rated nine of the rape vignettes and five filler or control vignettes. Three variables—setting (work, girl's home, party), force (threatened to "spread rumors" or to "tell lies"; threatened to "hurt her"; pushed her down, slapping and hitting her), and relationship (just met and previously unacquainted; known to each other and friendly but never having dated; in a dating relationship)—varied through three levels were systematically included in each vignette. All rape vignettes ended with the phrase "Though the girl does not want to, they have sexual intercourse." Examples of two vignettes follow.

A guy and a girl who are dating are at a friend's party one evening, and decide to sit out in the yard. It is very dark and after a while, they start to kiss and hug. The guy slips his hand under his girlfriend's blouse, but she pulls away and tells him to cut it out. Her boyfriend says that he wants to have sex with her, and when she refuses, he threatens to hurt her. Though the girl does not want to, they have sexual intercourse.

As part of her after-school job a girl is working alone in a basement checking supplies. A guy she has not met but who works in the same place comes into the room where she is and they start talking. They find they have many interests in common and, after a while, they hold hands and kiss. Then the guy grabs the girl and tries to slip his hand under her blouse. She struggles, but he holds her and tells her he wants to have sex with her. The girl refuses, but the guy hits her several times and forces her to the floor. Though the girl does not want to, they have sexual intercourse.

Respondents were asked to answer six questions about each rape.

   1 How much was the boy responsible for what happened? (expressed as a percentage: 0–100)
   2 How much was the girl responsible for what happened? (expressed as a percentage: 0–100)
   3 Do you think you would like the boy in this story? (Five-point rating scale)
   4 Do you think you would like the girl in this story? (Five-point rating scale)
   5 Do you think this was rape? (Five-point rating scale)
   6 Do you think this girl would want to see this boy again? (Five-point rating scale)

Toward the end of the survey a second set of six vignettes was read to each respondent. In this set of vignettes the boy and girl knew each other and two variables were manipulated: they did or did not have sex and they agreed or did not agree about having sex. Both consensual and conflictual simulations were presented, with the couple agreeing not to have sex, the couple agreeing to have sex, or the couple disagreeing. In the conflictual portrayals either the male or the female can be the initiator. An example of a vignette with the interchangeable phrases follows.

A girl and a guy who live in the same neighborhood know each other fairly well but have not dated. One evening the guy comes over to watch TV. The girl's parents are not at home. They sit on the couch and hold hands and begin to kiss. After awhile (he/she) starts to unbutton (her blouse/his shirt) but they both pull away. They agree that they like each other, but only as friends./(She/He) says that (she/he) doesn't want (him/

her) to do that, but (he/she) continues to touch and kiss (her/him), and then says that (he/she) wants to have sex with (her/him). The (girl/guy) says that (she/he) doesn't want (him/her) to, but the (guy/girl) says that (he/she) will tell lies about (her/him) if (she/he) doesn't. (They decide they do not want to have sexual intercourse, and they do not./Though the [girl/guy] does not want to, they have sexual intercourse.)

Questions similar to those asked about the rape vignettes were asked of each respondent following each of these six vignettes. Traditional questions asked as part of the survey included responses to situational and behavioral cues in which participants were asked to respond to a list of five things that "a guy and a girl might do together" and eight questions about how they might act when they were alone. Respondents were asked whether a variety of situations, verbal behaviors, physical behaviors, or romantic verbal behaviors provided a signal or cue that either the male or female target person wanted to have sex. Situations and verbal behaviors rated included: going to a guy's house alone when nobody was home, going to a park or beach at night, going to a party where there were drugs or the couple took drugs, going somewhere together after meeting for the first time in a public place, talking a lot about sex, telling someone that s/he is sexy, telling someone that s/he is good-looking, playing with the other person's hair, tickling/wrestling with the other person, continually looking at him/her or into his/her eyes, telling someone that you love him/her, and telling someone that s/he is understanding.

Questions were also asked about the circumstances in which it is all right for a guy to hold a girl down and force her to have sexual intercourse, and the extent to which attributes of a date such as attire and prior reputation signal sexual availability.

Unfortunately, findings from this study are reported in only two published articles and in papers from four presentations (Goodchilds et al., 1979; Giarrusso et al., 1979; Zellman et al., 1979; Zellman et al., 1981; Goodchilds and Zellman, 1983; Goodchilds and Zellman, 1987). Analysis of variance with sex as a grouping variable generally was used to analyze data, and many of the analyses reported included only the Anglo members of the sample, which precludes knowing the relative power of race and sex as predictive variables. Using only Anglo respondents, Giarrusso et al. (1979) reported on the situations and behaviors that boys and girls perceive as signals for sex, and the circumstances that they believe legitimize the use of force for sex. Using a three-way analysis of variance (sex of subject, sex of target, and activity), main effects were found for all three variables and two-way interactions with the activity portrayed were significant. Males were more likely than females to think *all* the locations presented were sexy and thought males and females were equally likely to want sex in each of the portrayed situations. Females thought (correctly) that males were more interested in sex in all situations. Differences between male and female respondents' perceptions that the males and females portrayed were interested in sex were most pronounced upon first meeting and when alone at a guy's house. When behavioral cues were analyzed in the same way, males perceived males and females to be intending the same thing and were more likely than females to think all behaviors are sexually oriented. Females differentiated between behaviors, with verbal behaviors intending the most sex and romantic verbal behaviors intending the least sex. In response to questions about the appropriateness of forced sex, only 34 percent said it was inappropriate in all circumstances listed and males were more likely than females to say that force is justifiable.

A second set of analyses reported in the same year (Zellman et al., 1979) examined how sexual experience, ethnicity, age, and the sex of the respondent influenced perceptions that attire and prior reputation, as well as the location and dating behaviors discussed above, were sexual cues. Males were more likely than females to mention physical appearance as a desirable attribute of a date while females mentioned personality and sensitivity. While clothes were generally not thought to be a sexual cue, females were significantly *less likely* than males to perceive any type of clothing—whether worn by men or women—to be a signal that the wearer was sexually available. Females were more likely than males to judge with leniency an innocent female dating an experienced male, and they were more likely to judge harshly a "bad girl."

Although no tabular data were reported, Zellman's was the only paper reporting analyses by race.

Black males reported the most sexual experience and were more likely than other males to view actor characteristics and behavior as indicating a desire for sex. Hispanic girls were the most different from males.

They reported the least sexual experience of all the girls and were the least likely of all sex and ethnic groups to attribute sexual meaning to actor characteristics or behavior. These ethnic differences probably represent cultural difference in socialization and social behavior as well as in norms for reporting sexual experiences.

Within ethnic groups, sex differences were generally smallest among Anglos. This may be a function of their greater exposure to the cultural mainstream, including women's liberation ideology, or it may simply reflect socioeconomic status differences in our sample—disproportionately more Anglos came from better educated families with professional backgrounds.

However, it is cross-ethnic group similarities rather than differences that are noteworthy. There were virtually no sex-by-ethnic-group interactions in the data presented above. (pp. 11–12)

Zellman et al. (1981) used vignettes to analyze the circumstances under which a sexual encounter was judged to be a rape, and Goodchilds et al. (1979) reported how responsibility for the sexual encounter was apportioned between the male and female portrayed in the vignette. Although the entire sample was included in the analyses, no analyses by race or sex of respondent were reported. Two of the three variables manipulated in the vignettes—level of force and degree of relationship—strongly influenced decisions that a rape had occurred. Both main effects and an interaction between the two variables were reported. The location of the incident had no effect. Vignettes that portrayed the lowest level of force (verbal threats to tell lies or blackmail) and a dating relationship were least likely to be judged a rape. Verbal threats elicited few judgments that a rape had occurred and respondents had difficulty labeling anything that occurred between dating partners to be a rape. Zellman et al. conclude "Adolescents appear reluctant to label nonconsensual sex within a dating relationship as rape, even when the guy slugs the girl" (p. 6).

Using both the rape vignettes and the set of six vignettes presented near the end of the survey, Goodchilds et al. (1979) were concerned with the different meanings of responsibility—most notably, responsibility implying control and responsibility implying blame. They noted the odd paradox of a person's being regarded "as responsible for outcomes as a direct consequence of having behaved irresponsibly" (p. 3). Four dependent measures were created: the boy's responsibility, the girl's responsibility, the boy's relative responsibility (which equals the boy's responsibility minus the girl's responsibility), and the total responsibility (which equals the boy's responsibility plus the girl's responsibility). Only results for the first three dependent variables were presented.

Interestingly enough, these adolescent boys and girls in Los Angeles did not differ in how they apportioned responsibility between the male and female portrayed in the vignette. Whoever initiated the sexual encounter was judged more responsible for the outcome regardless of whether or not the encounter ended in sexual intercourse. Boys were also assigned greater responsibility when the encounter resulted in intercourse and when it involved conflict.

In general, more responsibility was assigned to the male in the rape vignettes, but girls also were assigned responsibility for the rape. Both the kind of relationship portrayed and the amount of force portrayed affected decisions about responsibility, although force was the more powerful variable. Boys were assigned significantly more responsibility in high force portrayals and girls significantly less responsibility. More responsibility was assigned to the boy and less to the girl when they did not know each other, particularly when the boy was portrayed as using a high level of force.

Two major conclusions emerged from Goodchilds and colleagues' study of Los Angeles adolescents. First, at least among Southern California teenagers studied, males are much more likely than females to infer sexual meaning from anything involving the opposite sex—whether it is the girl's dress, where she is, what others think of her, or what she says or does. Although females do not infer sexual meanings from everything a male peer does, they seem well aware of the extent to which females differ from males in this regard. When asked to make direct comparisons between the males and females in the vignettes, both male and female respondents tended to say that the males intended a sexual action. In contrast, males perceive verbally romantic statements to be sexually seductive and females do not. This finding is consistent with data from other studies of young adults, with data from some attribution studies, and from observations of judicial processing. Koss and Oros (1983) and Kanin (1985) both report use of romantic promises by males in obtaining sexual acquiescence, while attribution studies report gender differences in the perception of rape motivation with males more frequently perceiving a sexual rather than an aggressive motivation (e.g., Krulewitz, 1981; Heilbrun, 1980).

The second major finding concerns perceptions of rape. The Los Angeles Adolescent Study, one of only four studies to ask respondents explicitly whether simulated encounters constitute rape, clearly shows the importance of force and victim-perpetrator relationship in such judgments. The findings that verbal force was not convincing evidence that a rape occurred and that rapes were rarely perceived to occur between dating partners complement Ageton's (1983) findings as well as those from other studies, particularly studies of adolescents (e.g., Kanin, 1985). Furthermore, the three studies are consistent in the extent to which males and females both agree and disagree as to the sexually explicit circumstances in which sexual aggression can be expected or even forgiven. Males and females in all three studies report sexual excitement of the male and sexual behaviors of the female as precursors—and even excuses—for the occurrence of sexual aggression. Likewise, all three studies are consistent in assigning some degree of responsibility to the female even when she is attacked with a significant amount of force by a stranger.

It is too bad that this data set was not analyzed further. Analyses of interest would include the relationship between attitudes measured using vignettes and those measured using traditional questions. Also of interest would be the extent to which combinations of sociodemographic and attitudinal variables combine to predict judgments that vignette scenarios portray rapes and the variables within the vignettes used in making those judgments.

Tuscaloosa Study

Klemmack and Klemmack (1976) surveyed women 18 and older in Tuscaloosa, Alabama. They gathered their subjects by randomly sampling 400 dwelling units selected out of the 1970 city telephone directory. Fifty-seven homes were no longer used as residences or contained no women. Sixty percent ($N = 208$) of the 343 women contacted in the other homes agreed to participate in the study. Data were collected using a combination of household interviews, hand-delivered questionnaires, and mailed questionnaires. Thirty-eight percent of the sample had completed high school, and 36 percent had post-high school educations. The average age was 44 years; 60 percent were married. The median number of children was 2.04 and 44 percent of the women worked outside the home. The purpose of the study was to determine whether normative standards are consistent with the legal definition of rape.

Respondents were asked to evaluate seven freestanding vignettes designed to portray sexual encounters that met legal requirements for rape. Briefly, the following situations were portrayed: a woman being accosted in a parking lot and beaten, a woman meeting a man in a bar and being taken to a deserted road, a man and a woman on a date in a man's apartment, a man with a knife entering through a window of a woman's home, a telephone repairman who slaps a woman, a woman with her boss after working late, and a date with a respectable bachelor. Situations were rated as rapes on a five-point scale on which the points were defined as "yes," "possibly," "uncertain," "probably not," and "no." Examples of two of the vignettes follow.

> A woman is walking to her car in a parking lot after finishing work at I I P.M. A man she does not know comes out of the shadows, beats her up, and drags her to a far corner of the parking lot. There he has sexual relations with her.

> A woman has been dating the same man for three months. They are at the man's apartment where they are kissing and embracing. After some period of time, the woman states that she wants to stop. The man continues and after a struggle, he has sexual relations with her. (p. 139)

Other data collected included sociodemographic characteristics, attitudes toward family, role definitions within the family, and attitudes toward premarital sex. Frequency distributions and correlations were used in analyzing the data.

Only 7 percent of the respondents said that all the scenarios portrayed a rape, while 3 percent said that none of them portrayed a rape. In general, women acknowledged situations as rapes when it was clear that the victim had no control over the event and no prior relationship with her assailant. Unfortunately, these differences are confounded with the amount of force the assailant used and the amount of resistance engaged in by the victim. Vignettes that portrayed women taken by surprise by strangers also described the strangers using weapons or physical force, as well as resistance on the part of the woman. Only 20 percent of the sample felt that the two dating situations portrayed a rape.

Decisions that the vignettes portrayed rapes were associated with higher socioeconomic status, higher education, greater tolerance toward premarital sex, having older brothers, and attitudes favorable to women. Kanin and Parcell (1977) also reported a relationship between having older brothers and attitudes about sexual assault (see chapter 2). College women with older brothers reported sexual assaults less often, leading Kanin and Parcell to speculate that women with brothers might formally or informally be socialized by brothers either to avoid sexually assaultive situations or to ignore them. To the extent that similar factors are present in both studies, women who grow up with brothers—particularly older brothers—may have more realistic perceptions of men, both their bad and good points. Their expectations in relationships with men may be better grounded in reality or they may be better able to read cues that warn of a dangerous situation and to avoid it.

Klemmack and Klemmack's findings are consistent with those of Ageton and Goodchilds and colleagues. Again, assaults between intimates and assaults in which low levels of force are portrayed are rarely judged to be rapes. Since only women were surveyed in this study, it highlights the extent to which women, differentiated by demographic and attitudinal characteristics, differ in their definitions of rape. Unfortunately no multivariate analyses are presented, and although non-Anglo women must surely be present in the sample, differences by race were not reported.

Minnesota Survey

Burt (1979, 1980) interviewed 598 Minnesota adults aged 18 and over during the spring of 1977. Random sampling points were purchased from a commercial survey organization and, with one exception, each sampling point yielded six interviews. The sample is not probabilistic in that interviewers were allowed to replace target households. Respondents within households were selected using the Kish tables.[2] Comparison samples of 110 social service workers and 36 rapists from treatment programs were also obtained.

Six out of ten respondents in the community were female, and the average age of participants was 42. On average they had completed 12.8 years of school, and had an average Duncan (1961) score of 42.9.[3] On average, the social workers were younger and better educated, earned more money, were more likely to be female, and had had more experience with both rape victims and assailants. Rapists were younger and less well educated, earned less money before conviction, and had more experience with both victims and assailants. Rapists had also experienced more violence as children and in their marriages, and perceived more violence in their parents' marriage.

Data collected included personality variables (own sex-role satisfaction, self-esteem, romantic self-image), experience variables (experience with intrafamilial violence, victim of an attempted or completed sexual assault, number of sexual assault victims known, exposure to media treatments of sexual assault), attitude variables (sex-role stereotyping, sexual conservatism, adversarial sexual beliefs, acceptance of interpersonal violence), rape myth acceptance, and vignettes. Item analyses and Cronbach's alpha were used to evaluate scalability within predetermined sets of questions;[4] no factor analyses or other procedures were used to determine whether constructs assumed to be independent actually were.[5] Thus the content overlap among six of the constructs is particularly troubling. These six are: own sex-role satisfaction, sex-role stereotyping, adversarial sexual beliefs, sexual conservatism, acceptance of interpersonal violence, and rape myth acceptance. As part of a separate study of college students, Koss et al. (1985) factor-analyzed parts of this battery of questions and reported roughly comparable constructs.

Each respondent was given a single, lengthy vignette in which three factors or elements (reputation, relationship, force) were varied at two levels to create 8 ($2^3 = 2 \times 2 \times 2$) unique vignettes. In the bad-reputation, no-relationship, low-force condition, the vignette read as follows:

On the evening of August 20, a young woman and her date went to a party at a neighbor's who lived in the woman's apartment building. After the party was well under way, she noticed that there wasn't much of a selection of albums, so she decided to go to her apartment to get some of her own. She told her date she would be right back with some more records. Not noticing the stranger who followed her from the party, she headed for her apartment on the third floor. The man had talked to some other men at the party who had told him that she had a reputation of being sexually "easy." Inside the apartment, she was sorting through records when the man stepped inside and quickly locked the door behind him. She screamed, but the man pulled her down on the couch, covering her mouth with his hand, and had sex with her. (Burt, 1979, pp. 27–28)

In the good-reputation, dating-relationship, high-force condition, the vignette read:

On the evening of August 20, a young woman and a man she had dated several times went to a party at a neighbor's who lived in the woman's apartment building. Having been raised in a very strict family, the woman did not drink alcohol and was still a virgin. After the party was well under way, she noticed that there wasn't much of a selection of albums, so she decided to go to her apartment and get some of her own. She told her date she would be right back with some more records. She did not notice that he followed her from the party as she headed for her apartment on the third floor. Inside the apartment, she was sorting through records when her date stepped inside and quickly locked the door behind him. Surprised, she started to say she was ready to start back, when he suddenly pulled a knife. She screamed, but he held it to her throat, threatening to kill her if she didn't obey him. He then pushed her roughly on the couch and had sex with her. (Burt, 1979, p. 28)

Respondents were asked to rate both the assailant and the victim using eight 7-point bipolar adjectives. They were also asked to judge whether the situation portrayed was a rape and whether they would or would not convict the man, using 7-point bipolar scales. Following the vignettes, two open-ended questions were asked. The questions and the coding frames created for their analysis follow.

1 We are interested in why people decided the way they did about whether or not the situation was a rape, in their opinion. Can you tell me some of the reasons you decided the way you did?
　　1 No particular or specific reasons given;
　　2 The woman's reputation made it seem more of a rape;
　　3 The woman's reputation made it seem less of a rape;
　　4 The amount of force used made it seem more of a rape;

5 The relationship between the man and the woman made it seem more of a rape;

6 The relationship between the man and the woman made it seem less of a rape;

7 The victim resisted or otherwise behaved in a way that indicated she did not precipitate the rape;

8 The victim did not resist, or otherwise behaved in a way that suggested she did precipitate the rape;

9 The man showed intent to rape, therefore it was rape;

2 Is there anything else you feel you would have liked to know about this case in order to make a better decision about it?

1 Nothing, had enough information;

2 More information of an unspecified nature, felt didn't have enough information to make decision;

3 Proof of resistance;

4 Proof of penetration;

5 What the man looked like, how he acted;

6 What the situation was like, who was at the party, what kind of party it was, etc.;

7 The interaction between the woman and the man immediately preceding the rape;

8 The prior relationship between the woman and the man, if any;

9 The woman's character and past history (desire for information about the woman's past sexual history was coded here, but the vast majority of requests for more information about the woman were general, not specifically sexual);

10 The man's character and past history, including any previous criminal or sexual assaults, history of violent behavior, etc.;

11 Signs of the man's intent to commit rape;

12 Whether the man was drunk, on drugs, or mentally ill;

13 What the woman did to precipitate the attack;

14 The "man's side" of the story. (Burt, 1979, pp. 30–31)

Staged multiple regressions and path analysis were used in evaluating predictors of rape myth acceptance and vignette decisions, but indirect effects were not evaluated. In evaluating predictors of rape myth acceptance, variables were entered in stages into the equation in the following order: (1) demographic characteristics, (2) personality measures, (3) experience variables, and (4) attitudes. Education (low), low exposure to media pornography, and attitudes supportive of sex-role stereotyping, adversarial sexual beliefs, and acceptance of interpersonal violence directly predicted high acceptance of rape myths. Age (older), education (low), occupational status (low), exposure to violence, low self-esteem, and low romantic self-image were indirect predictors of belief in rape myths: Their effects were mediated by personality and/or attitudinal variables (Burt, 1979, table 9, p. 61). Experiences with violence and sexual aggression did not have a direct effect on perceptions or decisions about rape. For reasons that are never explained, summary scores for the various indices are not provided for either the total sample or relevant subgroups, nor is sex of the respondent included in the total sample model. This makes it impossible to evaluate the influence of sex on rape myth acceptance relative to other demographic, personality, and attitudinal variables. Instead, noncontributing variables are eliminated and the model is replicated within each sex-defined subgroup. Results within subgroups generally replicate those reported for the total sample, except that education and age were of more importance for women, and occupational status for men. Having experienced violence has a slight indirect effect, making women less sexually conservative. Interestingly, exposure to media violence reduced rape myth acceptance by men. Of total variability in rape myth acceptance, 46 percent is explained by the direct effects of variables mentioned above, 42 percent and 46 percent respectively for females and males. Although attitudes favorable to both violence and sexual conservatism were predictive of rape myth acceptance, attitudes supportive of violence were stronger predictors of rape myths. Burt concluded that ". . . the data supported the hypothesis that rape myth acceptance forms part of a larger and complexly related attitude structure that includes sex role stereotyping, feelings about sexuality, and acceptance of interpersonal violence" (1980, p. 228).

Vignette responses were analyzed using procedures similar to those used in predicting rape myth acceptance. Two dependent variables —likelihood that the incident was a rape and decisions to convict—were predicted, and four additional covariates (perceptions of the assailant portrayed in the vignette, perceptions of the victim portrayed, the three factors manipulated within each vignette, and responses to the two open-ended questions that followed the vignette) were included in the model. Interestingly enough, unlike vignette ratings in Goodchilds' survey, variables manipulated *within* the vignettes predicted little variance in respondents' decisions about rape and conviction. Although unanswerable within the context of this study, this may result from the fact that the unmanipulated material in Burt's vignettes, unlike that of Goodchilds and colleagues, was very lengthy relative to the manipulated data, and vignettes were read to respondents, which may have interfered with comprehension. In addition, Burt's respondents rated only a single vignette while Goodchilds' respondents rated nine systematically varied vignettes and five "filler" vignettes.

Adding attitudinal and demographic data increases predictive ability slightly. Both acceptance of rape myths and acceptance of interpersonal violence reduce the propensity to judge the incident a rape or to convict the man portrayed. Respondents' perceptions of the male and female in the vignette also add to predictive power. Negative perceptions of the male and positive perceptions of the female increase propensity to judge the simulation a rape and to convict the male portrayed. Finally, respondents' statements about what information they used and/or their desires for further information affected decisions about whether the incident was perceived to be rape and/or decisions to convict. While answers to both open-ended questions are included in predictions of decisions to convict, only answers to the first open-ended question are included in predictions that a rape was portrayed. The reason for this difference is not given.

In the final model presented by Burt, decisions about whether the vignette portrays a rape were directly predicted by the respondents' perception of the amount of force portrayed in the vignette. Information about the victim's precipitative behaviors was not considered, but favorable perceptions of the woman portrayed and unfavorable perceptions of the male were considered. Variables having an indirect effect are the woman's reputation and the amount of force as portrayed in the vignette and the acceptance of rape myths, which are mediated by statements regarding the type of information used in making the rating.

Although analyses that clearly answer the question were not presented, variables such as education, age, occupation, media exposure, and attitudes about sex and violence, which were found to predict rape myth acceptance, must have some indirect effects on respondents' decisions about the rape portrayed in the vignette. Because all of these variables influenced rape myth acceptance, and rape myth acceptance indirectly affects the rating of the vignette, effects of these variables are probably being mediated by rape myth acceptance. Only 19 percent of the variance is explained in the decisions about whether or not the vignette portrays a rape. Similar variables explain decision to convict, but here the amount of variance explained increases to 28 percent.

The Minnesota study suggests that males and females are similar in their attitudes about rape. The interplay among attitudes about sexual behavior, attitudes about women, and rape myth acceptance is consistent with data reported by Koss et al. (1985) and the Klemmacks (1976). Persons who hold stereotyped or traditional attitudes about women and their roles and conservative attitudes about sex are more likely to believe in rape myths and less likely to judge simulated sexual encounters to be rape.

Burt's findings are somewhat inconsistent, however, with those of Ageton who reported no relationship between self-reported acts of aggressive sex and opinions about women. On the other hand, Ageton did report that both males and females say that sexual behavior of the man and/or the woman precedes and explains the occurrence of sexual aggression. Consistent with Ageton's findings are Burt's findings that acceptance of interpersonal violence correlates with acceptance of rape myths and decisions that a rape was not portrayed in a vignette. In Ageton's study, participation in delinquent behaviors—some of which implied use of violence—was the variable that most significantly differentiated perpetrators and victims from same-aged peers.

On the face of it, Burt's findings are also somewhat inconsistent with Goodchilds and colleagues' results. Both studies report an interplay between perceptions of sex and rape, but the Goodchilds study suggests that females' perceptions of rape and its sexual connotations intertwine with their perceptions of male sexuality and male-female interactions, whereas Burt's findings suggest a less complex intertwining of factors for females and few differences between men and women.

Although, as mentioned earlier, Burt apparently was disappointed with her vignettes and her inability to explain more of the variance in ratings, understandable methodological reasons explain her failure. Use of a single lengthy vignette that was read to respondents probably reduces the reliability of detecting differences of opinion. Most studies in the attribution tradition, where lengthy vignettes are frequently used, have respondents themselves read the vignette. In the Klemmacks' study (in which some respondents had vignettes read to them) the vignettes were much shorter, and subjects responded to seven vignettes; Goodchilds's study also used shorter multiple vignettes. Feild and Bienen (1980), who used an even longer vignette, had respondents read the vignette. Respondents probably have difficulty retaining all the relevant information when lengthy vignettes are read to them. In such cases responses to questions about the vignettes are probably less precise. The use of multiple vignettes has the additional advantage of allowing respondents to be involved in the same task for a period of time, and allows comparative judgments to be made across the set of stimuli presented.

Probably the single most influential study reported to date is Burt's study, which utilizes one of the most sophisticated analytical strategies. Given the study's high level of sophistication, it is too bad that greater efforts were not made to establish the construct validity of the wide variety of indices included. Item analyses and evaluation of homogeneity within indices, while necessary tasks in index construction, do not answer questions about cross-construct independence. Factor analysis combined with item and homogeneity analyses, both within and across construct areas, would determine whether constructs treated as independent are in fact independent. As reported in table 3 (Burt, 1980), correlations between indices assumed to be independent are as high as .623 and .525, significantly higher than many of the item-total correlations within the individual indices as reported in tables 1 and 2. Such findings suggest that the reported indices are, in fact, part of a single, broader construct. The larger construct could be unidimensional or multidimensional (McKennell, 1977). Burt shows her awareness of this when she reports data suggesting that sex-role stereotyping and sexual conservatism are not independent constructs (Burt, 1979, p. 43).

Another problem involves the procedure by which items contained in the rape myth acceptance index were scored and summed. Unlike the other indices, the rape myth acceptance index contains questions in two formats: 11 items have seven-point answer formats and 8 items have five-point answer formats. Unless answers were standardized to ensure that each item contributed an equal weighting to the index score, seven-point questions contribute proportionally more to the total score; they would add 7/5 or 1.4 relative to five-point questions. How this differential scoring might affect characteristics of the final index is unknown.

Finally, as noted earlier, Burt's rationale for deleting variables from her analytical models and her ordering of variables within the model is not always clear. The decision to exclude sex from the fully recursive model predicting acceptance of rape myths is particularly unclear.

Southeastern Community Survey

Feild (1978) and Feild and Bienen (1980) surveyed 1,056 community residents in a southeastern city, 254 police officers in two urban and two rural southeastern communities, 118 female counselors from rape crisis centers across the country, and 20 rapists committed to a state mental hospital. Details of sample selection were not provided. The community sample was evenly divided between males and females. More than eight out of ten (85 percent) were white; the average age was 34; 78 percent had been or were currently married; 24 percent knew a woman who had been raped. Ninety-three percent of the 254 police officers were male, 89 percent were white, 90 percent had been or were currently married, and 59 percent knew a woman who had been raped. Their average age was 32. All 118 rape counselors were women; 91 percent were white, 55 percent were married, and 78 percent knew a woman who had been raped. Their average age was 29.

Data collected included: demographic information, an *Attitudes Toward Rape* questionnaire developed by the investigator, the short form of Spence and Helmreich's (1972) *Attitudes Toward Women* scale, a rape knowledge test developed by the investigator, and a six-page written narrative or vignette that portrayed a legal rape case. Included in the narrative were photographs of both the victim and the defendant. The intent of the study was to examine the effects of selected victim, defendant, crime, and juror characteristics on jurors' decisions in a rape case (1980, p. 13). Six variables were systematically varied: race of the victim, physical attractiveness of the victim, moral character of the victim, race of the defendant, type of rape, and strength of evidence. Photographs were used to manipulate two levels of attractiveness and race (black, white). Moral character, type of rape, and strength of evidence were manipulated using the following lengthy descriptive statements.

> *Moral character (high)*: [W]hile being questioned, it was established by the prosecutor that Mary Harrington [the alleged victim] lived alone and had no previous sexual experiences (Feild and Bienen, 1980, p. 14).
>
> *Moral character (low)*: Mary Harrington had previously lived with a man to whom she was not married, and she admitted having had sexual relations with several men (Feild and Bienen, 1980, p. 14).
>
> *Nonprecipitory rape*: On Friday, August 12, at 10:00 P.M., Mary Harrington answered a knock at her apartment door. Harrington was confronted by a black male who explained that he had had some car trouble and asked if he could make a telephone call to a service station for help. Harrington said she would make the call for him. At this time, the man pushed the door open, dragged her into the bedroom, and then raped her (Feild and Bienen, 1980, p. 15).
>
> *Precipitory Rape*: On Friday, August 12, at 10:00 P.M., Mary Harrington answered a knock at her apartment door. Harrington was confronted by a black male who explained that he had had some car trouble and asked if he could make a telephone call to a service station for help. Harrington let him in to use her telephone. The service station indicated that it would be about two hours before a truck could be sent due to a shortage of station attendants. While waiting for the service truck, Harrington asked him if he would care to wait in her apartment and to have a cup of coffee. Approximately an hour and a half after Willoughby called the station, sexual relations occurred between the two individuals (Feild and Bienen, 1980, p. 15).

It should be noted that at least three variables were manipulated within the two levels of "type of rape": length of the presentation, information about force, and information about resistance. In addition, the term "rape" was used in one portrayal and replaced by "sexual relations" in the other.

Both prosecution and defense materials were manipulated in portraying the two levels of evidence. Because the total vignette was unusually lengthy, only those parts of the vignette that actually differed are reproduced here.

Strong Evidence: Mary Harrington was called to the stand. She told how Willoughby had forced his way into her apartment and raped her. She noted that he had verbally threatened her with physical violence if she did not comply. However, she had attempted to offer some resistance to him by fighting him. As she pointed out, her efforts were evidenced by the fact that his shirt was torn with a button ripped loose during the struggle, and by scratches on his face and back. . . . The prosecuting attorney noted that a button was found in Harrington's apartment. An examination of Willoughby's shirt at the time of his arrest revealed that a button was missing. The button located in Harrington's apartment matched those on Willoughby's shirt. Further, the prosecuting attorney pointed out that Willoughby fit the description given by Harrington to the police. In addition, she had positively identified him. . . .

David Willoughby, the defendant, took the stand and stated that he was innocent of the charges. He explained that the scratches on his face and back as well as his torn shirt had occurred when he was assaulted by two unidentified youths while walking alone through a park earlier in the evening. When asked if he had reported the incident to the police, Willoughby said "No, they didn't get my money, and the police probably wouldn't have caught them anyway." The defense attorney insisted that the fact that the button found in Harrington's apartment matched Willoughby's shirt and his resemblance to her assailant were mere coincidences. Willoughby maintained that he was watching television alone in his apartment at the time of the rape of Mary Harrington. . . .

Weak Evidence: Mary Harrington was called to the stand. She told how Willoughby had forced his way into her apartment and raped her. She noted that he had verbally threatened her with physical violence if she did not comply. . . .

Further, the prosecuting attorney pointed out that Willoughby fit the description given by Harrington to the police. In addition, she had identified him. . . .

David Willoughby, the defendant, took the stand and stated that he was innocent of the charges. He told the jury that he had never seen Mary Harrington before his arrest and had not forced his way into her apartment. Willoughby maintained that he was watching television alone in his apartment at the time of the rape of Mary Harrington. . . (Feild and Bienen, 1980, pp. 15–17).

It is also important to note the significant difference in length between the two presentations. Also, in the strong-evidence case there were several elements of evidence presented, but in the weak-evidence case the amount of evidence was reduced to the victim's identification, the physician's statement, and a reduced statement by the victim.

Each respondent in the community received one of the 64 (2^6) unique vignettes created and, unlike other community studies using vignettes, respondents read the vignette rather than having it read to them. Although all 64 vignettes were evenly distributed among male and female Anglo members of the sample, only 16 versions were distributed to the much smaller black subsample (1980, p. 106).

Unlike the three prior studies, respondents were not asked to decide whether they thought a rape had occurred. Rather, they were asked whether the defendant was or was not guilty (two-alternative answer), how sure they were of their judgment (five-alternative answer), and the number of years of sentence they would impose (0–99 years).

To begin his analysis, Feild, unlike Burt, performed principal components factor analyses with varimax rotations both within his total sample and within each of his respondent subgroups. Only the 32 items measuring attitudes toward rape were included in the later analysis; neither attitudes about women nor items measuring rape knowledge were included in the factor analyses. Eight factors were extracted and all were used in further analysis; neither item analysis nor tests of homogeneity were reported. The eight factors were labeled: women's responsibility in rape prevention, sex as a motivation for rape, severe punishment for rape, victim precipitation of rape, normality of rapists, power as a motivation for rape, favorable perception of women after rape, and resistance as a woman's role during rape. Attitude structures were similar for police officers, rape crisis counselors, and community residents. Correlations and stepwise regressions were used to assess correlations between the eight indices and characteristics of respondents.

Sex, race, marital status, and attitudes toward women predicted the various dimensions of attitudes toward rape. Feild concluded:

> These results point to the need for examining people's views of rape as something more than simply an act of sex; their perceptions of rape tend to be intimately tied to their views of women. . . . [For] male

citizens, there appeared to be significant relationships between their race and their rape attitudes. However, for women, attitudes toward the female role tended to explain more of their attitudes toward rape than did their race.

. . . In comparison to the counselors, rapists were more likely to have the following views: rape prevention is primarily women's responsibility, rape is motivated by a desire for sex, punishment for rape should not be severe, victims are likely to precipitate rape through their appearance or behavior, rapists are not mentally normal, rape is not motivated by a need for power, a raped woman is a less desirable woman, and women should not resist during rape. (pp. 70–73)

According to Feild, most of the people fared only slightly better than guessing on the fourteen-item rape knowledge test (p. 85). Scores on the knowledge of rape items differed significantly among community members, counselors, police, and rapists. Of the fourteen questions asked, counselors correctly answered a total of 5.3, police 4.8, community members 4.5, and rapists 3.5. Sex, race, and education predicted knowledge, and males, whites, and more highly educated persons were the most knowledgeable. However, once education was controlled, information about sex and race predicted no further variance in knowledge.

The type of rape committed, the amount of evidence presented, and the race of both victim and defendant affected sentencing decisions made about the vignette portrayals. In nonprecipitated cases of rape in which a great deal of evidence was presented, defendants were judged guilty. Black defendants were given longer sentences than whites and assailants of black victims were given lighter sentences.

Bivariate and simultaneous multiple correlations rather than staged regressions were used to determine the relative contribution of case characteristics, attitudes of respondents, and demographic characteristics to respondents' decisions about the length of prison term that should be given to the defendant. Bivariate correlations showed that Anglo respondents' sentencing decisions were affected by their age, education, and attitudes on four of the rape factors—race of the defendant, race of the victim, type of rape portrayed, and strength of the evidence. Within the much smaller black subsample, education, prior jury service, three of the rape factors, and the strength of evidence portrayed in the vignette affected sentencing decisions. After presenting a series of multiple correlations, Feild and Bienen (1980) concluded that attitudinal variables are more important in predicting jurors' sentences of the defendant than are background characteristics.

Their conclusions probably overstate the data. Sequences of simultaneous correlations make attitudes appear to be stronger than demographic characteristics in predicting simulated jury decisions. However, the strong associations among demographic characteristics, the eight dimensions of rape attitudes, and knowledge about rape reported earlier by Feild and Bienen (pp. 66–67) hint that attitudes mediate the effect of demographic variables. For example, while the respondent's sex is not significantly correlated with sentencing decisions, respondent's sex is significantly correlated with three of the four attitudinal measures (sex as a motivation for rape, victim precipitation of rape, and power as a motivation for rape). These measures show strong bivariate correlations with Anglo respondents' sentencing decisions and with two of the three attitudinal measures that show strong correlations with black respondents' sentencing decisions. Similar kinds of relationships exist among other demographic variables (e.g., age, education, marital status) and the attitude measures. Had staged regressions and path models similar to those reported by Burt been run, and indirect effects calculated (e.g., Alwin and Hauser, 1975), demographic characteristics might well have been found to be strong indirect predictors of sentencing decisions. An indirect effect is an effect that works through something else. For example, education predicts attitudes about rape which in turn predict sentencing decisions. Persons with higher education hold less stereotyped attitudes about rape; persons with less stereotyped attitudes about rape give shorter sentences. Education has an indirect effect on sentencing decisions that is mediated by attitudes toward rape. The effects are mediated by attitude measures, knowledge of rape, and the respondent's sensitivity to characteristics manipulated in the vignettes.

Two further problems in the design of this study make interpreting results difficult. Unlike the other studies, respondents were not asked whether the simulated encounter was a rape. Thus, inferences about respondents' images of rape can only be made by assuming that judgments of defendants' guilt and imposition of a long sentence equate with the judgment that the event portrayed is a rape. Equating a lengthy sentence with a judgment of rape is particularly problematic. As discussed in much greater detail in chapter 5, one objective of those working to reform rape laws has been to reduce sentences for convicted rapists. Thus, persons who do not hold stereotyped ideas about rape may also advocate reduced sentences for rapists. And indeed something of the sort appears to be happening in this data set. The bivariate correlations show more highly educated respondents as less likely to think women are responsible for rape prevention, less likely to think sex is a motivation for rape, more likely to support severe punishment for rape (p. 66), and more likely to be knowledgeable about rape (p. 87), but less likely to prescribe long sentences for the defendant portrayed in the vignette (p. 121). Although data necessary to judge are not presented, it would not be surprising if more highly educated respondents were more likely to decide that the defendant was guilty and to be relatively sure of that judgment even in vignettes that portrayed a precipitated rape and/or weak evidence.

A second unfortunate result of the study design is the inability to compare Anglo and black sentencing decisions. Because blacks were presented only 16 of the 64 vignettes created, blacks and Anglos cannot be combined in analyses. Analyses can only be conducted within racial subgroups; therefore, rigorous comparisons of findings cannot be made across the two racial strata.

San Antonio Survey

Williams and Holmes (1981) conducted a tri-ethnic survey of San Antonio residents to ascertain whether sex-role attitudes and perceptions of rape are the product of sexual and racial stratification. Interviews were conducted in 1976–77 with 335 non-Hispanic whites, 336 blacks, and 340 Hispanics. Equal numbers of males and females were studied. The mean age was 38 for whites, 41 for blacks, and 43 for Hispanics. Mean education completed was 14 years for whites, 11 years for blacks, and 7 years for Hispanics, with respective annual family incomes of $16,578, $8,232, and $6,231. Seventy-four percent of whites, 44 percent of blacks, and 65 percent of Hispanics were married, and the average number of children was, respectively, 2, 3, and 4. Blacks were overwhelmingly Protestant (85 percent) while Hispanics were Catholic (85 percent); 60 percent of Anglos were Protestant, 28 percent were Catholic.

Respondents were asked about attitudes toward rape, attitudes about sex roles, beliefs about male-female sexuality vis-à-vis rape, minority-related rape risks, and demographic characteristics. Three open-ended questions and nine freestanding vignettes were used to assess attitudes about rape. With the exception of a marital rape, all scenarios met the legal definition of rape and were designed to vary certain components that the literature suggests are integral to the concept of rape (i.e., victim's activity and/or reputation, use of a weapon, injury, victim-assailant relationship). Examples of two of the vignettes follow.

> A teenage female had an argument with her parents and left home. She wanted to go to another city to stay with a friend. Because she had no money, she decided to hitchhike. She accepted a ride with an older man who pulled a gun on her, took her to a wooded area, and forced her to have sexual intercourse with him. He then told her to get back in the car and that he would take her where she wanted to go.

> A young college student was forced at knife point to have sex with a man she had been dating for several weeks. They supposedly had an understanding that there would be no sexual involvement. The attack came after she refused to spend the weekend with him (Williams and Holmes, 1981, p. 61).

Respondents were asked to judge whether the situation was a rape, whether the female was at fault, and whether they would be willing to prosecute the alleged assailant. Composite scores were created across the three dimensions for each of the nine vignettes and across the nine vignettes for each of the three dimensions.

Items were adapted from other sources to measure sex role beliefs, sex role behaviors, women's liberation beliefs, and women's liberation behaviors. Thirteen items were developed by the authors to assess beliefs about female sexuality, male sexuality, and rape. Eight items were developed by the authors to measure perceptions of minority-related rape risks.

Staged regressions within racial strata were used to determine the sets of variables that best predicted respondents' decisions that the vignettes portrayed rape, that the victim was responsible, and that the assailant should be tried. To control for the high covariation among judgments that a rape was portrayed, perceptions of female responsibility, and willingness to prosecute, the latter two judgments made up the first stage in some regressions. For example, in predicting decisions that rapes were portrayed, respondents' perceptions about the woman's responsibility were first regressed on rape judgments, demographic characteristics of the respondents made up the second stage of the regression, and attitudinal variables made up the third stage. Within a given stage, stepwise regressions were allowed. Twenty-seven regressions—nine within each racial group—were computed. Within each racial group equations predicting rape perceptions, the woman's perceived responsibility, and likelihood of prosecution were computed for the group as a whole and within groups stratified by sex.

The decision to simplify equations within the six subgroups defined by race and sex without regard to the other groups, as well as the decision to allow variables to enter the equation in a stepwise fashion within stages, means that the relative importance of variables across race-sex subgroups cannot be evaluated. Further complicating comparison is the unavailability of correlation matrices for the six groups and the presentation of standardized rather than unstandardized coefficients. As in the studies by Burt and Feild, no effort was made to interpret indirect effects, and none of the intermediate stages of the equations was reported (e.g., regression of attitude measures on demographic characteristics). These caveats should be kept in mind when comparing predictors across the six respondent subgroups: white males, white females, black males, black females, Hispanic males, and Hispanic females.

Composite judgments concerning whether or not rapes were portrayed could range from 9 (all nine scenarios portray a rape) to 36 (none of the nine scenarios portrays a rape). Anglo males were most likely to judge all scenarios a rape ($\bar{x}$ = 14.8) followed by white females (15.2), black females (16.1), black males (16.7), Hispanic females (17.6), and Hispanic males (18.1). White males were also least likely to attribute responsibility to the female (20.0). White females (21.4), Hispanic males and females (21.7), black females (22.0), and black males (22.9) followed in that order. Black females were most likely to seek prosecution (14.9), followed by white males (15.0), white females (15.8), Hispanic females (16.8), black males (17.4), and Hispanic males (18.1).

Generally within sex-race subgroups, attitudes about sex roles, male-female sexuality, and rape predict perceptions of female responsibility.

Respondents in all sex-race subgroups consistently thought a rape had not occurred if they thought the female was responsible. Decisions that a rape occurred, in turn, consistently predict a willingness to prosecute.

Demographic characteristics other than race and sex generally are more relevant within ethnic subgroups (black and Hispanic) than they are for white respondents. This may be a result of sample stratification. Hispanics in this study have significantly less education and income than do blacks, who in turn have lower socioeconomic status than Anglos. Within each sex-race subgroup education and income are relatively homogeneous, leaving only attitudes that are unrelated to sex and race to explain differences within groups. This is particularly true for white males and females.

The amount of variance predicted in perceptions of female responsibility ranges from a low of 7 percent for Hispanic females to a high of 22 percent for black males. In contrast, the amount of variance explained in decisions about prosecution ranges from a low of 40 percent for black females to a high of 74 percent for white females.

Methods of data analysis and presentation make it difficult to summarize further study findings. Suffice it to say that differences defined by race and sex exist across groups. Anglos are more likely to consider all vignettes presented as rapes, and thus it can be assumed they consider a wider range of sexual assaults to be rape. Yet Anglos vary in the extent to which they have liberal attitudes about women's roles and male-female sexuality and, to the extent that those attitudes are conservative, their perceptions of rape are also more conservative. The relative importance of ethnicity, sex, education, and income in determining rape-supportive attitudes and culpability in sexual assaults is not clearly addressed in this study.

Summary, Caveats, and Implications for Future Research

Table 6.2 summarizes the six community surveys, the variables tested, and the extent to which each variable affected perceptions of rape. With the exception of the Ageton and Feild studies, the dependent variable is the respondent's decision that the sexual encounter portrayed in vignette(s) was rape. In the Ageton study the dependent variable is adolescent reports of involvement in sexual assaults and the type of assaults. In the Feild study the dependent variable is the length of sentence respondents gave the male in the vignette. Variables are grouped in stages relative to their distance from the vignette portrayal.

Stage One: Variables Manipulated within Vignettes

The first stage is the variables manipulated within the vignettes. Interpretations of the data must be only suggestive, because vignettes were constructed and administered in very different ways across the five studies. However, everyone manipulated information about the force used by the man, and everyone except Feild manipulated the degree of acquaintanceship between the man and the woman. Both variables affected definitions of rape in all five studies, with portrayals of high-force encounters between strangers being much more likely than low-force encounters between acquaintances or dating partners to be called rape. Moreover, information about the woman's reputation and/or sexual history was found consistently to affect definitions of rape. In contrast, location and physical appearance had no effect on judgments. Interestingly enough, no clear direct tests were made of the woman's resistance to the attack. To the extent that indirect information was presented, resistance on the part of the woman increased a respondent's propensity to judge the encounter a rape.

Future researchers might want to design studies to incorporate factors that were not assessed in these investigations. For example, in spite of evidence from studies such as Ageton's that sexual excitement and use of drugs and alcohol are factors, particularly in sexual assaults between adolescent acquaintances, none of these studies included vignettes manipulating either variable. Vignettes might also be used to test the extent to which people think rape is a sexual act, a violent act, or some combination of the two. Also surprisingly absent are efforts to test stereotypes about cross-racial and cross-social class rapes. Such information has direct relevance for judicial processing of rape cases where it has repeatedly been shown that black males and/or lower-class males are more frequently prosecuted and convicted. Only Feild tested respondents' use of such information in deciding whether or not a rape occurred. He found that the race

Table 6.2 Variables reported to predict rape behaviors or judgments in five community studies[a]

Sets of variables tested (grouped by distance from rape decision)	Ageton (1983)
Stage One: Variables portrayed within vignettes	
Force by man	Yes
Resistance by woman	Yes
Acquaintance level	Yes
Evidence presented	Not tested
Indicators of the woman's character	
Location: place/time of day	Not tested
Woman's behavior, dress, physical appearance	Yes
Woman's use of drugs/alcohol	Not tested
Woman's marital status/sexual history	Not tested
Woman's reputation	Not tested
Woman's sexual excitement	Yes
Indicators of man's character	
Man's use of drugs/alcohol	Yes
Man's sexual excitement	Yes
Indicators of social status	
Woman's race	No
Man's race	No
Woman's socioeconomic status	No
Man's socioeconomic status	No
Stage Two: Respondents' perceptions of the vignettes	
Perceptions of the man portrayed	Not tested
Perceptions of the woman portrayed	Not tested
Perceptions of what used in rating	Not tested
Perceptions of information wanted	Not tested
Stage Three: Nonvignette measures of attitudes toward rape	
Attitudes about rape and sexual assault	No
Perceptions of sexual cues	Not tested
Knowledge about rape	Not tested
Minorities and rape	Not tested
Stage Four: Personality measures	
Measures of sexual attitudes and behaviors	
Attitudes toward sex roles	No
Attitudes toward women	No
Sexual behaviors	Not tested
Sex role satisfaction	Not tested
Attitudes & exposure to violence/delinquency	
Attitudes toward violence/delinquency	Yes
Exposure to delinquent peers	Yes
Experience with intrafamilial violence	Not tested

Goodchilds & colleagues (1983)	Klemmacks (1976)	Burt (1980)	Feild & Bienen (1980)	Williams & Holmes (1981)
Yes	Yes	Yes	Yes	Yes
Not tested	Yes	Not tested	Yes*	Not tested
Yes	Yes	Yes	Not tested	Yes*
Not tested	Not tested	Not tested	Yes	Not tested
No	Not tested	Not tested	Yes*	Not tested
Not tested	Not tested	Not tested	No	Yes*
Not tested	Not tested	Yes	Not tested	Not tested
Not tested	Not tested	Yes	Yes	Not tested
Not tested	Not tested	Yes	Not tested	Not tested
Not tested	Not tested	Not tested	Not tested	Not tested
Not tested	Not tested	Not tested	Not tested	Not tested
Not tested	Not tested	Not tested	Not tested	Not tested
Not tested	Not tested	Not tested	Yes	Not tested
Not tested	Not tested	Not tested	Yes	Not tested
Not tested	Not tested	Not tested	Not tested	Not tested
Not tested	Not tested	Not tested	Not tested	Not tested
Yes*	Not tested	Yes	Not tested	Yes
Yes*	Not tested	Yes	Not tested	Yes
Not tested	Not tested	Yes	Not tested	Not tested
Not tested	Not tested	No	Not tested	Not tested
Not tested	Not tested	Yes	Yes	Yes
Yes*	Not tested	Not tested	Not tested	Not tested
Not tested	Not tested	Not tested	Yes*	Not tested
Not tested	Not tested	Not tested	Not tested	Yes
Not tested	Yes	Yes*	Not tested	Yes
Not tested	Yes	Yes*	Yes*	Yes
Not tested	Yes	Yes*	Not tested	Yes
Not tested	Not tested	Yes*	Not tested	Not tested
Not tested	Not tested	Yes*	Not tested	Not tested
Not tested	Not tested	Not tested	Not tested	Not tested
Not tested	Not tested	Yes*	Not tested	Not tested

Table 6.2 (continued)

Sets of variables tested (grouped by distance from rape decision)	Ageton (1983)
Victim of sexual assault	Not tested
Exposure to media treatments of sexual assault	Not tested
Other personality measures	
Romantic self-image	Not tested
Self-esteem	Not tested
Social isolation	No
Stage Five: Indicators of social stratification	
Age	No
Sex	Yes
Race	Yes
Income	No
Occupation	No
Educational achievement/aspirations	No
Family size and/or structure	Not tested
Marital status	Not tested
Religion	Not tested

a Interpretation of cell content is as follows: Yes = Explicitly tested within the context of the study and influenced decisions or, in the Ageton study, reported to differentiate those involved in assaults from peers or male offenders from female victims. No = Explicitly tested in study and did not predict characteristics of definitions of rapes. Yes* = Data available in study but not explicitly ana-

of both the male offender and the female victim had a significant effect on judgments. Racial information also interacted with other data manipulated in the vignettes to affect definitions.

Stage Two: Respondents' Perceptions of the Vignettes

Many of the researchers asked respondents what they thought about the female and male portrayed in the vignette(s). To the extent that they held negative perceptions of the man and positive perceptions of the woman, their propensity to consider the incident a rape increased. Because such information is not independent of the vignette itself, it cannot be considered apart from the manipulated information. Its greatest value is most likely as validation for the manipulated data. For example, if respondents say they used information about force in making their decisions, actual differences observed in the vignette data between high-force and low-

Goodchilds & colleagues (1983)	Klemmacks (1976)	Burt (1980)	Feild & Bienen (1980)	Williams & Holmes (1981)
Not tested	Not tested	Yes*	Not tested	Not tested
Not tested	Not tested	Yes*	Not tested	Not tested
Not tested	Not tested	Yes*	Not tested	Not tested
Not tested	Not tested	Yes*	Not tested	Not tested
Not tested	Not tested	Not tested	Not tested	Not tested
Not tested	No	Yes*	Yes*	Yes
Yes*	Not tested	Not tested	Yes*	Yes
Yes*	Not tested	Not tested	Yes*	Yes*
Not tested	Yes	Not tested	Not tested	Yes
Not tested	Yes	Yes*	Yes*	Not tested
Not tested	Yes	Yes*	Yes*	Yes
Not tested	Yes	Not tested	Not tested	Not tested
Not tested	Not tested	Not tested	Yes*	Yes*
Not tested	Not tested	Not tested	Not tested	Yes

lyzed as it affects vignette ratings; findings presented elsewhere in the study suggest that this variable associates with or predicts definitions of rape. Not tested = No data was collected, no tests made, or no findings reported.

force portrayals can be assumed to be real and not simply a statistical artifact.

When entered into regression equations where the dependent variable is "definitions of rape," such data must be handled carefully—either entered simultaneously with information intentionally manipulated within the vignette or immediately after such data.

Stage Three: Nonvignette Measures of Rape Attitudes

A major reason for using vignettes is to develop methods of measurement different from and better than traditional questionnaires. Three of the studies included one or more nonvignette measures of attitudes toward rape which were subsequently included in analyses of the vignettes. Like questions about the vignettes, such data are not independent of what we find out using the vignette. Rather, such data can be used to validate vignette data and as examples of triangulation of data collection (e.g., Denzin, 1970; Webb et al., 1966). Persons who rated vignettes in stereotypical ways should have high scores on a traditional index measuring rape myth acceptance and belief in coercive sex. It is not surprising, therefore, that studies that included such indices consistently found that they were highly correlated with vignette rating patterns. They are, after all, part and parcel of the same construct—attitudes toward and perceptions of rape. The most interesting index in this category, Feild's *Rape Knowledge Index,* is not reported as part of the study's vignette analyses (Feild and Bienen, 1980). One assumes that the rape knowledge of South Carolina residents correlates with their vignette ratings since it correlates with traditional questionnaire measures of their attitudes toward rape.

Stage Four: Personality Measures

Personality measures used are categorized by substantive type. Authorities differ in the extent to which they consider rape a sexual act, a violent act, an aspect of male-female relations, or some combination of these. Therefore, measures of sexual attitudes and behaviors are differentiated from measures of violent attitudes and behaviors which in turn are differentiated from all other personality measures. Four of the studies include one or more measures of sexual behaviors and attitudes. Unlike the mixed findings from attribution studies, in all cases such measures are reported to correlate with or influence respondents' definitions of rape.

Interestingly enough, and in spite of feminist views that rape is a violent act rather than a sexual one, only Burt included specific measures of attitudes toward, exposure to, and participation in violent or deviant activities. Discouragingly, she found such variables were less predictive of rape perceptions than were sexual behaviors and attitudes. On the face of it and based on minimal data, community members' perceptions of rape appear more closely tied to sexual behaviors and perceptions than to participation in and acceptance of violence. This may be a methodological artifact, because the measures of violence used suffer from one of two problems. Three of the measures are experiential (experience with intrafamilial violence, victim of sexual assault, and exposure to media treatments), with prevalence rates so low as to be almost unusable in multivariate analyses. The content of the attitudinal measures of violence is confounded with measures of attitudes toward sex, women, and rape in that many items ask about violence in heterosexual interactions. The relative importance of sex and violence as predictors of rape-supportive attitudes and behaviors and the interplay between them needs a great deal more investigation.

Burt is the only researcher who includes other personality measures in her study. Like some attribution researchers, she concludes that personality measures are not predictive of rape attitudes. Again, this is an area that deserves much more attention.

Stage Five: Social Indicators

It is remarkable that only cursory attention was paid to traditional measures of social status and life-style. Even when data exist, researchers frequently do not include one or more potentially important variables in their analyses. Only two surveys—those of the Klemmacks and Williams and Holmes—systematically explore the role of demographic characteristics in predicting or differentiating between rape perceptions. Age, sex, income, education, and religion are all found by Williams and Holmes (1981) to affect perceptions of rape. The Klemmacks similarly found that socioeconomic status predicts definitions of rape, with higher-status women adopting more feminist definitions. Although available in the other three vignette studies, the impact of demographic variables is not investigated or its importance is minimized.

Traditional emphasis on demographic variables, feminist assumptions of differential status by gender, and official statistics on rape all suggest that we need to carefully examine the impact of social stratification on rape. Socioeconomic status, race, and gender repeatedly have been found to be powerful predictors of intergenerational mobility, life-style, and family structure. Moreover, demographic variables generally have been found to be more powerful than personality variables in explaining resource utilization, leisure-time activities, child-rearing practices, family size, health behaviors, and migration, among other behaviors. The list is endless. To ignore the possible relevance of social stratification or to assume that it is irrelevant in studies of rape seems unwise.

Conclusion

Clearly, people use information about force, acquaintanceship, the woman's sexual history, and race of the victim and perpetrator to decide whether a sexual encounter is rape. In these studies, the location of the assault and the physical attractiveness of participants were not important determinants of decisions about rape. The impact of information about resistance, sexuality, and stimulants was not tested. People are consistent in their attitudes across different kinds of measures. To the extent that they change their decision about the sexual encounter as available information changes or increases, they are aware of the change and of the information they considered important. Information used to make decisions about vignettes mirrors attitudes about rape as measured using traditional questions.

Summary of Part II

To a large extent it is rape crisis center counselors and other practitioners—many of whom have roots in the feminist movement—who have defined theory and research on rape. Most of the programmatic changes made in the way rape victims are handled by medical personnel, police, and legal institutions evolved from the somewhat amorphous feminist sociocultural perspective. Feminist practitioners and researchers pointed out the extent to which rape was a significant social problem worthy of careful consideration by both service providers and researchers; they exerted pressure to ensure that scarce resources available were directed to programs and research efforts they considered worthy of funding.

Since its inception, research on rape has been in the eye of a hurricane. Miscommunication among practitioners, policymakers, and researchers has persisted, each group often failing to understand the goals, constituents, and the very language of the others. In spite of these problems, a significant amount of increasingly good work has evolved during the past fifteen years. Nevertheless, no well-defined cohesive body of findings or theory currently exists in the area. In fact, in many instances theories and findings continue to compete with one another for consideration and recognition.

At the same time we know that the rise in reported rapes has been relatively consistent over the twenty-year period 1960–80, and that it now appears to be plateauing. However, we do not know why official rape rates consistently rose between 1960 and 1980. Some hypothesize that increasing rates of all crimes during the 1970s reflect the fact that the post-World War II "baby boomers" reached their teens and twenties during the 1970s and that the majority of crimes (or at least those that are reported) are committed by young males. Others suggest the number of reported rapes may have increased because official statistics became more complete or because legal definitions of rape, at least for purposes of reports to police, broadened to include a wider range of assaults of males against females. Finally, the rising number of rapes during the 1960s and 1970s may reflect changing definitions of rape on the part of women who report it, persons they consult, or receptivity of institutions where rapes traditionally are reported, such as police, community mental health centers, and hospitals.

Whatever the reason, the subject of the incidence, prevalence, and correlates of rape among women as a group or among subgroups clearly merits continued attention. The literature review herein suggests recent efforts to assess the prevalence of sexual assault within specified populations of women and to locate self-identified rapists in general populations have expanded and enriched our knowledge of rape and its correlates. Contemporary definitions of rape, however, remain reflections of the groups from which they were obtained, and do not yet represent a full cross-section of the society. We need to know more about how nonvictimized community members of all ethnicities define rape before we can accurately assess cross-ethnic differences in the reporting of rapes over time. As Reiss notes, "One must collect information on exposed populations who constitute the base for rates as well as for the populations of victims" (1986, p. 251). Only by doing so will we have an accurate measure of the extent and nature of the problem and how to deal with it.

Part III **A Community's Definition of Rape**

In response to rising official rates of sexual assaults and pressures from the women's movement, all fifty states revised their sexual assault statutes in hopes that rape cases would receive more attention from the judicial system and, by inference, from the community. Yet evidence is mixed and inconclusive as to whether statutory changes resulted in greater numbers of reports, prosecutions, and convictions.

Prevalence studies suggest that large numbers of sexual assaults still go unreported—particularly those between friends or acquaintances that neither perpetrator nor victim may label as rape. Traditional beliefs about the distribution of sexual assaults by geographic area, social class, and ethnicity are both challenged and supported by these studies. Likewise, tests of popular hypotheses regarding the distribution of attitudes and behaviors supportive of violent sexuality have yielded inconclusive results. Although legal statutes emphasize the importance of force and consent or resistance to differentiate rape from an ordinary sexual encounter, clearly other factors influence almost all decisions at all levels—from those made by Supreme Court justices to those made by impoverished adolescent victims.

A host of studies in a wide variety of traditions arrive at the conclusion that women are assumed to be at least partly responsible for their own sexual victimization. Attribution of responsibility apparently varies with the woman's character, her appearance, characteristics of her attacker, the extent and nature of prior interactions with her attacker, and, possibly, with characteristics of her judges. From surveys including adolescents, victims, men who rape, and even Ann Landers, it has been shown that certain behaviors that some women would call "sexual assault" are viewed as expected or even justified given the circumstances. Responding in April 1987 to a letter from a woman who had been raped by a man she had dated twice, Ann Landers sympathized, suggested counseling, and said "too bad you didn't file charges against those creeps." Ten weeks later, after numerous letters challenging her response, Landers changed her mind. One writer said:

> Granted, "Date Raped" may not have intended to go all the way, but she certainly must accept responsibility for encouraging the guy and making him think she was a willing partner. The trouble starts when she changes her mind after his passions are out of control. Then it's too late.

Landers replied:

> Many readers picked up on this, and I believe they are on to something. When I made this point in the column several months ago, I got my ears slapped down. Now I'm convinced that I must rethink my position and go back to telling women, "If you don't want a complete sexual experience, keep a lively conversation going and his hands off you." (*Los Angeles Times*, April 13 and July 2, 1987)

In our pluralistic society, what determines rape is not clear. Ideal definitions exist but evidence suggests that they are applied to everyday situations only rarely. How do ordinary people decide whether a sexual encounter is a rape? What information do they use? Does the decisionmaking process reflect the pluralistic nature of our society or is there consensus across groups defined by gender, ethnicity, socioeconomic status, and criminal exposure?

The study reported in part III examines some of the information used by residents of Los Angeles County, California, to decide whether a coercive sexual encounter is a rape. The study shows the extent to which the information used and respondents' certainty that a rape did or did not occur differ with social structural characteristics, life-style, and feelings of criminal vulnerability. Respondents also were asked to give their own definition of rape, what they thought the legal definition was, their perceptions of what causes rape, what might reduce it, and their beliefs about men and women involved in rape.

7 Los Angeles Study

The Los Angeles study investigates how people in one community define rape. Using data collected in the spring and summer of 1979 from black and white Los Angeles County residents, the study examined the extent to which respondents use information about force, resistance, and characteristics of the female, male, and situation to decide whether a rape has occurred. The study's two major objectives were to find out what information was used in deciding a sexual encounter was a rape and the extent to which decisions and data used to make decisions systematically differed with social, demographic, and life-style characteristics of respondents. Of particular interest is the extent to which consensus about definitions of rape does or does not exist across persons differentiated by sex, race, age, socioeconomic status, and prior life experiences. Both traditional questionnaire items and vignettes or short written scenarios or descriptions were used to learn how residents of Los Angeles County describe and define rape.

Like many other studies of rape, the Los Angeles investigation was designed and conducted during the mid- and late 1970s. The study's orientation is generally feminist, but no explicit feminist hypotheses were tested. We assumed that perceptions would differ across the population sampled and would differ systematically with respondent characteristics. In particular, we anticipated that gender, race, age, and socioeconomic status would affect perceptions of rape.

Los Angeles Sample

A sample of 126 white and 125 black Los Angeles County residents was interviewed during the summer and fall of 1979.[1] Using the Los Angeles Metropolitan Area Survey (LAMAS) sample frame, primary sampling units (PSUs) in Los Angeles County were prestratified according to the proportion of black and white households each PSU contained. PSUs with high proportions of black and/or white residents were retained in the sample frame, while those with high proportions of Hispanic and/or Asian residents were dropped.[2] The resulting sample frame thus excludes Hispanics and Asians, oversamples blacks, and undersamples white residents of Los Angeles County.[3]

Households selected by random sampling off the sample frame were sent a letter approximately one week prior to the arrival of an interviewer from the Institute for Social Science Research at the University of California at Los Angeles. The letter explained the purpose of the study, identified who was doing the study, and informed all household residents that a UCLA interviewer would be asking them to participate in the study. Upon arrival at a designated household, interviewers first completed a household roster and screened residents to ensure that household residents were black and/or white. After the roster was completed, Kish tables were used to select the household resident that was to be interviewed (Kish, 1949). (See note 2 in chapter 6 for an explanation of Kish tables.)

As seen in table 7.1, a total of 436 addresses were approached to obtain a completed sample of 250 Los Angeles County residents equally divided between blacks and whites. Of those respondents both eligible and selected for interview, 69 (16 percent) refused. When analyzed by race, 16 percent of whites and 15 percent of blacks refused to participate. Although sex of refusers was not recorded, experience in prior surveys suggests that refusers were disproportionately male.

Characteristics of the sample are summarized in table 7.2. Since respondents were intentionally selected to have even numbers of blacks and whites, data presented in table 7.2 are stratified by race. Females compose 64.3 percent of the sample while 35.7 percent are males; 39.9 percent of the respondents had from one to seven children under the age of 18 in the household; 61.7 percent of the respondents were currently working. Their median annual income was between $12,000 and

Table 7.1 Response rate and reasons for household exclusion by race of household, Los Angeles study, 1979

	Race of household		
Basis for sample exclusion	Anglo	Black	Unknown/other
Addresses approached	163	148	125
Not a dwelling unit			9
Vacant			8
Language barrier[a]			4
Refused to be screened			21
Never home[b]	3		31
Not a qualified respondent[c]			45
Incapable	5		5
Miscellaneous[d]	3	1	2
Designated respondent refused	26	22	
Completed interviews	126	125	

a Languages were Dutch (1), Lebanese (2), and Greek (1).

b Includes 20 households in security buildings.

c Household or respondent defines self as Spanish (36), Oriental (3), Asian (1), Hawaiian (1), Cuban (1), or unknown (3) rather than black or Anglo.

d Household not contacted or ineligible because dog in yard (1), not a permanent residence (1), terminated by respondent (1), or wrong respondent (1).

$14,000. The average age of respondents was 38 years. Almost four out of five (39.8 percent) were married.

Demographic characteristics differed by race; black respondents were significantly more likely to be younger, female, currently unmarried, employed full time, or unemployed, and of lower income, education, and socioeconomic status. Black respondents lived in neighborhoods with higher official rates of robbery, burglary, and rape. They perceived their neighborhoods as having more crime, and themselves as being more vulnerable to crime. In addition, household income and perceived vulnerability to crime differed with sex of the respondent. Black females had significantly lower household incomes in 1978 than black males, and females of both races perceived themselves to be more vulnerable to crime than did male counterparts.

Table 7.2 Demographic characteristics of sample,
Los Angeles study, 1979

Demographic characteristics	Race Black	White	Total unweighted sample
Percentage female	68.0	60.3	64.1
Mean age[a]	39.9	46.2	43.1
Percentage Protestant[a]	84.8	49.2	66.9
Household characteristics			
Number of years in home	5.3	6.4	5.9
Mean number of adults	1.7	1.7	1.7
Mean number of children less than 18 years[a]	1.1	0.4	0.75
Percentage currently married[a]	29.6	50.0	39.8
Socioeconomic status			
Percentage working full-time[a]	56.0	47.6	51.8
Percentage working part-time[a]	4.8	15.1	10.0
Percentage professional, technical, or managers[a]	13.6	38.1	25.9
Percentage operatives, laborers, or service workers[a]	47.2	14.3	30.7
Mean Duncan score[a]	34.4	50.0	42.3
Highest grade completed[a]	12.3	13.5	12.9
Percentage high school degree or more[a]	69.6	86.5	78.1
Median household income	$8,500–9,999	$14,000–16,999	$12,000–13,999
Perceived and actual vulnerability to crime			
Crime in area[a,c]	0.78	– 0.77	0.0
Perceived crime in area[a,d]	2.9	2.1	2.5
Perceived vulnerability to crime[b,e]	4.9	3.9	4.4
Preventive behaviors taken[f]	0.78	0.66	0.72
Total *N*	125	126	251

a Significant difference by race.

b Significant difference by race and sex.

c The official rates of burglary, robbery, and rape in each respondent's area were summed using the formula in note 9 and standardized to have a mean of 0 and a standard deviation of 1. Thus, negative scores represent safer areas and positive scores represent more dangerous areas.

Table 7.2 (continued)

d Mean answer to question 22, "Compared to other neighborhoods in Los Angeles, do you think that crime in your neighborhood is much more serious, more serious, about as serious, less serious, or much less serious?," where "much less serious" received a code of 1 and "much more serious" received a code of 5.

e Nine-item vulnerability index created from questions 8–13, 16, 17, and 18 using factor analysis with orthogonal rotation followed by testing with Cronbach's alpha (1951). See note 7 for the content of the nine questions. Scores range from 1 to 9.

f Summation of answers to question 24, "When you go out *at night*, do you ever take steps to protect yourself such as taking a dog along, asking someone to walk with you, or carrying a whistle or something like that?" (yes = 1; no or other answer = 0); and question 28A, "Some people have taken steps to protect their home against burglary, others have not. How about you? In the last *five* years have you put additional locks on the doors and windows?" (yes = 1; no or don't know = 0). Scores range from 0 to 2.

Data Collection

Measuring the Dependent Variable: Definitions of Rape

Vignettes were used in the Los Angeles study to portray sexual encounters.[4] Information in the vignettes was selected to represent the domain of information people consider in deciding whether a given sexual encounter is a rape. Respondents were asked to evaluate whether each sexual encounter portrayed was a rape. The pattern of answers given by each respondent represented his or her perception of the circumstances under which rape occurs. A major hypothesis of the study was that respondents would differ both in the extent to which they thought a given vignette or set of vignettes portrayed rape, and also in the amount and type of information used to arrive at their decision.

Eight kinds of information were included in the vignettes: force, resistance, race of the male, race of the female, marital status of the female, occupation of the male, location of the encounter, and whether the male and female were acquainted with each other. These eight variables represent four dimensions of information thought to be used by individuals and groups to decide whether a sexual encounter is rape. These four dimensions are the relationship between victim and offender, the circumstances surrounding the sexual encounter, characteristics of the victim, and characteristics of the offender.

As we saw in part II, an infinite number of factors have been hypothesized to influence decisions about rape. Consequently, each of the four dimensions can be operationalized in an infinite number of ways. At the same time, obviously, every possible component of the four dimensions cannot easily be described and controlled within a single set of vignettes without the number of combinations becoming astronomically high. The exact content of the eight elements selected was guided by a combination of theoretical concerns and research available at the time the study was designed.

Both lay and legal systems emphasize "force" and "consent" as characteristics differentiating rape from other sexual encounters, and due to the continuing debate about what constitutes sufficient force and evidence of nonconsensual sex, we felt that these two variables should be included in the vignettes. Since consent often is operationalized as resistance, the vignettes included information on whether the woman resisted as the measure of consent.

As reported in part II, numerous writers suggest, and studies of judicial processing and simulated juries often find, that characteristics of the male, female, and situation are used as cues in determining responsibility for rapes and probably as surrogates in judging whether the woman consented to or resisted the sexual encounter. Six kinds of information about the man, woman, and situation were, therefore, included in the vignettes. Selection of the information was guided by past research and legal concerns. While statistics suggest that most rapes are intraracial, stereotypes and research suggest that sexual encounters involving black males and white females are most likely to be judged rapes. Race of both the male and the female was included to test the accuracy of the stereotype. The male's occupation also was specified in the vignette, both to minimize the use of race as an indicator of social class and to allow the effect of race to be separated from that of social class. Marital status of the woman was included as an indirect indicator of her sexual history. To differentiate stranger rape from acquaintance rape, information about whether the man and woman knew each other was included in the vignette. And finally, the site of the encounter was included as an indication of provocation or the extent to which the woman had precipitated the attack because of where she was or what she was doing.

Each element or variable contained within the vignette can assume two levels. Figure 7.1 presents an example of a single unique vignette, the variables or elements contained within the full set of vignettes, and the levels they could assume. All elements were fully crossed to create a universe of 256 or 2^8 unique, parsimonious vignettes. Vignettes were

Format of vignette on IBM card

(Level of provocation) a (Marital status) (Race) woman was approached by a (Race) man who is a (Male's occupation) and who (Level of knowing). The man (Level of force). She (Level of resistance).

Two levels of content varied within each vignette element

Race: black *or* white

Level of provocation: coming out of a bar *or* coming out of a supermarket

Marital status: married *or* divorced

Occupation: janitor *or* lawyer

Level of knowing: lives on the same block *or* she had never seen before

Level of force: threatened her and forced her to have sex *or* told her he was going to have sex with her

Level of resistance: was unwilling but did not fight *or* struggled with him

Example of an actual vignette

As she was coming out of a bar, a divorced white woman was approached by a black man who is a janitor and who she had never seen before. The man told her he was going to have sex with her. She struggled with him.

Figure 7.1 Design of the vignettes used in the Los Angeles study. 1970 U.S. census and Duncan (1961) Socioeconomic Index Scores for the janitor are 903 and 13, and for the lawyer are 031 and 92 (Featherman, Sobel, and Dickens, 1975).

assigned to respondents using fractional replication (e.g., Alexander and Becker, 1978; Cochran and Cox, 1957; appendix 2). In this study, eighth replicates were used to assign vignettes to respondents. An "eighth replicate" contains 32 different vignettes out of the universe of 256. Each respondent received one of the eight unique replicates or sets of 32 vignettes. Since eighth replicates were used, seven of the possible interactions that could be computed between the eight variables contained within the vignettes are confounded with the way the 256 vignettes are assigned to the eight blocks or replicates and, subsequently, with respondents to whom that set of vignettes is assigned.[5]

Unlike vignettes commonly used in attribution research and some of the community studies discussed in part II, vignettes were intentionally designed to be sparse. Information relevant to variables being manipulated was maximized, and extraneous information was reduced to a minimum on the premise that extraneous information influences subjects' responses in unknown and uncontrollable but potentially significant ways (see appendix 2).

Respondents were asked to read each vignette (printed on an IBM card by computer) and to decide, using a six-point, bipolar rating scale, whether the situation definitely was or was not a rape. Interviewers read vignettes to respondents who had difficulty reading. The two polar categories were defined, but categories between were not. After the respondent decided whether the vignette portrayed a rape, s/he placed the vignette in a pocket on a vignette board that corresponded to the rating selected. (See appendix 1 for the full set of instructions used in administering the vignettes.)

Immediately following administration of the 32 vignettes, respondents were asked a series of five questions about their ratings.

2 Was there any rating (envelope or number) that you used more than the others?
3 Was there any additional information that you would have found particularly helpful in deciding how to rate the cards?
4 Was there any information that you did *not* use in making up your mind?
5 Were there any cards that you found particularly difficult to rate?
6 Was there anything that you found particularly upsetting or that made you uncomfortable about rating the cards?

The questions were designed to find out whether respondents' perceptions of how they rated the vignettes matched their actual ratings, what if any difficulties they had in rating the vignettes, and whether the contents of the vignettes upset them.

Questionnaire

Following administration of the vignettes, a questionnaire containing 47 items was administered in a face-to-face interview. It included traditional questions on opinions about rape, items on criminal victimization, and standard demographic data. (Appendix 1 contains the questionnaire.)

Vulnerability to Crime. The first set of 21 questions asks about feelings of vulnerability to crime. Designed by Tyler (1978) for an earlier study in Los Angeles County, these questions solicit information on perceived vulnerability to burglary and robbery, the number of burglaries and robberies that have occurred in the immediate neighborhood, and precautions taken by the individual or household in the last five years to prevent burglary or robbery.[6] The 21 items were factor-analyzed, and a nine-item vulnerability index was created for later analyses.[7] Items asking about preventive behaviors and exact information (e.g., number of crimes within the neighborhood) were dropped from the index because they did not add to its reliability and homogeneity as measured using Cronbach's alpha (1951).

Traditional Questions about Rape. Questions 29–40 were adapted from Williams and Holmes's (1981) tri-ethnic study of San Antonio residents. This section was modified in four ways: open-ended questions were moved to the front of the series to minimize contamination, closed questions were made open-ended, administration procedures were modified, and questions were added. Question 29, "When you hear the term *rape*, what is the *first* word that comes to your mind? Just give me *one* word that you first associate with rape," directly replicates question 40 in the Williams and Holmes schedule. Questions 30–33, which read as follows, expanded items 41 and 42 from Williams and Holmes.

    30 Do you think a woman who gets raped is *different* from other women *before* she is raped?
    31 Do you think she is different *after* she is raped?
    32 Do you think a man who commits rape is *different* from other men *before* he rapes?
    33 Do you think he is different *after* he rapes?

Whereas the two original items asked respondents whether "a man who commits rape" and "a woman who gets raped" are different from other men or women, the revised questions specify two time periods—before and after the rape.

In the San Antonio study, respondents were asked to select the correct legal definition of rape from among four statements. Because we thought it would be difficult to distinguish between the statements, and because we were curious about what kinds of unsolicited responses we would get, we asked two open-ended questions (questions 35 and 36). First, "In your own words, how would you define rape (i.e., what do you think rape is?)" and second, "What do you think the legal definition of rape is in California?"

Questions 37 and 39 are modified versions of items 38 and 39 in the Williams and Holmes's schedule:

37 In your opinion, what is the *main* cause of rape?
39 In your opinion, what is the one thing that would *reduce* rape the most?

The stem phrases are identical to those of the San Antonio study. However, while Williams and Holmes asked respondents to select their responses for questions 37 and 39 from a card, we had the interviewer first record spontaneous answers verbatim. Respondents who did not give a spontaneous answer were provided with a card identical to the ones used in the San Antonio study. Responses on the card for question 37 were:

Rapists are mentally ill, "sick," or emotionally disturbed
Pressure put on males in our society (by women or in general)
Women's behavior (e.g., teasing, inappropriate dress, false accusations, "leading men on," etc.)
Women being where they should not be (e.g., out late at night, in a bar, hitchhiking, etc.)
Sex (e.g., strong desire, need, lust, frustration, or lack of sex)
Drugs or alcohol
A part of the violence in our society.

Responses on the card for question 39 were:

Harsher punishment for rapists (e.g., death sentence, longer imprisonment)
Stricter laws or better police protection
Women being more careful (e.g., how they dress, where they go, etc.)
Women learning self-defense or protecting themselves from attack
Education (e.g., sex education, public education about rape)

Treatment for rapists or people with sex problems

Better family life (better marriage relations, parents raising mentally healthy children, etc.).

Our changes in the questions reflected our desire to find out whether our spontaneous answers would match the prespecified coding categories used in the San Antonio study. In question 37, which asks "In your opinion, what is the *main* cause of rape?" follow-up questions were used in two instances. If sexual desire/need, etc., was specified as the cause of rape, we asked whether it was on the part of the male or the female. If mental illness was specified as a main cause, we asked whether rapists should be hospitalized or imprisoned.

Question 38, "When men rape women, do you think they rape women who are from their own race or ethnic group or from a race or ethnic group that is different from their own?" was slightly modified from Williams and Holmes' question 36 with the same objective, i.e., to minimize giving the respondent any cues as to possible answers.

Finally, question 40, "Do you think the number of rapes in Los Angeles has increased, decreased, or stayed about the same in the last *5 years*?" essentially replicates Williams and Holmes's question 36 with the exception of format. Answer categories were modified to make it easier for interviewers to differentiate among them.

Demographic Questions. Demographic questions (41–45) and their numerous subparts directly replicate questions used in all surveys of Los Angeles County conducted by the Institute for Social Science Research, University of California at Los Angeles. They read as follows:

41 What is your *current* employment status?

42 What was the highest grade in school you *completed* and *received* credit for?

43 What is your religious preference?

44 How long have you lived in this (house/apartment)?

45 Now, thinking of your household, in 1978 was the total income from *all* sources and *before* taxes, for this household, under $10,000 or over $10,000?

Crime Statistics

It has been theorized that persons perceive their own neighborhood to be safer than other neighborhoods. In order to determine whether this was true of these respondents and whether reported crimes helped to predict feelings of vulnerability and the instigation of protective behaviors, questionnaire data were compared to police reports of crime. Statistics for Part One Crimes by census tract were gathered from the Los Angeles County sheriff's department and the Los Angeles police department for 1978 and 1979. Part One Crimes include criminal homicide, forcible rape, robbery, aggravated assault, burglary, larceny, theft, and grand theft auto.[8]

Respondents were assigned to census tracts which were then plotted onto precinct maps in order to determine the crime statistics for each respondent's area. An estimate of the total population of a precinct or sheriff's area was obtained and crime statistics were computed for a base of 10,000 persons. After preliminary examination of the rates, attention was restricted to rape, burglary, and robbery since those were topics presented in the questionnaire. These three rates were highly intercorrelated and, when factor-analyzed using a principal components solution, 89 percent of the variance was explained by the first factor. Using the factor score coefficients, a composite crime statistics variable was created for each respondent.[9] When necessary for purposes of analyses, the composite variable was standardized to correct for skew. When the variable is standardized, respondents with crime scores of zero live in areas with average crime rates. Respondents with positive crime scores live in high-crime areas, and respondents with negative crime scores live in low-crime areas. When unstandardized, a low-crime score represents a low-crime area and a high-crime score represents a high-crime area.

Preliminary Studies

Two preliminary studies were conducted prior to the Los Angeles study. In the first study vignettes were developed and pretested. In the second study these vignettes were revised, and reliability tests were conducted.

Developmental Pilot Study

The objective of the first pilot study was to develop and test vignettes, paying particular attention to their form and content. Questions addressed included the kinds of information that should be included in vignettes, the kind of rating procedure that should be used, the length and complexity of vignettes, and respondents' and interviewers' reactions to vignettes. Data were collected from a convenience sample of 112 respondents evenly divided across four shopping areas. Shopping areas were selected because of their proximity to residential areas that could be assumed to be white upper-class, white lower-class, black upper-class, and black lower-class. Forty-eight vignettes and a questionnaire identical to the one described above were administered to each respondent.

Results were used to revise and finalize content and structure of vignettes and questionnaires. As discussed in greater detail in appendix 2, results suggested that the inclusion of information extraneous to the variables under study influences respondents' ratings of vignettes.

Reliability Study

Using information gathered in the developmental pilot study, vignettes were modified and tested for reliability on four community groups (Bourque, 1978). Groups were selected to represent upper- and lower-socioeconomic-status blacks and whites. The content and format of vignettes tested for reliability were identical to those described earlier in this chapter. Each block or set of vignettes was given to a minimum of six persons in each of the four community groups. Each respondent received the same vignette cards at both administrations (which were one week apart). To minimize sequencing effects, the cards were randomly reordered for the second administration. The first card in each packet briefly reiterated instructions given verbally. The last card in each packet invited the respondent to write down any comments s/he had. Vignettes were placed in pockets on a vignette board as they were rated. Respondents were asked to rate cards in the order presented and not to change their ratings. Since this was a group administration, however, control over individual respondents could not be maintained to the same degree that it might be in a face-to-face interview.

Immediately following the first administration, respondents filled out a brief, self-administered questionnaire and initialed a consent form. Of the 189 persons who rated vignettes at time 1, 155 persons returned one week later for the second administration. When examined by group, no significant demographic differences were found between those who returned and those who did not.

As discussed in somewhat greater detail in appendix 2, ratings of vignettes were found to be highly reliable over a one-week period.

Analysis

The Los Angeles study has four sets of variables. For purposes of analysis, variables in the first set—the self-reported demographic and social-psychological data collected with the questionnaire—are always treated as independent variables. The second—respondents' ratings of the 32 vignettes—is always treated as a dependent variable. The third and fourth —respondents' attitudes toward rape as elicited using traditional questionnaire items, and the vignette information used by respondents in deciding whether or not the sexual encounter was a rape—assume both independent and dependent variable status at different stages of analysis.

Analysis of Vignettes

The two kinds of data on rape—vignettes and traditional questions—were kept separate for most analyses. (Chapters 9 and 10 report analyses of vignettes, and chapters 10 and 11 report analyses of traditional questions about rape.) Analyses of vignettes were conducted in four stages. In the first, procedures used to generate vignettes were tested for both block and respondent effects that might confound and obscure substantive findings, and contrast matrices were used to develop a summary measure of the information each respondent used in deciding whether vignettes they rated portrayed a rape. Appendix 2 describes procedures used in these analyses.

In the second stage, analysis of variance and multiple regressions were used to determine the extent to which each variable included in the vignette—either singularly or in combination—predicts decisions that the encounter is rape. Both one-way and multivariate analyses of variance were computed.

Once methodological and substantive analyses restricted to vignettes were completed, discriminant analysis and multiple regression were used to investigate the relationship between vignette ratings, vignette rating patterns, and various demographic and attitudinal characteristics of respondents.[10] Discriminant analysis was used to determine the extent to which decisionmaking styles could be clearly differentiated using demographic and life-style characteristics of Los Angeles County residents. Regression analyses were used to determine the extent to which decisions that the vignette portrayed a rape could be predicted from demographic and life-style characteristics of respondents and information they used in making decisions.

Both discriminant and regression analyses were conducted using both the respondent and the vignette as the unit of analysis, and with both the full set of demographic and life-style variables and with only those that most efficiently predicted respondents' decisions about whether the vignettes were rapes.[11] When the respondent was the unit of analysis and the full sample was included, regressions were computed using both the unweighted and weighted samples (see note 3 in this chapter).

Findings were generally the same regardless of the unit of analysis selected, the number of variables included in an equation, or whether the sample was weighted or unweighted. (Reduced equations using the vignette as the unit of analysis are presented in chapter 9. Correlation matrices, full set equations, and weighted and unweighted regressions in which the respondent is the unit of analysis are reported in appendix 3.)

Analysis of Traditional Questions on Rape

Once vignettes had been analyzed both alone and in relationship to characteristics of respondents, crosstabular analyses examined responses to traditional questions on rape and the extent to which responses differed with demographic and vignette rating pattern characteristics of respondents. (These analyses are reported in chapters 10 and 11.)

⑧ When a Sexual Encounter Becomes a Rape

Community Perceptions of Sexual Encounters

Vignettes used to evaluate how the 126 white and 125 black Los Angeles County respondents decided whether a sexual encounter was rape included eight kinds of information:

Whether the man used physical or verbal force
Whether the woman physically resisted the sexual encounter
Whether the encounter occurred outside a market or a bar
Whether the man and woman lived on the same block or had never seen each other before
Whether the man was black or white
Whether the woman was black or white
Whether the man was a janitor or a lawyer
Whether the woman was married or divorced.

Each respondent evaluated 32 of the 256 unique vignettes using a six-point bipolar scale to decide whether the vignette "definitely was not a rape," "definitely was a rape," or fell somewhere in between.

Respondents were remarkable in their general tendency to think that sexual encounters portrayed in most of the vignettes probably or definitely were rape. Almost half (49.5 percent) of the 8,032 responses were "definitely was a rape," and an additional 17 percent of the responses

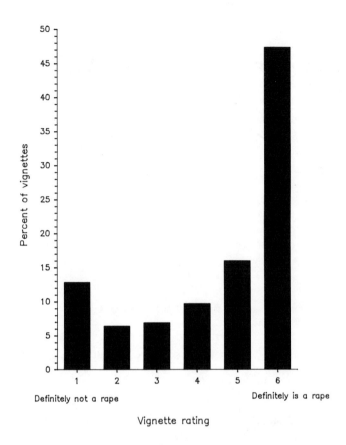

Figure 8.1 Distribution of vignettes by rating given to vignette, Los Angeles study, 1979

indicated that the vignettes portrayed situations which respondents viewed as highly likely to be rape (figure 8.1).

What Makes It a Rape?

The data indicate that physical force and physical resistance, and to a lesser extent whether the victim knew the assailant and where it occurred, made it rape. If he "threatened her and forced her to have sex," participants thought very probably that rape had occurred (table 8.1). Even when he "told her he was going to have sex with her," participants were not convinced it "definitely was not a rape." If the woman "struggled

Table 8.1   Mean vignette rating by level of vignette variable portrayed, Los Angeles study, 1979

Variable and level	Mean rating[a]	Standard deviation	Signifi- cance[b]
Level of force			
Threatened her and forced her to have sex	5.2	1.4	.0001
Told her he was going to have sex with her	3.8	1.9	
Level of resistance			
Struggled with him	4.9	1.7	.0001
Was unwilling but did not fight	4.2	1.9	
Acquaintanceship level			
Lives on the same block	4.5	1.8	.0854
She has never seen him before	4.6	1.8	
Location of encounter			
Coming out of a bar	4.5	1.8	.2134
Coming out of a supermarket	4.6	1.8	
Marital status of female			
Married	4.5	1.8	.8972
Divorced	4.5	1.8	
Race of female			
Black	4.5	1.8	.6292
White	4.5	1.8	
Occupation of male			
Lawyer	4.5	1.8	.8330
Janitor	4.5	1.8	
Race of male			
Black	4.5	1.8	.2857
White	4.5	1.8	
Total vignettes[c]	8,032		

a Ratings can range from 1 (definitely is not a rape) to 6 (definitely is a rape).

b One-way analysis of variance was used to test whether the ratings differ across the two levels of each of the eight variables, force, resistance, acquaintanceship, location, marital status, race of female, occupation and race of male.

c Each respondent rated 32 vignettes that represent an eighth replicate of 256 unique vignettes.

with him," respondents thought rape was more probable ($\bar{x} = 4.9$) than if she "was unwilling but did not fight." However, even when she did not physically resist, Los Angeles residents were not convinced that rape had *not* occurred ($\bar{x} = 4.2$).

Is Available Information Combined?

A series of analyses starting with a multivariate analysis of variance was used to investigate whether respondents combined available information, how they combined it, and the impact the combination had on decisions about the sexual encounters.

As in the one-way analysis of variance (anova) discussed above, an eight-way anova again demonstrated that information about force and resistance strongly affected decisions about the sexual encounters (figure 8.2), while acquaintanceship again had a marginally significant influence·on decisions (p = .085) with couples who lived on the same block being slightly less likely ($\bar{x}$ = 4.5) to have been involved in a rape than those

Figure 8.2 Vignette rating by level of force and level of resistance portrayed in the vignette, Los Angeles study, 1979

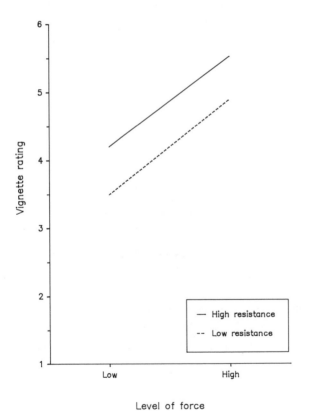

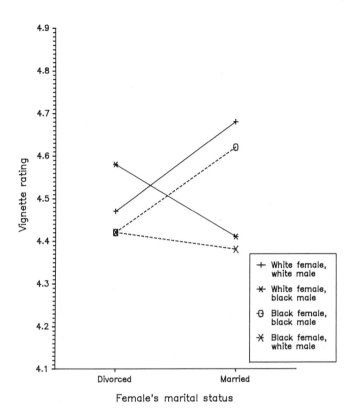

Figure 8.3 Vignette rating by vignette's portrayal of the male's race, the female's race, and the female's marital status, Los Angeles study, 1979

who had never seen each other before ($\bar{x} = 4.6$). If the man used physical force to obtain sex and the woman physically resisted him, respondents as a group were almost positive a rape had occurred ($\bar{x} = 5.52$). Respondents were fairly sure a rape had occurred ($\bar{x} = 4.89$) when the man used force even if the woman portrayed did not physically resist. If, on the other hand, the woman physically resisted a verbal threat, certainty about rape occurring dropped substantially ($\bar{x} = 4.20$). And if the woman did not physically resist a verbal threat, participants as a group were neutral ($\bar{x} = 3.49$) about what had occurred.

Clearly, force and resistance are important cues in deciding whether a sexual encounter is a rape. But the multivariate analysis of variance yielded other information as well. Whereas the one-way anovas implied that information about race, occupation, and marital status was not considered by

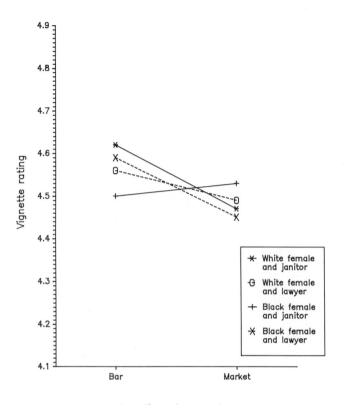

Location of encounter

Figure 8.4 Vignette rating by vignette's portrayal of the female's race, the male's occupation, and the location of the encounter, Los Angeles study, 1979

respondents in making their decisions, the eight-way anova hints that such information may be important to some people.

Two significant three-way interactions were found: the first between the male's race, the female's race, and the female's marital status; the second between the male's occupation, the female's race, and the location of the encounter (figures 8.3 and 8.4). If the woman is married, Los Angeles County residents as a group are more likely to decide she was raped *if the man who attacks her is of her own race* than if he is a man of a different race ($\bar{x} = 4.68$). In contrast, if the woman is divorced, respondents are more likely to decide she was raped *if the man who attacks her is of a different race* ($\bar{x} = 4.65$). For respondents as a whole, these three variables have no independent effect on decisions about whether or not a rape occurred, nor do any of the three variables interact with information about force or resistance to influence decisions about rape.

A similar but weaker three-way interaction is observed among the male's occupation, the female's race, and the location of the encounter. Again, none of the three variables has a significant main effect on decisions, nor are two-way interactions between the three variables significant, nor does any of the three variables interact with the two major variables—force and resistance—to influence decisionmaking. For Los Angeles respondents, a white female who is attacked outside a market by a janitor is judged most likely to have been raped ($\bar{x} = 4.62$), while a black female who is attacked outside a bar by a lawyer is judged least likely to have been raped ($\bar{x} = 4.45$).

Given the large number of vignettes ($N = 8,032$) being rated, the small number of interactions observed in the data, and the small absolute differences in decisions caused by these three-way interaction terms, it is of course possible that the observed interactions are statistical artifacts.[1] On the other hand use of force and/or resistance by a large proportion of the sample as the sole and/or primary information in decisionmaking, in combination with high absolute differences across vignettes (differing in force and resistance), may obscure the influence and subtle use of other information.

All legal definitions of rape unequivocally state, and normative community definitions are assumed to state, that if intercourse is accomplished through force or violence, it is rape. At issue is what constitutes force. Nonconsent is also assumed to be a characteristic that differentiates rapes from consensual sex. But here again, what constitutes nonconsent? Physical resistance is most frequently used as the primary indication of nonconsent. Other information—such as the socioeconomic status of the man and woman, where they were, and whether they knew each other—while technically irrelevant, is widely assumed and has been documented to influence perceptions that rape has or has not occurred.

It certainly is within the realm of possibility that the Los Angeles County residents used force as their major source of information to label a sexual encounter rape, that resistance was used as their secondary source of information, and that they generally ignored other information. If this were true, the other differences observed above would simply be statisti-

Table 8.2 Distribution of respondents and mean vignette rating by vignette rating pattern, Los Angeles study, 1979

Vignette rating pattern used by respondents	Unweighted sample		Weighted sample		Mean vignette rating[a]
	N	Percentage	N	Percentage	
Nonrater	30	12.0	38	15.1	5.59
Nonnormative rater	29	11.6	24	9.6	3.78
Force only	34	13.5	36	14.3	4.55
Force with other variables	95	37.8	98	38.7	4.38
Resistance only	20	8.0	14	5.7	4.97
Resistance with other variables	43	17.1	42	16.5	4.36
Total N	251		253		4.35

a One-way analysis of variance comparing the mean ratings across the six groups in the unweighted sample is significant at p<.0001.

cal artifacts. It is also possible—social norms being what they are—that persons who use less acceptable kinds of information in making decisions attempt to censor or conceal their use, thus yielding the two three-way interactions and the marginally significant main effect for acquaintanceship. Or it is possible that different people use different combinations of information with use of force and resistance being both most prevalent and, when used, most influential in differentiating rapes from other sexual encounters.

Patterns of Information Used to Decide about Rapes

Contrast matrices (described in detail in appendix 2) showed that people use different combinations of information to differentiate rape from other sexual encounters. Six patterns were identified. Four of the six were dominated by force and/or resistance (table 8.2). Thirty-four (13.5 percent) Los Angeles respondents used only information about force as a major determinant of whether the sexual encounter was rape. For these 34 people, the encounter was definitely a rape ($\bar{x}$ = 5.96) if the man "threatened her and forced her to have sex" (table 8.3). Conversely, if he "told her he was going to have sex with her," they were at best undecided about the encounter ($\bar{x}$ = 3.14), tending to think the encounter was not a rape (table

Table 8.3 Mean rating by vignette rating pattern used and level of vignette variable portrayed, Los Angeles study, 1979 (unweighted sample)[a]

Variable and level	Vignette rating pattern					
	Non-rater	Non-normative rater	Force-only rater	Force-plus rater	Resistance-only rater	Resistance-plus rater
Force						
Physical	5.60	3.93*	5.96**	5.51**	5.03	4.63**
Verbal	5.59	3.64	3.14	3.25	4.92	4.10
Resistance						
Struggled	5.60	3.95*	4.58	4.59**	5.95**	5.26**
Did not	5.59	3.62	4.53	4.18	4.00	3.46
Acquaintanceship						
Same block	5.60	3.72	4.57	4.35	4.97	4.29
Not seen	5.59	3.84	4.54	4.42	4.98	4.40
Location						
Bar	5.60	3.69	4.56	4.34	4.98	4.38
Market	5.59	3.88	4.55	4.43	4.97	4.34
Female's marital status						
Divorced	5.60	3.70	4.55	4.36	4.96	4.36
Married	5.59	3.87	4.55	4.41	4.99	4.36
Female's race						
Black	5.59	3.78	4.55	4.40	4.98	4.35
White	5.60	3.79	4.56	4.37	4.97	4.38
Male's race						
Black	5.59	3.68+	4.55	4.37	4.99	4.35
White	5.60	3.89	4.55	4.40	4.96	4.38
Male's occupation						
Janitor	5.60	3.77	4.55	4.39	4.97	4.39
Lawyer	5.59	3.79	4.56	4.38	4.98	4.34
Mean rating	5.59	3.78	4.55	4.38	4.98	4.34
Total *N*	30	29	34	95	20	43

** $p < .01$
* $p < .05$
+ $p < .10$

a This table is analogous to table 8.1 in which the vignette was the unit of analysis. Here the respondent is the unit of analysis. Respondents are grouped according to the rating pattern used and one-way analysis of variance is used within groups to test whether ratings differ across the two levels of each of the eight variables portrayed within the vignettes.

Table 8.4 Two-way analysis of variance of effect of force and resistance on vignette ratings by vignette pattern groups, Los Angeles study, 1979 (unweighted sample)[a]

Variable and level	Vignette rating pattern					
	Non-rater	Non-normative rater	Force-only rater	Force-plus rater	Resistance-only rater	Resistance-plus rater
Force high						
Resistance high	5.60	4.10	5.99	5.72	5.96	5.41
Resistance low	5.60	3.75	5.93	5.31	4.09	3.84
Force low						
Resistance high	5.59	3.79	3.16	3.46	5.93	5.12
Resistance low	5.58	3.49	3.13	3.05	3.91	3.08
Main effects						
Force	NS	$p=.03$	$p<.01$	$p<.01$	NS	$p<.01$
Resistance	NS	$p=.01$	NS	$p<.01$	$p<.01$	$p<.01$
Interaction	NS	NS	NS	NS	NS	$p<.01$
Mean rating	5.59	3.78	4.55	4.38	4.98	4.34
Total N	30	29	34	95	20	43

a The 251 respondents were stratified by vignette rating pattern. Within each group, two-way analysis of variance was used to examine the extent to which the amount of force and resistance portrayed within a vignette influenced respondents' decisions that a rape had occurred and, thus, their rating of the vignette.

8.3). This group may use other information occasionally, but since its use only becomes evident when an eight-way analysis of variance is computed within the group, the influence of other variables may simply represent statistical artifacts (tables 8.4, 8.5, and 8.6). The influence of other information on decisions by the force-only raters is both subtle and minimal. Decisions of these 34 Los Angeles County residents most closely fit the ideals advocated by persons who believe that decisions about rape ought to be premised exclusively on the use of force by men. Within this context, rape is strictly a violent act, never a sexual act.

Twenty people (8.0 percent) cued their decisions exclusively to information about resistance. If the woman "struggled with him," the encounter was judged a rape ($\bar{x} = 5.95$); if she "was unwilling but did not fight" respondents were generally indecisive ($\bar{x} = 4.0$). As a group, however, these 20 people were more likely to consider all encounters rape ($\bar{x} = 4.97$) than were the 34 who cued their decisions to information about force ($\bar{x}$ = 4.55). Thus even when the woman did not struggle, these respondents thought rape likely ($\bar{x}$ = 4.00). None of the other information was ever used by these respondents in making decisions. For this group of respondents, what the man does is largely irrelevant in the judgment of rape. Although we cannot know whether these respondents would ignore more specific information about use of force—such as weapons—had such information been presented, it seems clear that decisions are cued primarily to the woman's behavior. Specifically, the woman must physically resist the encounter. The impact that a woman's verbal resistance might have on these respondents' decisions cannot be evaluated with this set of data.

Over half the respondents (54.9 percent) combined information about force or about resistance with other information to decide whether a sexual encounter was rape. Ninety-five (37.8 percent) respondents used force as their major piece of information while 43 (17.1 percent) used resistance as their major piece of information. In both groups, the most common secondary source of information was information about the other variable, force or resistance. The relative importance of the second variable to decisionmaking was, however, much more important to the resistance-plus raters than to the force-plus raters (tables 8.4, 8.5, 8.6).

Both groups were almost certain that encounters in which the man "threatened her and forced her to have sex" and the woman "struggled with him" were rapes. Those whose decisions were more strongly influenced by force were somewhat surer ($\bar{x}$ = 5.72) than those whose decisions were influenced primarily by resistance ($\bar{x}$ = 5.41) (table 8.3). When either piece or both pieces of information changed, both groups' confidence that a rape occurred lessened significantly. Whereas those whose decisions were dominated by resistance combined information about resistance with information about force to the extent that the two kinds of information were almost equally important and interacted in decisionmaking, those whose decisions were dominated by force relegated information about resistance to a clearly secondary status.

Although force and resistance were the primary sources of information used in these two groups, other information was used at least some of the time by some members of the two groups. Information on acquaintanceship was particularly relevant to resistance-only raters in that a man who lived on the same block was thought to be less likely to have raped. In

Table 8.5 Pearson product moment correlations between vignette characteristics and vignette ratings by vignette rating patterns, Los Angeles study, 1979 (unweighted sample)

	Vignette rating pattern[b]		
Vignette characteristics[a]	Nonrater	Nonnormative rater	Force-only rater
Force (1 = high)	.005	.07**	.74**
Resistance (1 = high)	.003	.08**	.01
Acquaintanceship (1 = same block)	.005	−.03	.007
Location (1 = bar)	.00	−.05*	.00
Male's race (1 = black)	−.002	−.05**	.00
Female's race (1 = black)	−.002	.004	.00
Marital status (1 = divorced)	−.005	.04*	.00
Occupation (1 = lawyer)	−.005	.005	.004

** Significant at $p < .05$
* Significant at $p < .10$
a Codes used are 1 and 0.

contrast, the location of the encounter was relevant for force-plus raters with encounters occurring near a bar less likely to be judged rape (tables 8.5 and 8.6). Other information appears to influence decisions of these two groups subtly, but as in the case of the force-only raters, findings observed in eight-way anovas may result from statistical artifacts.

Both the size of these two groups and information used suggest they represent the decisionmaking norm about rape at least among whites and blacks in Los Angeles County. They acknowledge the importance of force and resistance (or consent) in differentiating rape from other sexual encounters, but they are not averse to letting other, less legally and morally relevant information have some influence over their decisions. Such information is, however, used less frequently, and influences decisions less than information about force and resistance. The relative influence of extra information is lower for force-plus raters than for resistance-plus raters.

The remaining two groups of Los Angeles respondents seem to pay little attention to information about force or resistance in decisionmaking. However, their reasons for ignoring such information and how this affected their decisions are quite different. Thirty people (12.0 percent) decided that either all or the majority of the sexual encounters they evaluated were definitely or probably rapes. Twenty-seven of the 30 said that all

(Vignette rating pattern)			
Force-plus rater	Resistance-only rater	Resistance-plus rater	Total
.63**	.04	.15**	.38**
.12**	.66**	.51**	.18**
−.02	−.003	−.04*	−.02*
−.03*	.003	.01	−.01
−.01	.01	−.008	−.01
−.01	.01	−.008	−.01
−.01	.01	.001	.001
−.003	.005	−.01	−.002

b Within each vignette rating group, eight correlations were computed between the ratings selected, which ranged from 1 to 6, and use of each of the eight kinds of information portrayed in making decisions.

of the vignettes—including those in which "he told her he was going to have sex with her" and she "was unwilling but did not fight"—"definitely were a rape." One person who gave all vignettes a rating of four effectively said that all the sexual encounters were, more likely than not, rape. Two persons mixed one high or low rating in with a predominant pattern of 3s. Assuming that these respondents were serious—and there is no reason to doubt their seriousness (see appendix 2)—these are the people prosecuting attorneys, date-rape victims, and feminists would most likely want on a jury.

The last group of respondents was least cognizant, or most rejecting, of what ideally defines a rape. Twenty-nine people (11.6 percent) minimized their use of information about force and resistance in deciding about rapes. They, more than others, used information about location and acquaintanceship. Moreover, they were the only group that clearly used information about marital status and the man's race. Although force and resistance influenced these respondents, they were significantly less likely to think that any encounter is rape. To the extent that they were willing to judge a sexual encounter to be rape, such a decision was made only when a white man used force, a married woman resisted, the encounter was outside a market, and the two did not live on the same block. Unlike persons in the resistance- and force-dominant groups who denied using

Table 8.6 Regression of vignette rating on characteristics of vignettes within vignette rating pattern groups, Los Angeles study, 1979 (unweighted sample)[a]

	Vignette rating pattern					
	Nonrater		Nonnormative rater		Force-only rater	
Vignette characteristics	B	Beta	B	Beta	B	Beta
Force (1 = high)	.01	.005	.29**	.07**	2.82**	.74**
Resistance (1 = high)	.01	.003	.33**	.08**	.04	.01
Acquaintanceship (1 = same block)	.01	.005	−.12	−.03	.03	.01
Location (1 = bar)	.01	.005	−.20	−.03	.004	.0001
Female's race (1 = black)	−.01	−.005	.02	.004	−.004	−.0001
Male's race (1 = black)	−.004	−.002	−.21*	−.05*	.00	.00
Marital Status (1 = divorced)	−.004	−.002	.17	.04	.00	.00
Occupation (1 = lawyer)	−.01	−.005	.02	.005	.01	.004
Constant	5.59**		3.64**		3.10**	
R^2	.00		.02**		.54**	
Adjusted R^2	.00		.01		.54	
Total vignettes	960		928		1088	
Total respondents	30		29		34	
Mean vignette rating	5.59		3.78		4.55	

** Significant at $p < .05$
 * Significant at $p < .10$

morally questionable information, only two of these nonnormative raters denied using such information. Persons interested in reducing rape and increasing official reporting and convictions when rapes do occur should be most concerned about this group, while accused rapists and their attorneys would probably be eager to have them on their juries.

Combining Ratings and Patterns

Using information from the vignettes only to predict differences in decisionmaking, quite different amounts of variance are explained within the different groups (table 8.6). For the sample as a whole only 18 percent of the variance is explained, largely due to the variety of rating patterns that are obscured when the sample is not stratified. When stratified by rating pattern the most variance in ratings is explained for those per-

(Vignette rating pattern)

Force-plus rater		Resistance-only rater		Resistance-plus rater		Total	
B	Beta	B	Beta	B	Beta	B	Beta
2.26**	.63**	.10	.04	.53**	.15**	1.36**	.38**
.42**	.12**	1.95**	.66**	1.80**	.51**	.67**	.18**
−.07	−.02	−.01	−.003	−.15*	.04*	−.06	−.02
−.09*	−.03*	.01	.003	.04	.01	−.05	−.01
−.03	−.01	.003	.001	−.03	−.01	−.02	−.004
−.03	−.01	.03	.01	−.03	−.01	−.04	−.01
−.05	−.01	.03	.01	.004	.001	.005	.001
−.01	−.003	.02	.01	−.05	−.01	−.01	−.002
3.19**		3.90**		3.30**		3.59**	
.42**		.44**		.28**		.18**	
.42		.43		.28		.18	
2976		640		1376		8032	
95		20		43		251	
4.38		4.97		4.36		4.35	

a Within strata defined by rating pattern, the vignette rating is regressed on the eight kinds of information provided within each vignette.

sons for whom there was substantial variability across vignettes and who used a single piece of information, either force or resistance, to decide. Unexplained variance, however, remains higher for resistance-only raters ($1 - .44 = .56$) than for force-only raters ($1 - .54 = .46$). Conversely, because no variability exists in decisions of nonraters, no variance is explained. For groups using multiple kinds of information in different combinations, success in explaining variability in ratings solely with vignette information ranges from quite good for force-plus raters (.42) to less good for resistance-plus raters (.28) to terrible for nonnormative raters (.02).

The variability in success reflects three differences between groups: the absolute range over which decisions vary, the number of kinds of information used in making decisions, and the complexity with which information is combined by respondents. For force-plus raters whose decisions are clearly dominated by one variable and vary over a relatively wide range, significantly more variance in decisions can be explained. For non-normative raters whose decisions are influenced by at least six kinds of information, little variance is explained.

Summary

As a group, Los Angeles residents think that the sexual encounters portrayed in vignettes are probably rapes. Information about the amount of force used, and to a lesser extent, physical resistance on the part of the woman combine to determine whether Los Angeles County residents think that a rape occurred. Respondents differ, however, in the extent to which they use these two pieces of information and the importance they place upon them. An unusual exception to the rule are those respondents who cue all their decisions exclusively to what the woman does: if she struggles, they decide it is rape; if she does not, it is not rape. Persons in this group apparently believe that women are responsible for controlling men's sexual passions. Victims, such as those described by Kanin, who are immobilized by fear would be in a bad way if these resistance-only raters predominated on their juries. The fear and unwillingness of such victims is not likely to be recognized or validated by this group. In contrast, the subgroup that cues decisions exclusively to force displayed by the man apparently consider men responsible for rape. These persons probably are more likely to consider rape a violent rather than a sexual act. The remaining respondents, while heavily influenced by information on force and resistance, also used less appropriate information in making decisions. This is the situation in which most respondents found themselves. Decisions were determined primarily by legally and morally correct information about force and resistance, but were also influenced by information about location, acquaintanceship, ethnicity, prior sexual history, and socioeconomic status.

⑨ Ethnic, Gender, and Social-Class Differences in Perceptions of Rape

I t is widely believed that attitudes toward rape and beliefs about its occurrence vary systematically as social and psychological character-istics vary. Findings from some of the community studies presented in chapter 6 suggest that attitudes and perceptions vary with gender, ethnicity, age, and socioeconomic status. Sociological literature demonstrates that most if not all attitudes and behaviors vary substantially with one's loca-tion in the social structure. Practitioners' best and most determined efforts to overcome, reverse, or neutralize the impact of social class and family of origin on one's ideals, norms, and behaviors have often been frustrated.

In this chapter we investigate the extent to which the Los Angeles County residents' decisions about rape vary with their social, demo-graphic, life-style, and environmental characteristics. No personality data were collected, but respondents' perceptions of crime in their neighbor-hood, their feelings of vulnerability to crime, and their adoption of pre-ventive behaviors within the past five years, as well as traditional demo-graphic data, were collected as part of the interview. In addition, data on official crime rates for each respondent's area of residence were collected from relevant criminal justice agencies.

Gender, Ethnicity, and Age

One does not have to be a sociobiologist to know that race, age, and gender are ascribed at birth and, henceforth, prescribe certain degrees of freedom in an individual's life. Whereas the roles, behaviors, and opportunities considered appropriate for men and women or blacks and whites differ over time and with social class and opportunity, norms defining appropriate sexual and racial behaviors tend to transcend time and determine the range of alternatives available at any given point in any given range of opportunity. We expect that information used by Los Angeles County residents to decide whether a sexual encounter is a rape and the relevance ascribed to different types of information might well differ among respondents of different gender, race, and/or age.

Age, Gender, Ethnicity, and Rating Pattern

Older respondents, particularly older black respondents, were less likely to think any of the vignettes portrayed rape ($r = -.16$, $p < :01$). Age was not, however, related to the pattern of information used to decide whether a rape had occurred for either black or white respondents.

Black respondents were consistently less sure that the sexual encounters portrayed were rapes (4.35 vs. 4.70), and men (4.45) tended to be less certain than women (4.56). White women had the highest average rating ($\bar{x} = 4.77$) while black males had the lowest ($\bar{x} = 4.29$). However, with the exception of two rating groups, respondents were surprisingly evenly distributed by race and sex across the six decision patterns (table 9.1). Whites were twice as likely as blacks to be nonraters and, therefore, to think all the sexual encounters were rapes. The overrepresentation of white respondents among nonraters contributed to whites' higher overall scores on the vignettes. Conversely, black males were overrepresented among the resistance-only raters. Eight (40 percent) of the 20 people who premised all their decisions on whether or not the woman struggled with the man were black males. Recall that resistance-only raters, as a group, were second only to nonraters in thinking that most of the sexual encounters were probably rapes ($\bar{x} = 4.97$). In contrast to nonraters, however, the woman's behavior was key to the decisions of resistance-only raters.

Table 9.1 Distribution of respondents and mean vignette ratings by vignette rating pattern, race, and sex of respondent, Los Angeles study, 1979 (unweighted sample)[a]

Vignette rating pattern	Race and sex of respondent [means and percentages (in parenthesis)]						
	All blacks	Black males	Black females	All whites	White males	White females	Total
Nonraters[b]	4.9 (7.2)	3.5 (5.0)	5.3 (8.2)	5.9 (16.7)	5.8 (18.0)	6.0 (15.8)	5.6 (12.0)
Nonnormative raters	4.1 (15.2)	4.6 (15.0)	3.8 (15.3)	3.3 (7.9)	3.1 (10.0)	3.5 (6.6)	3.8 (11.6)
Force-only raters	4.5 (11.2)	4.2 (15.0)	4.7 (9.4)	4.6 (15.9)	4.7 (10.0)	4.5 (19.7)	4.6 (13.5)
Force-plus raters	4.3 (37.6)	4.2 (27.5)	4.3 (42.4)	4.5 (38.1)	4.7 (38.0)	4.3 (38.3)	4.4 (37.8)
Resistance-only raters[c]	4.8 (10.4)	4.4 (20.0)	5.6 (5.9)	5.2 (5.6)	5.4 (4.0)	4.7 (6.6)	5.0 (8.0)
Resistance-plus raters	4.2 (18.4)	4.3 (17.5)	4.2 (18.8)	4.5 (15.9)	4.5 (20.0)	4.5 (13.2)	4.4 (17.1)
Total mean[b]	4.4	4.4	4.3	4.7	4.6	4.8	4.5
Total N	125	40	85	126	50	76	251

a Respondents are similarly distributed by race, sex, and rating pattern when the sample is weighted. When three-way analysis of variance of race, sex, and rating pattern on vignette rating is computed in the unweighted sample, main effects for race and vignette rating pattern, the two-way interactions between race and rating pattern, and sex and rating pattern are significant at $p < .05$; the three-way interaction of race, sex, and rating pattern has a p value of .08; and the R^2 is .28. When three-way analysis of variance is computed in the weighted sample, the same two two-way interactions are significant but significant main effects are found for sex and vignette rating pattern.

b Within the category of nonraters, respondents are differentially distributed by race, $p < .01$; when the weighted rather than unweighted sample is used, $p = .065$ for race and $p = .073$ for sex. When the vignette sample is used, $p < .01$ for both main effects of race and sex. Similar patterns are found for the vignette rating by race and sex of respondent.

c Within the group of resistance-only raters, the interaction of race and sex on the distribution of respondents is significant at $p = .02$.

While significant differences by race and sex do not exist across the other four decision groups, blacks are somewhat more likely than whites to be nonnormative raters (to use information other than force and resistance in deciding about rape), and least often thought sexual encounters were rapes. White females were least likely to use nonnormative decisionmaking.

Within the three remaining groups—those using force by itself, force

Table 9.2 Regression of vignette ratings on characteristics portrayed in vignette within subgroups stratified by race and sex, Los Angeles study, 1979 (unweighted sample)[a]

	Black respondents					
	Total		Males only		Females only	
Vignette characteristics	B	Beta	B	Beta	B	Beta
Force (1 = high)	1.36*	0.36	1.23*	0.31	1.43*	0.38
Resistance (1 = high)	0.93*	0.25	1.36*	0.35	0.73*	0.20
Male's occupation (1 = lawyer)	0.03	0.007	0.003	0.0008	0.04	0.01
Male's ethnicity (1 = black)	−0.09	−0.02	−0.09	−0.02	−0.09	−0.02
Female's ethnicity (1 = black)	0.03	0.001	0.05	0.01	0.02	0.004
Location (1 = coming out of bar)	−0.03	−0.008	0.04	0.01	−0.07	−0.02
Female's marital status (1 = divorced)	0.01	0.003	−0.03	−0.01	0.03	0.01
Acquaintanceship (1 = same block)	−0.06	−0.02	−0.12	−0.03	−0.03	−0.01
R^2	0.19*		0.22*		0.19*	
Constant	3.21*		2.99*		3.31*	
Number of vignettes	4000		1280		2720	
Number of respondents	125		40		85	
Mean rating	4.35		4.29		4.38	

* Coefficients are significant at $p < .01$.

a The vignette is the unit of analysis in these equations. Vignettes first are stratified by the respondent's race and sex, and then the vignette rating is regressed on the eight characteristics portrayed in

in combination with other information, and resistance in combination with other information—insignificant trends can also be seen. White females are somewhat more likely than the other three race-sex groups to cue their decisions exclusively to the amount of force exhibited by the man. For them, use of physical force almost guarantees that the situation will be judged a rape, while use of verbal force makes judgment difficult. Black males are less likely than others to use force in combination with other information to make decisions about rape.

| White respondents | | | | | | | |
| Total | | Males only | | Females only | | Total | |
B	Beta	B	Beta	B	Beta	B	Beta
1.37*	0.40	1.41*	0.39	1.34*	0.41	1.36*	0.38
0.40*	0.12	0.54*	0.15	0.32*	0.10	0.67*	0.18
−0.04	−0.01	−0.07	−0.02	−0.02	−0.01	−0.01	−0.002
0.01	0.004	0.03	0.009	0.001	0.0003	−0.04	−0.01
−0.06	−0.02	−0.08	−0.02	−0.04	−0.01	−0.02	−0.004
−0.06	−0.02	−0.07	−0.02	−0.06	−0.02	−0.05	−0.01
−0.0005	−0.0002	0.04	0.01	−0.03	−0.01	0.005	0.001
−0.06	−0.02	−0.15*	−0.04	−0.006	−0.002	−0.06	−0.02
0.17*		0.18*		0.17*		0.18*	
3.88*		3.77*		3.95*		3.59*	
4032		1600		2432		8032	
126		50		76		251	
4.70		4.60		4.77		4.5	

the vignette; the eight vignette characteristics or independent variables are simultaneously entered into the regression equation.

Gender, Ethnicity, Rating Patterns, and Decisions Made

Both analysis of variance and regression were used to ascertain whether race, sex, and the pattern of information affected decisions made (tables 9.1 and 9.2). While ratings are quite comparable by race and sex within 3 pattern groups (force-only, force-plus, resistance-plus), they differ quite substantially by race and sex within the resistance-plus, nonrater, and nonnormative groups (figure 9.1). Among nonraters—those who gave all vignettes identical ratings—the two black males did not think the sexual encounters were rapes while other nonraters thought they were. In contrast, black males in the nonnormative group were more likely than others in the group to think a rape had occurred. Among resistance-only raters eight black males and two white females gave moderate ratings, while black females and white males gave atypically high ratings.

Within the total sample, 18 percent of the variance is explained when vignette ratings are regressed on characteristics portrayed in the vignettes. When groups are stratified by race and sex little additional variance is explained within the race-sex strata (table 9.2). Although both the decision itself and the kind of information selected differ with a respondent's race and sex, the importance of force and resistance for the vast majority of respondents (76.4 percent) and the failure to account for differences that do not vary with race and sex obscure contributions made by other variables. Racial and sexual differences in the relative importance of force

Figure 9.1 Vignette rating by rating pattern used and respondent's race and sex, Los Angeles study, 1979

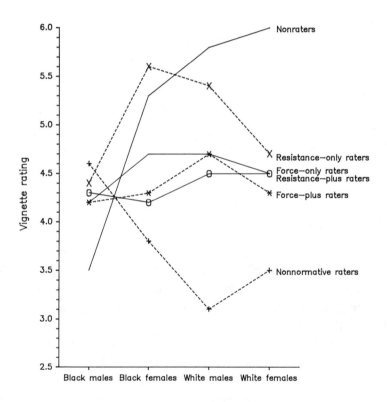

Race and sex of respondent

and resistance within the various subgroups can, however, be observed. The importance of resistance for black males is particularly noteworthy. Unlike other race-sex groups, resistance is more important than force for black men and significantly more important for black men than for black women, white men, or white women.

For black females, white males, and white females, the man's use of physical force is the most important piece of information used in deciding whether a sexual encounter is rape. The importance of force to their decisions is about equal for the three groups, while resistance is second in importance for all three groups with black females putting such information to greatest use in deciding. White women use information about resistance least. Black women's greater use of information about resistance may reflect black men's heavy dependence on the woman's behavior as a major cue in differentiating rapes from other sexual encounters. One can interpret this either as evidence of a skeptical sexism about rape on the part of black men with which women must acquiesce in self-defense, or as evidence that women control sexual encounters between black males and females with males acquiescing to that control. The first interpretation seems more viable because the latter interpretation is inconsistent with both findings from other studies where black males most often agreed with rape-supportive attitudes (e.g., Williams and Holmes, 1981) and official statistics on rape where black males are found to be substantially overrepresented as perpetrators of reported rapes.

Although table 9.1 suggests that blacks in Los Angeles were more likely than whites to ignore information about force and resistance and base decisions on other, more questionable sources of information, a significant contribution of such information is seen only for white males. Evidence that the woman never saw the man before, while of some importance for all respondents, reached significance only for white males. Consistent with findings of Goodchilds et al., sexual encounters with strangers were more likely than those with acquaintances to be judged by white males to be rapes.

Other noteworthy trends failing to reach significance were those regarding ethnicity, occupation, and marital status. Black respondents tended to see white lawyers as rapists and black females as victims, while white respondents tended to see black janitors as rapists and white females as victims. Interestingly, black females and white males are slightly more likely to think divorced women are rape victims, while white females and black males tend to see married females as victims.

Nonnormative, Force-Multiple, and Resistance-Multiple Raters

Since we know that three groups of respondents thought all the sexual encounters were rapes (nonraters) or used only information about force (force-only raters) or resistance (resistance-only raters) in deciding whether a rape occurred, regressions were recomputed using only the other three groups of respondents—those who had used multiple pieces of information to make decisions (see appendix 3).[1] Results generally confirmed or elaborated on trends observed in table 9.2 with little additional variance in decisions within these three groups being explained. Elimination of the nonraters who thought all encounters were rapes, and the two groups who exclusively used force or resistance, reduced the constant or intercept to the midpoint or below on the six-point range for all race-sex subgroups. By eliminating the resistance-only raters—a group disproportionately comprised of black males—resistance still remained the most important piece of information used by black males in deciding whether or not a rape occurred.

Whether the man and woman are strangers or acquaintances appeared at first to be relevant for everyone in these three decisionmaking groups, but we later found that it was relevant to males only—white males in particular. As before, black respondents in these three groups paid attention to the race of the man, and consistent with historical reality experienced by blacks in the United States, blacks thought that the presence of a white male increased the probability that rape was committed. Interestingly enough, the tendency seen earlier for white respondents to think black males more likely to be rapists is not strengthened by eliminating from the analysis the three low-variance groups. However, the tendency for males of both races to think rape more likely when the woman is of the same race does become stronger: Black males are somewhat more likely to think black women are victims, while white males are somewhat more likely to think white women are victims.

Although respondents' marital status influenced the judgment of nonnormative raters, its effect is not evident in these regressions. Occupation, as before, appeared irrelevant in decisionmaking.

Socioeconomic Status, Life-Style and Criminal Vulnerability, and Perceptions of Rape

Gender and ethnicity generally correlate with or predict other characteristics of individuals such as their level of completed education, income, socioeconomic status, area of residence, and vulnerability to crime. At the same time, education is often considered and often works as a passport to higher social status and more liberal social attitudes. To the extent that blacks and males seem to have slightly more restrictive definitions of rape and acknowledge fewer sexual encounters to be rape, such proclivities may be neutralized or reversed by education and income, or may change over generations. Similarly, greater exposure to crime or feelings of vulnerability to crime may affect the kinds of information used in deciding about rapes and the propensity to consider a particular sexual encounter a rape. To investigate the effect that socioeconomic status, age, lifestyle, and criminal environment have on decisions about rapes, bivariate associations using correlation, analysis of variance, and chi square were computed followed by regression and discriminant analyses.

Predicting Whether Sexual Encounters Are Judged Rapes

In our correlation analyses, decisions by whites that rape occurred are associated only with the kind of information they use to arrive at a decision. Among blacks decisions are associated only with age (see tables A3.1–A3.3 in appendix 3). Consistent with information presented in figure 9.1, white respondents who are nonraters are significantly more likely than other whites to think that sexual encounters are rapes ($r = .58$). Although a similar trend exists for blacks, the relatively small number of them who are nonraters and the atypical tendency of black male nonraters to think that many of the sexual encounters were not rapes both work to prevent the correlation from reaching significance. Similar relationships by race exist between being a nonnormative rater and decisions about the sexual encounters. White nonnormative raters are significantly less likely than other whites to think that any of the sexual encounters are rape. While a similar trend exists for black respondents, the tendency of black male nonnormative raters to give atypically high ratings neutralizes low ratings given by black female nonnormative raters, and keeps the correlation from reaching significance.

Although a participant's sex, age, education, income, and exposure to crime correlate with his or her propensity to decide that many sexual encounters are probably rapes, none of the direct associations reaches significance. Such information is of greater relevance in understanding black decisionmaking than it is for whites. The correlations suggest that younger, better-educated blacks with higher incomes who live in low-crime areas and who do not feel vulnerable to crime consider more sexual encounters to be rape. But of these factors, only age is a significant predictor of rape decisions, with younger blacks significantly more likely to label encounters as rape ($r = -.26$, $p < .01$). While younger white females are also more likely than other whites to think more encounters are rapes, the associations are not significant. Within the correlation matrix, there is little evidence that black females differ from black males in their propensity to consider sexual encounters as rape. Sex differences within racial groups occur only in the relative importance assigned to force and resistance in making decisions.

To ascertain how demographic, life-style, crime vulnerability, and information usage combine to predict decisions, the vignette rating or the decision as to whether the sexual encounter was a rape was regressed on all variables. Table 9.3 reports the set of variables that best predicted decisions about sexual encounters for the total unweighted sample and for race and race-sex strata using the vignette as the unit of analysis.[2]

In general, adding demographic and life-style information to regression equations explains only an additional 5 percent of the variance in decisions for either the total sample or within race-sex strata. For all Los Angeles respondents as a group, their sex, age, religion, number of children, area crime rates, perceived neighborhood safety, perceived vulnerability to crime, adoption of preventive behaviors, and use of information about force and resistance combine to determine whether a sexual encounter is rape. Twenty-one percent of the variance in decisions can be explained using this combination of information. Younger non-Protestant women without children are more likely to decide that sexual encounters are rape, while older Protestant males with children are less likely to think that a rape occurred. The decision that these vignette encounters are rape is predicted by living in low-crime areas, combined with perceiving one's neighborhood as safer than other neighborhoods, while simultaneously perceiving oneself as vulnerable to crime, and taking preventive behaviors. Conversely, persons living in high-crime areas who nevertheless do not feel vulnerable to crime judge few encounters to be rape. Consistent with earlier findings, information that force was used and resistance attempted increases the likelihood of judging that a rape occurred. Although respondents' race does not show up as a significant direct determinant of rape decisions in this equation, race indirectly influences decisions through its association with official crime rates with black respondents generally living in more dangerous areas.

Twenty-three percent of the variance in black respondents' decisions is predicted. While sex and adoption of preventive behaviors does not influence ratings, education, income, Duncan scores, the number of adults in the household, and the number of years lived in the same house influence decisions. Black males who decide that a rape occurred are characterized as being younger non-Protestants who are less educated but have higher incomes. They are more likely to live with children under 18 in high-crime areas which they nonetheless perceive to be safer than other neighborhoods while still feeling vulnerable to crime. In spite of the addition of demographic and life-style information, the heavy dependence by black males on information about the woman's resistance continues to be prominent in this equation. Black females' decisions also correlate with being younger, but are not correlated with education or income. Like black males, black females who decided that rapes were portrayed are unlikely to be Protestant, and perceive their neighborhood to be safer than those of others. Unlike black males, they do not have children under 18 and do live in crime-free neighborhoods where they have adopted crime-protective behaviors.

Consistent with what was observed in the correlation matrix, fewer demographic and life-style characteristics influence the decisions of whites in Los Angeles. In contrast to blacks, decisions about rape do differ by sex with white females judging more sexual encounters to be rape. Like black respondents, higher ratings are correlated with being younger but, unlike black respondents, higher ratings are correlated with completing

Table 9.3 Regression of vignette ratings on best set of predictor variables by race and sex using the vignette as the unit of analysis, Los Angeles study, 1979 (unweighted sample)[a]

Independent variables	Black respondents					
	Total		Males only		Females only	
	B	Beta	B	Beta	B	Beta
Demographic characteristics						
Race (1 = black)	—	—	—	—	—	—
Sex (1 = male)	−.19	−.05	—	—	—	—
Age	−.02	−.19	−.02	−.16	−.02	−.15
Years of schooling completed	−.02	−.04	−.06	−.09		
Yearly income in $100s	.0008	.04	.00	.10		
Duncan score	−.004	−.05			−.01	−.06
Protestant	−.28	−.07	−.24	−.06	−.30	−.08
Catholic						
Life-style characteristics						
Married						
Number of adults in household	−.09	−.05				
Children under 18 in household	−.04	−.03	.13	.09	−.11	−.09
Number of years in house	.02	.05				
Criminal vulnerability						
Official crime rate in area (unstandardized)	−.12	−.04	.31	.11	−.36	−.12
Neighborhood safety (1 = safer; 5 = less safe)	−.13	−.07	−.34	−.17	−.07	−.04
Feelings of vulnerability (1 = none; 9 = very)	.07	.06	.23	.23		
Crime-preventive behaviors						.27	.06
Vignette characteristics						
Force (1 = high)	1.36	.36	1.23	.31	1.43	.38
Resistance (1 = high)	.93	.25	1.36	.35	.73	.28
Acquaintanceship (1 = same block)						
Location (1 = bar)						
Female's race (1 = black)						

| White respondents | | | | | | Total | |
| Total | | Males only | | Females only | | | |
B	Beta	B	Beta	B	Beta	B	Beta
—	—	—	—	—	—		
−.34	−.10	—	—	—	—	−.19	−.05
−.01	−.12	−.02	−.18	−.01	−.09	−.01	−.12
.02	.03	.05	.08				
				.004	.05		
		−.62	−.11	.27	.04	−.24	−.06
				.14	.06		
−.11	−.05	−.27	−.10			−.06	−.04
		.03	.12	−.03	−.12		
−.11	−.04			−.17	−.07	−.14	−.08
−.08	−.04	−.16	−.08	−.09	−.05	−.11	−.06
						.03	.03
.30	.08	.27	.07	.45	.13	.21	.05
1.37	.40	1.41	.39	1.34	.41	1.36	.38
.40	.12	.54	.15	.32	.10	.67	.18

Table 9.3 (continued)

Independent variables	Black respondents					
	Total		Males only		Females only	
	B	Beta	B	Beta	B	Beta
Male's race (1 = black)						
Female's marital status (1 = divorced)						
Male's occupation (1 = lawyer)						
Equation statistics						
Constant	4.78		3.89		4.72	
R^2	.23		.28		.24	
Adjusted R^2	.23		.27		.24	

a All coefficients and equation statistics are significant at $p < .05$. Vignettes are the unit of analysis.
  Variables were entered in four stages with demographic characteristics of the respondents entered

more years of schooling. As with black females, the absence of children under 18, residence in safe neighborhoods, and the adoption of crime-preventive behaviors all correlate with higher ratings. Income, socioeconomic status, number of adults in the household, and years of residence in the house do not influence decisions of whites as a group.

The influence of education, socioeconomic status, religious affiliation, years in home, and crime rate on rape decisions differs for white males and females whereas age, perceived neighborhood safety, and adoption of preventive behaviors does not. Although women's decisions do not differ with greater education, but do differ with higher socioeconomic status, those of men are reversed. Religion influences decisions differently for males and females, with Protestant affiliation increasing the propensity of white females to decide that a rape occurred and decreasing it for white males. Similarly, the more adults in the household, the higher the ratings of females, while those for white males are not influenced by living with other adults but are influenced by the presence of children.

White respondents							
Total		Males only		Females only		Total	
B	Beta	B	Beta	B	Beta	B	Beta
4.14		3.86		3.88		4.19	
.20		.22		.21		.21	
.19		.22		.21		.21	

first and vignette characteristics entered last. Variables included in the these analyses were selected on the basis of prior analyses within the race-sex group of interest.

Predicting the Information Used

To see whether information used to make decisions varies with social status and life-style, bivariate associations between demographic characteristics, life-style, criminal vulnerability, and the decisionmaking patterns were examined (table 9.4).

Race, education, and the official crime rate for the respondent's precinct differ across the vignette pattern groups in unweighted analyses, with income and religion becoming relevant in weighted analyses. As we already know, nonraters are disproportionately likely to be white, but here we see that they are substantially more likely to have a college education and to be professionals or managers. They are neither younger nor older than other respondents, but their incomes are lower than might be expected given their age, education, and professional status. They live in moderately safe neighborhoods, perceive their neighborhoods to be safe, and do not feel unusually vulnerable to crime.

Nonnormative raters are in many respects the exact opposite. They are disproportionately black and are among those with the lowest levels of education, income, and occupational status. They live in high-crime areas,

Table 9.4 Relationship between vignette rating patterns and demographics, life-style, and criminal vulnerability, Los Angeles study, 1979 (unweighted sample)[a]

Demographics, life-style, and criminal vulnerability	Vignette rating pattern	
	Nonraters	Nonnormative raters
Demographic characteristics		
Percentage female	53.3	62.1
Percentage black*	30.0	65.5
Mean age	43.4	42.8
Mean years of education*	13.0	12.2
Percentage college or more	33.3	6.9
Percentage no degree*	16.7	13.8
Percentage income > $10,000	56.7	41.4
Mean Duncan score	49.3	35.8
Percentage professional or manager	46.7	13.7
Percentage Protestant	63.3	79.3
Percentage Catholic	20.0	17.2
Life-style characteristics		
Mean number of years in house	4.7	8.0
Percentage married	20.0	27.6
Mean number of adults in household	1.7	1.8
Mean number of children in household	0.3	0.8
Vulnerability to crime[b]		
Official crime in area*	−0.59	0.59
Perceived safety of neighborhood (1 = safe; 5 = unsafe)	2.07	2.59
Perceived vulnerability to crime (1 = not; 9 = very)	4.1	4.6
Preventive behaviors (range: 0−2)	0.63	0.81
Total *N*	30	29

* One-way analysis of variance significant at p<.001.

a When bivariate analyses are computed using the weighted sample, differences by race are not significant but the proportion of persons who are Protestant, those with incomes over $10,000, and those with college degrees differ significantly with vignette rating pattern. Mean years of schooling

perceive their neighborhoods to be unsafe, and see themselves as vulnerable to crime.

Resistance-only raters are also disproportionately younger blacks with low educational levels, but because they are also disproportionately male they have somewhat higher incomes. They also live in moderately unsafe neighborhoods, but are less likely to perceive themselves to be vulnerable to crime.

| (Vignette rating pattern) | | | | |
Force-only raters	Force-plus raters	Resistance-only raters	Resistance-plus raters	Total
67.6	68.4	50.0	60.5	64.1
41.2	49.5	65.0	53.5	49.8
39.1	42.2	37.9	46.6	42.4
14.2	13.1	12.9	11.8	12.9
29.4	24.2	5.0	9.3	19.5
11.8	23.2	30.0	30.2	19.9
85.3	54.7	45.0	51.2	56.2
52.3	41.0	40.0	36.5	42.1
43.2	20.1	25.0	16.3	25.9
52.9	64.2	60.0	81.4	66.9
26.5	14.7	30.0	11.6	17.9
5.9	5.0	5.0	7.6	5.9
20.6	29.5	20.0	27.9	25.9
1.7	1.6	1.6	1.8	1.7
1.0	0.8	0.7	0.7	0.7
−0.23	0.02	0.16	0.23	0.00
2.38	2.63	2.25	2.49	2.47
4.2	4.6	4.1	4.6	4.4
0.76	0.78	0.65	0.71	0.74
34	95	20	43	251

completed, the proportion with no degrees, and official crime rates differ significantly with vignette rating pattern in both weighted and unweighted analyses.

b Eight respondents refused to complete the questionnaire items. Hence, total N is 243 for non-demographic and nonvignette items.

As a group, force-only raters have the highest social status. They are generally younger with good educations and high incomes. Their neighborhoods are safe, and they do not perceive themselves to be vulnerable to crime.

Respondents in the last two groups—those that use force and/or resistance in combination with other information—are not easily distinguished from the sample as a whole. The only thing that distinguishes between the

Table 9.5 Discriminant analysis of vignette decision groups, Los Angeles study, 1979 (unweighted sample)[a]

A. Means and standard deviations of the discriminating variables by vignette decision groups

Vignette rating pattern	Total cases	Years of education	Vignette rating
Nonrater	30	12.9	5.59
Nonnormative rater	29	12.1	3.78
Force-only rater	34	14.2	4.55
Force-plus rater	94	13.2	4.38
Resistance-only rater	20	12.9	4.97
Resistance-plus rater	42	11.8	4.34
Total	249[a]	12.9	4.52

B. Classification of cases (in percentage)

Actual group	Predicted group					
	Non-rater	Non-normative	Force-only	Force-plus	Resistance-only	Resistance-plus
Nonrater	90.0	6.7	0.0	0.0	0.0	3.3
Nonnormative rater	0.0	10.3	0.0	89.7	0.0	0.0
Force-only rater	8.8	0.0	0.0	91.2	0.0	0.0
Force-plus rater	3.2	0.0	0.0	92.6	0.0	4.3
Resistance-only rater	20.0	0.0	0.0	80.0	0.0	0.0
Resistance-plus rater	4.8	0.0	0.0	90.5	0.0	4.8

Total cases correctly classified: 47.8%

C. Standardized canonical discriminant function coefficients of discriminating variables

	Function 1	Function 2
Education	.028	1.004
Vignette rating	.997	−0.117

D. Pooled within group correlations of discriminating variables and canonical discriminant functions

	Function 1	Function 2
Education	.12	0.99
Vignette rating	1.00	−0.03

E. Relative location of six vignette decision groups as determined by discriminant analysis

Vignette rating pattern	Function 1	Function 2
Nonraters	1.30	−0.14
Nonnormative raters	−0.90	−0.16
Force-only raters	0.05	0.44
Force-plus raters	−0.17	0.11
Resistance-only raters	0.55	−0.08
Resistance-plus raters	−0.22	−0.34

a Analysis used listwise deletion of cases with missing data. Two cases, therefore, are not included in this analysis.

two groups is the tendency for those who use resistance as the most important cue to have significantly less education and to live in areas with higher crime rates.

Discriminant analysis was used to determine whether trends noted above can successfully differentiate between the six decision groups. A series of stepwise discriminant analyses was computed using both weighted and unweighted respondent samples and the vignette sample. In general the six decision groups cannot be effectively differentiated. Because it is easier to interpret, discriminant analysis using the unweighted respondent sample is reported in table 9.5.

The first and by far the most powerful discriminating function is defined by a single variable—decisions that the sexual encounters were rapes (table 9.5). That piece of information alone significantly differentiates nonraters and nonnormative raters from the remaining four groups. Confirming what we already know, nonraters are significantly more likely to say that all or most of the sexual encounters are rapes, while nonnormative raters are significantly more likely to say that few of the sexual encounters are definitely rapes. This variable alone effectively differentiates those who use resistance by itself from both those who use force by itself and those who use either force or resistance in combination with other variables.

The second and less powerful discriminant factor is the number of years of schooling completed. Consistent with what was shown in table 9.4, persons using force as their only or major cue are most readily differentiated from the other four decision groups using this factor. As can be seen, however, in section B of table 9.5, those who use force alone in deciding

Table 9.6 Regression of vignette ratings on best set of predictor variables by vignette rating group using the vignette as the unit of analysis, Los Angeles study, 1979 (unweighted sample)[a]

Independent variables	Vignette rating pattern					
	Nonrater		Nonnormative rater		Force-only rater	
	B	Beta	B	Beta	B	Beta
Demographic characteristics						
Race (1 = black)	−.69	−.25	.89	.21		
Sex (1 = male)	.23	.09	.24*	.06*	−.44	−.11
Age	−.02	−.35	−.01	−.09	−.02	−.16
Years of schooling completed	−.17	−.40	.09	.15	.07	.09
Yearly income in $100s	−.003	−.33				
Duncan score	−.01	−.24			−.005	−.05
Protestant	−1.58	−.53				
Catholic			−.47	−.08		
Life-style characteristics						
Married					.26	.07
Number of adults in household	.18	.13	.27	.16	.23	.08
Children under 18 in household			−.36	−.20	−.08	−.05
Number of years in house					−.02	−.06
Criminal vulnerability						
Official crime rate in area	.43	.27				
Neighborhood safety (1 = safer; 5 = less safe)	−.12	−.08				
Feelings of vulnerability (1 = none; 9 = very)	−.21	−.27	.17	.18		
Crime-preventive behaviors (range: 0–2)	.45	.16	.40	.09	.30	.07
Vignette characteristics						
Force (1 = high)			.29	.07	2.82	.74
Resistance (1 = high)			.33	.08		
Acquaintanceship (1 = same block)						
Location (1 = bar)						
Female's race (1 = black)						
Male's race (1 = black)						
Female's marital status (1 = divorced)						
Male's occupation (1 = lawyer)						

| (Vignette rating pattern) | | | | | |
| Force-plus rater | | Resistance-only rater | | Resistance-plus rater | |
B	Beta	B	Beta	B	Beta
		.53	.17		
−.27	−.07	−1.20	−.41		
		−.01	−.09	−.01	−.15
.02	.03				
		.002	.14		
−.004	−.05	−.01	−.17	.00*	.05*
−.20	−.05	−.60	−.18	−.54	−.15
−.24	−.03				
.30	.08	−.37	−.13		
.07*	.03*	−.95	−.38		
.08	.06	.28	.19	−.12	−.10
−.10	−.06	−.16	−.09	.19	.11
−.09	−.05	−.47	−.21	−.23	−.12
		−.20	−.17		
.20	.05				
2.26	.63			.53	.15
.42	.12	1.95	.66	1.80	.51

Table 9.6 (continued)

Independent variables	Vignette rating pattern					
	Nonrater		Nonnormative rater		Force-only rater	
	B	Beta	B	Beta	B	Beta
Equation statistics						
Constant	11.14		0.75*		3.02	
R²		.55		.15		.62
Adjusted R²		.55		.14		.61

* Coefficients marked are significant at p<.10; all other coefficients and equation statistics are significant at p < .05.

a Vignettes are the unit of analysis for these regressions. After stratification by vignette rating pattern,

about rapes cannot be clearly distinguished with this information from those using force in combination with other information. In fact, data show that only nonraters can be clearly distinguished from the other five groups. The remaining five decision groups cannot be distinguished from each other using available demographic and life-style information. Overall, only 48 percent of the cases can be correctly classified using the information at hand.

Although the six decisionmaking groups are not readily differentiated with available demographic, life-style, and criminal vulnerability information, it is possible that within a given group such information may differentiate those who think many of the sexual encounters are rapes from those who do not. Using the vignette as the unit of analysis, table 9.6 reports the set of variables that best predicts decisions about sexual encounters within groups defined by the decisionmaking information used. (Equations containing all variables examined are available in appendix 3.)

For nonraters who gave all or most of their vignettes identical ratings, the results of the regression are largely meaningless and simply differentiate the few persons who gave universally low ratings from the rest of the group. Since by definition this group did not vary decisions with information available in the vignette, only the nonvignette characteristics can differentiate those with high ratings from those with low ratings. Such nonvignette factors explain 55 percent of the variance in ratings, with low

(Vignette rating pattern)					
Force-plus rater		Resistance-only rater		Resistance-plus rater	
B	Beta	B	Beta	B	Beta
2.91		8.15		4.47	
.45		.66		.33	
.45		.66		.33	

variables are entered in four stages starting with demographic characteristics and ending with vignette characteristics. Only variables found to be significant predictors in earlier analyses within each group are included in these analyses.

ratings associated with being older, black, female, Protestant, having more education and higher income, living in low-crime areas perceived to be less safe, and feeling vulnerable to crime without taking protective behaviors.[3]

Although the total variance in ratings explained among nonnormative raters remains a low 15 percent, significant additional information is obtained about this group of respondents. As was noted earlier, decisions by black males in this group were atypical in that they saw more of the vignettes portrayed to be rapes. Also associated with higher ratings is being younger, having more education, not being Catholic, living with other adults but not children under 18, feeling vulnerable to crime, and having adopted preventive behaviors. In spite of the fact that nonraters minimized the importance of force and resistance in their decisions, both variables do differentiate higher raters and higher ratings from lower raters within the group while other information in the vignettes does not.

Among force-only raters, information that physical force was used by the man remains by far the most important characteristic differentiating high from low ratings. Sex and age (with younger females being more certain rapes occurred) most clearly differentiate respondents who thought that many of the vignettes portrayed rape from those who thought few did. Also relevant was being married and living with other adults but with no children, completing more years of schooling, having lower socioeconomic status, living in the same house for fewer years, and adopting crime-preventive behaviors.

Many of the same kinds of information differentiate high raters in the force-multiple group from low raters with little overall additional variance in ratings being explained. High raters are more highly educated females who are married but with children and who engage in crime-preventive behaviors. Age and length of residence do not differentiate high raters from low raters, but religion and safety of the neighborhood do. As would be expected, sexual encounters judged to be rapes are those that portray physical force by the man and physical resistance by the woman.

Addition of demographic and life-style information is most helpful in differentiating high raters from low raters within the group of resistance-only raters, explaining an additional 23 percent of the variance and a total of 66 percent of the variance in ratings. Judging more of the vignettes to be rapes is associated with being black, female, and younger, having higher incomes but lower socioeconomic status, being unmarried with children, being a non-Protestant living in a safer neighborhood, and not feeling vulnerable to crime.

In contrast, little additional variance is explained for resistance-plus raters. Those who think that more of the vignettes portray rape live in high-crime areas without children. They are younger non-Protestants of somewhat higher socioeconomic status. As expected, the amount of resistance engaged in by the woman combined with the amount of force used by the man differentiates the sexual encounters they judge to be rape from those judged not to be rape.

Summary

Information used to decide whether rape occurred and the number of portrayed sexual encounters judged to be rape differ to some extent with demographic, life-style, and criminal vulnerability characteristics of Los Angeles residents. White females use information about force as their primary cue and are most likely to judge sexual encounters to be rape. Black males, in contrast, make the greatest use of information on resistance, and are least likely to label sexual encounters as rape. Educational level marginally differentiates the kind of information used in decision-making; persons with more schooling tend to emphasize force alone or in combination with other factors; those with less school emphasize resistance and other information. Age and actual and perceived criminal vulnerability affect rape judgments; younger persons in safer neighborhoods who, nonetheless, think they are vulnerable to crime are most likely to think that most of the sexual encounters are rapes. As exposure to crime increases and as feelings of vulnerability decrease, the number of sexual encounters judged to be rape decreases. As exposure to crime decreases and feelings of vulnerability increase, the number of sexual encounters judged to be rape increases. This pattern is consistent for all race-sex groups except black males. Although black males generally did not think the portrayed sexual encounters were rape, black males who lived in high-crime areas and felt vulnerable to crime were more likely than other black males to decide that sexual encounters were rape.

Other variables such as income, living arrangements, and religion are more useful for understanding black respondents' decisions or for differentiating males from females than for describing the sample as a whole or explaining the decisions of whites. While income differentiates rape-responsive males (who are likely to judge a given situation to be a rape) from rape-unresponsive males, it has no influence on female perceptions. Low-income black males and high-income white males are more likely to think rape occurred. While the presence of children decreases black women's and white men's responsiveness to the vignettes and has no influence on white women's perceptions, it increases responsiveness of black men to the sexual encounters. Conversely, being Protestant, which decreases the responsiveness of most respondents, increases the likelihood that white women will decide rape occurred. Although decisions do differ with demographic and life-style characteristics—particularly race, sex, age, education, and actual and perceived vulnerability to crime—much of the variance remains unexplained. While young, highly educated, white females who live in crime-free neighborhoods and feel vulnerable to crime are most likely to use only force to decide about rape and to consider most sexual encounters to be rape, the associations are imperfect. While black residents of high-crime neighborhoods are more likely to cue their decisions to the woman's behavior and be unsure that encounters are rapes, some white females are also unsure about appropriate information and conclusions. Decisions vary systematically but imperfectly with one's place in society. Knowing a respondent's ethnicity, gender, education, and criminal vulnerability increases our ability to know how they define rape, but does not tell us their exact definition.

Combining demographic and life-style information with information used in making decisions increases our ability to predict the proportion and types of sexual encounters that are judged to be rape. This ability differs, however, across decisionmaking groups, with behavior and characteristics of force-only and resistance-only raters most easily described while nonnormative and resistance-plus raters are least easily described.

10 **Actors, Causes, and Solutions**

While the Los Angeles County study revealed that respondents use different kinds of information to decide whether sexual encounters are rapes, it also provided information, not directly related to definitions of rape, that clarified how rape is thought to affect the social fabric. This broader view came from using traditional questions to probe areas such as respondents' beliefs about what causes rape, whether rape is increasing, opinions about solutions, and perceptions of its victims and perpetrators.

First Word

The first question asked of each Los Angeles participant was, "When you hear the term 'rape,' what is the *first* word that comes to your mind?" Most answers were easily coded into one of the categories described in table 10.1. The largest number of respondents (36.2 percent) answered with a word that described the act of rape. Generally the word described rape in terms of violence, harm, or hurt, e.g., respondents used words such as "hate," "weapon," "assault," "attack," "violence," "violate," "brutal," "vicious," "abuse," "hurt," "pain," "crime," "bad," "disgusting," "sue," "rotten," "terrible," "sorrow," "beating," "molestation," "angry," and "kill." An additional 16.5 percent of respondents answered with some variant of the word "force."[1]

Table 10.1 Distribution of responses to nonvignette questions on rape by race and sex, Los Angeles study, 1979 (unweighted sample)[a]

Question and answer category

A. *When you hear the term rape, what is the first word that comes to your mind?*

Reference to sex
Reference to sickness/illness
Force specifically mentioned
Negative reference to the man
Description of/identification with the woman
Negative/violent description of the act
Other/don't know
No answer

B. *Characteristics of the males and females involved in rapes*

Do you think a woman who gets raped is different *before* she is raped?
Yes
No
Don't know
No answer

How is she different?
Takes unnecessary chances
Provocative
Other response
Woman is not different
No answer/don't know

Do you think a woman who gets raped is different *after* she gets raped?
Yes
No
Don't know
No answer

How is she different?
Negative about self
Negative about society
Afraid
Physically hurt/afraid
Other
Woman is not different
No answer/don't know

Do you think a man who commits rape is different from other men *before* he rapes?[c]
Yes
No
Don't know

Table 10.1 (continued)

Black respondents (in percentage)			White respondents (in percentage)			Total (in percentage)
Total	Males	Females	Total	Males	Females	
7.2	12.5	4.7	17.5	22.0	14.5	12.4
7.2	7.5	7.1	4.0	4.0	3.9	5.6
16.8	25.0	12.9	15.1	18.0	13.2	15.9
2.8	7.5	4.7	6.3	8.0	5.3	6.0
21.6	5.0	29.4	11.1	2.0	17.1	16.3
32.0	27.5	34.1	38.1	40.0	36.8	35.1
8.0	12.5	5.9	3.2	4.0	2.6	5.6
1.6	2.5	1.2	4.8	2.0	6.6	3.2
20.8	20.0	21.2	12.7	18.0	9.2	16.7
76.8	75.0	77.6	82.5	82.0	82.9	79.7
0.0	0.0	0.0	0.8	0.0	1.3	0.4
2.4	5.0	1.2	4.0	0.0	6.6	3.2
1.6	5.0	0.0	1.6	2.0	1.3	1.6
18.4	12.5	21.2	11.1	16.0	7.9	14.7
0.8	2.5	0.0	0.0	0.0	0.0	0.4
76.8	75.0	77.6	83.3	82.0	84.2	80.1
2.4	5.0	1.2	4.0	0.0	6.6	3.2
77.6	72.5	80.0	82.5	82.0	82.9	80.1
19.2	22.5	17.6	12.7	16.0	10.5	15.9
0.0	0.0	0.0	0.8	2.0	0.0	0.4
3.2	5.0	2.4	4.0	0.0	6.6	3.6
12.0	17.5	9.4	19.0	12.0	23.7	15.5
23.2	25.0	22.4	23.8	24.0	23.7	23.5
25.6	15.0	30.6	24.6	24.0	25.0	25.1
11.2	7.5	12.9	12.7	18.0	9.2	12.0
2.4	2.5	2.4	0.8	0.0	1.3	1.6
19.2	22.5	17.6	13.5	18.0	10.5	16.3
6.4	10.1	4.7	5.6	4.0	6.6	6.0
71.2	77.5	68.2	85.7	86.0	85.5	78.5
24.8	17.5	28.2	8.7	10.0	7.9	16.7
0.8	0.0	1.2	1.6	4.0	0.0	1.2

Table 10.1 (continued)

Question and answer category
No answer

How is he different?[b,c]
  Reference to sick
  Reference to sex
  Reference to anger
  Poor/faulty socialization
  Reference to women
  Other answer
  Man is not different
  No answer/don't know

Do you think a man who commits rape is different from other men *after* he rapes?[e]
  Yes
  No
  Don't know
  No answer

How is he different?[d]
  Feels dominant
  Feels remorse/shame
  Reference to sick
  Will rape again
  Sexually satisfied
  Other referent
  Man is not different
  No answer

Do you think that rapists should be . . .
  Hospitalized for treatment
  Put in prison
  Both
  Neither
  Alternative answer
  Don't know
  No answer

When men rape women, do you think they rape women who are from their own race or ethnic group or from a different group?[b]
  Same
  Different
  Doesn't matter
  Don't know
  No answer

Table 10.1 (continued)

Black respondents (in percentage)			White respondents (in percentage)			Total (in percentage)
Total	Males	Females	Total	Males	Females	
3.2	5.0	2.4	4.0	0.0	6.6	3.6
32.0	27.5	34.1	31.7	20.0	39.5	31.9
7.2	7.5	7.1	7.1	10.0	5.3	7.2
1.6	2.5	1.2	4.8	2.0	6.6	3.2
24.0	35.0	18.8	27.0	42.0	17.1	25.5
4.8	5.0	4.7	13.5	10.0	15.8	9.2
0.8	0.0	1.2	1.6	4.0	0.0	1.2
24.8	17.5	28.5	8.7	10.0	7.9	16.7
4.8	5.0	4.7	5.6	2.0	7.9	5.2
46.4	47.5	45.9	42.9	54.0	35.5	44.6
49.6	47.5	50.6	51.6	42.0	57.9	50.6
0.0	0.0	0.0	1.6	4.0	0.0	0.8
4.0	5.0	3.5	4.0	0.0	6.6	4.0
5.6	5.0	5.9	4.8	4.0	5.3	5.2
11.2	10.0	11.8	8.7	12.0	6.6	10.0
7.2	10.0	5.9	6.3	12.0	2.6	6.8
17.6	15.0	18.8	13.5	14.0	13.2	15.5
1.6	2.5	1.2	5.6	4.0	6.6	3.6
3.2	5.0	2.4	5.6	12.0	1.3	4.4
49.6	47.5	50.6	51.6	42.0	57.9	50.6
4.0	5.0	3.5	4.0	0.0	6.6	3.9
31.2	30.0	31.8	28.6	30.0	27.6	29.9
24.8	32.5	21.2	19.8	24.0	17.1	22.3
35.2	25.0	40.0	38.1	40.0	36.8	36.7
1.6	2.5	1.2	3.2	2.0	3.9	2.4
1.6	2.5	1.2	1.6	2.0	1.3	1.6
2.4	2.5	2.4	4.0	2.0	5.3	3.2
3.2	5.0	2.4	4.8	0.0	7.9	4.0
12.8	7.5	15.3	18.3	32.0	9.2	15.5
7.2	5.0	8.2	8.7	8.0	9.2	8.0
72.0	70.0	72.9	58.7	46.0	67.1	65.3
4.0	12.5	0.0	9.5	14.0	6.6	6.8
4.0	5.0	3.5	4.8	0.0	7.9	4.4

Table 10.1 (continued)

Question and answer category

c. *Causes of and solutions for rape*

What is the *main* cause of rape?[b]
    Social problems
    Mental problems
    Character of the male
    Reference to sex
    Character of the female
    No answer

In your opinion, what is the one thing that would *reduce* rape the most?
    Laws/punishment
    Treatment
    Change society's values
    Education
    Women learn to behave differently
    No answer

Do you think the number of rapes in Los Angeles County has . . .[b]
    Increased
    Decreased
    Stayed about the same
    Don't know
    No answer

---

a Eight respondents (5 white females, 1 white male, 1 black female, and 1 black male) refused to answer any of the questions in this table.

b Main effect by race significant at $p < .05$.

Forty respondents (16.9 percent) described or identified with the woman in their answer, using words such as "shame," "sorrow," "degradation," "threatened," "help," "trapped," "victim," "lady," "unwilling," "fear," "fright," and "fight." Fifteen respondents (6.0 percent) referred to the male perpetrator by using words such as "bastard," "hate," "the fucker," "savage," "animal," "beast," "fool," and "sadistic." The remaining respondents referred to concepts of sex and illness using words such as "sick," "ill," "crazy," "degenerate," "madness," "sex" ($N = 23$), "lust," "intercourse," and "fuck."

As with decisions about the sexual vignettes, words volunteered dif-

Table 10.1 (continued)

Black respondents (in percentage)			White respondents (in percentage)			Total (in percentage)
Total	Males	Females	Total	Males	Females	
15.2	15.0	15.3	18.3	16.0	19.7	16.7
24.8	17.5	28.2	33.3	22.0	40.8	29.1
8.8	7.5	9.4	7.9	12.0	5.3	8.4
13.6	20.0	10.6	13.5	18.0	10.5	13.5
28.0	27.5	28.2	10.3	14.0	7.9	19.1
9.6	12.5	8.2	16.7	18.0	15.8	13.1
27.2	25.0	28.2	33.3	28.0	36.8	30.3
8.0	7.5	8.2	7.1	8.0	6.6	7.6
18.4	15.0	20.0	19.0	18.0	19.7	18.7
2.4	2.5	2.4	9.5	14.0	6.6	6.0
31.2	35.0	29.4	15.1	14.0	15.8	23.1
12.8	15.0	11.8	15.9	18.0	14.4	14.4
67.2	67.5	67.1	80.2	84.0	77.6	73.7
8.8	10.0	8.2	1.6	0.0	2.6	5.2
8.8	12.5	7.1	6.3	8.0	5.3	7.6
12.0	5.0	15.3	7.9	8.0	7.9	10.0
3.2	5.0	2.4	4.0	0.0	6.6	3.6

c Main effect by sex significant at $p < .05$.

d Main effect by sex for white respondents only, significant at $p < .05$.

e Main effect by sex for black respondents only, significant at $p < .05$.

fered with the race and sex of respondents. Words used by whites compared to those used by blacks were much more likely to describe the act of rape (40 percent) or refer to sex (18 percent). Women of both races were more likely to identify with the woman while men were more likely to respond with sexual terms. Black males were somewhat more likely than other respondents to use the words "force," "forced," or "forcefully." While there was a relationship between income, education, and age of respondents and their answers, these differences correlated with and were explained by race and sex. Younger, highly educated respondents with high incomes (e.g., white males) referred to sex, while older, less well educated respondents with lower incomes referred to illness (i.e., by using the word "sick"). References to force and/or descriptions of the act also correlated with higher education and income.

Males and Females Involved in Rapes

The extent to which men and women who have been involved in rape differ from other men and women has been widely debated. Historically, research on rape was based on the assumption that rapists had deviant sexual needs (e.g., Rada, 1978). Feminists challenged that assumption arguing that the typical rapist was the man next door or the man who worked in the next room. Recent research tends to support feminist rather than traditional views (e.g., Koss, 1985; Scully and Marolla, 1985; Kanin, 1985).

Similarly, many hypothesize that society in general and males in particular think that some women deserve to be raped, implying that women who are raped are somehow different from other women. Kanin's studies of college students, Ageton's studies of young adults, and Goodchilds's studies of high school students found that some respondents believe a woman whom they perceive as exploiting a man or leading him on is fair game for rape. Attribution studies find that characteristics of a woman's appearance, background, and behavior affect observers' judgments about responsibility for rape.

To see what residents of Los Angeles County believe, we asked them whether they thought persons involved in rape are different from other persons—before and after the rape. In general respondents did not think raped women were different from other women before the rape (80 percent), but did think they were different after the rape (80 percent) (see table 10.1). Men who committed rape were thought to differ from other men before the rape (78 percent), but less than half (45 percent) thought they differed after the rape. In other words, the man did not change as a result of the rape; he was already "different."

Of those who thought the woman was "different" before the rape, most thought she was "provocative" and a few thought she was different in that she took "unnecessary chances." Black females were most likely to think the woman was "different" before she was raped, while white women were least likely to think so. After the rape had occurred, women involved were perceived to be "different" in that they were afraid of other persons or had negative feelings toward others. In contrast to opinions expressed about women previous to rape, postrape opinions of women did not differ with race or sex.

Whites are more likely than blacks to think that males who rape differ from other males before the rape, while black females are least likely to think they differ from other males. Females say rapists differ from other men in that they are sick, while males imply that problems during socialization led to "twisted values," "poor self-image," and "lack of control." Postrape, respondents are less united in their opinions about rapists. White males most frequently perceive them as different while white females least frequently perceive them as different. Those that perceive them as different mention a wide range of differences that are not easily summarized. Thirty-nine respondents stated that the male is different in that he "will rape again." Thirteen cited feelings of dominance, 25 cited feelings of remorse, 17 cited "sick," and 9 cited "sexual satisfaction" to explain how rapists differ from other males after the rape.

Disposition of Rapists

Suggested disposition of rapists was divided between hospitalization (30 percent), incarceration (24 percent), and both hospitalization and imprisonment (38 percent). Eighty of the 196 respondents who said rapists were "different" also said they were "sick." Almost half of the 80 said that rapists should be hospitalized for treatment and should also be put in prison. As we will show later, Los Angeles County residents consistently suggest that rapists should be both punished and treated. Answers to the question above and others suggest that even when mental problems are considered a major cause of rape, changes in the legal system or punishment are considered the solutions of choice.

Answers to the four questions about women and men before and after rape were examined for common patterns. We identified five patterns and two residual categories. The most common or normative pattern among Los Angeles residents is to think that women are different only after the rape, and that men are different only before the rape. Eighty-seven persons (34.7 percent) adhere to this pattern. An additional fifty-seven (22.7 percent) agree, however, that the man differs after the rape as well as

Table 10.2   Perception of what would most reduce rape by perception of main cause of rape, Los Angeles study, 1979 (unweighted sample)[a]

Perception of what would reduce rape	Main cause of rape (in percentage)				
	Issues related to socialization	Mental problems	Character of the male	Sexual referent	Character of the female
Changes in the legal system	38.5	42.0	25.0	28.6	26.2
Psychological treatment	5.1	14.5	12.5	7.1	2.4
Change values and/or society	25.6	18.8	37.5	35.7	14.3
Education	12.8	5.8	12.5	3.6	2.4
Women learn or change behavior	17.9	18.8	12.5	25.0	54.8
Total *N*	39	69	16	28	42

a Significant at $p < .01$. Percentages and statistical tests exclude "don't know" and "no answer" categories.

before. Because it is unlikely that the first group thought the man somehow was abnormal before the rape and normal afterward, these two groups can be combined, suggesting that a majority of respondents fall into this pattern of thinking. The three deviant patterns are: those who consider both the male and female to differ from other men and women both before and after the rape (8.4 percent); those who never perceive the woman as different, but always perceive the man as different (6.4 percent); and those who perceive only the woman after the rape to be different (5.2 percent). Responses of remaining subjects (18.3 percent) do not fall into any discernible pattern.

Whites were more likely (85.2 percent) than blacks (71.2 percent) to answer all four questions. Whites were also more likely (66.7 percent) than blacks (48 percent) to believe that women are not different before the rape but are different after the rape, and that men who rape are different before the rape and either different or not after the rape (48 percent) (table 10.2). Black females are more likely (10.6 percent) to say the woman is not different either before or after the rape, while white females are least likely (2.6 percent) to say so.

Prevalence and Ethnic Identity of Participants

The majority of respondents (74 percent) thought rape was increasing in Los Angeles County (see table 10.1). Whites, particularly white males, were more likely than blacks to perceive the number of rapes to be increasing. This is a realistic perception in that reported rapes did increase in Los Angeles County during the 1970s, and certainly public attention on rape increased significantly during the period.

To test the stereotype that rapes are race-related and specifically cross-ethnic, respondents were asked whether they thought that rapes were between males and females of the same race or different races. In answering the question respondents could also indicate that race is irrelevant or does not matter. Less than 10 percent of the Los Angeles respondents felt that rapes generally occur between people of different races. The majority (65 percent) felt that race was irrelevant (see table 10.1). If the category indicating concern with race is broadened to include all answers except those that said race does not matter, close to 30 percent of the sample indicate possible concern with race in deciding about rapes.

Respondents who believe rapes are cross-racial may adhere to some of the social stereotypes surrounding rape. Given the races of this sample, the stereotype logically and reasonably can be seen to work in either direction. Respondents may either believe that black men rape white women or white men rape black women. Since respondents who said rapes were cross-racial were not asked what the relevant races of the male and female would be, we cannot be sure what they would have said. If, however, the stereotype exists in the way it is thought to, white respondents would say white women are raped by black men and blacks would say black women are raped by white men. (This interpretation is consistent with this sample's slight tendency to judge as rape sexual assaults in vignettes portraying opposite-race males and same-race females.)

White males were most likely to believe that race is a relevant issue regarding rape. This is consistent with feminist theories of the social and political evolution of rape (e.g., Williams and Holmes, 1981) which suggest that rape is not only a way for males to control women but also a specific product of white males' need to control other men. The finding above is, however, inconsistent with other data available from this study. Contrary to what responses to this question suggest, white males were no more likely than any other race-gender subgroup to actually use race to decide whether sexual encounters portrayed in vignettes were rapes or, if used, to deny its usage.

Los Angeles respondents' perceptions of the relevance of ethnicity to rape contrast sharply with those of San Antonio residents in the study discussed in chapter 6. No San Antonio black respondents and only 15 percent of white males and 10 percent of white females thought race was irrelevant to discussion of rape (Williams and Holmes, 1981, p. 140). San Antonio blacks were evenly divided as to whether rapes were interracial or intraracial, while 56 percent of white males thought they predominantly occurred between men and women of the same race, and 48 percent of white females thought that different races were most common.

Main Cause of Rape

Los Angeles residents are in no more agreement than the experts on what causes rape. Twenty-nine percent thought mental problems were the main cause, with most ($N = 42$) specifically stating that "mental illness" was the cause (see table 10.1). Others (17 percent) thought that "social problems," including the "breakdown of the family" ($N = 14$), "permissiveness" ($N = 6$), drugs, changing sexual attitudes, lack of respect for others, the media, etc., were the major cause of rape while 8.4 percent referred to the male's character and cited inferiority complexes, a need to prove himself, loneliness, etc. Specific references to sex were given as the main cause by 13.5 percent. Included in this category were suggestions that rapists had unfulfilled sexual lives, lack of access to prostitutes, feelings of sexual superiority, loneliness for women, and hatred of women. Finally, 19.5 percent cited characteristics of the victims including references to dress, behavior, flirtation, attitudes, and vulnerability.

Answers differ with race, sex, and age of respondents, but not with income or education. Younger blacks of both sexes are more likely to cite characteristics of the female as a major cause of rape, while younger males of both races are more likely to refer to sexual problems. References to women as a major cause of rape are consistent with black respondents' somewhat greater propensity to see women who are raped as different (e.g., more provocative) from other women prior to a rape, and to base their decisions about the sexual encounters portrayed in vignettes on the woman's behavior (e.g., amount of resistance she engaged in). Consistent with their perception that males who rape are different from other males and are sick prior to the rape, 40 percent of white females think mental problems are the major cause of rape. A substantial proportion of black females also see mental problems as a major cause of rape.

Males in Los Angeles and San Antonio are generally comparable in their perceptions of the main cause of rape, but females in the two cities differ sharply (Williams and Holmes, 1981, p. 117). Black females in Los Angeles are much more likely than those in San Antonio to cite women (28 percent vs. 20 percent) and men or sex (20 percent vs. 5 percent) as the major cause of rape. In contrast, white females in Los Angeles cite women much less frequently (8 percent vs. 23 percent) and men or sex somewhat less frequently (16 percent vs. 21 percent).

Opinions regarding the main cause of rape are not associated with respondents' overall perceptions of whether rape victims and rapists differ from other men and women (table 10.3). But persons who view society and its values as a major cause of rape are less likely to see women who are raped as different either before or after the rape. Those who see mental problems as the cause of rape are less likely to see women as different before the rape and men as different after the rape. Those citing males' character as the problem see men as different before the rape, while those who cite sexual causes are less likely to see men as different before the rape but more likely to see them as different after the rape. Finally, those who see women as a major cause of rape are more likely to perceive women as different before a rape, somewhat less likely to perceive men as different before a rape, and somewhat more likely to see men as different postrape.

When asked "When you hear the term rape, what is the first word that comes to mind?" persons who see mental problems as a major cause of rape (32 of 73) supply a negative term descriptive of the act itself. Nine of the twenty who cite the male's character as a major cause of rape referenced "force" and 13 of the 48 who cite the female's character used a word describing or identifying the woman.

Table 10.3 Relationship of questions on rape to vignette rating, Los Angeles study, 1979 (unweighted sample)

Question and answer categories	Mean vignette rating
First word mentioned	
Sexual referent	4.33*
Sick referent	4.37
Force referent	4.63
Describes man	4.18
Describes woman	4.45
Describes act	4.80
Perceptions of man and woman	
Woman different pre-rape?	
Yes	4.07*
No	4.65
Woman different postrape?	
Yes	4.59
No	4.37
Man different pre-rape?	
Yes	4.61*
No	4.26
Man different postrape?	
Yes	4.43
No	4.65
Woman not different before and different after; man different before and either different or not different after	4.71
Both woman and man different before and after rape	4.23
Woman not different either before or after; man different before but not after	4.80
Woman not different before but different after; man not different before but different after	4.33
All other	4.20
People involved in rapes are	
Same race	4.61
Different race	4.46
Doesn't matter	4.54
Don't know	4.65
No answer	3.87
Rapes in Los Angeles have	
Increased	4.63
Decreased	4.27

Vignette rating pattern (in percentage)

Nonrater	Nonnormative rater	Force-only rater	Force-plus rater	Resistance-only rater	Resistance-plus rater
3.6	7.4	18.8	19.8	16.7	5.3
0.0	11.1	3.1	4.7	11.1	10.5
14.3	7.4	25.0	19.8	11.1	18.4
3.6	7.4	3.1	5.8	5.6	13.2
21.4	25.9	3.1	19.8	22.2	15.8
57.1	40.7	46.9	30.2	33.3	36.8
10.0	21.0	12.0	18.0	20.0	19.0
93.0	68.0	85.0	80.0	85.0	72.0
83.0	61.0	94.0	77.0	80.0	74.0
37.0	50.0	41.0	46.0	40.0	49.0
70.0	48.3	64.7	58.9	50.0	44.2
3.3	10.3	8.8	8.4	15.0	7.0
3.3	3.4	8.8	2.1	5.0	11.6
10.0	3.4	2.9	5.3	10.0	9.3
13.3	34.5	14.7	25.3	20.0	27.9
14.8	12.0	19.4	24.4	16.7	7.5
7.4	16.0	3.2	9.8	11.1	7.5
77.8	72.0	77.4	65.9	72.2	85.0
93.1	87.5	88.9	85.2	63.2	86.5
0.0	4.2	7.4	3.7	15.8	10.8

Table 10.3 (continued)

Question and answer categories	Mean vignette rating
Same	4.42
No answer/don't know	4.19
Main cause of rape	
Issues of socialization	4.56
Mental problems	4.63
Character of male	4.80
Sexual referent	4.30
Character of female	4.44
How to reduce rape	
Laws/punishment	4.56
Treatment	4.53
Change values/society	4.44
Education	4.65
Women change behavior	4.59

* $p < .05$

Reduction of Rape

Opinions regarding what would reduce rape were as diverse as those about what causes it. Thirty percent stated that changes in legal or judicial practices would be most effective in reducing rape. Included were harsher laws ($N = 15$), longer sentences ($N = 12$), imprisonment ($N = 11$), police protection ($N = 11$), stricter punishment ($N = 19$), easier reporting ($N = 9$), vasectomy, castration, getting rapists off the streets, and more convictions. Treatment, suggested by 18 percent, included identification of potential rapists, better communication, psychiatric help, and hospitalization. Changing society was thought to be the solution by 19 percent who cited changing values, more emphasis on people, greater emphasis on Judeo-Christian principles, provision of jobs, stable home life, increased respect for family, changes in the media, nonexploitive sex, legalization of prostitution, etc. Six percent suggested that rapes could be reduced by education, including more education in general, sex education, education of parents, education about rape, counseling in high schools, and/or education targeted at females (including how to avoid

Vignette rating pattern (in percentage)

Nonrater	Nonnormative rater	Force-only rater	Force-plus rater	Resistance-only rater	Resistance-plus rater
6.9	8.3	3.7	11.1	21.1	2.7
15.4	20.0	13.8	16.0	25.0	30.0
38.5	24.0	48.3	30.9	31.3	32.5
15.4	8.0	10.3	11.1	0.0	5.0
7.7	24.0	13.8	17.3	6.3	17.5
23.1	24.0	13.8	24.7	37.5	15.0
34.6	34.8	27.3	28.9	72.2	38.5
7.7	13.0	9.1	10.5	5.6	5.1
23.1	17.4	24.2	27.6	5.6	17.9
7.7	8.7	6.1	6.6	5.6	7.7
26.9	26.1	33.3	26.3	11.1	30.8

rapes, self-defense, etc.). And 14 percent thought women needed to learn to behave differently. Included in this last category were suggestions that women learn self-defense ($N = 8$), carry a weapon, not travel alone ($N = 9$), learn to recognize danger ($N = 13$), not show fear, avoid threatening situations ($N = 7$), not ride with strangers, not let strangers in the house, change how they present themselves publicly including how they dress ($N = 8$), and give up their freedom ($N = 2$).

With the exception of white females in the two cities, Los Angeles residents are only half as likely as San Antonio residents to think that increased law and order will reduce rape (Williams and Holmes, 1981, p. 121). San Antonio blacks, in particular, give little attention to the possibilities of reducing rape through fundamental social change, bettering family life, and/or religion (3 percent). In contrast, 18 percent of Los Angeles black residents think such changes would be effective. Los Angeles whites (16.6 percent) are somewhat more likely than San Antonio whites (10 percent) to think that education and treatment are reduction strategies.

Although people's views regarding what will reduce rape relate to their perceptions of its cause and the first word that comes to mind, unlike responses to earlier questions, strong differences by race and sex do not exist (tables 10.1 and 10.2). However, white females are somewhat more likely than other respondents to state that laws and punishment will reduce rape. This is particularly interesting given their propensity to think of rapists as mentally ill. In spite of that perception white females do not think that psychological treatment is an effective treatment. Consistent with attitudes examined earlier, blacks, particularly younger black males, think that the major way to reduce rape is to change the behavior of women. This is consistent with blacks' perception that women are instrumental in the occurrence of rape.

While an absolute one-to-one relationship does not exist between Los Angeles residents' perception of the major cause of rape and its solution, a single solution predominates for what are perceived to be two of the major problems—mental problems and women's behavior (table 10.2). Persons who see mental problems as a major cause of rape tend to think that laws and punishment, rather than treatment, are most effective in reducing rape. Persons who think women's behavior is the major cause of rape think changes in women's behavior would solve or reduce the problem. To the extent that the first group is dominated by white females and the second by blacks, differences in perceptions of what causes rape and what might reduce it correlate with race and gender.

Association with Vignette Ratings

Discernible patterns, but few significant overall associations, exist between respondents' perceptions of vignettes and their responses to traditional questions about rape. Nonraters of vignettes—those who gave identical scores to all their vignettes—generally gave a first word that described the act of rape or the woman involved. In response to questions about the main cause of rape and what would reduce it, nonraters most frequently said that mental problems are the cause of rape and changes in the legal system would reduce it. A number of nonraters think that women are the main cause and/or that changes in women's behavior would reduce rape. Nonraters' perceptions of males and females involved in rape are normative for the sample. Males who rape are thought to be different from other males before the rape; women who are raped are thought to be different after the rape. Nonraters are most likely to think that rapes in Los Angeles increased.

Consistent with their minimal use of force or resistance in their vignette ratings, nonnormative raters do not mention force as a first word. Like nonraters, they give a word that describes the act of rape or the woman involved. Nonraters' perceptions of the main cause of rape are evenly divided among socialization, mental problems, sex, and women. But they view laws and punishment as the most effective solution, followed by changes in women's behavior. In spite of a tendency to see women as responsible for reducing rape, nonnormative raters are not particularly prone to think that women who are raped differ from other women. An exception is the 15 percent in the group who think males and females involved in rapes are different both before and after a rape.

Persons who used only force to decide about sexual encounters were most likely to give force or a synonym as their first word. While almost 50 percent of force-only raters said mental problems were the major cause of rape, only 9 percent thought treatment was a solution. Their most commonly proposed solution was for women to change their behavior (33 percent), followed by laws and punishment (27 percent), and changing society or social values (24 percent). For these persons women who are raped do not differ from other women but men who rape do differ from other men.

The largest number of Los Angeles County respondents used force in combination with other information to decide whether a sexual encounter was rape. Consistent with the size of the group and their use of multiple information, force-multiple raters were highly diverse in their responses to open-ended questions. In contrast to the force-only group, when giving the first word that came to mind force-multiple raters were more likely to use a word that described or identified with the woman. The combination of main causes and solutions selected by this group covered almost every possibility as did their perceptions of the male and female involved. This group was, however, least likely (66 percent) to see race as irrelevant in that they believed that rapes either occurred between men and women of the same race or men and women of different races. In fact, persons in this group were more likely than persons in any other group to say that rapes occur between people of the same race.

Consistent with their use of resistance as the determinant of vignette ratings, the resistance-only group generally does not use the word "force" or a synonym as their first word. Relative to other groups they are most likely (37.5 percent) to think that women cause rape, but, unlike other groups who cite such a cause, they think laws and punishment (72 percent) are the solution. Other causes cited are mental problems and socialization. Consistent with their perception of cause, resistance-only raters were somewhat more likely than other respondents to see women who are raped as different from other women before the rape occurs.

Like first words selected by persons who used force and other information in rating vignettes, first words selected by persons who rated vignettes with information about resistance and other information were diverse. In contrast to other groups, resistance-plus raters were most likely to see society as the cause of rape (30 percent) and laws (38.5 percent) followed by women changing their behavior (31 percent) as solutions. Like resistance-only raters, more than 30 percent of this group perceived mental problems as the major cause of rape. Their perceptions of men and women involved in rape were diverse, and showed no prominent pattern. But they were most likely (85 percent) to think race irrelevant.

To the extent that associations exist between rating patterns used in judging vignettes and traditional questions about rape, similar patterns exist in the association between the magnitude of the ratings and the questionnaire data. To the extent that force-only, resistance-only, or nonraters tended to give a specific response to a question, the mean rating for that response was higher. To the extent that nonnormative raters differentially selected a response, the average score was lower. Because, in general, few patterns existed, few associations were observed. Respondents who referred to the act of rape as their first word (consistent with their tendency to be nonraters or force-only raters) were more likely to think more of the vignettes portrayed rape ($\bar{x} = 4.8$). The tendency of these two groups to see women as different after rapes but not before, and men as different before, similarly resulted in higher scores ($\bar{x} = 4.71$) for this combination of answers. The remaining questions, whether examined alone or in combination, yield only minor differences in decisions about vignettes.

Summary and Discussion

White females' opinions about rape are most easily summarized with information provided in this chapter. White females are more likely than any other racial or gender group in the sample to answer questions in ways that might be defined as normative for this sample of Los Angeles residents. That is, they think men who rape are somehow different from other men, but that women they rape do not differ from other women until after they have been raped—when they become fearful and suspicious. Sixty-eight percent of the white women in this study were of this opinion. Forty percent of the white females interviewed responded with a negative description of rape when asked their first response to the word "rape." White females consider mental problems to be a major cause of rape, and changes in the legal system to be a major solution.

For no other race and gender group is the structure of opinions so readily defined. Thirty-three percent of black females agree with white females who think mental problems are a major cause of rape; and 44 percent of black females ($N = 10$) agree that the judicial system is the major solution. Another major cause of rape for black females, however, concerns the woman's behavior and character (29 percent). For this group, the major solution is for women to change their behavior (14 of 20). Black females' reference to women as a major cause of rape is consistent with their greater tendency to use information about the woman's resistance in judging sexual encounters in the vignettes.

Opinions of males cannot be summarized. Males are somewhat more likely than females to refer to sexual inadequacies, etc. as the major cause of rape and more likely than white females to cite women as the major cause. For males, however, the cited cause of rape does not predict the solution sought. Black males, like black females, think that women should change their behavior. As a solution this tactic may reflect the realities of rape in the black community where both official and, until recently, unofficial statistics have consistently shown prevalence of rape to be higher than in the white community. In contrast, a plurality of white males (11 of 34) see the legal system as the major way to reduce rape regardless of the cause cited. In contrast to black males, only five of 34 white males think that rapes would decrease if women changed their behavior.

In general, few associations exist between respondents' answers to the traditional questions examined in this chapter and their responses to the vignettes. Opinions of force-only and resistance-only raters are most easily characterized. Resistance-only raters are more likely than other groups to cite women as a cause (37.5 percent), but (perhaps strangely) think laws and punishment are the best solution (72 percent). They are least likely to think rapes are increasing in Los Angeles County (63 percent). Force-only raters are distinctive in thinking that mental problems (48 percent) are a major cause, while also thinking that women need to change (33 percent). Resistance-plus raters are more likely than others (30 percent) to see society and its values as a major cause of rape and are most likely to think that race is irrelevant (85 percent) to rape. In contrast, force-plus raters are most likely (24 percent) to say that rape occurs between persons of the same race.

Responses to these questions neither duplicate nor clearly elaborate upon the information obtained from the vignettes. At best, one can conclude that the two kinds of information are complementary.

Clearly, while patterns exist in opinions about men and women involved in rape, rape's causes, and how it might be reduced, such patterns are not particularly strong. The opinions of the Los Angeles residents in this study are more diverse and often contrast sharply with those in the San Antonio study. In general, Los Angeles residents' perceptions of the causes, solutions, and participants in rape are more liberal and sophisticated than those of San Antonio residents. The apparent inconsistency and fluidity in opinion structures, both within Los Angeles County and between Los Angeles and San Antonio, probably reflect differences in public knowledge about rape, rapidly changing attitudes on the part of some community subgroups, and the open-ended nature of questions asked. Since rape was formerly a taboo topic that received little public attention until 1970, opinions regarding rape may have been verbalized only rarely by the respondents in our sample. Many may not even have thought about such questions. Others' opinions may have been undergoing significant change as the issue received greater attention in the media and other public forums. One objective in asking open-ended questions was to reduce response bias and constriction by minimizing the transmission of cues regarding appropriate or socially acceptable answers.

Certainly professionals are not united in their beliefs about the major cause(s) of rape, its solution, or treatment. Even if they could identify a cause or a solution, they would not necessarily agree as to the appropriate match between perceived cause and solution. Therefore it is not surprising that community members too fail to arrive at precise, neatly described perceptions of rape and its solutions.

11 Respondents' Personal and Legal Definitions of Rape

A s part of each interview in the Los Angeles County study, respondents were asked to define rape and state their concept of the legal definition. Each definition was coded based on how closely it matched the California statute in force in 1978 and whether it referred to five concepts contained in the legal definition: use of force, specific mention of sex or intercourse, nonconsent or lack of willingness, conflict between the two persons, and women as victims. In 1979 the California statute defined rape as ". . . an act of sexual intercourse accomplished with a person not the spouse of the perpetrator, under any of the following circumstances . . . (1) Where it is accomplished against a person's will by means of force or fear of immediate and unlawful bodily injury on the person or another . . ." (*West's California Codes*, 1983). In other sections of relevant statutes it was emphasized that rapes were limited to sexual acts of a man or men against a woman.

Each respondent's definition was coded on a scale of 1 to 5, where 1 was equated with being close to the legal definition and 5 was equated with having little resemblance to the legal definition. Examples of answers coded "1" were: "intercourse without consent," "heterosexual intercourse without consent," and "a man having intercourse with a woman without her consent." Answers such as "sex without consent," "forceful entry," "sex between a man and woman without consent," and "forceful entry of the vagina" were coded as "2." "Forced sex" and "force" were coded "3." Terms such as "attack," "sex," "violent," and "sadistic" were coded as "4." Statements such as "sex and illness," "sick," and a variety of miscellaneous phrases were assigned a code of "5."

Definitions of Rape

All but eight respondents gave their own personal definition of rape, but only 50 percent volunteered a legal definition (table 11.1). Personal definitions generally contained many of the elements of the California statute with errors being omissions rather than inclusions of incorrect information.

Content of Definitions

Most respondents referred to sex (72 percent), conflict (66 percent), and lack of consent (57 percent) in their personal definitions of rape. In spite of the use of the term "forced" in the vignettes, only 30 percent of the respondents specifically used the term "force" or a variant as a component of their own definition of rape. Including this 30 percent, 74 percent mentioned force or a synonym for force as part of their personal definition of rape. Interestingly, only 22 percent of participants specified a woman's presence as part of their personal definition. And very few specified that women are, by definition, the victims of rapes.

Similar content was contained in the legal definitions given by respondents. Again, the most frequently cited characteristics were force or a synonym (75 percent) and sex (75 percent). Somewhat over half of our respondents specified nonconsent (56 percent) and conflict between the two people was mentioned by 42 percent. Again, only 22 percent specifically mentioned women as part of their legal definition.

Ethnicity, Gender, and Socioeconomic Status as Predictors

Closeness of personal definitions to the California statutes differed with race, education, and age of respondents, but not gender or income. Older black respondents who failed to complete high school gave personal

Table 11.1 Characteristics of respondents' personal and legal definitions of rape by race and sex, Los Angeles study, 1979 (unweighted sample)

Question and answer category	Black respondents (in percentage)			White respondents (in percentage)			Total (in percentage)
	Total	Males	Females	Total	Males	Females	
A. *Personal definitions of rape*							
Personal definition's closeness to California legal definition[a]							
close 1	15.1	8.1	18.3	11.1	12.2	10.3	13.1
2	29.4	37.8	25.6	35.9	36.7	35.3	32.6
3	25.2	27.0	24.4	27.4	28.6	26.5	26.3
4	16.8	16.2	17.1	22.2	18.4	25.0	19.5
distant 5	13.4	10.8	14.6	3.4	4.1	2.9	8.5
Mean closeness score[a]	2.84	2.84	2.84	2.71	2.65	2.75	2.78
B. *Legal definitions of rape*							
Percentage who gave a legal definition[a]	40.8	50.0	36.5	57.1	62.0	52.6	51.4
Legal definition's closeness to California legal definition							
close 1	11.8	10.0	12.9	15.3	16.1	15.0	13.2
2	35.3	35.0	32.3	40.3	45.2	37.5	36.4
3	27.5	30.0	22.5	23.6	22.6	25.0	24.8
4	17.6	20.0	12.9	11.1	9.7	12.5	13.2
distant 5	7.8	5.0	22.5	9.7	6.5	10.0	12.4
Mean closeness score	2.74	2.92	2.75	3.03	2.61	2.45	2.73
C. *Components included in personal definitions*							
Force is specifically mentioned	26.4	27.5	25.9	32.5	34.0	31.6	29.5
Force or synonym is mentioned	73.6	72.5	74.1	73.8	82.0	68.4	73.7
Conflict is mentioned	47.2	45.0	48.2	41.3	48.0	36.8	44.2
Presence of woman specified	24.0	25.0	23.5	20.6	20.0	21.1	22.3
Sex specified	68.0	62.5	70.6	75.4	76.3	74.0	71.7
Nonconsent specified	54.4	55.0	54.1	59.5	64.0	56.6	57.0

Table 11.1 (continued)

Question and answer category	Black respondents (in percentage)			White respondents (in percentage)			Total (in percentage)
	Total	Males	Females	Total	Males	Females	
Mean number of components mentioned	2.94	2.88	2.96	3.03	3.22	2.91	2.98
D. *Components included in legal definitions*							
Force is specifically mentioned	27.5	30.0	25.8	38.0	41.9	35.0	33.6
Force or synonym is mentioned	70.6	75.0	67.7	78.9	87.1	72.5	75.4
Conflict is mentioned	43.1	45.0	41.9	40.8	45.2	37.5	41.8
Presence of woman specified	19.6	20.0	19.4	23.9	25.8	22.5	22.1
Sex specified[b]	66.7	85.0	54.8	80.3	80.6	80.0	74.6
Nonconsent specified	47.1	45.0	48.4	62.0	64.5	60.0	55.7
Mean number of components mentioned	2.75	3.0	2.58	3.24	3.45	3.08	3.03

a Race significant at $p < .05$.
b Sex significant at $p < .05$ for black respondents only.

definitions that came closest to the California statutes or definitions least resembling California statutes. In spite of the greater accuracy of some black respondents' personal definitions, many black respondents refused to provide a legal definition of rape. Whereas 62 percent of white males and 53 percent of white females attempted a legal definition, only 50 percent of black males and 36.5 percent of black females attempted a legal definition.

Older, less well-educated white respondents were significantly more likely to give a legal definition ($p < .05$). While some black respondents' personal definitions were less complete than those of white respondents, the differences were not significant enough to explain why volunteering a legal definition was differentially distributed by race and gender, with the majority of black females refusing to give a legal definition.

Neither the number of coded components mentioned in personal definitions nor their distribution differed by race or sex. They did differ by age and education of respondents. Younger persons included more concepts in their definitions and were more likely to mention force as part of their personal definition. More highly educated respondents either included none or many specified concepts in their definitions.

Because significantly fewer black respondents volunteered a legal definition of rape, fewer differences existed by race, sex, or socioeconomic status in characteristics of respondents' legal definitions. Black respondents were less likely to mention nonconsent as a component, while black females were much less likely than all other groups to refer specifically to sex in their legal definitions. When variables were analyzed one at a time, no differences were found by demographic characteristic in closeness of definitions to actual legal statutes or number of concepts mentioned.

Comparison of Personal to Legal Definitions

There was a tendency for persons who provided legal definitions to have given personal definitions that more closely resembled the 1979 California statute than the 1978 laws, but the trend was not significant (table 11.2). A similar tendency existed regarding the number of concepts included in personal definitions with persons who included more components being somewhat more likely to volunteer a legal definition. Again, however, the trend is not significant.

When both personal and legal definitions were given, both tended to be similarly close to the California statute. To the extent that a particular component was mentioned in a respondent's personal definition of rape it was also likely to be mentioned in his or her legal definition (table 11.2). There was a tendency for respondents with the least legally correct personal definitions to provide more correct legal definitions. Whereas sex and nonconsent were often part of legal definitions when they were not in a person's personal definition of rape, references to force, conflicts, and women were apt to be omitted from Los Angeles residents' legal definitions though included in their personal definitions.

As more components were mentioned in a definition, the closer that

Table 11.2 Relationship between the California statute in / respondent's own definition of rape, and his or her perceptio/ legal definition, Los Angeles study, 1979 (unweighted samp..,

Closeness of respondent's legal definition to California statute	Closeness of personal definition to California statute (in percentage)				
	(close)				(distant)
	1	2	3	4	5
close 1	29.0	6.6	1.7	4.4	0.0
2	16.1	31.6	10.2	13.3	10.5
3	9.7	7.9	23.7	11.1	10.5
4	0.0	5.3	5.1	20.0	0.0
distant 5	3.2	5.3	8.5	6.7	10.5
Refused to give legal definition	41.9	43.4	50.8	44.4	68.4
Total N	32	79	64	47	21

a Chi square is 61 with p < .001; gamma is .23 and increases to .45 if those who refused to give a legal definition are deleted from the calculation.

definition came to reflecting California law at the time. Definitional components which most strongly differentiated close responses from less close responses were mentions of sexual activity, nonconsent, and presence of women. Persons who mentioned all three were most likely to have personal and/or legal definitions close to the California statute. But, as noted above, persons whose personal definitions contained many of the coded characteristics were only slightly more likely to volunteer a legal definition than those whose definitions contained few of the components. Whether or not a legal definition was given, the relationship between a respondent's own definition of rape and the characteristics s/he incorporated in the legal definition did not change when controlled by race and sex.

The extent to which respondents' own definitions of rape resembled California law was not a significant predictor of willingness to give a legal definition. But once respondents decided to attempt a legal definition, characteristics in their personal definitions combined with demographic characteristics to increase the likelihood that the legal definition volunteered would resemble the actual California law. White males with lower incomes whose personal definitions were close to the legal definitions but did not include reference to use of force gave the most adequate legal definitions ($R^2 = .33$). Personal definitions of those who also gave legal definitions were more likely than other respondents' personal definitions to mention women and lack of consent specifically. Three facts explain this finding.

First, a majority of the sample (78 percent) included force or a synonym in their personal definitions. Thus its presence or absence was not a useful discriminating variable between respondents who did and did not give a legal definition. Second, a significant subgroup (44 percent) of those who included force in their personal definitions actually used the term "force," "forced," "forceful." This subgroup was less likely than other respondents to include other concepts in their definitions, such as references to women or consent. Its definitions, in general, were less likely to resemble the California law. There is reason to think that inclusion of the concept "force" by this subgroup was as much a product of having been exposed to the use of the word "forced" in the vignettes as it was commitment to the notion that presence of some kind of force is an integral part of a definition of rape. And finally, most respondents did not include specific references to women or consent in their personal definitions of rape. To the extent that a respondent did include these concepts, his or her personal definition was both more complete and closer to California law.

Definitions and Vignette Ratings

A mild association existed between Los Angeles respondents' personal definitions of rape and their decisions about the sexual encounters portrayed in the vignettes. None of the six groups was consistently more accurate than others in the personal or legal definitions it gave, but the decision to give a legal definition and the content of the decision did differ across the six groups. Force-only raters were most likely to volunteer a legal definition (73.5 percent) followed by nonnormative raters (51.7 percent), nonraters (50 percent), resistance-multiple raters (44.2 percent), force-multiple raters (43.2 percent), and resistance-only raters (35.0 percent).

Nonraters and nonnormative raters, consistent with their perceptions of the vignettes, tended to use all information coded or none of it to define rape. Although nonnormative raters had a tendency to think women were both the cause of and solution to rape, they did not mention women in their personal definitions of rape. The two groups that used force as a major cue in deciding about the sexual encounters overwhelmingly (90 percent) included force in their definitions. Resistance-only raters most frequently gave definitions that used none of the coded content. No one in this group included all the coded content in his or her definition. In contrast, resistance-multiple raters most often included all the coded content in their personal definitions of rape. The relationship between respondents' legal definitions of rape and their vignette rating patterns was consistent with that found between personal definitions and rating patterns, with the exception that associations became somewhat clearer.

Summary

Neither the closeness of a person's own definition to California statute or the number of components included in defining rape raised the probability that a legal definition would be given. Race of the respondent, however, did have an effect on giving a legal definition. Older whites were more likely than other respondents to provide a legal definition. The extent to which a respondent's personal definition resembled California statute and contained references to sexual activity slightly increased the likelihood that a legal definition would be attempted. When a legal definition was given, white females with lower incomes were more likely than others to incorporate multiple components into their legal definitions. Black females with high incomes were most likely to provide legal definitions resembling California statute.

Characteristics of the definitions given by Los Angeles residents have a mild but consistent association with the kinds of information used and the certainty of decisions about sexual encounters portrayed in the vignettes. Consistent with their relative education and social status, force-only raters were most likely to volunteer a legal definition. Inconsistent with their education, resistance-only raters, in contrast, were least likely to volunteer a legal definition. The reason for this finding is not clear, but may reflect differences in general sophistication, sophistication and knowledge about rape, or simply the race-sex composition of the two groups.

12 Rape in Los Angeles

C learly, Los Angeles County residents do not agree about when to label a coercive encounter rape. The six decisionmaking groups identified in our study form a continuum from liberal to conservative. At the most liberal end are 27 nonraters who thought all encounters described were rape. At the conservative end are 29 nonnormative raters who thought few encounters were rapes and 20 resistance-only raters who thought an encounter was a rape only when the woman resisted. In between are force-only raters, force-multiple raters, and resistance-multiple raters. As one moves across the continuum, respondents' certainty that a rape occurred decreases, dependence on violence as the key discriminator of rape declines, and use of information other than force and consent increases. Perceptions of the man and woman involved and the balance between sexuality and violence also change as one moves across the continuum. At the liberal end men and society are more likely to be thought responsible for rape, and rape is more likely to be thought a violent act. At the conservative end women and the characteristics of the encounter are considered as responsible or more responsible than men, and rape is more likely to be considered a normal expression of sexuality.

The liberal nonraters and force-only raters had higher educations and were younger than respondents in other groups. As one moves from liberal to conservative, education of respondents decreases significantly while age tends to increase slightly.

Identifiable differences by race and gender were also more noticeable at the conservative end of the continuum. Among conservatives, black males and females differed considerably from each other and from white males and females in conclusions they reached using similar information. Black male nonnormative raters and black female resistance-only raters gave atypically high ratings for their respective groups. Comparable differences in decisionmaking were not found between white males and females.

Nonraters

Most of the 27 nonraters who judged all encounters rapes thought that women were affected by rape and that rapists differed from other men. None said rapists and their victims were of different races, and all thought the number of rapes in Los Angeles had increased.[1]

When asked what causes rape and how it might be reduced, nonraters' answers reverted to traditional beliefs. While some said that rape was a product of social conditions, and believed society would have to change for rape to disappear, more common beliefs were that rape resulted from men's mental problems and women's behaviors. The most popular solutions within this group were that women should change their behavior or more laws and punishments should be enacted. Thus, in spite of this group's acceptance of more sophisticated definitions of rape, its members distanced themselves from its perpetrators by believing rapists were different from themselves and that solving the problem was the responsibility of law enforcement.

Disproportionately made up of white males, nonraters had high educations and good jobs and lived in safe neighborhoods.

Nonnormative Raters

The reluctance of nonnormative raters to think any of these sexual encounters were rapes suggests that they held traditional definitions of rape and limited their definitions to highly stylized, historical definitions. Consistent with this perception was their tendency to think women's behavior was the cause of rape, and to exclude any mention of women in their personal definitions. Inconsistent with their views was the fact that they were no more likely than other respondents to think that changes in women's behavior would reduce rape, and that they were more likely than others to volunteer a legal definition of rape.

The seeming discrepancies in opinions among nonnormative raters may reflect in part the disproportionate number of males of both races and black females in the group, and the group's low socioeconomic status. This subgroup of black females either actively rejected or had not been exposed to more enlightened views of rape. Consistent with studies of political attitudes in which black females frequently refuse to volunteer opinions, black females in this study refused to volunteer a legal definition of rape. This refusal may reflect an unsophisticated level of political knowledge, uneasiness with what they perceived to be a political system dominated by the white majority culture, or a practiced cynicism about realities of life in the ghetto and doubts that white liberal women are really interested in rapes suffered by their black sisters.

These women were among the poorest in the sample. They often were unmarried and lived with other adults and children in high-crime neighborhoods. They knew about crimes in their neighborhood and felt vulnerable to them. Their perception that women are a major cause of rape and that women must change their behavior if rape rates are to be reduced reflects realities of their lives. Consistent with historical evidence and contemporary statistics, these women perceived both black males and white males to be likely rapists. In their opinion black men and white male-dominated political institutions are not going to save them from rape: These women know that they are going to have to do it for themselves.

The few black men in the nonnormative group were atypical. In contrast to all other men in the sample, they felt vulnerable to crime. Most Los Angeles males, regardless of where they lived, felt invulnerable to crime; Los Angeles females, regardless of where they lived, felt vulnerable to crime. Something apparently had happened to this subgroup of black males to make them feel vulnerable. Possibly they or a friend or relative had been the victim of a violent crime in the recent past. But regardless of the causes, their feelings of vulnerability were reflected in their decisions about rapes. In spite of a tendency to ignore information about force and resistance in making a decision, they were more likely than other nonnormative raters to think that the vignettes portrayed rapes. Like black women in this group, they thought white men were probable rapists. Unlike black women, however, they denied that black men were rapists.

Violence and Consent: Force-Only Raters

Most Los Angeles black and white residents fell between the two extreme groups of nonraters and nonnormative raters. Most also used information about violence and consent to make decisions. They did not, however, agree about the relative importance of these two kinds of information. Most liberal within this large group were the 34 people whose decisions were determined strictly by the amount of violence portrayed in the vignette. If the man used physical force these people were fairly certain that a rape had occurred. Even when only verbal force was portrayed, members of the group were at least ambivalent. This group was most likely to provide a legal definition of rape, which suggests they may be the most sophisticated and knowledgeable group in the sample. This impression is consistent with their youth, high education, high-status jobs, and residence in low-crime areas. But they saw rapists as different from other men, believed mental problems are the major cause of rape, and saw the legal system rather than social change as the solution to rising rape rates. Should they, their friends, or relatives be raped, they would probably report the rape to police and expect arrest, conviction, and punishment of the rapist to occur.

Violence and Consent: Resistance-Only Raters

Resistance-only raters were second only to nonnormative raters in conservatism. For these people, use of violence in a sexual encounter did not make it a rape. It was a rape only if the woman actively objected, and verbal resistance probably was not sufficient. Passive acquiescence by the female to intercourse was clearly equated with consent. Consistent with their perception that the woman's behavior determines whether a rape occurs, resistance-only raters thought women were the cause of rape; they had a greater tendency than others to think that the behavior, appearance, or demeanor of a woman who is raped differs from that of other women before the rape and at least contributes to causing it to occur.

Like the nonnormative raters, these people lived in high-crime areas, had low educations, and worked in poorly paying jobs. What differentiates resistance-only raters from nonnormative raters is the disporportionate number of black males in the first category and the disparate rating patterns of black males and females across the two groups. While the least sophisticated or most skeptical black females were nonnormative raters, the least sophisticated or most skeptical black males were resistance-only raters. Black males in the resistance-only group remained skeptical that a rape occurred even when the woman physically resisted sexual intercourse. Men in both groups were apparently reluctant to label any sexual encounter a rape, and nonnormative women were very likely to agree with them.

In contrast, black female resistance-only raters were very sure a rape occurred if the woman physically resisted. This difference suggests that black female resistance-only raters either had more confidence in their own ability to avoid rape, had more liberal attitudes than black female nonnormative raters, or were more idealistic. Whereas black female nonnormative raters thought that women were going to have to take care of themselves, and were skeptical that resistance would stop a rape or result in authorities believing them, black female resistance-only raters thought that they *could* resist a rape attempt and that sufficient resistance on their part would make authorities believe them should they fail to prevent the rape. When self-reliant people fail to prevent a disaster, the trauma may be greater than for those who attribute evils to forces outside themselves. Resistance-only women who are internally oriented in locus of control might, if raped, be very vulnerable to extended postrape trauma (Janoff-Bulman, 1979).

Violence and Consent: The Majority

The majority of the sample ($N = 133$) sought multiple kinds of information which they combined to make a decision about whether a rape had occurred. Information about both violence and consent was incorporated into decisionmaking. But while information on force was most influential for most respondents ($N = 95$), others thought resistance more important ($N = 38$). Other aspects of their attitudes differed accordingly. Resistance-plus raters were more likely to include information on consent in the definitions they volunteered, to see women as unaffected by rapes, and to believe that changes in the judiciary and in women are ways to reduce rape. Yet they did not tend to blame women. Rather, they took the more sophisticated route of blaming society for increased rape. The force-plus raters, interestingly enough, were quite likely to see women as the main cause of rape, less likely to think laws and punishment were the solution, and more likely to think social change was a solution.

Where perceptions most diverged, however, was on the ethnic make-up of rapes. In a sample where a strong majority of all respondents thought ethnicity did not matter, resistance-plus raters were the most likely to take this position (85 percent). Force-plus raters were the least likely to think race was irrelevant (66 percent) and most likely to think people involved in rape had the same race (24 percent).

Both groups were heterogeneous in life-style and demographic characteristics. However, resistance-only raters were older, had less education and less income, and lived in unsafe neighborhoods. Unlike nonnormative and resistance-only raters and like force-only raters, identifiable subgroups within these two groups did not differ in their decisionmaking behavior. The magnitude and range of ratings, across and within both groups, were similar.

Los Angeles Adults and Adolescents

Both adults and adolescents have been studied in Los Angeles. Vignettes used with the two age groups, while not identical, were comparable. Having these two data sets allows us to make tentative comparisons across age cohorts. To directly compare responses of adults in our study with those of adolescents studied by Goodchilds et al., the mean score at each level of three variables (force, acquaintanceship, and location) was converted to the proportion it represented of the range between 0 percent, definitely is not a rape, and 100 percent, definitely is a rape. Thus, in the adult sample a mean score of 4.5 in a range of 1 to 6 becomes 70 percent in a range of 0 percent to 100 percent. This compares with a mean of 63.8 percent for the adolescents.

All vignettes in both studies technically represented rapes. Within the adult sample younger respondents were slightly more likely to think more vignettes were rapes and much more likely to think that force, by itself, differentiates rape from consensual sexual encounters. Those two trends in the adult sample suggest that adolescents would be more likely than young adults to judge more of the encounters rapes and to use force as their major discriminating variable. Contrary to this prediction, adolescents were, if anything, more conservative than young adults and only reluctantly called a sexual assault a rape. When decisions of adults and adolescents are examined only by the amount of force portrayed (figure 12.1), adolescents are seen to be consistently less likely than adults to think a rape occurred. This difference persists at every level of force portrayed. According to reported findings, adolescent decisions—unlike adult decisions about rape—did not vary with respondents' sex, race, education, age, sexual experience and attitudes, or exposure to violence (Zellman et al., 1981). Among adolescents, the point at which a sexual assault might be called a rape was similar for all subgroups. Furthermore, similar information was used by all adolescents to make decisions.

As with adults, the most important clue to decisionmaking by adoles-

Figure 12.1 Probability that a vignette was judged a rape by the age cohort of the respondent and the level of force portrayed in the vignette. Data from the Los Angeles study, 1979, and Goodchilds et al., 1979.

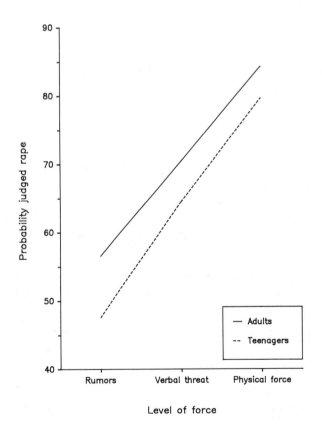

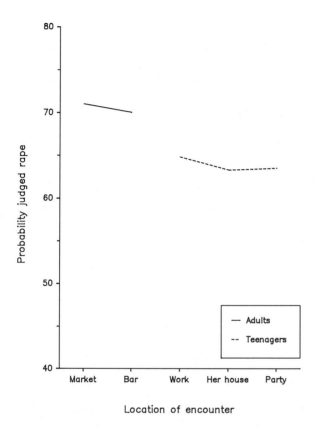

Figure 12.2 Probability that a vignette was judged a rape by the age cohort of the respondent and the location of the encounter portrayed in the vignette. Data from the Los Angeles study, 1979, and Goodchilds et al., 1979.

cents was the type and amount of violence that occurred during the encounter. But, as already noted, force or violence was not as definitive a clue for adolescents as it was for adults. Furthermore, adolescent assurance that a rape had occurred was seriously weakened by information that the girl and boy dated regularly or were friends. The location of the encounter had little or no effect on their perceptions. In contrast, both acquaintance and locale affected adults' perceptions of sexual assaults, but neither variable affected adults' perceptions as strongly as the relationship itself affected adolescent perceptions. Even among adults who used such information to decide, the information simply added to information

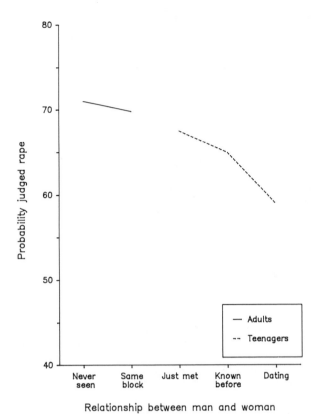

Figure 12.3 Probability that a vignette was judged a rape by the age cohort of the respondent and the relationship portrayed in the vignette. Data from the Los Angeles study, 1979, and Goodchilds et al., 1979.

about force; it did not interact with information about force as it did among teenagers.

One explanation for differences between adults and adolescents is that the two studies measured perceptions at two different points along the same continuum. The assumption here would be that the differences in acquaintanceship and location, as portrayed in the adults' vignettes, were too innocuous to have much effect on adult decisions, and were far too weak to interact with force to determine judgments about rape. Figures 12.2 and 12.3 show the influence that the location and relationship had on the decisionmaking of both adults and adolescents. In both figures it is assumed that the kind of information given to adolescents would be of greater relevance to decisionmaking about rapes and affect ratings more than the information given to adults. It is, for example, assumed that an encounter outside a market is less likely to lead to a sexual encounter than one that occurs at work. It is also assumed that a man and woman who happen to live on the same block are less likely to engage in sexual relations than a boy and girl who just met.

To be fully consistent with the interpretation proposed above, both the relationship and the location would have to influence decisions about rape significantly and interact with force to predict judgments. Contrary to this expectation, adolescents reacted differently to information about location than to information about the relationship. Whereas adults were mildly

Figure 12.4 Teenager's assurance that vignettes are rapes by relationship between male and female portrayed and level of force portrayed in vignette, Goodchilds et al., 1979

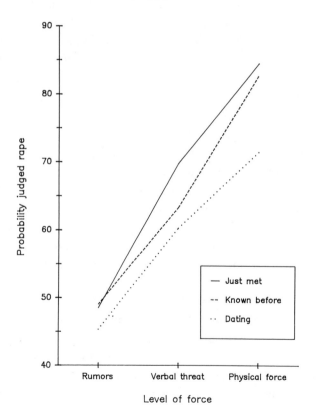

sensitive to both location and relationship, adolescents ignored information about location and were quite sensitive to information about the relationship. For adolescents, work, a girl's house, or a party were equally
likely locations for sex and, by implication, rape. Furthermore, all locations were neutral in their likelihood of being the scene of a rape. Rape
and, by implication, sex, was no more likely to occur at a girl's house or a
party than at work. In contrast, for adolescents the influence of being in a
dating relationship was clear. They considered rape or inappropriate sex
much less likely to occur in a dating relationship. It seems that adolescents equate rape with inappropriate sexuality rather than with violence.

Assuming that differences between adults and adolescents are real and
not methodological artifacts, what possible explanations are there for these
differences? Three can be identified. These explanations imply the existence of cohort differences and incomplete socialization on the part of
teenagers. First, it is possible that the adolescents studied were not as
homogeneous as implied by the reported analyses. The use of contrast
matrices or other techniques similar to those used in analyzing the adult
sample might demonstrate that adolescents also differ in the kinds of information they use in deciding about rapes and in their level of assurance that
a rape did or did not occur. Information available from other sections of
the study by Goodchilds et al. suggests that rape perceptions might differ
by sex, with adolescent females' decisions being more strongly and exclusively influenced by information on force.

If strong sex-linked differences transcending race were found in the
amount and type of information used by adolescents in making decisions,
they would contrast sharply with the Los Angeles County adults, who
showed only weak gender differences in their selective use of information.
Such a finding would suggest that intergenerational changes in sexual
norms exist that might exacerbate male-female miscommunication and
increase male attempts at nonconsensual sex that would be labeled rapes
by women.

If, in contrast, strong race-linked differences were found that tran-
scended gender, this would suggest the same diverging class stratification
in sexual scripts reported by Reed and Weinberg (1984) who found over a
thirty-year period that men's and women's sexual attitudes and behaviors
converged within social strata but diverged between strata. Such results
would forecast a likely decline in reports of intraracial rape and a possi-

ble increase in reports of interracial rape. In any case, discovery of strong racial or class-linked differences in adolescent perceptions would be in great contrast to findings concerning race-sex patterns among Los Angeles adults, because we failed to find any clearly definable differences by race and sex in our adult sample.

A second possibility is that Los Angeles adolescents' perceptions of rape are as homogeneous as presented. If this is the case, then the question becomes whether adolescent attitudes toward and perceptions of sexual assault are fully formed or are subject to further development and change. If the homogeneous patterns reported are fully formed, this suggests an interesting cohort effect. Unlike Los Angeles adults, attitudes of adolescents are both unisex and uniethnic. Such unanimity between men and women would suggest that miscommunication about sex should not occur within this cohort, and that the number of rapes occurring and reported would decline. Also contributing to a decline in rapes within the adolescent cohort would be their conservative definition of rape, which strongly reduces the possibility of rape.

A final possibility is that teenage perceptions of rape are largely unformed and subject to change should events occur that influence change. Adolescents' rejection of information about location might support this explanation. Either they have yet to learn society's perceptions of the appropriate location for sexual intercourse, or their perceptions of rape limit its occurrence to dark alleys and its perpetration to strangers. Although many of these adolescents had been sexually active, each one probably has had at most one extended sexual relationship. National norms as well as data from Los Angeles County show that the modal age for first intercourse is between 15 and 16 years of age, with lower-status non-Hispanic white and black females most active at the earliest ages and lower-status Hispanic females least active at young ages (Aneshensel, Fielder, and Becerra, 1988).

The reluctance among adolescents to label sexual assaults between dating couples as rape suggests that they have difficulty with the ambiguity of the situation being presented to them. To begin with, rape appears to be a foreign term from which they wish to distance themselves. To ask whether a sexual assault within an intimate relationship is a rape presents them with an incongruity that they find difficult to comprehend. Rapes are bad, violent things that happen to strangers. They are not events that occur in the context of what to adolescents are romantic relationships. To admit the possibility of rape between intimates, one first must think sexual assault is wrong and, second, one must have a definition that is broad enough to include the possibility that sexual assault could happen to oneself or someone one knows. For adolescents involved in their first close cross-sexual relationships, sexuality itself is scary enough without incorporating the possibilities for violence into the situation.

It is possible that adolescents' perceptions provide a barometer of society's norms to the point that they become an archetype or even stereotype of what they have absorbed from the culture they were exposed to while growing up. Children and adolescents are notoriously egocentric and engrossed in themselves, and generally hold conservative attitudes. Until challenged by events, peers, parents, or the institutional demands of school or work, an adolescent may not even verbalize a belief, let alone question it. Behaviors are cleanly characterized as good or bad, with no disturbing ambiguities.

In the study by Goodchilds et al., Los Angeles adolescents were challenged to deal with what was to them an ambiguity or perhaps even an absolute contradiction: sexual assault between intimates. Unlike other tasks with which they were presented in the study (in which they were asked to judge whether a boy and girl thought something sexual in connotation or denotation, or to apportion responsibility for sexuality), the vignettes suggested that enough violence might have occurred in a sexy situation to call it a rape. It may simply not have occurred to them that this could happen. Their repertoire of experience was insufficient to the task at hand.

If incomplete socialization explains the differences seen between adults and adolescents, then adolescents' perceptions of rape will change over the next few years as they are exposed to new experiences and ideas. To the extent that situations to which adolescents are exposed resemble those to which Los Angeles adults were exposed, we expect them to develop perceptions of rape resembling those of the Los Angeles adults.

13 Los Angeles in Context

In 1979, the diversity of attitudes about rape among residents of Los Angeles County resembled those of persons who were studied in other communities. What we learned in Los Angeles can be compared with what others have learned about Alabama females, blacks and whites in South Carolina, whites in Minnesota, black, white, and Hispanic residents of San Antonio, a nationwide sample of adolescents, and a tri-ethnic group of adolescents in Los Angeles (Klemmack and Klemmack, 1976; Feild and Bienen, 1980; Burt, 1980; Williams and Holmes, 1981; Ageton, 1983; Goodchilds et al., 1979). Direct comparisons between the samples are, however, complicated by the fact that sample means were rarely reported and the ways in which questions were asked, vignettes constructed, and answers solicited often differed significantly. As a result, and with the exception of the study of Los Angeles adolescents reviewed in the last chapter, the overall tendency of each group of respondents to think that vignettes they evaluated portrayed rape cannot easily be summarized and compared. We can, however, compare the demographic characteristics of Los Angeles respondents to those of the other adult samples. We can also compare Los Angeles respondents' rating behavior and what influenced it to respondents in all studies.

Demographic Comparison of Adult Samples

Los Angeles respondents and females studied in Alabama were the same age, but white subjects in Los Angeles were older than respondents studied in Minnesota, South Carolina, and Texas. Black respondents were comparable in age to blacks studied in Texas. Los Angeles residents had the same education as Alabama females, more education than Minnesota residents, and less education than South Carolina residents. Whites in Los Angeles had comparable education to whites in San Antonio; blacks in Los Angeles were more highly educated than blacks in San Antonio. The average income of whites and blacks in Los Angeles and San Antonio was comparable. Black and white men and women in Los Angeles were substantially less likely to be married, and had fewer children than residents in any of the other four adult studies. White Los Angeles residents were less likely than white San Antonio residents to be Protestant, but black respondents in the two cities were equally likely to be Protestant.

Methodological Differences across Studies

Differences in sampling and methodology across the seven studies must be kept in mind when evaluating the validity of interpretations made in this chapter. Specifically, we need to remember that:

1 The goal of the Ageton study, unlike the six other studies, was to investigate the extent to which young adults involved in sexual assaults differ from their peers.

2 The kinds of vignettes used in Los Angeles and in the other six studies differed substantially. Burt (1980) and Feild and Bienen (1980) asked each respondent to evaluate a single long vignette. Williams and Holmes and the Klemmacks asked each respondent to evaluate sets of short free-standing vignettes. Vignettes used by Goodchilds et al. to study adolescents in Los Angeles in 1979 most resembled those used in our study of Los Angeles adults in the same year. In both Los Angeles studies, each respondent was asked to evaluate a series of parsimonious vignettes including information that was fully crossed across the set of vignettes. The two Los Angeles studies differ in the number of variables included within a vignette, the number of vignettes given to each respondent, and the

number of levels each variable assumed. Whereas adolescents were asked to evaluate the full set of available vignettes (in which each of three variables assumed three different levels) and three filler vignettes, adults were asked to evaluate a one-eighth replicate of the full set of vignettes (in which each of eight variables assumed two different levels).

3 With the exception of Burt, all researchers report that information contained in vignettes significantly predicted respondents' decisions about sexual assaults portrayed.

The Influence of Information Contained in Vignettes

All studies found that force or violence had a major impact on decision-making. Sexual encounters involving high (usually physical) force were more likely to be judged rape. Ageton found that adolescents also were more likely to call a sexual encounter a rape if the man used physical force. With the exception of our study of adults in Los Angeles, none of the community studies directly examined the impact of resistance on decisionmaking. However, among Ageton's adolescents, as among adults in Los Angeles, the amount of resistance attempted differentiated rape from nonrape, and Feild and Bienen found indirect evidence that resistance influenced respondents' decisions.

The influence of prior acquaintanceship on decisionmaking was tested and found to have a significant impact on decisionmaking in five of the six studies. This was true even when, as in the adult Los Angeles study, the two levels at which it was tested varied between two seemingly innocuous conditions. The influence of acquaintanceship on decisions about rape increased as the intimacy of the portrayed relationship increased. Respondents in all studies consistently reported rape less when the man and woman knew each other. Differentiating friends from strangers or dating couples from acquaintances had a more powerful influence on decisions than did the innocuous distinction made in the Los Angeles study. Additionally, Ageton's adolescents were less likely than adults in the other studies to label an assault a rape if it involved a couple who dated regularly.

Information about sexual history was given to adults in Minnesota, South Carolina, and Los Angeles. In each study, sexual history influenced decisions of at least some respondents. The sexual encounters which portrayed the woman as already sexually experienced were generally not seen as rape.

Only in South Carolina and Los Angeles were adults asked to evaluate how the man's and woman's race affected decisionmaking. In both studies race influenced decisionmaking, but somewhat differently. Although some blacks in Los Angeles thought that black women were more likely to be victims and white males were more likely to be rapists, blacks in South Carolina did not use the race of either victim or defendant to make decisions. Whites in Los Angeles, like those in South Carolina, thought white women were more likely to be victims and black males more likely to be rapists. However, the magnitude of the racial influence on decisionmaking was much greater in South Carolina than in Los Angeles. In differentiating young adults who had been involved in sexual assaults from those who had not, Ageton found no racial differences. Other studies and official statistics have found intraracial rape to be much more common than crossracial rape. When interracial rape does occur, it has been found that black males rape white females more often than white males rape black females (LaFree, 1980, 1982).

The socioeconomic status of the man, found salient in the decisions of Indianapolis jurors (e.g., LaFree, Reskin, and Vischer, 1985), was tested only in Los Angeles where it did not influence decisionmaking.

Only in the adult and adolescent studies in Los Angeles were respondents asked directly to evaluate whether the location of the encounter influenced decisionmaking. However, investigators in South Carolina assessed its influence indirectly. While both groups of adults used location, in part, to arrive at decisions, adolescents did not.

While researchers in Los Angeles did not ask respondents to evaluate the influence of the woman's appearance on decisionmaking, Ageton did, and found that the woman's physical appearance, dress, and behavior did influence decisions about rape. Williams and Holmes found indirect evidence in support of this finding, but Feild and Bienen reported no influence of appearance on rape decisions.

Comparison of Nonvignette and Vignette Data on Rape

All the community studies used both vignettes and traditional questions to assess respondents' attitudes and opinions about rape. Most researchers tested associations between attitudes assessed with questionnaires and those obtained with vignettes, and found they were related. However, questionnaire data obtained from Los Angeles adults were not clearly associated with information obtained from their vignette ratings, and in some respects the two conflicted. This probably reflects differences in the way questions were structured for Los Angeles adults. In contrast to other studies, indices and scales could not be formed from the questions administered to Los Angeles adults. Compared with attitudes in San Antonio, attitudes in Los Angeles were both more liberal and more diverse. Los Angeles adults were much more likely than San Antonio adults to think that the race of the man and woman was irrelevant to rape. Females in the two cities differed sharply in their perceptions of the main cause of rape. Black females in Los Angeles were more likely than those in San Antonio to think that women's behaviors or male sexuality cause rape. White females from Los Angeles were less likely than white females from San Antonio to think that women's behaviors or male sexuality cause rape. Residents of the two cities also differed in their selection of solutions. Los Angeles residents selected a more diverse set of solutions. With the exception of white females, all Los Angeles residents were much less likely than San Antonio residents to think increased law and order would reduce rape. Los Angeles residents were more likely than San Antonio residents to think that rape could be reduced through fundamental social change, improved family life, religion, education, and treatment.

Differences found between residents in Los Angeles and San Antonio and Los Angeles and South Carolina suggest that race of victim and perpetrator is a salient factor in decisionmaking about rapes, but its saliency is more pronounced in the South than in the West.

Influence of Attitudes Toward Sex and Violence

Unlike many other studies, no data were collected about Los Angeles adults' attitudes toward sexuality, sexual behavior, or sex roles. The

Klemmacks, Burt, and Williams and Holmes all report that more conservative attitudes toward rape are predicted by or associated with more conservative attitudes toward sex and sex roles. Ageton, however, did not find that such attitudes differentiated persons involved in assaults from persons not involved. As in attribution studies, the findings are inconclusive and contradictory. It may be that the importance of such attitudes differs for observers and actors and that such attitudes are of more salience in predicting the kind of judgment an observer will make than in predicting the sexually assaultive behaviors of actors. To increase our understanding of the role played in decisionmaking by attitudes toward sex and sex roles, further study is needed.

Curiously underrepresented in data from community studies is the assessment of how attitudes toward violence and exposure to violence are associated with or predict definitions of rape. Only Ageton and Burt included such information. Both found that participation in violence, exposure to violence, or attitudes supportive of violence were related to attitudes about rape or were associated with being a victim or perpetrator of rape. However, associations were not always in the direction predicted. In particular, Burt found that exposure to violent pornography decreased men's belief in rape myths. In contrast, all other exposure to and evidence of violent or delinquent behavior and attitudes increased belief in rape myths and involvement in sexual assaults.

Definitions of rape among Los Angeles adults also were influenced by exposure to violence. Respondents who lived in high-crime areas were less likely than other subjects to think that sexual assaults were rapes, while respondents who felt vulnerable to crime and took measures to prevent it were more likely to think that sexual assaults were rapes. The tentative association between violence and sexual assault and the tendency to confuse sexuality with violence need to be more carefully tested in future community studies and in case-control studies of self-identified victims and rapists. If such relationships are replicated over time and are differentially distributed within the social structure, this might support Curtis's (1976) hypothesis that rape is the product of a violent counterculture, or Simpson's (1986) impression that men's need to demonstrate masculinity by sexually denigrating women has a long history traceable to the effects of European industrialization on urbanizing peasant families.

Demographic and Life-Style Influences

Although often ignored or minimized in community studies of rape, demographic and life-style characteristics do influence definitions of rape. Younger Los Angeles residents, like those in Minnesota, South Carolina, and Texas (but unlike those in Alabama) were more liberal in their definitions —saw more situations as rape—than did older residents. Consistent with Los Angeles adolescents and adults in South Carolina and Texas, Los Angeles women defined rape more liberally than men. The direct influence of race was tested only by Ageton and Williams and Holmes.

Definitions of rape differ with race or ethnicity in other studies, but patterns are not easily summarized. The general pattern is for blacks, particularly black men, to have more conservative attitudes about rape and to be less likely to think that sexual assaults are rapes. This tendency may be reduced or even reversed across different age groups and through exposure to education, religion, or crime.

Attitudes differ more consistently and more strongly with education than with any other demographic or life-style variable tested. Apparently, conservative attitudes about rape can be liberalized simply through exposure to further education. These findings suggest education as an intentional intervention tool, either with groups whose attitudes are not yet clearly formed or with groups such as police or judges whose attitudes and behaviors are relevant to the well-being of victims and to dealing with rapists.

To the extent that they have been tested, occupational status and income show a similar but weaker relationship with rape definitions. Persons with higher-status jobs or higher incomes have more liberal attitudes. Such associations are consistent for Alabama females, and adults in Los Angeles, Texas, Minnesota, and South Carolina. Income and social status do not, however, differentiate young adults who are assaulted from those who are not. As noted earlier in our discussion of the influence of sex-role attitudes and sexuality on rape judgments, income and social status may influence observers' judgments about sexual assaults without differentiating those involved in assaults from others.

Only a few researchers have investigated the influence of religion, marital status, number of children, and characteristics of the family of origin on perceptions of rape. When reported, these life-style characteristics appear to influence attitudes, but data are insufficient to know how this influence occurs. In Los Angeles marital status and household composition influenced decisions differently in the six rating groups. Most intriguing are reports that women who were raised with brothers differ in their exposure to and attitudes about sexual assault (Kanin and Parcell, 1977; Klemmack and Klemmack, 1976). When combined with Burt's observations about exposure to violence during childhood, this suggests that longitudinal cross-generational studies might be useful to determine how attitudes and behaviors supportive of sexual assault are transmitted across generations.

Part IV Conclusions and Implications

14 Defining Rape in the United States

The premise underlying this book is that definitions of rape are more diverse than is generally acknowledged. This diversity has ramifications for reporting, preventing, intervening in, and treating rape, as well as for conducting research on the topic. Diverse definitions were found in all areas of research reviewed and in all community studies examined. Although we found regular differences across studies and areas of research, we were unable to ascertain from them precisely who is at greatest risk of rape, who is most likely to commit rape, and who holds opinions and attitudes supportive of rape. Definitions varied with respondents' location in the social structure, education, perceptions of and attitudes towards violence and sexuality, and perceptions of attitudes and behaviors of those around them. At the same time, substantial numbers of persons across the nation use technically irrelevant, extra-evidentiary information to decide whether a rape occurred or find it difficult to call any sexual assault rape.

While our inability to understand why men rape and some women tolerate it may in part reflect inadequate knowledge within this relatively new area of research, our lack of understanding also may have something to do with our extreme reluctance to think of rape as just one of many violent and sexual behaviors in which humans engage. Clearly many persons find it difficult to call even a violent sexual encounter a rape.

The tendency to separate rape from other human behavior has two unfortunate results. First, it ignores the wide variety of behaviors between men and women that technically meet the definition of rape. Second, it ignores the fact that rape differs in degree but not in kind from other violent and sexual interactions. If we are to lower the tolerance for rape and develop consistent sanctions for dealing with violators, we must understand the wide range of behaviors rape encompasses. As matters stand, large segments of the population, if not the majority, continue to equate rape with attacks by strangers in dark alleys. Acceptance and application of such a narrow definition of rape allows people to distance themselves from rape, and to see it as irrelevant to their lives and as an activity for which they have no responsibility.

Deciding It Was Rape

When a man forces intercourse on a woman it is rape. Rape is a crime, an act society says it will not tolerate and whose perpetrators it will punish. Many states include a variety of other forced sexual behaviors within the category of acts they define as intolerable and worthy of punishment. In spite of extensive efforts by reformers, it is still unclear whether persons understand or agree with the original, common-law definition of rape, let alone with expanded statutory definitions. Among those who disagree are many persons who play crucial roles in deciding whether a sexual encounter is a rape. These include the potential victim, the alleged offender, family and friends, health personnel in hospitals and clinics, counselors, and police.

The Possible Victim

Without a victim, there is no crime. If it never occurs to the assaulted woman that she was the recipient of antisocial behavior, if she does not complain to the perpetrator or tell a relative or friend what occurred, the sexual assault will not be defined as rape. Research reviewed in this book repeatedly reports that women vary in the extent to which they define sexually demeaning or assaultive behavior as criminal. Probably only a very few define repeated sexual innuendo or continued brushing up against them in a work area as deserving of formal sanction. Even when such behavior makes the woman consciously uncomfortable, concerns for herself or the man often result in action being delayed or repressed.

Even more problematic from the point of view of those wishing to increase women's autonomy and freedom from physical victimization are some women's tendencies to ignore or excuse increasingly sexually coercive behaviors by men they know. Apparently, some women continue to tolerate unwanted sex in exchange for the security or status of a stable relationship. Evidence suggests that in an ongoing relationship women often tolerate coercion that they would not tolerate on a first date. A man's excuses that he could not control himself because he became too excited or because he thought the woman was excited may serve for some women as a status symbol or a symbol of continued desirability and attractiveness. So these women do not protest.

Perceptions that sexual coercion and assault are unacceptable and intolerable differ somewhat with a woman's location in society and probably with her access to other methods of obtaining status and recognition from society in general and from men in particular. Younger, highly educated women are most likely to define assaultive behavior as inappropriate and worthy of sanction; however, they are not necessarily more likely to report sexual assaults to police or other authorities. These women are most likely to have been exposed to, and to have accepted, contemporary feminist perceptions regarding roles of men and women. They are more likely to have access to resources that promote self-determination and free them from dependence on husbands or fathers for status or economic well-being. In spite of their greater recognition that sexual assault is rape, their continued tendency to distance themselves from rape may lead them to ignore cues indicative of imminent sexual assault. The relatively high prevalence of date rape among college students indicates that, in spite of the presumed greater sexual sophistication of college women, something is awry in the relationships of some college-age men and women.

Among less sophisticated women with more restrictive definitions of rape, three possible explanations exist for their belief that rape is a highly unusual and extreme behavior of little relevance to their own lives. The first interpretation is that these women have never been assaulted and they therefore conclude that rape is limited to the lunatic fringe portrayed by the stereotype of the classic rape. The little research evidence available suggests that this reasoning may be most characteristic of older, majority-culture women.

The second interpretation is that these women have been assaulted to a lesser or greater extent, but fail or refuse to identify the assault as a rape because it occurred within a long-term or intimate relationship. In this instance, recognition of the assault as criminal could threaten not only the woman's relationship with the man but also her definition of herself and possibly her interactions with an entire social network. This reaction may be characteristic of rarely studied, nonblack minorities. Certainly data on Hispanic women, reported by Williams and Holmes, are consistent with this interpretation.

The third interpretation is that women indeed recognize the violence of their sexual encounters, but accept it as within the bounds of normal sexuality and see sexual violence as just another variant of the violence that permeates their lives. Like the prior group of women they see no escape from their life situations but, unlike the prior group, they may adopt a variety of behaviors to protect themselves from the effects of sexual and other kinds of violence in interactions with men. Lower-class black women's perceptions of rape as reported in Los Angeles and San Antonio appear to fit this pattern of reasoning. Williams and Holmes (1981) suggested that black women's reactions to rape are pragmatic and oriented to the basic survival of the individual (p. 172).

Male Perpetrators

Like females, males differ in their recognition and acceptance of the normality of sexual assault. Education and social status tend to differentiate males who recognize sexual assault as demeaning and criminal from those who do not. At the same time, date rapes by college males, and admission by some that they would rape if they thought they could get away with it, indicate that education alone does not prevent sexual assault (Kanin, 1984; Koss and Leonard, 1984; Malamuth, 1986).

It may be that men who feel inadequate in their ability to compete with peers or to develop satisfying heterosexual relationships are at greatest risk of being sexually coercive. Some have suggested that the mystique of masculinity and the need to feel "macho" is greatest among those who have the least autonomy over their own lives (e.g., Simpson, 1986). Others suggest that men who resort to sexual violence are "wimps" who are chronic failures in other areas of their lives (Sanders, 1980). Such perceptions of rapists are consistent with clinical studies that find incarcerated rapists often have inadequate or poorly developed social skills. Such perceptions are also consistent with studies in which self-identified rapists reported atypically high needs for coital sex, perceptions of support by peer groups for their activities, and greater exposure to, participation in, and acceptance of other types of nonsexual violence or deviance (e.g., Ageton, 1983; Kanin, 1984).

Male feelings of inferiority may be absolute or relative. Lower-class high school dropouts, for example, are definitely at a disadvantage even within communities where their fathers and grandfathers similarly failed to complete high school. Unlike past generations, failure to obtain a high school degree or its equivalent may preclude upward mobility, or steady employment, except in menial or illegal jobs. Reasons for college date rapists to feel deprived are much less obvious to an observer. But these men may feel inferior to or unable to compete successfully with male peers.

Unfortunately, there continues to be a population of women for sexually coercive men to victimize. Like their victimizers the most vulnerable women may be those who have poor self-concepts and are unable to see themselves interacting with men on other than a sexual basis. Effective resistance, even in situations where slight resistance might suffice, appears to be beyond these women's psychological means even when it is within their physical ability. The consequence is that an initially unsure male adolescent's sexually coercive behavior is rewarded by lack of resistance. Each further success reinforces his image that such behavior is both possible and appropriate. If sexual assault also enhances his self-perception of his standing among his peers, further assault is likely.

Support Groups of Families and Friends

Clearly the social network of which young men and women are part influences perceptions and decisions about sexual assault. It seems clear that women who cannot admit even to themselves that they were assaulted will not discuss the event with family or friends. Women who recognize on some level that they were assaulted or coerced into sex may purposely or inadvertently tell relatives or friends about it in an effort to define and deal with the experience. Others, knowing that family and friends think women are responsible for rape, may intentionally avoid such discussions. This would be particularly likely if the woman herself thought her own behavior had contributed to the assault. Family and friends, when told, can reinforce the woman's perception or even define the assaultive or coercive behavior as criminal for her. Conversely, family and friends may attempt to dissuade the woman from identifying the behavior as unusual or from reporting it.

The role of friends and family in the development of attitudes about sexuality and violence should not be overlooked. Parents, older siblings, and other older relatives serve as models for adolescents when they are first experimenting with adult sexuality. Observations of sexually demeaning or coercive behavior between parents or siblings and their friends undoubtedly influence an adolescent's perception of what constitutes appropriate heterosexual interaction. Friends likewise serve as models for behavior and probably as the major sounding board for discussion of early sexual experimentation and exploits. Although some studies have investigated the influence of family and friends on women's reporting of rape and postrape recovery, the extent to which women's attitudes and definitions about rape match those of best friends and family is unknown. Evidence indicating that peer groups do influence the sexually coercive behavior of men suggests that similar interactions occur within women's peer groups.

Police

Police control a rape victim's entry into the judicial system. A policeman's receptivity to investigating a charge of rape strongly influences its later judicial status. Immediate and careful collection of evidence increases the probability that the offender will be arrested and charged. Although rape laws have undergone extensive revision, the influence of these revisions on police is largely unknown. When educational programs targeting police officers were not incorporated into reform legislation, new legal statutes may have had little direct or indirect influence on their behavior and attitudes. The working-class family background of many police officers suggests that their attitudes would be conservative, and the few studies of attitudes about rape among police officers confirm that their attitudes are among the community's most conservative. They frequently express skepticism about women who report rapes and often deny the violence inherent in the act (e.g., Feild and Bienen, 1980; Battelle Institute, 1977). Such opinions clearly act to discourage a sexual assault victim from pursuing a rape complaint.

Rape Counselors

In contrast to police, rape counselors are more likely to include a broad range of sexually coercive and assaultive behaviors within their definition of rape. Rape counselors generally come from the majority culture, are often highly educated white women, and often were themselves rape victims. As Williams and Holmes (1981) cogently point out, the predominance of white women among rape counselors presents a potentially dysfunctional match between counselor and client. To the extent that recognition of sexual assault differs with ethnicity and education, uneducated minority women may feel particularly hesitant about utilizing available services. Moreover, research in other health care areas has shown repeatedly that unavailability of money and lack of knowledge about how to gain access to services has been found to restrict minority women's use of medical and psychological services. A woman's propensity to use other kinds of health services probably influences her propensity to seek assistance after sexual assault.

Since victims at counseling centers have been a major focus of study by rape researchers, little is known about how victims who have identified themselves to authorities compare to those who have not. The few studies available have focused on college women whose knowledge of and ability to gain access to services can be assumed to be high.

Once a woman gets to a rape counseling program, the kind and duration of assistance needed probably reflects her images of rape and the extent to which pre-assault attitudes and assumptions are undergoing change. Whereas some women may need help to decide whether to report the assault or press charges, others may need help to revise and restructure their perceptions of what constitutes normal heterosexual behavior.

Implications for Policy and Practice

Research reviewed in this book emphasizes the diversity that exists in rape definitions, and the difficulty men and women in all socially definable subgroups have in recognizing rape within their own environments. As with crimes of all types, residents of the United States want to believe that rape only occurs in other people's neighborhoods. Before rape and other kinds of sexually coercive behaviors can be eliminated, their existence must be recognized.

Rape has received increased public attention over the last ten years, largely due to antirape activists. In order to catch public attention many presentations are, of necessity, simplistic in nature. Little effort is made to recognize the complex, diverse, and often highly emotional attitudes about sexuality, violence, and male-female interactions that predict whether an individual can recognize rape, let alone cope with it. Too often, presentations portray rape as a singular, extreme behavior differentiated from other behaviors both in kind and in degree. Such presentations simply reinforce many recipients' need to deny the relevance of such information for themselves. That part of the audience which is lost may well be made up of those persons most vulnerable to rape. Even if such people are able to hear the message, they may not have the resources to use the information. It is of little value to tell a teenager that he or she is at risk of being a victim or perpetrator of date rape if he or she does not have the skills to recognize and extricate him- or herself from such situations.

The situation is not unlike that found when discrepancies exist between diagnosis and treatment of physical illness. Debates about the efficacy of developing sophisticated screening programs for diseases for which we have no effective treatment are endless. Often, diagnostic screening can discern persons in the early stages of a disease (e.g., AIDS and ARC), but the ethical considerations of telling the patient must be balanced against the benefits.

Research reviewed in this book suggests that two interrelated problems permeate the way the study of rape has been approached over the last ten years. First, significant numbers of the population are so threatened by the word "rape" that they simply avoid information that might lead them to see rape as an act that encompasses a wide range of sexually coercive behaviors, some of which apply to them. Second, recognizable but not necessarily insurmountable dangers exist in encouraging people to see rape as only the endpoint of a range of sexually coercive behaviors. To the extent that people are encouraged to broaden their definition of rape to include an increasingly broad range of nonconsensual sexual behaviors, they must be provided with skills to help them rectify or extricate themselves from situations they now define as wrong.

Social Change

Heterosexual violence will be reduced only when an increased societal concern with human dignity allows women the right to control their own destiny, when the debilitating effects of violence are confronted, and when inequities in resource allocation are put right. Heterosexual assault has a long tradition whose beginnings are lost in the dust of history. Although social change sometimes appears to take an interminably long time, the value placed on human life has increased over the last 200 years and the quality of relationships between males and females has improved markedly. Historians and other researchers differ in their explanations of these changes, their predictions regarding the direction of future change, and the extent to which they think social change can be actively influenced. Always of interest and actively debated is the extent to which social change can be orchestrated. One solution is not to attempt to orchestrate changes in discrete specific behaviors, but to concentrate on larger social movements. This scenario suggests that heterosexual violence will not decline or disappear until certain structural conditions of society change. Alternatively, Williams and Holmes (1981) and others argue that the momentum for social change will stop or its direction reverse if social pressure is not maintained within certain carefully targeted areas.

Effective social intervention involves legal reform, efficient communication with constituencies, and control over allocation of resources. In contrast to numerous other areas of social legislation, reform of rape legislation occurred early and with remarkable ease. Rape reform, like school desegregation, has the potential to be an area in which efforts to legislate social change can be evaluated. Although a plurality of respondents in both Los Angeles and Texas thought tougher laws and punishment were the most effective way to reduce rape, these same respondents' perceptions of rape are often too conservative to allow them to take full advantage of currently reformed statutes. To date, the new legal definitions appear to have had little effect on people's perceptions of rape or their propensity to define sexual assaults as criminal behaviors.

Public Education

Public education is one method that might increase people's understanding of revised legislation while simultaneously bridging the chasm that many think exists between rape and normal sexual relationships. Public education campaigns that explain the four degrees of sexual assault found in statutes such as Michigan's law would help demonstrate the continuum that exists between mutually consensual sex and rape. Such campaigns could simultaneously provide recipients with information about how to approach and negotiate the judicial system.

Within the judicial system, judges and attorneys could be encouraged to include questions in voir dire to sensitize potential jurors to their own preconceptions regarding rape. Expert witnesses could be called to testify to the range of perceptions held about rape and the extent to which people deny the existence of rape (e.g., Feild and Bienen, 1981; Borgida and White, 1981).

In making presentations, those who disseminate information to the public should be encouraged to soften their message and try to include within it some recognition of the complexities that underlie perceptions of rape. One suggestion would be to avoid the highly charged word "rape." Terms like "date rape" are catchy, but when combined on the cover of a pamphlet with a menacing dark shadow, the viewer may decide not to read the pamphlet. Incorporating information on date rape into more general information about dating behaviors might alleviate initial aversion. Using terms such as nonconsensual or coercive sex, or even sexual assault, or incorporating discussion of sexual assault into more general discussions of criminal behavior might make it easier for people to hear the messages being delivered. Recognizing that excuses used to deny the occurrence or responsibility for rape are used widely by both men and women might increase audience receptivity and involvement. The point here is to encourage people to see rape as simply the extreme point on a behavioral continuum of sexual and violent behaviors in which human beings unfortunately choose to engage. The assumption is that if people can accept rape as one of a continuum of activities, they will be better able to examine their own attitudes and behaviors and change those that are destructive to themselves or others.

Adolescent Education

Adolescents and their parents are probably the best groups to target for educational programs. Teenagers are appropriate targets for two reasons. First, they are beginning their adult sexual lives and are probably more concerned with sexuality than older adults. Second, evidence from the two Los Angeles studies suggests that adolescent perceptions of what constitutes appropriate sexual behavior are only partially formed and thus, if properly approached, teenagers may well be more receptive than adults to competing points of view and possible change.

Ideally, programs would be available as part of the normal school curriculum, would be provided more than once during junior high and high school, and would involve all students. Emphasis would be on getting students to understand the diversity of their preconceptions about sexuality, violence, and sexual violence and to understand the extent to which miscommunication occurs between boys and girls. Techniques that might be used include role-playing, vignettes, group discussion, and the adaptation of measures such as those used by Goodchilds et al. and Koss in their research.

Problems include finding the time, resources, and support for such programs. The support of parents, teachers, school boards, and community institutions such as the church would be essential for establishing specific programs. Given many adults' continued reluctance to acknowledge sexual assault, and continued community disapproval of school-based health clinics and sex education classes, parents may see heterosexual violence as a low-priority curricular concern. They may feel that attention might more profitably be focused on drugs or other prevalent adolescent behaviors.

To counter these barriers, we might convince teachers to merge the study of sexual violence into a broader health curriculum. A second solution would be to defuse parental objections by attempting to involve them in program development and administration. A third solution would be to develop programs outside schools in health clinics and community centers serving large numbers of adolescents. The disadvantage of the last approach is that it would probably significantly reduce the number of adolescent boys who were exposed to such information.

Educational programs aimed at other groups in the community also merit consideration and expansion. The general disadvantage of programs targeted at nonadolescents is that they are less likely to reach members of the community who could most profit from such information.

Future Research

Throughout this book we have identified gaps in knowledge and possibilities for future research. Of greatest urgency is the need to develop a consistent terminology that is used across studies. Prevalence needs to be clearly differentiated from incidence; attempted rape needs to be clearly differentiated from completed rape; and rape needs to be clearly differentiated from all other kinds of coercive sexual behavior. The methods used must assure that both acknowledged and unacknowledged events are being reported, and that questions are sufficiently explicit without being unduly threatening. A constant age boundary needs to be established for differentiating childhood sexual molestations from adult molestations.

Ageton (1983) rightly pointed out that little effort has been made to integrate information about causes, consequences, and findings across studies. One reason is the difficulty of making comparisons across studies that use different sampling procedures and focus on different age groups, different ethnicities, and different social classes. Response rates differ as do data collection and measurement techniques. Comparison becomes particularly problematic when studies differ in their theoretical perspectives and study different populations. For example, problems are obvious in any attempt to compare findings from an attribution study using college students with those from a clinically oriented study of rape victims.

Not only are problems related to lack of consistency across community studies; there are also significant discrepancies between findings in the community and official crime statistics. Research as reviewed in this book suggests that groups defined by ethnicity and social class differ in the extent to which they acknowledge rape. Black respondents in Los Angeles were less likely to consider a sexual encounter a rape. Yet, consistent with other areas of the country, black females were more likely to report completed or attempted rapes to officials or to the National Crime Panel. Why do these discrepancies exist? Do discrepancies reflect differences in methodology? Do they reflect differences in willingness to acknowledge and report sexual assault, or perhaps differences in the severity of the assault or intensity of the relationship between victim and offender? Much more research needs to focus on explicating these differences. Creative multimethod or crossover designs might be used to resolve some of the discrepancies. For example, items used in the National Crime Panel might be administered with those used in one or more research studies. Either a crossover design could be used or two or more equivalent samples might be drawn from the same population.

Measures of exposure to the cultural mainstream need to be developed and related to studies of rape. As in much of the sex role research, middle-class white women have most frequently been studied in their roles as members of families, housewives, students, and workers. Rape research-ers know most about white females and least about nonwhite men and women. Assumptions about men and women of all ethnicities and races are probably buried within many of the studies. Unstructured or semistructured interviews should be conducted with all groups, but partic-ularly with nonwhites. Interviews similar to those conducted by Spence and Sawin (1985) might explore the attitudes and expectations men and women bring to heterosexual relationships; their images of consensual, nonconsensual, coercive, and assaultive sex; and their concepts of mascu-linity and femininity. Findings could be compared with current knowledge about rape and used to modify research instruments used to elicit informa-tion from respondents.

More detailed and varied studies are needed to assess whether and how rape relates to measures of personality, sexuality, and violence, and the extent to which such characteristics are amenable to change. We need to study the roles that peer groups and families play in overtly and covertly encouraging solicitation and acceptance of heterosexual violence. In addi-tion, we need innovative ways to study the dynamics of male-female interactions.

The community studies reviewed in this book could appropriately be replicated and expanded. Good baseline data exist for Texas, Minnesota, South Carolina, and California. Replicating all or part of each study would enable us to estimate the extent and pace of social change. Expansion of each study to include material from other studies, comprehensive measures of prevalence and incidence, and relevant new material would allow researchers to make direct rather than inferential comparisons across geographic areas of the country. We might also want to include measures developed in attribution studies. Samples of respondents might be expanded to include family members, friends, and significant others, the better to study interactions between persons and similarity of attitudes within definable social groups.

By designing and implementing longitudinal studies on perceptions about rape, we could evaluate the extent to which new legal statutes and increased publicity have helped change attitudes and behaviors. We also need careful studies of judicial processing. Such investigations should be conducted across jurisdictions, across time, and across crimes. They should not depend exclusively on statistical records, but should include data collected using ethnographic observational methods and attitude surveys.

Finally, much more sophisticated vignettes could be developed and used more widely to study rape and sexual assault as well as other violent crimes. Vignettes used in Los Angeles and in the other studies reviewed were quite primitive. Instead of varying three to eight variables between two to three levels, vignettes could be constructed for which each variable took on a large variety of content (e.g., Nock and Rossi, 1984). Whereas vignettes in Los Angeles portrayed a range from consensual sex to rape, future studies could be done in which vignettes were first used to screen out subgroups. Then subgroups at the extremes, such as nonraters and nonnormative raters in Los Angeles, could be reinterviewed with sets of vignettes designed to identify the threshold at which they differentiate rape from other sexual behaviors.

Vignettes could be used to explore how violent sexual acts contrast with violent nonsexual acts, and how sexual excitement, drugs, and alcohol influence decisions about rape. Identical sets of vignettes could be designed and used to compare perceptions of rape victims, police, rape counselors, and rape perpetrators. Carefully designed vignettes might help untangle the ways in which indicators of force, resistance, and consent are confused with each other and with other technically irrelevant aspects of sexual encounters. Such vignettes could also be used to differentiate among consensual, nonconsensual, coercive, and assaultive sex.

Although our study in Los Angeles and other studies across the nation have begun to elucidate how Americans feel and think about rape, clearly we still have much to learn. The possibilities for research are endless. Like most research projects, our investigation ends with more questions than it had in the beginning.

Appendix 1 Questionnaire Used in the Los Angeles Study

Confidential Questionnaire
Respondent I.D. number:
Vignette I.D. number:
AI Interviewer:
I.D.
A2 Time beginning:
Time ending:
Number of minutes:

Your opinions are very important. You have been scientifically chosen to represent other people like yourself. Your cooperation in this interview will be a definite public service. *Everything you tell us will be strictly confidential. Your name will not be connected in any way with the findings of this important study.* We will be asking you to rate a stack of cards that have short statements about sexual contacts between men and women. Each card describes a possible rape. The information you provide will be treated with the utmost confidentiality by the University of California. Nothing will be published except numerical summaries.

Before we continue with this interview, I would like you to read and sign this form. It contains some information about the project. It also indicates that you understand the nature of the study and that you agree to participate, with the option of dropping out of the study at any time.

Circle one: Respondent signed form   I
                 Respondent initialed form   2
                 Respondent did not *sign or initial form*   3

1 I would like you to rate a stack of cards that have short statements about sexual contacts between men and women. Each card describes a possible rape. Read the top card that describes what you are going to do while I read the instructions.

Allow respondent to read carefully.
Now show respondent board and explain . . .

As you can see, there are six envelopes on this board, numbered one (1) through six (6). Each card describes a possible rape. If you feel that a rape *was definitely not* committed, you would rate it "1". If you feel a rape *definitely was* committed, rate it "6". Use the envelopes labeled "2", "3", "4", or "5" to rate cards that you are less sure about. If you tend to think a rape *was not* committed, use "2" or "3". If you tend to think a rape *was* committed, use "4" or "5". After you have rated a card, put it in the envelope with the number that matches your rating. Each card is different; similar cards will differ by at least one word, so please read each card carefully and base your rating on *only* the information on the card you are reading. There is no right or wrong answer. It is *your* opinion as to whether or not there was a rape.

When respondent has read card with instructions, read:

Now read the second card. This is the first card that you are going to rate.

Allow respondent to rate card.

Now please rate these cards as you did the first card. Rate each card in the order given to you. Do *not* rearrange the cards, or go back to reread a card you have already rated.

Hand respondent rest of deck for rating.
Record time respondent begins to rate vignettes
Record time respondent ends rating vignettes
Number of minutes

Move vignette board and packets so that they are out of respondent's direct line of vision.

Now that you have finished rating all the cards, I would like to ask you a few questions.

2 Was there any rating (envelope or number) that you used more than the others? (*Do not let respondents look at packets.*)
 Yes (*Ask* A)
 No (*Skip to* Q3)
 Don't know (*Ask* A)

A Which rating (did/do) you think you use(d) most often?
    One
    Two
    Three
    Four
    Five
    Six
    Don't know (*Skip to* Q3)
    No answer (*Skip to* Q3)
B Why do you think you used that rating the most?
    Don't know

3 Was there any additional information that you would have found particularly helpful in deciding how to rate the cards?
    Yes (*Ask* A)
    No (*Skip to* Q4)
    Don't know (*Ask* A)
A Can you tell me what that would be?
    Don't know

4 Was there any information that you did *not* use in making up your mind?
    Yes (*Ask* A)
    No (*Skip to* Q5)
    Don't know (*Ask* A)
A Can you tell me what that was?

5 Were there any cards that you found particularly difficult to rate?
    Yes (*Ask* A)
    No (*Skip to* Q6)
    Don't know (*Ask* A)
A Can you describe them?
    Don't know

6 Was there anything that you found particularly upsetting or that made you uncomfortable about rating the cards?
    Yes (*Ask* A)
    No (*Skip to* Q7)
    Don't know (*Ask* A)
A What was that?
    Don't know

Now I am going to ask you some questions about how you feel about crime. We are interested in citizens' opinions about the nature of crime in Los Angeles.

7 Is there any area right around your home—that is, within five blocks in any direction—where you would be afraid to walk alone at night?

Yes

No

Don't know

8 To what extent are you *afraid* of being robbed, or having somebody take or try to take something from you by force when you are *outside your home and in your neighborhood*? Would you say:

A great deal,

Some,

A little, or

Not much at all?

Don't know

No answer

9 How much do you *worry* about being robbed while *you are in your home*? Would you say:

A great deal,

Some,

A little, or

Not much at all?

Don't know

No answer

10 How much are you *afraid* of being assaulted or physically attacked when you are *in your neighborhood but not in your home*? Do you worry:

A great deal,

Some,

A little, or

Not much at all?

Don't know

No answer

11 How much are you *afraid* about being assaulted or physically attacked *in your home*? Do you worry:

A great deal,

Some,

A little, or

Not much at all?

Don't know

No answer

12 How *likely* do you think it is that you will be robbed or assaulted *in your neighborhood*—but not in your home—in the coming year? Would you say:

Very likely,
Likely,
Somewhat likely,
Not very likely, or
Not likely at all?
Don't know
No answer

13 How *likely* do you think it is that you will be robbed or assaulted *in your own home* in the coming year? Would you say:
Very likely,
Likely,
Somewhat likely,
Not very likely, or
Not likely at all?
Don't know
No answer

14 Now, thinking about the *number of assaults and robberies* that have occurred in your neighborhood in the *past six months*, would you say that you have a:
Good idea of how many there have been,
A fair idea,
Some idea of how many, or
Not much of an idea at all?
Don't know
No answer

15 In your opinion, how many assaults and robberies have occurred in your neighborhood in the last six months?
(*Record as given*)
Don't know
No answer

Now I would like to ask you some questions about burglary, that is, about a person breaking into or somehow illegally getting into someone else's home or apartment so that they can take someone else's property.

16 How *afraid* are you of someone burglarizing or breaking into your (home/apartment)? Would you say:
A great deal,
Some,
A little, or
Not much at all?
Don't know
No answer

17 How *likely* do you think that it is that your (home/apartment) will be burglarized or broken into *at night* when you are away during the next year? Do you
think that it is:
> Very likely,
> Likely,
> Somewhat likely,
> Not very likely, or
> Not likely at all?
> Don't know
> No answer

18 How *likely* do you think that it is that your home would be broken into *during
the day*? Do you think that it is:
> Very likely,
> Likely,
> Somewhat likely,
> Not very likely, or
> Not likely at all?
> Don't know
> No answer

19 Now thinking about the *number of burglaries* that have occurred in your neighborhood in the past six months, would you say that you have:
> A good idea of how many there have been,
> A fair idea,
> Some idea, or
> Not much of an idea at all?
> Don't know
> No answer

20 In your opinion, how many burglaries have occurred in your neighborhood in
the past six months?
> (*Record as given*)
> Don't know
> No answer

Next I am going to ask you some questions about crime in general.

21 Do you think that being a victim of a crime *in your own neighborhood* depends
on how much you do to try and protect yourself? Would you say:
> A great deal,
> Some,
> A little, or
> Not much at all?

Don't know
No answer

22 Compared to other neighborhoods in Los Angeles, do you think that crime in
your neighborhood is:
Much more serious,
More serious,
About as serious,
Less serious, or
Much less serious?
Don't know
No answer

23 Who do you think is more to blame for crime, the individual or society?
Individual
Society
Both about the same
Neither
Don't know
No answer

People do different things to protect themselves against crime. We are interested in whether or not you have done anything to protect yourself against
crime.

24 When you go out *at night* do you ever take steps to protect yourself such as
taking a dog along, asking someone to walk with you, or carrying a whistle
or something like that?
Yes
No
Do not go out at night
Don't know
No answer

25 When you *leave your home*, do you lock up *both* the doors and windows?
Would you say:
Always,
Usually,
Sometimes,
Seldom, or
Never?
Don't know
No answer

26 How often do you lock your front door when you are *at home* in the *evening*? Would you say:

Always,
Usually,
Sometimes,
Seldom, or
Never?
Don't know
No answer

27 How often do you leave your lights burning when you are *not* at home for the purposes of protection? Would you say:

Always,
Usually,
Sometimes,
Seldom, or
Never?
Don't know
No answer

28 Some people have taken steps to protect their home against burglary. Others have not. How about you? In the last *five* years have you done any of the following:

A Put additional locks on the doors and windows?
B Put bars on the doors and windows?
C Put an alarm in your home or car?
D Bought a dog for protection?
E Bought a gun for protection?
F Is there anything (else) that you have done to protect yourself from crime?

Yes (specify)
No
Don't know
No answer

Now I am going to ask you a few questions about your opinion on rape.

29 When you hear the term *rape*, what is the *first* word that comes to your mind? Just give me *one* word that you first associate with rape. (*Record.*)

30 Do you think a woman who gets raped is *different* from other women *before* she is raped?

Yes (*Ask* A)
No (*Skip to* Q31)

A How is she different? (*Probe for up to three responses; record verbatim.*)

31 Do you think she is different *after* she is raped?
   Yes (*Ask* A)
   No (*Skip to* Q32)
   A How is she different? (*Probe for up to three responses; record verbatim.*)

32 Do you think a man who commits rape is *different* from other men *before* he rapes?
   Yes (*Ask* A)
   No (*Skip to* Q33)
   A How is he different? (*Probe for up to three responses; record verbatim.*)

33 Do you think he is different *after* he rapes?
   Yes (*Ask* A)
   No (*Skip to* Q34)
   A How is he different? (*Probe for up to three responses; record verbatim.*)

34 Do you think that rapists should be hospitalized for treatment for mental illness, or do you think rapists should be put in prison?
   Hospitalized, treated
   Put in prison
   Both
   Neither
   Don't know
   No answer

35 In your own words, how would you define rape (i.e., what do you think rape is)?
   Don't know
   No answer

36 What do you think the legal definition of rape is in California?
   Don't know
   No answer

37 In your opinion, what is the *main* cause of rape? (*Probe for up to three responses; record verbatim.*)

   Refer to Q37.
   If only one response to Q37, skip to Q38.
   If more than one response to Q37, ask A.

   A Of those things mentioned, (*Repeat responses from Q37*), which *one* thing do you think is the main cause of rape?

38 When men rape women, do you think they rape women who are from their own race or ethnic group or from a race or ethnic group that is different from their own?

From their own race or ethnic group (i.e., both rapist and victim are white, or both are black), or

From a race or ethnic group different from their own (i.e., black men raping white women, or white men raping black women)?

It doesn't matter/Race not important

Don't know

39 In your opinion, what is the one thing that would *reduce* rape the most? (*Probe for up to three responses; record verbatim.*)

Refer to Q39.
If only one *response to Q39, skip to Q40.*
If more than *one response to Q39, ask* A.

A Of those things you mentioned, (*Repeat responses from Q39*), which *one* thing do you think would reduce rape the most? (*Record number of the response given.*)

No one thing/About the same

40 Do you think the number of rapes in Los Angeles has increased, decreased, or stayed about the same in the last *5 years*?

Increased

Decreased

Stayed about the same

Don't know

No answer

Now I would like to ask some background information about you and your household.

41 What is your *current* employment status? Are you:

Working full-time,

Working part-time,

Unemployed,

Retired,

Keeping house,

In school, or

Something else? (specify)

A Have you ever been employed?

Yes (*Ask about* usual *or* last *employment in* B)

No (*Skip to* Q42)

B Do/did you work as:

Self-employed in your own business (not incorporated) (or farm),

Self-employed in your own business (incorporated),

For a private company, business, or individual for wages, salary, or commissions,

For the *government* (federal, state, county, or local), or
Without pay in a family business or farm?

C What kind of business, industry, or organization is that? What do/did they do or make? (*Examples: TV manufacturer, retail shoe store, state labor dept.*) Is it wholesale, retail, manufacturing or what?

D What kind of work do/did you do? What is/was your main occupation? [*Examples: electrical engineer, shoe clerk, janitor, teacher (school level)*]

E What are/were your most important duties, or activities? What do/did you actually do? (*Examples: type, keep account books, sell shoes*)

F Do/did you supervise the work of others?
Yes
No

42 What was the highest grade in school you *completed* and *received* credit for? (*Recorded as given.*)

A Have you had any trade, technical, or vocational training?
Yes
No

B What degrees or diploma, if any, do you have? (*Code highest degree.*)
High school diploma (equivalent)
Junior college degree (A.A.)
Bachelor's degree (B.A., B.S.)
Master's degree (M.A., M.S.)
Doctorate (PH.D.)
Professional (M.D., J.D., D.D.S., etc.)
Other (specify):
None

43 What is your religious preference?
Protestant (*Ask* A)
Roman Catholic (*Skip to* B)
Jewish (*Skip to* B)
Other (specify) (*Skip to* B)
None (*Skip to* Q44)

A (*If Protestant:*) What is your denomination?
Baptist
Methodist
Episcopalian
Presbyterian
Lutheran
Congregational
Other (specify)

B How important is your religion to you? Would you say:
Very important,

> Fairly important,
> Fairly unimportant, or
> Not important at all?

44 How long have you lived in this (house/apartment)?
  (*Record as given.*)
  Don't know
  No answer

45 Now, thinking of your household, in 1978 was the total income from *all* sources and *before* taxes, for this household, under $10,000 or over $10,000?
  Under (*Ask* A)
  Over (*Ask* A)
  Refused (*Skip to* Q46)
  Don't know (*Skip to* Q46)
  A (*Hand appropriate income card: If under $10,000 use income card 45A-1. If over $10,000, use income card 45A-2.*) Please look at this card and tell me the letter of the income group that includes the total income for your *entire* family, all those related, before taxes for 1978.
    Refused
    Don't know
  B Including yourself, how many people were dependent on the total income in 1978? (*Interviewer: Does roster agree?*)

46 Finally, were there any questions in the survey that you felt were unnecessary or irrelevant?
  Yes (*Ask* A)
  No (*Skip to* Q47)
  A Which ones? Please explain.

47 Any other comments about the interview?
  Yes (*Skip to* A)
  No (*Terminate*)
  A Please explain.

Thank you for your cooperation. May I have your name and telephone number in case my office wants to make sure that I was here to do this interview?
Respondent's name:
Telephone number:
Interviewer's name:
Interviewer's I.D. number:
Date completed:
Label I.D. number:

Thank you for helping in this research project. The questions that you were asked were designed to learn what you and others think is acceptable sexual behavior.

We believe that sexual relationships should occur when both people desire it, not when one person in a couple does not consent. Crimes such as rape are frightening acts and we do not believe that any one race or occupational group is more likely to be involved in crime. In order to prevent crime, when possible, and to provide the greatest help to the victims of crime, we need to understand more about what causes it.

If for any reason, at any time, you feel that your participation in this study has raised any concerns for you, an appointment for you to discuss your feelings with Joshua Golden, M.D., will be provided without cost. You may contact him by calling (213) 825-0243.

Interviewer: Go to screener and complete observation page, Q1 through Q8 after leaving household.

Appendix 2 Designing and Analyzing Vignettes

V ignettes are used increasingly as an instrument for measuring attitudes, both in small group experiments and surveys. Their design and administration vary widely and are not determined or restricted by the subject of the research or the goals of the study (Converse and Presser, 1986). While literature on the definition, role, and measurement of attitudes is extensive, issues relevant to the design and analysis of vignettes are scant (Burstein, Doughtie, and Raphaeli, 1980). Only Giovannoni and Becerra (1979) have used standard psychometric techniques to evaluate vignettes, and only Rossi and Nock (1982) have summarized the procedures they used to design vignettes for surveys.

Because a major focus of the Los Angeles study was methodological, a pilot study, a reliability study, and a validity study were conducted as part of the process of designing and evaluating vignettes to be used in the community survey. Information from the three studies is reported later in this appendix. First we define vignettes, review substantive areas in which they have been employed, and describe how they have been used for a variety of purposes. In the second section, we discuss fractional replication, procedures used to design vignettes for the Los Angeles study, and then outline data processing procedures used to analyze vignettes.

Vignettes in Social and Psychological Research

Description of Vignettes

Sometimes called "scenarios," "scripts," or "simulations," vignettes are short descriptive statements of a situation. Usually they contain a central event that the respondent is asked to evaluate. Respondents judge the situation portrayed or answer a series of questions relating to the vignette. Their judgments and answers are then assumed to represent their attitudes or opinions.

Developed by social psychologists for use in place of laboratory experiments criticized for their use of deception, vignettes have been employed to investigate cognition, cognitive dissonance, decisionmaking, role theory, attribution, and victimology (e.g., Abelson, 1968, 1976; Aronson and Carlsmith, 1968; Brown, 1962; Brunswick, 1956; Fishbein and Ajzen, 1973; Forward, Canter, and Kirsch, 1976; Freedman, 1969; Kelman, 1974; Landy and Aronson, 1969; Miller, 1972; Mixon, 1971; Prytula, Whiteside, and Davidson, 1975; Rasch, 1974; Walster, 1966). Rossi and other sociologists have used vignettes to investigate how judgments or decisions are made and the extent to which there is consensus across social groups about assumed social norms such as the assignment of status, the seriousness of various crimes, and issues of distributive justice (Alves and Rossi, 1978; Garrett, 1982; Jasso and Rossi, 1977; Nock and Rossi, 1978; Rossi et al., 1974; Sampson and Rossi, 1975). Several articles have involved studies of rape (e.g., Joe, McGee, and Dazey, 1977; Smith et al., 1976; Seligman, Brickman, and Koulack, 1977; Rumsey and Rumsey, 1977).

Every vignette or set of vignettes has three identifiable parts: element(s), level(s) of elements, and a context. Elements are analogous to variables, thus it is the elements and interactions between them that are of interest to the investigators. For example, in the Los Angeles study, the following elements or variables were portrayed in vignettes to assess definitions of rape: force, resistance, victim provocation, ethnicity of the male and female, prior sexual history, relationship between the man and woman, and the location of the encounter. Selection of elements can be determined by theoretical issues, evidence from prior research, or other relevant constraints imposed by the study design.

Each element can assume one or more levels. For example, ethnicity can be varied between black and white; black, Hispanic, and white; or among or between any other combination of ethnic groups. An element also may be varied by portraying it in some vignettes and omitting it from others. For example, the race of the female might be specified in some vignettes but not in others. Theoretically, the number of elements and levels for each element can vary infinitely; in practice, variations are finite.

A vignette also may include information that provides a context for the elements of interest or to make the situation portrayed more realistic. For example, time of day, location, descriptions of the weather (or other pieces of information irrelevant to the variables under study) can be added to increase the reality of the situation. When included, such information generally is held constant across all respondents or all vignettes.

Use of Vignettes in Surveys and Social Psychology

To some extent, techniques used to vary elements, to assign vignettes to respondents, and the amount of extra information added correlate with the area under investigation and the investigator's professional discipline. Sociologists and psychologists generally include multiple elements or variables in each vignette and vary them systematically across all vignettes. Based upon the researcher's theoretical framework and previous empirical findings, the investigator decides which elements to include, and designs the range variable levels to be assigned to each element. For example, if we wish to portray household social status, prior research suggests that occupation, education, and income of the head of the household are major determinants of social status. Thus, these three elements might be selected as variables in the vignette being designed. Also, we might want to include sex of the head of the household or other household characteristics.

Once the set of elements is selected, the number and content of the levels that each element is allowed to assume must be decided. In the simplest example, education can be varied between "high" and "low." In the most complicated example, the exact number of years of schooling or the highest educational degree obtained can be described in the vignette. When both the number of elements and the number of element levels have been determined, it is possible to create a universe of vignettes representing all possible combinations of elements and element levels. If education, occupation, and sex of the head of the household are the elements, and if each element varies between two levels (e.g., high/low; male/female), the universe defined by all possible combinations would be represented by $2^3 = 8$ unique vignettes.

Procedures by which vignettes have been administered have varied (Bourque and Engelhardt, 1979). Experimental social psychologists generally design a universe of vignettes in which three or four variables are fully crossed. Each usually is varied between two levels, and is presented in combination with a large amount of contextual information held constant across the universe of vignettes. Resulting vignettes are quite long.

In psychology, each respondent usually is presented with a single, lengthy vignette. Frequently each vignette is given to only one respondent. Vignettes are assigned to respondents using fractional replication (Alexander and Becker, 1978) or other techniques allowing investigators to insure that a certain mix of respondent characteristics—frequently sex and race—is balanced relative to variations within the universe of vignettes. All elements or variables contained within the universe are fully crossed. For example, in a study of rape one might decide to include three variables: force, resistance, and location, and to vary each element between two levels. Force could be varied between "he held a gun to her head" and "he told her he would hurt her." Resistance could be varied between "she hit him in the face" and "she was unable to move." And location could be varied between "outside a bar at midnight" and "outside a grocery at noon." Fully crossing all combinations of the three elements, each at two levels, would create eight vignettes ($2^3 = 2 \times 2 \times 2 = 8$) each containing a different combination of elements (variables) and levels of elements. In most social psychological experiments each respondent is given only one of the eight vignettes. The three elements of interest —force, resistance, and location—would be embedded in a lengthy paragraph containing other irrelevant information to increase the reality of the portrayal.

Other investigators create a number of lengthy, freestanding vignettes in which elements and levels are neither constant across vignettes nor crossed (e.g., Williams and Holmes, 1981; Klemmack and Klemmack, 1976). In such cases, each subject responds to all the vignettes developed for the investigation. In her study of attitudes toward the mentally disabled, Shirley Star (1952) used such a procedure. "Six thumb-nail sketches, describing the personality and behavior of hypothetical individuals in terms which actually typified one degree or another of mental disorder were presented to the public" (Star, n.d., chapter 4, p. 2). The sketches or vignettes were designed to portray persons suffering from paranoia, simple schizophrenia, anxiety, alcoholism, compulsivity, and childhood conduct disturbance. After each description was read, each person was asked a series of open-ended questions. All respondents were presented with all six vignettes, and no effort was made to use parallel construction or systematic inclusion or exclusion of material across the six vignettes.

Following presentation of a vignette, respondents answer a series of questions or make judgments about the vignette. To assess results, most investigators compare means or analyze variance. Alexander and Becker (1978), Shotland and Goodstein (1983), and Ruch and Chandler (1983), however, are among the few social psychologists who have used multivariate measures other than analysis of variance. Alexander and Becker used a one-half replication of a 2^5 factorial design to assign vignettes to respondents, and analyzed responses using regression techniques similar to those of Rossi and associates. Shotland and Goodstein constructed a causal model, and tested it using path analysis of vignette-generated data.

In contrast to social psychologists, sociologists generally give respondents large numbers of parsimoniously constructed vignettes. Rossi and associates have respondents read several parsimonious vignettes (Rossi and Nock, 1982). The elements of interest are fully crossed within the vignette universe. Because vignettes designed by Rossi and associates include as many as eight elements (each of which is allowed to assume a large number of levels), the universe of unique vignettes is large — so large that it remains hypothetical. Rather than creating a series of vignettes, the researchers generate vignettes by computer through sequential random draws from the various elements and levels they can assume. Each set of vignettes assigned to a respondent is, thus, randomly selected from the available universe. For a detailed description of their techniques see Rossi and Nock, 1982.

Rossi and associates have used vignettes more often than any other investigator. In their investigations of assignment of social status, perceived seriousness of various crimes, and distributive justice (e.g., Rossi, Sampson, et al., 1974; Nock and Rossi, 1978; Alves and Rossi, 1978;

Garrett, 1982), they have varied procedures by which they select the content of vignettes and the process by which they assign vignettes to respondents, and have explored numerous ways to use regression techniques to analyze vignette data. They have not detailed issues surrounding the selection of variables or the number of variables to include. They have, however, studied the impact of the number of levels each variable contains. In recent investigations they allowed each variable to assume an essentially unrestricted number of levels (Nock and Rossi, 1978; Alves and Rossi, 1978).

Rossi and associates have alluded to difficulties in design and analysis that may result from decisions about how variables are selected, the number of variables selected, and subjects' response patterns. But because the impact of these potential problems in their own research has been minimal, they have not conducted a detailed examination of ramifications of such potential difficulties.

Because using vignettes deviates from classical experimental methods, the methodology has been criticized (e.g., Cronkite, 1980); nevertheless, nothing in the literature describes difficulties encountered in determining format or content of a vignette.

Vignettes in the Los Angeles Study

Use of Fractional Replication in Designing Vignettes

In the Los Angeles study, we used fractional replication to assign subsets of the universe of vignettes to respondents. As is true of any technique, fractional replication has both strengths and weaknesses. In this case its strength is its assumption that all variables or elements are equally important. (Although it has been suggested that some variables may be more powerful than others in defining rape, empirical evidence remains sparse.) We assessed interactions between variables to eliminate those that were insignificant predictors in order to replace them with variables that the literature suggested might be more viable predictors. We were willing to accept the limitations that fractional replication places on the number of element levels because, as Cochran and Cox (1957) note, the chief appeal of fractionally replicated designs is ". . . they enable five or more factors [variables] to be included simultaneously in an experiment of a practicable size, so that the investigator can discover quickly which factors have an important effect on the product" (p. 244).

According to experts in experimental design, the major disadvantage to fractional replication is that "this welcome reduction in the size of the experiment is not obtained without paying a price . . . the results . . . of fractional replication . . . are open to misinterpretation in a way that does not arise with fully replicated designs . . . the outcome of using a half-replicate is to lose one factorial effect, ABC, entirely and to leave each main effect inextricably mixed with one of the two-factor interactions" (Cochran and Cox, 1957, pp. 244–46).

From our point of view, the greater disadvantage is that the nature of the design necessitates limiting the number of levels that an element or variable can assume. This limitation may enable the respondent to perceive what the objective of the variation is. This would be particularly likely in a situation such as ours in which respondents are presented vignettes in which the same phrase representing a variable level appears in more than one vignette. On the other hand, the assignment of multiple vignettes allows us to obtain a more stable rating on each respondent and to investigate within-respondent effects.

In the Los Angeles study, vignettes contained eight elements, each with two levels. When all combinations of the eight variables were fully crossed, 2^8 or 256 unique vignettes were created. Because it is unreasonable and unnecessary to have each respondent rate 256 vignettes, eighth replicates were created. Each respondent rated a packet of 32 vignettes analogous to one of the eighth replicates. To create the eighth replicates, attempts were made to maximize balance between vignettes and to minimize difficulty in our ability to tell which factor (variable) or interaction between factors (variables) caused an effect.

To analyze data from a fractionally replicated design, one must first address the extent to which replicates are equivalent both in terms of their substantive content and in terms of the characteristics of the subjects to which each replicate was assigned. Investigating characteristics of respondents assigned to each group of vignettes is analogous to analyzing block effects. Using block designs is similar to using fractional replication in that one block (a set of treatment combinations) is similar to a fractional replicate. In the Los Angeles study, each packet of 32 vignettes is both a block and a fractional replicate. In the Los Angeles study, several respondents received packets that replicated the same block. The vignettes contained within these packets are identical except for randomized order.

Using fractional replication to assign vignettes should not produce different patterns of main effects or interaction effects between blocks. In other words, if we observe that certain characteristics within vignettes result in higher ratings across the entire sample of respondents, that pattern should be replicated within each of the eight blocks. Because the ultimate question of interest in the Los Angeles study was to determine whether respondents who had different social characteristics would or would not differ in their judgments of rape we were anxious to eliminate any differences that might be determined by characteristics of the design, such as sample selection, assignment of vignettes to respondents, poor construction of vignettes, etc. If differences were found, we wanted to be able to conclude that the differences were real, resulting from social structural characteristics of the respondents rather than from methodological artifacts. To do so we used contrast matrices to test for block effects and within-respondent effects, and as a procedure to summarize within-respondent patterns of rating vignettes.

Data Processing Using Contrast Matrices

Each respondent in the Los Angeles study received 32 vignettes comprising an eighth replicate of the 2^8 factorial design. Within the respondent's ratings, 31 orthogonal contrasts can be computed. An orthogonal contrast for the main effect of a variable is simply the difference between the average of the sixteen ratings given at one level of the variable and the average of the sixteen ratings given at the other level of the variable. For example, if a respondent rated all vignettes portraying a high level of force as "6" (definitely is a rape) and all vignettes portraying a low level of force as "2" (probably is not a rape), then for that respondent the orthogonal contrast for the main effect of force would equal "4."

Orthogonal contrasts for interactions between two or more variables were also computed, but are more difficult to describe. A two-way interaction effect occurs when the ratings for the two levels of one variable are not the same across levels of another variable. For example, if the vignettes with a low level of force are rated "3" when knowledge is also at the low level, but "2" when knowledge is at a high level, and if vignettes with a high level of force are all rated "6" regardless of level of knowledge, then there is an interaction between force and knowledge. That is, knowledge is rated differently depending upon the level of force in the vignette. This example portrays only the simplest, least complex interaction that might be found in a data set where eight-way interactions are possible, but fortunately rarely occur.

The actual computation of contrasts involved several steps, the end result of which was to produce a data set for each respondent that contained 31 contrast scores. Each score represented the extent to which one variable (e.g., force used by the man) by itself or in combination with other variables influenced a respondent's decisions about whether their 32 vignettes portrayed rape. If a respondent's contrast score was zero, then his or her ratings were not affected by the variable (e.g., force) represented for that particular contrast.

Although the 31 within-respondent contrast scores summarized each respondent's reaction to each of the eight variables and selected interactions among them, a straightforward summary of the individual's response pattern was still needed. This composite variable would summarize each respondent's 31 contrast variables, provide a shorthand representation of what he or she used to rate vignettes, and provide an indirect measure of his or her attitudes about rape.

The ideal respondent for which such a score could be computed would be someone who used only one or two variables to make decisions about rape. For example, a respondent might ignore all information except level of force. Or someone might use no information to rate vignettes, but rather rate them at random or give all vignettes the same score. In these instances, response patterns could easily be summarized to classify respondents. To the extent that any response pattern is used by substantial numbers of respondents, the composite variable can be used to investigate theoretically interesting associations between rating patterns and demographic characteristics of respondents.

To develop a composite variable for each respondent, we first sorted the contrast variables in descending order. The sort ignored the sign (direction) of the contrast, because our objective was simply to discover which of the eight variables respondents selected as a rating criterion. Tables A2.1 and A2.2 show the distribution of respondents based upon the magnitude of their three highest contrast scores and the values of those first

Table A2.1 Distribution of respondents by identity of the three contrasts on which they had the largest values, Los Angeles study, 1979

Contrast	First contrast (in percentage)	Second contrast (in percentage)	Third contrast (in percentage)
Main effects			
Male's race	2.4	6.4	2.8
Male's occupation	2.8	4.8	5.2
Male and female know each other	0.4	4.0	3.2
Resistance	27.5	21.1	5.6
Force	49.0	9.6	2.8
Location	1.6	4.0	2.4
Female's marital status	0.4	2.0	3.2
No contrasts (value = 0.0)	9.2	15.5	15.5
Interactions			
Male's race and occupation	0.4	2.4	2.4
Male's race and knowledge	0.4	1.2	4.8
Male's race and resistance	0.4	0.8	2.4
Male's race and provocation	0.8	1.2	4.0
Male's race and marital status	0.4	2.8	0.8
Male's race and female's race	0.4	2.4	2.8
Occupation and force	0.4	1.2	3.2
Knowledge and resistance	1.2	1.2	1.6
Knowledge and force	0.4	—	0.4
Knowledge and provocation	0.4	0.8	2.0
Knowledge and marital status	0.4	3.6	2.0
Resistance and provocation	0.4	4.0	13.5
Male's race, knowledge, and female's race	0.8	15.5	5.5
Contrasts that appeared only after the first level			
Female's race	—	3.2	1.6
Female's race and force	—	2.4	2.4
Occupation and knowledge	—	0.4	2.8
Occupation and resistance	—	1.2	2.0
Occupation and provocation	—	1.2	2.4
Resistance and force	—	0.8	0.6
Resistance and marital status	—	0.4	2.0
Provocation, marital status, and female's race	—	1.2	0.8
Male's race, resistance, female's race	—	0.4	1.6
Resistance and female's race	—	—	2.0

Table A2.2   Value of three highest contrasts, Los Angeles study, 1979

Value	First contrast (in percentage)	Second contrast (in percentage)	Third contrast (in percentage)
Less than −4.0	0.4	0.0	0.0
−3.0 to −3.9	0.4	0.0	0.0
−2.0 to −2.9	0.8	0.0	0.0
−1.0 to −1.9	5.5	13.0	10.0
−0.50 to −0.99	1.6	12.0	17.1
−0.01 to −0.49	2.8	8.8	9.2
0	9.8	15.5	15.5
+.01 to +0.49	0.8	12.7	13.5
+.50 to +0.99	11.2	16.3	22.4
+1.0 to +1.99	26.3	20.8	10.4
+2.0 to +2.99	19.5	0.8	0.0
+3.0 to +3.99	11.6	0.0	0.0
+4.0 and greater	10.0	0.0	0.0
Total N	251	251	251

three contrasts. Because most respondents used only three contrasts in a meaningful way, we used variables represented by those contrasts to create the composite variable. Table A2.3 shows the association between the highest contrast used by a respondent and the absolute value of that contrast. Information in these tables highlights the following rating patterns: use of force alone, use of resistance and force in combination, use of variables other than force and resistance, use of force or resistance in combination with one of the other variables, and few or no differentiations made between levels of variables. Given the distribution of the contrast scores, a contrast of less than 0.4 was defined as meaningless or the result of random noise. Thus, 0.4 was selected as the cutoff point for considering a particular contrast as meaningful. The resulting composite variable and distribution of respondents among the twelve rating patterns created is shown in table A2.4.

Summarizing Rating Patterns for Analysis

Although contrast matrices allowed us to summarize each respondent's rating pattern, the resulting twelve-category nominal variable was awkward and difficult to use in further analyses (because of its large number of categories and the size of some of the groups). Six characteristics or dimensions describing the twelve-category variable were used to collapse it further. Stated as questions, the six characteristics were:

1 In rating vignettes, did the respondent differentiate between vignettes?
2 In rating vignettes, did the respondent differentiate between vignettes in a systematic way?
3 In rating vignettes, did the respondent use force and/or resistance in deciding whether or not a rape is described?
4 Was force or resistance the major variable used in rating vignettes?
5 Did respondents who used force as the major determinant of their ratings use any other information in making ratings?
6 Did respondents who used resistance as the major determinant of their ratings use any other information in making ratings?

As each question was examined, respondents were placed in groups. Figure A2.1 demonstrates how this dispersed the sample.

The first question differentiates group 11, the 23 persons who gave identical ratings to all vignettes, from the rest of the sample; the second question differentiates group 12, the seven persons who interspersed a few random ratings among mostly identical ratings; the third question differentiates group 10, the 29 persons who do not use force or resistance in rating their vignettes. The fourth question separates out those who used force as the major determinant (highest contrast) from those who used resistance as the major determinant (highest contrast). Here an arbitrary decision was made to assign group three (six persons) and group nine (one person) to the force dominant group. The last two questions separate those who used only force or only resistance from those who used force or resistance in combination with other variables. This procedure left us with seven groups, all but one of which contained 20 or more respondents.

To decide whether further collapsing should be done and to ascertain the validity of responses made by persons who gave identical ratings to all or most of their vignettes, we then examined interviewers' observations of respondents and respondents' own reports of information they used. As table A2.5 shows, persons who gave identical ratings to all or most vignettes do not differ significantly from the other groups in the amount of time taken to rate vignettes. Nor did interviewers' perceptions of their interest and honesty differ across groups. The distribution of respondents

Table A2.3 Content of highest contrast by value of highest contrast, Los Angeles study, 1979

Highest contrast (in percentage)

Value of contrast	Male's race	Occu-pation	Knowl-edge	Resist-ance	Force	Provo-cation	Fe-male's marital status	Male's race by occu-pation	Male's race by knowl-edge	Male's race by resist-ance
0										
1.0–1.9	17	43	100	23	34	100	100	100	100	100
2.0–2.9	0	14	26	25	0	0	0	0	0	0
3.0–3.9	0	0	0	13	16	0	0	0	0	0
4.0+	0	0	0	7	0	0	0	0	0	0
Total N	6	7	1	69	123	4	1	1	1	1

across the final, six-category rating pattern variable is reported in table A2.5.

Because force and resistance are key components of all discussions of rape, respondents who use force or resistance alone or in combination with other variables are called "normative" raters. Subgroups differentiate those who cue ratings to force from those who cue ratings to resistance. Similarly, respondents who use force or resistance alone are differentiated from those who use multiple variables. Normative raters, therefore, are comprised of four subgroups: force-only raters, force-multiple raters, resistance-only raters, and resistance-multiple raters. Persons who differentiated between few or none of their ratings are called "nonraters" (in recognition of their universally high ratings with low or nonexistent variance). Persons whose ratings vary but who fail to use force or resistance to decide are called "nonnormative" raters.

Pilot Study

During the process of designing vignettes we conducted a pilot study to learn how best to operationalize variables of interest within the vignettes, to investigate respondents' ability to rate multiple vignettes, to assess their

Highest contrast (in percentage)

Male's race by force	Male's race by provocation	Male's race by female's marital status	Occupation by female's race	Knowledge by resistance	Knowledge by female's race	Knowledge by force	Knowledge by provocation	Resistance by force	Male's race by knowledge by female's marital status	No contrasts
										100
50	100	0	0	100	0	100	100	100	50	0
0	0	0	0	0	100	0	0	0	0	0
0	0	100	0	0	0	0	0	0	0	0
0	0	0	0	0	0	0	0	0	0	0
2	1	1	1	3	1	1	1	1	2	23

reactions to short parsimonious vignettes, and to examine the influence that extra information might have on respondents' ratings. Unlike the later survey in the community, the universe of vignettes in the pilot study was split into two sets (which greatly complicated assigning vignettes through fractional replication). In the first set of vignettes, force was varied between two levels; in the second, force was held constant at the lower level (see table A2.6). Other elements included in the vignettes were the male's race (varied between black and white), the female's race (varied between black and white), the male's occupation (varied between assembly-line worker and business executive), the female's occupation (varied between topless dancer and actress), context, and complexity. Depending on whether respondents were asked to evaluate a set of vignettes in which force was held constant or one in which force was varied, they rated either 32 or 48 vignettes (figure A2.3).[1]

The last two elements, context and complexity, were included in vignettes to find out what happens when material unrelated to the objective of the study is added to make a vignette more realistic or to reduce respondent fatigue and boredom.[2] The context in which the encounter occurred was varied between a telephone-borrowing encounter and a flat tire on a freeway. Both situations had been informally pretested against

Table A2.4 Distribution and description of rating patterns, Los Angeles study, 1979

Category	Description of category	Percentage
Force	Force is the first and only contrast > 0.4	13.5
Resistance	Resistance is the first and only contrast > 0.4	8.0
Force & resistance	Force and resistance and/or the interaction between them are tied and > 0.4	2.4
Force > resistance +	Force is highest contrast, resistance in the logically consistent direction (high level of resistance yields a rating of rape) is the second contrast	12.4
Force > resistance −	Force is the highest contrast & resistance in the inconsistent direction (low level of resistance yields a rating of rape) is the second contrast	4.4
Resistance > force +	Resistance is the highest contrast & force in the logically consistent direction is the second contrast	4.8
Combinations: force first	Force is the highest contrast & some set of variable(s) other than resistance is second	17.9
Combinations: resistance first	Resistance is the highest contrast & some set of variable(s) other than force is second	12.4
Combinations: force & resistance first	The interaction between force & resistance is the highest contrast OR force and resistance are tied for first; other variables are valid contrasts in the second or third order	0.4
Other variables	Variables other than force or resistance are used in the ratings	11.6
Nonraters	All contrasts are zero	9.2
Random raters	All contrasts are < 0.4	2.8
Total		251

three other possible situations, and appeared to be most neutral and most similar. Complexity was produced by including extra descriptive information in some vignettes (see figure A2.2). Information was selected to be as neutral as possible to ensure that it would not add unintended, subtle cues that would affect responses. For this reason we did not include information about the make and model of cars (which might be perceived as denoting socioeconomic or marital status), or references to evening or night. Compared to vignettes used in many studies, the amount of material added in the pilot study was minimal and totaled no more than seventy words.

Table A2.5 Average time taken to rate vignettes and complete the interview by vignette rating patterns, Los Angeles study, 1979

Vignette rating pattern	Percentage	N	Rate vignettes*	Complete interview*
			Average time in minutes	
Nonrater	12.0	30	14.9	52.2
Nonnormative raters	11.6	29	19.9	54.0
Normative raters				
Force dominant				
Single variable	13.5	34	14.2	51.0
Multiple variables	37.8	95	18.0	53.3
Resistance dominant				
Single variable	8.0	20	14.4	57.9
Multiple variables	17.1	43	19.2	57.9
Total	100.0	251	17.2	54.1

*One-way analysis of variance, not significant.

Figure A2.1 Allocation of respondents to vignette rating pattern typology

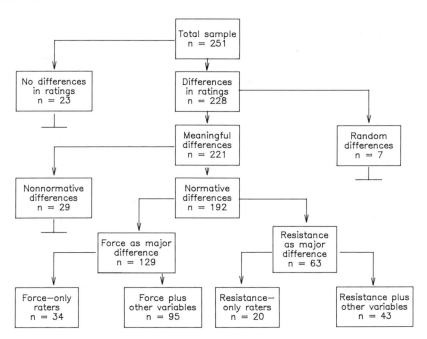

Table A2.6 Mean ratings of vignettes by selected vignette elements across pilot study, reliability study, and Los Angeles study, 1979

Study and vignette element	Mean	SD	No. of vignettes[a]
Pilot study[b]			
Level of force varied[c]	2.74	0.95	2,914
High level of force[c]	2.99	0.95	1,456
context: telephone[c]	2.76	0.95	708
context: freeway	3.20	0.95	748
Low level of force	2.49	0.95	1,458
context: telephone[c]	2.21	0.95	726
context: freeway	2.77	0.95	732
Level of force constant and low	2.50	0.95	2,278
context: telephone[c]	2.18	0.95	1,128
context: freeway	2.84	0.95	1,150
Reliability study[d]			
Time 1	4.6	1.8	6,048
high level of force[c]	5.3	1.9	3,024
low level of force	3.9	1.4	3,024
Time 2	4.6	1.8	4,960
high level of force[c]	5.4	1.3	2,480
low level of force	3.8	1.9	2,480
Los Angeles study[d]	4.5	1.8	8,032
high level of force	5.2	1.4	4,016
low level of force	3.8	1.9	4,016

a Since each unique vignette rating in this case is an observation, the N is very large; this increases statistical significance. All differences shown as significant remain significant, however, when analyses are made using within-respondent score where there is an N of 112, 189, or 251.

b Ratings were made using a 4-point scale where 1 = definitely is not a rape, 2 = probably not a rape, 3 = probably is a rape, and 4 = definitely is a rape. In comparing levels of vignette elements, mean ratings and standard deviations were computed across all respondents for each level of each of the eight variables. Since a strict experimental design was used in construction and assigning vignettes, analysis of variance was used to estimate a full model in which all interactions were controlled.

c Difference of means is significant at $p < .05$.

d Ratings were made using a scale from (1) definitely is not a rape to (6) definitely is a rape. Points (2) through (5) were not identified. In cases of strong indecision, respondents were allowed *not to rate vignettes*.

e Ratings were made using a scale from (1) definitely is not a rape to (6) definitely is a rape. Points (2) through (5) were not identified.

Findings

As shown in table A2.6, respondents failed to perceive the two situations or contexts as neutral or identical. Varying the situation between a freeway encounter and a telephone-borrowing encounter strongly influenced

Basic telephone vignette

A (race) man, who works as a(n) (occupation), knocked on the door and asked to use the phone. A (race) woman, who is a(n) (occupation), answered the door and showed him to the phone. She claims that, after he had come into the house, (level of force).

Complex form of telephone vignette

A (race) man, who works as a(n) (occupation), knocked on the door of an apartment near an elementary school on a cloudy weekday afternoon and asked to use the phone. A (race) woman, who is a(n) (occupation), answered the door. The sound of a television set could be heard from the other room. She claims that, after he had come into the house, (level of force).

Basic form of freeway vignette

A (race) woman, who is a(n) (occupation) was stopped because of a flat tire on a freeway. She accepted a ride from a (race) man, who works as a(n) (occupation). He drove her to an isolated area where he (level of force).

Complex form of freeway vignette

A (race) woman, who is a(n) (occupation) was stopped because of a flat tire on a freeway that goes through a residential neighborhood. It was a smoggy summer weekday and the sound of a factory whistle could be heard signaling the changing of the shift. She accepted a ride from a (race) man, who works as a(n) (occupation), and who was driving a light-colored car. He drove her to an isolated area where he (level of force).

Figure A2.2   Vignettes used in pilot study of the Los Angeles study showing variations in scenario and complexity

respondents' perceptions of the behavior. While the level of force portrayed in a vignette was a strong predictor of whether or not it was perceived as rape, the situation or context had an even stronger influence on the rating. Respondents clearly thought that the sexual encounter on the freeway was much more likely to be rape than the encounter in the telephone-borrowing situation. Although varying the context was intended to reduce boredom and increase verisimilitude, not to influence judgments

Race: black *or* white

Male's occupation: janitor *or* office worker *or* lawyer

Female's occupation as an indicator of SES: assembly line worker *or* business executive

Female's occupation as an indicator of provocativeness: topless dancer *or* actress

Level of force in telephone vignette: he forced her to have sex with him *or* he told her he was going to have sex with her

Level of force in freeway vignette: he threatened her and forced her to have sex *or* he pressured her into having sex with him

Figure A2.3 Content of pilot study vignette elements, other than scenario and complexity, used in the Los Angeles study

about the likelihood of rape, respondents considered portrayals of telephone-borrowing unlikely to be rape regardless of what else was described.

Moreover, varying the level of force, rather than holding it constant, also elevated ratings. Regardless of context, respondents whose sets of vignettes included both levels of force gave all vignettes higher average ratings. When force was held constant, the mean rating across vignettes was 2.5 (the exact midpoint of the available 1 to 4 range). When force was varied, the mean rating was 2.74. In contrast, the extra information had little influence on ratings when the level of force was not varied within the set of vignettes ($p > .50$), but had a highly significant effect when force was varied within the set of vignettes ($p < .001$). No clear reason for these differences can be suggested, but they suggest that extra material should not be included in vignettes unless its effect can be controlled or systematically evaluated.

Implications for Design of Vignettes

Findings from the pilot study suggest that the design of a vignette or set of vignettes affects study results. The selection of variables or elements, the number of levels across which elements are varied, and the amount and nature of extraneous information included affect respondents' ratings. Consistent with findings from the Los Angeles study as reported in part III, the amount of force portrayed in the pilot study strongly predicted whether respondents thought rape had occurred. Despite the consistency of this finding, ratings clearly also were sensitive to other properties of vignettes. Results of the pilot study suggest that even a powerful predictor like force varies with, and can be overpowered by, contextual characteristics of the portrayed event. This observation has ramifications for the design of future vignettes.

Ideally, prior to finalization of a set of vignettes, effects of variations in design should be tested systematically in a series of methodological studies. In the absence of such a set of studies, careful attention should be given to: (1) the selection of variables, (2) whether or not additional information, other than that being systematically manipulated in the variables, should be included in vignettes, (3) the selection of the number and content of levels to be included in each variable, and (4) the number of vignettes to be administered.

The addition of contextual material seems risky at best. In most studies it is impossible to tell whether a respondent reacted to the variables under investigation or to some part of the contextual data. Eliminating or reducing irrelevant material also would allow each respondent to react to multiple, parsimonious vignettes. Psychometric theory suggests that better and more stable measures will be obtained if multiple items are presented to a respondent. Obviously, if long vignettes are used and multiple questions asked about each vignette, it is impossible to give a single respondent a large number of vignettes. By asking research subjects to make single judgments about short vignettes including only material of interest, respondents can be asked to evaluate multiple vignettes.

Our pilot study also suggests that each variable portrayed should be allowed to assume a potentially infinite number of levels in the manner used by Rossi and colleagues (Alves and Rossi, 1978; Nock and Rossi, 1978). This is consistent with the above recommendation regarding the deletion of nonessential contextual information. One way of "making up" for the realism lost in dropping nonvaried contextual material is to allow each element to vary freely across the available range of possible levels. When multiple, parsimonious vignettes are given to a respondent, but variables are restricted to only a few levels, it is possible that respondents will consciously or unconsciously recognize the task and dissemble accordingly. This may explain differences in pilot study ratings between portrayals in which force was varied and those in which it was held constant.

Rossi and associates have successfully used vignettes with infinite variable levels to study distributive justice and the assignment of social status. The major drawback to using such vignettes in the study of rape is the assumption that levels of a given element form interval-level variables (e.g., completed education, income, etc.). Elements of interest in studies of rape (such as force, resistance, and attribution of responsibility) do not form intuitively obvious interval scales. However, careful pretesting of the levels of interest prior to incorporating them into vignettes should allow interval or ordinal rankings to be inductively assigned to each level.

Reliability of Vignettes

As with the design of vignettes, little has been reported on the psychometric and measurement characteristics of vignettes. When vignettes are used to measure attitudes, and each respondent is asked to evaluate multiple vignettes, each vignette is analogous to a single item in a more traditional questionnaire, scale, or index. To test the reliability of vignettes, we can thus test the reliability of the universe of vignettes and the relationship of a single vignette to that universe. The units of interest are the unique vignette (tested in exactly the same way as a single item in any psychometric test would be handled) and the composite or summary scores representing the universe of vignettes. As in any psychometric examination, inter-item correlations, test-retest, and homogeneity analyses can be done using the entire population of vignettes and respondents, or within subgroups defined by respondent or vignette characteristics (Cronbach, 1951; McKennell, 1977; Nunnally, 1967).

Design of the Reliability Study

After completing the pilot study and finalizing their structure we tested the reliability of the vignettes before we administered the survey in Los Angeles. The vignettes and procedures used were identical to those used in the actual community survey. Vignettes were administered twice,[3] at one-week intervals, to members of five community groups (two groups

Table A2.7 Types of groups, number of respondents at each administration, and demographic characteristics of Time 2 respondents, reliability study, Los Angeles study, 1979

Group	Number of respondents		Per-centage male	Median age group	Median education	Median income group
	Time 1	Time 2[a]				
Black, upper socio-economic status church group	40	29	69.0	45−54	college graduate	$25,000−$29,999
Black, lower socio-economic community action group	50	45	77.8	35−44	high school graduate	$5,000−$5,999
White, upper socio-economic status church group	50	41	56.1	45−54	post-college	$20,000−$24,999
White, lower socio-economic status retirement group[b]	23	18	61.1	65+	some college	$3,000−$3,999
White, lower socio-economic status housing project[b]	26	22	63.6	25−34	some college	$12,000−$13,999
Total N	189	155				

a N on which reliability testing is done.
b Groups are combined in latter analyses.

were combined to represent lower socioeconomic status whites) (see table A2.7). The 256 unique vignettes were divided into eight balanced groups of 32 vignettes each utilizing a fractional replicate design where only fourth- or fifth-order interaction terms are confounded or aliased with other main effects or interaction terms (Cochran and Cox, 1957). Each of the eight groups of balanced vignettes was assigned in random order to either 19 or 20 respondents. The 19 or 20 respondents who received each set were equally distributed across the four race-SES groups (i.e., five or six respondents from each group). Thus, within a single group, three to seven people received 32 identical vignettes, and each of the eight sets of 32 vignettes was received by at least five subjects in each group.

Table A2.8 Means, standard deviations, and test-retest correlations across all vignettes for total sample and by subgroup, reliability study, Los Angeles study, 1979

Group	Number of vignettes, Time 2	Number of people, Time 2
Total sample	4,960	155
Upper SES black	928	29
Lower SES black	1,440	45
Lower SES, white elderly	576	18
Lower SES white, housing projects	704	22
Upper SES white	1,312	41

a The fact that the means are high is surprising and suggests existence of a ceiling effect. On the face of it, we would not have expected this set of vignettes and the elements included in them to have yielded such a large number of high ratings (e.g., decisions that the incident portrayed was "definitely a rape"). Attenuation will not greatly affect tests of means but will affect tests involving correlations or variance (Scheffe, 1959). The probable impact of attenuation is to reduce the correlation. In order to normalize the distribution and use the respondent rather than the vignette as the unit of analysis, correlations between Time 1 and Time 2 ratings were computed for each respondent. An average correlation was then computed for each group. The null hypothesis that p = 0 was tested

Findings

Both internal consistency and test-retest reliability of the vignettes were analyzed. As noted earlier, each vignette can be treated as if it were a single item in an index. An average rating for each respondent, community group, replicate, block, or time period can be computed by summing ratings across vignettes, respondents, or both, and dividing by the number of vignettes or respondents. Once mean ratings or some other analogous composite score have been created, it is possible to compute variances and correlations. Test-retest reliability or stability was examined using Pearson's product-moment correlations between Time 1 and Time 2 ratings (see table A2.8). Cronbach's alpha was used to examine internal consistency within replicates at both Time 1 and Time 2. Because each replicate consisted of a balanced set of 32 vignettes, received by 155/8 = 19 or 20 respondents, the eighth replicates could be compared as replications of the same test or experimental design.

Demographic characteristics of respondents participating in both time periods were analyzed to ascertain whether the respondent characteristics, vignette characteristics, and the interaction between the two were similar

Mean[a]		Standard deviation		Correlation across time[b]	Mean correlation within group[a]
Time 1	Time 2	Time 1	Time 2		
4.63	4.64	1.80	1.83	.58[d]	.45[d]
4.59	4.45	1.78	1.85	.45[c]	.32[c]
4.29	4.36	1.99	1.95	.50[d]	.38[c]
4.31	4.25	1.94	2.07	.45[d]	.27[c]
5.07	5.28	1.38	1.29	.49[d]	.51[d]
4.90	4.91	1.66	1.68	.87[d]	.68[d]

using student's *t*.

b Although correlations are computed using the vignette rating as the unit of analysis, the degrees of freedom used in testing for significance are determined by the number of respondents. This provides a conservative estimate and, to some extent, controls for the lack of independence between the vignette ratings obtained from a single respondent.

c $p < .05$.

d $p < .001$.

in all groups. Our evaluation showed that no significant differences existed between persons who returned for Time 2 and those who did not.

Because each group of vignettes (each eighth replicate) was designed to be heterogeneous, as were subjects assigned to each replicate, demographic imbalances across replicates due to differential attrition between Time 1 and Time 2 could have been problematic. In fact, our chi square test indicated this was not the case. We found no differences among groups in the sex, ethnic, educational, occupational, or income distributions by replicate. Only the relationship between replicates and presence or absence of children in the household approached significance ($p = .12$).

Stability: Test-Retest Reliability

Test-retest reliabilities using the vignette rating as the unit of analysis were computed across the total sample of respondents and within each subgroup. Correlations were consistently significant, and ranged anywhere from .27 to .87 (see table A2.8). Test-retest correlations also differed by replicate; all correlations were significant, and once again the range was wide—from .38 to .71. Differences across groups and replicates may reflect block effects, respondent rating characteristics, or interactions between respondent and vignette characteristics.

However, when test-retest correlations across vignettes were examined within levels of each of the eight elements, patterns were consistent. While correlations within variable levels were remarkably similar for most variables and did not differ between levels, correlations did differ for two variables: force and resistance. At both Time 1 and Time 2, mean ratings of all vignettes portraying low force were lower (3.95 and 3.85) than those portraying high force (5.30 and 5.44). When vignettes were split into subgroups on the basis of whether low force or high force was portrayed, the test-retest correlation was higher for low-force vignettes (r = .54) than for high-force vignettes (r = .41). Similar but less dramatic results were observed when tests were run within levels of high and low resistance.

Internal Consistency and Unidimensionality

Both homogeneity of content and the number of items in a test determine the internal consistency of the test. In testing for internal consistency, the concern is with the extent to which a set of items can be said to represent a single conceptual space. Due to the design of the Los Angeles study, homogeneity had to be examined within each of the eight replicates in which the set of vignettes rated was the same for each respondent. At the same time, characteristics imposed by using fractional replication to assign vignettes allowed us to compare results across replicates. Such comparisons provide insight into the extent to which the eight subsets of vignettes are equivalent. To the extent that all eight sets of vignettes demonstrate similar levels of internal consistency, we can generalize from individual replicates to the entire population of vignettes. However, because each replicate contained only 19 or 20 respondents and each respondent rated 32 vignettes, to avoid creating an overdetermined matrix in computing Cronbach's alpha, we split each respondent's set of 32 vignettes into two sets of 16 vignettes each (see table A2.9). Because ethnicity of the female portrayed in the vignette was not significant as a predictor of ratings (see Bourque and Engelhardt, 1980), the groups were created by placing all vignettes with black females in the first subset and those with white females in the second subsets. Thus, instead of computing Cronbach's alpha within eight subsets of vignettes at each time period, we computed it within sixteen subsets of vignettes. While Cronbach's alpha was high within all subgroups defined in table A2.9, there was some evidence that the Time 1 vignette administration described an index with different kinds of characteristics than that of the Time 2 administration. The standard deviation for each item was broader and more consistent across items at Time 2. The homogeneity or average inter-item correlation was higher at Time 2, and Cronbach's alpha was slightly higher at Time 2.

Discussion and Conclusions

In the absence of comparable information from other studies, evidence reported here suggests that studies employing vignettes can provide viable, innovative, and reliable data on respondents' attitudes. Our findings also suggest that the set of vignettes developed for the Los Angeles County study of rape meets sufficient tests to conclude that these vignettes can be used to collect data on definitions of rape from representative samples of community residents. Although the universe of vignettes tests as unidimensional, some evidence suggests that the construct is multidimensional and that perceptions of force and resistance help define the multiple dimensions.

Further, we cannot be sure that we are measuring the reliability of the substantive content of the vignettes (i.e., perceptions of when rape occurs) rather than the technical characteristics of the task of assessing and manipulating vignettes printed on IBM cards. We cannot be sure whether we are, in fact, eliciting a respondent's attitude toward an object or his/her reactions to aspects of the technique used (such as the content of items, the context in which they were administered, or other characteristics of the instrument). This difficulty, however, applies to all studies in which vignettes are used and, for that matter, to many, if not all, data collection instruments. Scott (1968) suggests that the use of unusual stimuli such as pictures may allow for a greater degree of misunderstanding between the respondent's perception of the task and the experimenter's interpretation of responses. At the same time, Scott suggests that "the usual practice with verbal, pictorial, or other symbolic stimuli is to include many items relating to the same attitudinal object but phrased differently or set in

Table A2.9 Homogeneity by block assignment, time of administration, and race of woman portrayed in vignette, reliability study, Los Angeles study, 1979

| | Block 1 | | | | Block 2 | | | |
| | Time 1 | | Time 2 | | Time 1 | | Time 2 | |
	WF[a]	BF[b]	WF	BF	WF	BF	WF	BF
Cronbach's alpha	.95	.86	.82	.96	.86	.88	.98	.98
Mean rating of vignettes in set	4.07	4.90	4.8	4.0	1.8	4.6	3.8	3.9
Average inter-item correlation within set of vignettes	.57	.28	.23	.58	.30	.31	.72	.72
Analysis of variance								
Significance level between vignettes	.001	.001	.001	.001	.001	.007	.001	.001
Significance level of interaction between vignettes and respondents	NS	.001	.001	NS	NS	NS	.06	.06
Tukey's estimate of power to which ratings must be raised to achieve additivity (i.e., eliminate interaction)	1.06	4.08	3.85	.99	1.64	1.86	.57	.51
N of respondents	23	23	23	23	23	23	23	23
N of vignettes per respondent	16	16	16	16	16	16	16	16

a WF is white female

different contexts'' (p. 239). This takes into consideration the fact that respondents approach identical tasks differently. To minimize the effect of these differences we can state the task in a variety of ways or in multiple presentations. To date this has not been done using vignettes.

We would argue that our data provide some support for Scott's suggestion that the number of items should be increased when atypical stimuli are being used. While we show relatively high stability or test-retest reli-

| Block 3 | | | | Block 4 | | | |
| Time 1 | | Time 2 | | Time 1 | | Time 2 | |
WF	BF	WF	BF	WF	BF	WF	BF
.92	.90	.99	.99	.87	.90	.98	.98
4.6	4.6	3.95	4.0	4.7	4.7	4.1	4.2
.43	.37	.81	.83	.29	.35	.77	.79
.001	.001	.001	.001	.001	.001	.001	.001
.001	.001	.07	.04	.001	.001	NS	NS
2.64	2.32	.63	.63	3.23	3.20	.95	1.03
24	24	24	24	24	24	24	24
16	16	16	16	16	16	16	16

b BF is black female

ability, the somewhat different ratings and more homogeneous variance found at Time 2 may reflect a learning effect.

Contrary to our original expectations, respondents did not make full use of the six-point rating scale provided, and high ratings more frequently were used than low ratings. Whether this attenuation is a result of the substantive area under study, variables selected for inclusion, the rating scale provided, or characteristics of the technique itself cannot be discerned in this data set.

Table A2.9 (continued)

	Block 5				Block 6			
	Time 1		Time 2		Time 1		Time 2	
	WF	BF	WF	BF	WF	BF	WF	BF
Cronbach's alpha	.89	.87	.98	.98	.87	.88	.97	.97
Mean rating of vignettes in set	4.6	4.6	3.6	3.5	4.4	4.4	3.7	3.67
Average inter-item correlation within set of vignettes	.32	.30	.75	.73	.30	.30	.67	.66
Analysis of variance								
Significance level between vignettes	.001	.001	.001	.001	.001	.001	.001	.001
Significance level of interaction between vignettes and respondents	.01	.001	.001	.001	.001	.001	.01	.02
Tukey's estimate of power to which ratings must be raised to achieve additivity (i.e., eliminate inter-action)	2.13	2.61	.49	.38	2.75	3.0	.66	.65
N of respondents	24	24	24	24	23	23	23	23
N of vignettes per R	16	16	16	16	16	16	16	16

a WF is white female

The above are among the numerous questions that remain to be investigated more fully. Nevertheless, we argue that the test-retest reliability shown in our analyses indicates that vignettes can be used as a viable, innovative technique for measuring attitudes. Although insufficient attention has been devoted to their psychometric characteristics, nothing in these analyses suggests that vignettes should be abandoned. Rather, their construction, characteristics, and usage merit further attention and evaluation.

Block 7				Block 8			
Time 1		Time 2		Time 1		Time 2	
WF	BF	WF	BF	WF	BF	WF	BF
.74	.77	.97	.97	.89	.89	.98	.98
4.6	4.6	3.93	3.99	4.51	4.43	3.23	3.21
.14	.18	.67	.70	.34	.32	.72	.74
.001	.001	.001	.001	.001	.001	.001	.001
.001	.001	NS	NS	.001	.001	.001	.001
3.06	2.89	.69	.77	2.63	2.82	.47	.57
24	24	24	24	24	24	24	24
16	16	16	16	16	16	16	16

b BF is black female

Validity of Vignettes

As a partial test of the validity of vignettes used in the Los Angeles study, respondents were asked a series of questions (questions 2–6 in appendix 1) about vignettes and their ratings of them. The extent to which respondents' ratings corresponded to what they said they did in rating vignettes was used to evaluate the validity of the ratings. Answers to open-ended questions were coded to match the eight pieces of information contained in and manipulated in the vignettes: force, resistance, location (provoca-

Table A2.10 Agreement between respondents' perceived rating pattern and actual rating pattern used, Los Angeles study, 1979

| | Perceived rating pattern used | | | | | | | |
| | Normative rating patterns | | | | | Other categories | | |
Rating pattern used	force-only	force-plus	resist-ance-only	resist-ance-plus	Other valid pat-terns	all are rape	not enough infor-mation	not applica-ble[a]
Nonraters percentage	3.3	10.0	23.3	10.0	0.0	50.0	3.3	0.0
Nonnormative raters percentage	3.8	7.7	15.4	11.5	15.4	19.2	7.7	19.2
Normative raters								
Force dominant								
Force-only percentage	40.6	12.5	3.1	3.1	0.0	18.8	12.5	9.4
Force-plus percentage	35.7	16.8	6.3	8.4	0.0	20.0	7.4	7.4
Resistance dominant								
Resistance-only percentage	5.0	25.0	30.0	5.0	0.0	15.0	0.0	20.0
Resistance-plus percentage	14.6	9.8	19.5	12.2	0.0	22.0	12.2	9.8

a Includes respondents who gave miscellaneous responses, don't know, no answer, or on a prior screen said that they did not use one rating.

tion), relationship between male and female, race of female, marital status of female, race of male, and occupation of male.

The great majority of respondents (90 percent), regardless of vignette rating pattern, reported that they had tended to use one rating more than others. When asked which rating they used and why, it was clear that many respondents had a pretty good idea of what they did (table A2.10). For example, 27 of the 30 nonraters said they used a "6" (definitely is a rape), most of the time. The mean rating over the 32 vignettes rated by each of the 27 persons was 5.98. When asked why they used that rating, 15 of the nonraters said it was because "all the vignettes are rapes." Most force-only raters also said that they used "6" as their rating but, consistent with what they in fact did, the amount of force portrayed in the vignette was the reason given for using a "6" for many or most of their ratings.

Respondents in general were aware of which ratings and variables they used to rate vignettes. It was also clear that as patterns used became more complex, respondents' ability to reconstruct or describe the pattern used decreased. Persons who used a single variable to rate their vignettes more often reconstructed their rating patterns correctly than those who used multiple variables. Forty percent of the force-only raters and 30 percent of the resistance-only raters correctly stated that they used a single variable (force or resistance) to rate their vignettes. In contrast, 36 percent of the force-multiple raters and 19.5 percent of the resistance-multiple raters also reported that they had used a single variable in their ratings; only 17 percent and 12 percent respectively of the two groups correctly reported the use of multiple variables.

Responses of nonraters are most subject to questions of validity. The fact that nonraters used a single rating most of the time suggests that the individual vignettes were never read. Yet the average time taken by nonraters to rate the vignettes (14.9 minutes) was not significantly less than that taken by other respondents. This suggests that they did, in fact, read the vignettes and, after reading them, concluded that they all should be rated with a "6"—"definitely is a rape." Fifteen of the nonraters stated that they used "6s" because "all the vignettes are rapes." Another nonrater stated that s/he gave all the vignettes "4s" because "there was not enough information." In the absence of further information, we must conclude that the ratings of these 16 nonraters were valid: they correctly told the interviewer which rating they used and why. In contrast, the remaining 14 nonraters correctly reported which rating they usually used, but were not able to tell the interviewer which information they used to arrive at their decision or why they made it.

This same observation can be made about a substantial proportion of respondents in the other groups. As many as 70 percent of the respondents in the other groups were at least partially incorrect in their perceptions of how they rated vignettes. Only 41 percent of the force-only group correctly reported what they used to rate vignettes, and only 15 percent of the nonnormative raters correctly reported their rating pattern.

This leaves us with a question: Does a respondent's inability to correctly report how he or she rated vignettes invalidate his or her ratings?

But is this a good question? If, in fact, every respondent could accurately report exactly which variables and interrelationships he or she would use in deciding a vignette was a rape, why would we bother having him or her rate vignettes? Why wouldn't researchers simply list components of vignettes, and then have respondents tell them which kinds of information they would use to decide if a rape had occurred? One objective of using vignettes is to tap complex constructs and interrelationships between concepts that are not easily summarized in traditionally formatted questionnaire items. Thus, if all respondents accurately told us how they rated vignettes, it would suggest that employing vignettes was either an unnecessarily complex way to find out how people define rape or that the particular vignettes used were either an overly simple representation of what is relevant in deciding whether a rape happened or that the researchers' objective was transparently obvious to respondents. The fact that a significant portion of respondents could not describe their rating pattern suggests that vignettes in general and these vignettes in particular are a valid way to find out about what information people use to decide a rape has occurred.

What conclusions can we draw from this information? Clearly, persons use different kinds and numbers of cues to rate vignettes. Furthermore, people are at least somewhat aware of the number and types of cues they use and the conclusions they reach with those cues. At the same time, the task given to them—namely to rate this set of simply structured vignettes—is not so self-evident that respondents can, with complete accuracy, report what they did. Thus, the rating of this set of vignettes continues to have benefits similar to those of a projective test. Vignettes tap into a complex structure of attitudes and opinions regarding definitions of rape about which they are not completely aware. Apparently people are not completely conscious of how they combine information on force, resistance, race, marital status, etc., to decide whether a rape has occurred.

Even within this simple set of vignettes, rating patterns range from the very simple single responses to remarkably complex response patterns that utilize much of the information provided and the range of answers available. It makes sense that respondents who had simple rating patterns had an easier time reconstructing their ratings afterward. The clarity of their ratings and their ability to accurately reconstruct them may mean that they have a stronger, better thought out, more clearly reasoned definition of rape. Conversely, it may mean that they are more responsive to social or cultural definitions of rape, less able to recognize or deal with ambiguous definitions, or more narrow-minded than persons with more complex rating patterns. Regardless of what the underlying explanation is, as people vary in how they rate vignettes, they vary in their ability to tell you what they did. These variations interact with the substantive content of vignettes being rated, and as seen in chapter 8, with the demographic characteristics of the raters.

Appendix 3 Supplementary Tables from the Los Angeles Study

Table A3.1 Correlation matrix, Los Angeles study, 1979 (unweighted sample) (N = 251)

	Sex	Age	Educa	Duncan	Income	Protes	Cath	Mar	Adults
Race (1 = black)	-.08	-.17	-.21	-.35	-.28	.38	-.28	-.21	.00
Sex (1 = female)		-.08	.16	.00	.22	-.13	.06	.12	.13
Age			-.27	-.07	-.13	.13	-.11	.05	-.22
Education				.56	.39	-.26	.13	.15	-.01
Duncan score					.35	-.22	.12	.08	.00
Income						-.18	.11	.37	.22
Protestant							-.66	-.05	.00
Catholic								.09	.04
Married									.34
Adults in household									
Children under 18 in household									
Years in house									
Official crime rate in area									
Perception of neighborhood safety									
Vulnerability index (1 – 9)									
Preventive behaviors									

Chil	Years	Crime	Neigh	Vulner	Prevent	NR	Non	Force	Force +	Resist	Resist +	Rating
.28	−.08	.78	.37	.29	.13	−.15	.11	−.07	−.01	.09	.03	−.18
−.13	.02	−.05	−.12	−.27	−.16	.01	.02	−.03	−.07	.09	.03	−.06
−.23	.43	−.11	−.08	.07	−.09	.01	.03	−.08	.01	−.08	.08	−.16
−.01	−.16	−.29	−.10	−.17	.07	.00	−.09	.17	.07	−.01	−.16	.11
−.07	.00	−.36	−.16	−.14	.00	.12	−.10	.18	−.03	−.03	−.12	.08
−.06	.02	−.38	−.22	−.13	.00	.02	−.06	.16	.04	−.04	.14	.17
.12	.19	.27	.11	.18	.01	−.03	.10	−.12	−.05	−.05	−.04	−.14
−.07	−.12	−.21	−.04	−.13	−.10	.02	−.01	.09	−.06	.09	−.07	.10
−.01	.11	−.27	−.25	−.19	.01	−.05	−.04	.08	.00	.03	−.02	.07
.06	−.01	−.08	−.16	−.02	−.02	.04	.00	−.04	−.05	.07	.02	.00
	−.12	.15	.32	.08	.04	−.14	.00	.07	.06	−.01	−.01	−.08
		−.03	−.15	−.03	−.03	−.06	.11	.00	−.09	−.04	.11	−.05
			.42	.26	.13	−.22	.17	−.09	.00	.05	.09	−.22
				.46	.18	−.14	.04	−.03	.12	−.06	.01	−.13
					.28	−.07	.03	−.06	.07	−.06	.04	−.05
						−.07	.03	.04	.03	−.04	−.02	.00

Table A3.1 (continued)

	Sex	Age	Educa	Duncan	Income	Protes	Cath	Mar	Adults
Nonraters									
Nonnormative raters									
Force-only									
Force-multiple									
Resistance-only									
Resistance-multiple									

Note: Correlations > .16 are significant at p < .01 using a two-tailed test of significance.

Chil	Years	Crime	Neigh	Vulner	Prevent	NR	Non	Force	Force +	Resist	Resist +	Rating
							−.13	−.15	−.29	−.11	−.17	.42
								−.14	−.28	−.11	−.16	−.28
									−.31	−.12	−.18	.01
										−.23	−.35	.01
											−.13	.14
												−.08

Table A3.2 Correlation matrix, Los Angeles study, 1979 (weighted sample) (*N* = 253)

	Sex	Age	Educa	Duncan	Income	Protes	Cath	Mar	Adults
Race (1 = black)	−.09	−.15	−.13	−.26	−.16	.25	−.19	−.12	.03
Sex (1 = female)		−.16	.14	.06	.27	−.07	.02	.07	.17
Age			−.23	.04	−.17	.18	−.14	.01	−.24
Education				.52	.37	−.26	.08	.20	.00
Duncan score					.30	−.19	.13	.16	.07
Income						−.17	.07	.43	.25
Protestant							−.62	.00	−.07
Catholic								.04	.06
Married									.40
Adults in household									
Children under 18 in household									
Years in house									
Official crime rate in area									
Perception of neighborhood safety									
Vulnerability index (1−9)									
Preventive behaviors									
Nonraters									
Nonnormative raters									
Force-only									
Force-multiple									
Resistance-only									
Resistance-multiple									

Note: Correlations > .16 are significant at p < .01 using a two-tailed test of significance.

Chil	Years	Crime	Neigh	Vulner	Prevent	NR	Non	Force	Force +	Resist	Resist +	Rating
.24	−.08	.66	.28	.21	.12	−.10	.11	−.06	−.01	.06	.04	−.11
−.13	−.01	.02	−.08	−.28	−.12	.04	.03	−.12	−.02	.00	.08	−.10
−.22	.43	−.09	−.06	.08	−.05	−.02	.08	−.11	−.02	−.01	.09	−.12
.02	−.10	−.19	−.07	−.16	.13	−.05	−.12	.16	.16	−.08	−.17	.08
−.05	.13	−.26	−.12	−.15	.01	.03	−.10	.16	.00	.02	−.11	.07
.08	.02	−.23	−.14	−.15	.03	.02	−.05	.18	.04	−.03	−.20	.12
.04	.23	.08	−.07	.08	−.08	−.00	.10	−.12	−.11	.05	.15	−.10
.00	−.13	−.11	.06	−.07	−.08	−.02	−.01	.13	−.03	.04	−.08	.03
.17	.11	−.26	−.24	−.18	.06	−.04	−.08	.12	.07	.00	−.11	.07
.19	−.02	−.01	−.05	−.16	.03	−.02	−.02	.02	.04	−.03	−.01	.00
	−.06	.08	.19	.03	.06	.12	−.07	.13	.07	.02	−.06	−.05
		−.02	−.18	−.05	−.05	−.12	.16	.04	−.09	.07	.03	−.08
			.39	.26	.13	−.17	.16	−.08	.01	.02	.08	−.19
				.39	.15	−.14	−.03	−.03	.15	−.02	.01	−.04
					.26	−.11	.01	−.08	.09	.03	.04	−.04
						−.09	.01	.13	.03	−.06	−.04	−.03
							−.14	−.17	−.34	−.10	−.19	.53
								−.13	−.26	−.08	−.15	−.40
									−.33	−.10	−.18	−.02
										−.20	−.35	−.14
											−.11	−.13
												−.08

Table A3.3 Correlation matrix for black and white respondents (black respondents = top diagonal), Los Angeles study, 1979 (unweighted sample) ($N = 251$)

	Sex	Age	Educa	Duncan	Income	Protes	Cath	Mar	Adults
Sex (1 = female)		.05	.13	−.13	.10	−.19	.14	.16	.07
Age	−.23		−.39	−.31	−.19	.21	−.17	.03	−.23
Education	.15	−.23		.55	.37	−.15	.11	.01	−.02
Duncan	.06	.05	.50		.31	−.06	−.11	−.17	−.08
Income	.29	−.18	.34	.26		.09	−.08	.21	.21
Protestant	−.05	.22	−.25	−.14	−.17		−.66	−.02	.10
Catholic	−.01	−.17	.05	.11	.06	−.62		.09	.02
Married	.06	−.00	.21	.18	.43	.06	.00		.28
Adults in household	.23	−.22	.02	.10	.27	−.11	.07	.47	
Children under 18 in household	−.11	−.20	.04	.03	.20	−.06	.08	.29	.23
Years in house	−.04	.43	−.08	.17	.03	.26	−.15	.14	−.02
Official crime rate	.03	.00	−.06	−.11	−.13	−.10	−.01	−.21	−.09
Perception of neighborhood safety	−.04	−.05	.00	−.06	−.10	−.21	.16	−.21	−.04
Vulnerability index	−.27	.09	−.18	−.11	−.16	.00	−.01	−.22	−.16
Preventive behaviors	−.10	−.01	.16	.04	.03	−.10	−.06	.08	.03
Nonraters	.03	−.03	−.09	−.02	.00	.03	−.05	−.06	−.03
Nonnormative raters	.06	.15	−.10	−.09	−.02	.06	.01	−.06	−.09
Force-only	−.13	−.15	.17	.13	.16	−.12	.16	.13	.03
Force-multiple	.00	−.03	.20	.02	.06	−.15	−.03	.10	.10
Resistance-only	−.06	−.00	−.12	.07	−.04	.11	.00	−.03	−.05
Resistance-multiple	.09	.12	−.20	−.11	−.21	.18	−.08	−.13	−.04
Vignette rating	−.10	−.12	.04	−.06	.06	−.05	−.02	.04	−.02

Note: Correlations > .22 are significant at p < .01 using a two-tailed test.

Chil	Years	Crime	Neigh	Vulner	Prevent	NR	Non	Force	Force +	Resist	Resist +	Rating
−.13	.08	.02	−.15	−.25	−.21	−.06	−.00	.08	−.14	.22	.02	−.05
−.21	−.21	.42	.05	.00	.15	−.16	.01	−.02	−.03	−.12	.07	−.26
.07	−.31	−.33	−.04	−.06	.04	.05	−.05	.15	−.06	.11	−.12	.10
.03	−.26	−.20	−.03	.01	.06	.21	−.05	.21	−.08	−.05	−.10	−.01
−.08	−.06	−.44	−.18	.07	.05	−.05	−.03	.11	.02	.01	−.06	.21
.09	.21	.04	.17	.15	−.01	.03	.06	−.06	.10	−.29	.09	−.12
−.06	−.16	.07	−.05	−.12	−.07	.04	.05	−.10	−.15	.31	−.05	.18
−.09	.05	−.13	−.17	−.07	−.03	−.11	.02	−.01	−.11	.12	.10	.01
.13	.14	.04	−.12	−.17	−.06	−.01	.10	−.02	−.13	−.06	.13	.04
	−.17	−.11	.34	.02	−.02	−.14	.00	.06	.05	−.06	.03	−.04
−.02		.09	−.04	.04	.01	.09	.03	−.03	−.10	−.15	.20	−.04
−.15	.00		.16	−.10	−.11	−.23	.20	−.11	.03	−.11	.11	−.10
.03	−.22	.32		.44	.14	−.05	.06	−.09	.14	−.15	.01	−.14
−.05	−.06	.24	.35		.29	.06	−.03	−.03	.08	−.19	.07	.02
.03	−.04	.17	.15	.24		.00	.07	−.11	.06	−.07	.01	.10
−.09	−.16	−.13	−.14	−.11	−.08		−.12	−.10	−.22	−.09	−.13	.17
−.11	.21	.03	−.10	.04	−.04	−.13		−.15	−.33	−.14	−.20	−.14
.16	.02	−.01	.08	−.05	.18	−.19	−.13		−.28	−.12	−.17	.04
.09	−.08	−.01	.13	.07	.01	−.35	−.23	−.34		−.26	−.37	−.08
.01	.09	.05	−.02	.08	−.04	−.11	−.07	−.11	−.19		−.16	.18
−.11	.04	−.19	−.02	−.01	−.05	−.19	−.13	−.19	−.34	−.11		−.06
−.02	−.10	−.13	.01	−.01	−.04	.58	−.45	−.04	−.17	.14	−.08	

Table A3.4 Regression of vignette ratings on characteristics portrayed in vignette for nonnormative, force-multiple, and resistance-multiple raters within subgroups stratified by race and sex, Los Angeles study, 1979 (unweighted sample, unstandardized coefficients)

Vignette characteristics	Black respondents		
	Total B	Males only B	Females only B
Force (1 = high)	1.44*	1.14*	1.55*
Resistance (1 = high)	0.97*	1.22*	0.88*
Male's occupation (1 = lawyer)	−0.03	−0.008	−0.04
Male's ethnicity (1 = black)	−0.12*	−0.16	−0.11
Female's ethnicity (1 = black)	0.04	0.10	0.01
Location (1 = bar)	−0.05	0.05	−0.08
Female's marital status (1 = divorced)	0.01	−0.08	0.05
Acquaintanceship (1 = same block)	−0.08	−0.20	−0.04
R^2	.22*	.21*	.23*
Constant	3.02*	3.17*	2.96*
Number of respondents	89	24	65
Number of vignettes	2,848	768	2,080
Mean rating	4.21	4.34	4.15

*$p < .01$.

| White respondents | | | |
Total B	Males only B	Females only B	Total B
1.49*	1.60*	1.41*	1.46*
0.52*	0.66*	0.41*	0.76*
−0.06	−0.10	−0.03	−0.02
0.01	0.04	0.01	−0.06
−0.09	−0.12	−0.08	−0.02
−0.11*	−0.10	−0.11	−0.07
0.006	0.04	−0.04	0.005
−0.12*	−0.24*	−0.03	−0.10*
.20*	.23*	.18*	.20*
3.45*	3.31	3.56*	3.22*
76	33	43	165
2,432	1,056	1,376	5,280
4.35	4.23	4.44	4.27

Table A3.5 Regression of vignette ratings on all variables by race and sex using the vignette as the unit of analysis, Los Angeles study, 1979 (unweighted sample)

Independent variables	Black respondents					
	Total		Males only		Females only	
	B	Beta	B	Beta	B	Beta
Demographic characteristics						
Race (1 = black)	—	—	—	—	—	—
Sex (1 = male)	−.07	−.02	—	—	—	—
Age	−.02*	−.18*	−.02*	−.21*	−.02*	−.16*
Years of schooling completed	−.02	−.03	−.06*	−.09*	.01	.02
Yearly income in $100s	.0009*	.05*	.002*	.11*	.0004	.02
Duncan score	−.005*	−.05*	−.003	−.03	−.01*	−.09*
Protestant	−.30*	−.08*	−.38*	−.10*	−.34*	−.09*
Catholic	−.17	−.02	—	—	−.23	−.03
Life-style characteristics						
Married	−.04	−.01	.48*	.12*	−.08	−.02
Number of adults in household	−.09*	−.05*	−.28*	−.16*	−.08*	−.04*
Children under 18 in household	−.04	−.04	.21*	.15*	−.11*	−.09*
Number of years in house	.02*	.06*	.04*	.12*	.01	.03
Criminal vulnerability						
Official crime rate in area	−.11*	−.04*	.36*	.12*	−.33*	−.12*
Neighborhood safety (1 = safer; 5 = less safe)	−.13*	−.07	−.23*	−.11*	−.08*	−.05
Feelings of vulnerability (1 = none; 9 = very)	.06*	.05*	.20*	.20*	−.01	−.01
Crime-preventive behaviors	.03	.01	−.05	−.01	.27*	.06*
Vignette characteristics						
Force (1 = high)	1.36*	.36*	1.23*	.31*	1.43*	.38*
Resistance (1 = high)	.93*	.25*	1.36*	.10*	.73*	.29*
Acquaintanceship (1 = same block)	−.06	−.02	−.12	−.03	−.03	−.01
Location (1 = bar)	−.03	−.01	.04	.01	−.07	−.02
Female's race (1 = black)	.03	.01	.05	.01	.02	.00

White respondents

Total		Males only		Females only		Total	
B	Beta	B	Beta	B	Beta	B	Beta
—	—	—	—	—	—	−.09	−.02
−.35*	−.10*	—	—	—	—	−.20*	−.05*
−.01*	−.12*	−.02*	−.18*	−.01*	−.10*	−.01*	−.12*
.02*	.03*	.06*	.09*	.02	.03	.01	.01
.00	.01	.0005	.04	−.0002	−.01	.00	.01
.001	.01	.00	−.01	.004*	.05*	.00	−.02
−.11	−.02	−.58*	−.11*	.25	.04	−.24*	−.06*
−.11	−.01	−.04	−.01	−.18	−.02	−.16	−.02
.11	.03	.06	.02	.19*	.06*	.03	.01
.07	.03	.02	.01	.12*	.05	.01	.01
−.12*	−.06*	−.27*	−.10*	−.09*	−.05*	−.06*	−.04*
.00	−.02	.02*	.10*	−.03*	−.13*	.002	.01
−.09	−.03	.04	.01	−.16*	−.06*	−.11*	−.06
−.11*	−.06*	−.19*	−.08*	−.11*	−.06*	−.11*	−.06*
.05*	.04*	.04	.03	.02	.02	.04*	.04*
.25*	.07*	.19	.05	.41*	.12*	.19*	.05*
1.37*	.40*	1.41*	.38*	1.34*	.41*	1.36*	.38*
.40*	.12*	.54*	.15*	.32*	.10*	.67*	.18*
−.06	−.02	−.15[+]	−.04[+]	−.01	.00	−.06	−.02
−.06	−.02	−.07	−.02	−.06	−.02	−.05	−.01
−.06	−.02	−.09	−.02	−.04	−.01	−.02	.004

Table A3.5 (continued)

Independent variables	Black respondents					
	Total		Males only		Females only	
	B	Beta	B	Beta	B	Beta
Male's race (1 = black)	−.09	−.02	−.09	−.02	−.09	−.02
Female's marital status (1 = divorced)	.01	.00	−.03	−.01	.03	.01
Male's occupation (1 = lawyer)	.03	.01	.00	.00	.04	.01
Equation statistics						
Constant	4.82*		4.17*		4.90*	
R^2	.23*		.29*		.24*	
Adjusted R^2	.23		.28		.24	

* Coefficients and equation statistics are significant at $p < .05$.

White respondents							
Total		Males only		Females only		Total	
B	Beta	B	Beta	B	Beta	B	Beta
.01	.00	.03	.01	.00	.00	−.04	−.01
.00	.00	.04	.01	−.03	−.01	.004	.001
−.04	−.01	−.07	−.02	−.02	−.01	−.01	−.002
3.93*		3.76*		3.69*		4.26*	
.20*		.23*		.22*		.21*	
.20		.22		.21		.21*	

+ Significant at p < .10.

Table A3.6 Best set of predictor variables for vignette rating for regressions conducted on total weighted and unweighted respondent samples and within groups stratified by race and sex, Los Angeles study, 1979[a]

Independent variables	Total weighted		Total unweighted		All whites	
	B	Beta	B	Beta	B	Beta
Demographic characteristics						
Race (1 = black)						
Sex (1 = male)	−.29	−.15	−.23	−.12		
Age			−.01	−.13		
Education						
Income						
Duncan score	.01	.14	.01	.16		
Protestant						
Catholic						
Life-style characteristics						
Married						
Adults in house						
Children under 18 in house						
Years in house						
Criminal vulnerability						
Official crime rate						
Neighborhood safety						
Vulnerability						
Preventive behaviors						
Vignette patterns						
Nonrater	1.32	.51	1.19	.41	1.36	.55
Nonnormative	−.94	−.30	−.58	−.20	−1.25	−.36
Force-only						
Force-plus						
Resistance-only	.66	.17	.59	.17	.70	.17
Resistance-plus						
Equation characteristics						
Constant	4.40		4.53		4.53	
R^2	.45		.30		.52	
Adjusted R^2	.43		.29		.49	

a Unmarked coefficients and statistics significant at $p < .05$.

All blacks		White females		White males		Black females		Black males	
B	Beta	B	Beta	B	Beta	B	Beta	B	Beta
−.01	−.27								
−.01	−.20								
.02	.23					.02	.24	.03[+]	.36[+]
								.49[+]	.32[+]
.86	.24	1.18	.47	1.60	.66	1.11	.33		
		−1.54	−.42	−.91	−.29				
.47[+]	.16[+]	.80	.22			1.41	.36		
4.78		4.63	4.38			4.38		3.42	
.19[+]		.49	.58			.26		.14[+]	
.15		.46	.56			.23		.09	

[+] p < .10.

Table A3.7 Regression of vignette ratings on all variables within vignette pattern groups, Los Angeles study, 1979 ($N = 8,032$ vignettes)

Independent variables	Nonraters		Nonnormative raters		Force-only raters	
	B	Beta	B	Beta	B	Beta
Demographic characteristics						
Race (1 = black)	−.71*	−.26*	1.26*	.30*	.27	.07
Sex (1 = male)	.23*	.09*	.33*	.08*	−.41*	−.10*
Age	−.02*	−.36*	−.01	−.08	−.03*	−.17*
Education	−.17*	−.40*	−.11*	.17*	.06*	.08*
Income in $100s	−.004*	−.35*	.00	−.02	.00	.00
Duncan score	−.01*	−.24*	.00	−.03	−.005	−.05
Protestant	−1.65*	−.55*	.39	.09	−.12	−.03
Catholic	−.06	−.01	−.39	−.07	.11	.01
Life-style characteristics						
Married	−.07	−.02	−.22	−.05	.26*	.07*
Adults in household	.18*	.13*	.34*	.20*	.19*	.06*
Children under 18 in household	.06	.03	−.40*	−.22*	−.05	−.04
Years in house	.005	.03	.01	.03	−.03*	−.08*
Vulnerability to crime						
Official crime rate	.43*	.27*	−.40	−.19	−.22	−.10
Safety of neighborhood	−.11*	−.07*	.16	.10	.04	.02
Index of vulnerability	−.21*	−.27*	.15*	.16*	.05	.04
Preventive behaviors	.45*	.16*	.36	.08	.22	.05
Vignette characteristics						
Force (1 = high)	.01	.00	.29*	.07*	2.82*	.74*
Resistance (1 = high)	.01	.00	.33*	.08*	.04	.01
Relationship (1 = same block)	.01	.00	−.12	−.03	.03	.01
Location (1 = bar)	.01	.00	−.20	−.05	.00	.00
Female's race (1 = black)	.00	.00	.02	.00	.00	.00
Male's race (1 = black)	.00	.00	−.21	−.05	.00	.00
Marital status (1 = divorced)	−.01	.00	.17	.04	.00	.00
Occupation (1 = lawyer)	−.01	.00	.02	.00	.01	.00
Equation characteristics						
Constant	11.14*		.24		2.81*	
R^2	.55*		.17*		.62*	
Adjusted R^2	.54		.14		.61	

* $p < .01$.

Force-plus raters		Resistance-only raters		Resistance-plus raters	
B	Beta	B	Beta	B	Beta
.06	.02	1.10*	.36*	−.13	−.04
−.26*	−.07*	−1.36*	−.46*	−.01	.00
.00	−.01	−.01*	−.09*	−.01*	−.16*
.02	.03	.00	.01	.00	.01
.003*	−.01	.00	.00	.00	−.02
−.003*	−.05*	−.02*	−.24*	.004	.05
−.22*	−.06*	−1.00*	−.29*	−.57*	−.16*
−.22	−.03	—	—	—	—
.32*	.09*	−.58*	−.20*	−.02	−.01
.07	.03	−.97*	−.39*	−.09	−.05
.08*	.06*	.31*	.21*	−.09	−.07
.00	.00	.03	.17	.01	.03
−.13*	−.07*	−.22*	−.13*	.24*	.14*
−.09*	−.06*	−.78*	−.35*	−.24*	−.13*
.01	.01	−.20*	−.17*	.01	.02
.20*	.05*	.40*	.13*	.04	.01
2.26*	.63*	.10	.04	.53*	.15*
.42*	.12*	1.95*	.66*	1.80*	.51*
−.07	−.02	−.01	.00	−.15	−.04
−.09	−.03	.01	.00	.04	.01
−.03	−.01	.00	.00	−.03	−.01
−.03	−.01	.03	.01	−.03	−.01
−.05	−.01	.03	.01	.00	.00
−.01	.00	.02	.01	−.05	−.01
3.03*		8.55*		4.76*	
.45*		.67*		.34*	
.45		.66		.32	

Table A3.8 Significant effects of eight-way analysis of variance of vignette characteristics on vignette rating within vignette pattern groups, Los Angeles study, 1979 (unweighted sample of vignettes)

Vignette characteristics	Vignette rating pattern					
	Non-rater	Non-normative rater	Force-only rater	Force-plus rater	Resistance-only rater	Resistance-plus rater
Force (1 = high)		**	**	**		**
Resistance (1 = high)		**		**	**	**
Acquaintanceship (1 = same block)		**				*
Location (1 = bar)				*		
Male's race (1 = black)		*				
Two-way interactions						
Force and resistance		**				
Male's race and marital status		*				
Three-way interactions						
Force, resistance, and location			*			
Resistance, location, and male's race		**				
Resistance, location, and occupation				**		
Resistance, marital status, and occupation		**				
Location, female's race, and occupation						**
Female's race, male's race, and marital status			*			
Four-way interactions						
Force, acquaintanceship, marital status, and occupation						**
Force, location, female's race, and occupation				*		
Force, female's race, male's race, and marital status		**				
Resistance, acquaintanceship, location, and male's race			**			

	Vignette rating pattern					
Vignette characteristics	Non-rater	Non-normative rater	Force-only rater	Force-plus rater	Resistance-only rater	Resistance-plus rater
Resistance, acquaintance-ship, female's race, and occupation				**		
Resistance, acquaintance-ship, marital status, and occupation			**			
Resistance, female's race, male's race, and marital status						**
Acquaintanceship, location, female's race, and marital status				**		**
Acquaintanceship, female's race, male's race, and marital status				*		
Location, male's race, marital status, and occupation		**				**
Female's race, male's race, marital status, and occupation		*				
Five-way interactions						
Force, resistance, acquaint-anceship, location, and male's race						**
Force, resistance, aquaint-anceship, marital status, and occupation						**
Force, resistance, location, female's race, and occupation						**
Force, resistance, location, marital status, and occupation						*

Table A3.8 (continued)

Vignette characteristics	Vignette rating pattern					
	Non-rater	Non-normative rater	Force-only rater	Force-plus rater	Resistance-only rater	Resistance-plus rater
Force, resistance, female's race, male's race, and marital status						*
Resistance, location, male's race, marital status, and occupation				**		

** Main effect or interaction is significant at $p < .05$.
 * Main effect or interaction is significant at $p < .10$.

Notes

1 Rape and Society

1 Attribution theory evolved during the late 1960s in psychology. Attribution theorists and researchers want to know how the average person explains the things that happen both to himself and others, and the process by which responsibility is assigned for events. See chapter 4 for a more detailed description of attribution theory as it applies to research on rape.

2 My perspective is "sociological social psychology" or what House (1977) calls psychological sociology, ". . . which relates macrosocial phenomena (e.g., organizations, societies and aspects of the social structures and processes thereof) to individuals' psychological attributes and behavior, usually using quantitative but nonexperimental (often survey) methods" (pp. 161–62). The social-psychological theoretical perspective, briefly outlined here as relevant to study of and specific to rape, is explicated in greater detail by Back (1972), Turner (1976, 1978), House (1977), and Stryker (1977, 1980, 1987). My father, W. B. Brookover (1975), first exposed me to symbolic interaction theory and sociological social psychology.

Part II

1 Some writers (e.g., Weis and Borges, 1973; Russell, 1974; Williams and Holmes, 1981) argue that the women's movement has caused (or will cause) the increased incidence of reported rapes. Two arguments are made in support of this opinion. First, the women's movement encourages women to act in untraditional and "liberated" ways, thus increasing women's exposure to

situations and men who will victimize them. Secondly, as rape's visibility as a social issue increases, women are more likely to report rapes. According to this argument, increased rates of reported rape are largely the result of increased reporting. Neither argument has been supported by systematic testing (e.g., LaFree, 1982; Williams and Holmes, 1981).

2 More extensive discussions of the women's movement and the development of the antirape movement can be found in Geis (1977); Largen (1976, 1985); Rose (1977); and Williams and Holmes (1981).

2 Feminist Theory and Victims of Rape

1 Klein (1981) and Clark and Lewis (1977), among others, present extended discussions of women as property and how this perception of male-female relationships relates to social definitions of women's roles.

2 Victim precipitation is the idea that the victim, either consciously or unconsciously, precipitates or contributes to the crime. Over the last fifty years, a number of typologies have been proposed for specifying the variety of relationships that may exist between the victim, the crime, and the perpetrator. Many of the typologies attempt to assign to the victim legal responsibility that ranges from none to full culpability; others attempt to account for dispositional and circumstantial factors of the victim and the situation. Hindelang (1976) briefly reviews the history of the concept and the various typologies of victims proposed by criminologists. The term is not, however, restricted to criminology but has been adopted in many areas including attribution theory in psychology (see chapter 4; Frieze and Bar-Tal, 1979; and Coates, Wortman, and Abbey, 1979).

3 A number of recent articles thoughtfully review the development, strengths, and weaknesses of feminist theory and methodology. See, for example, Fine (1985), Cook and Fonow (1986), Rosenblum (1986), and Farganis (1986).

4 Other summaries of recent research on women and rape can be found in Burt and Katz (1985) and Allegeier (1986).

5 For a thorough discussion of the development and methodological inadequacies of the National Crime Surveys and the *Uniform Crime Reports* see Argana (1975), Biderman (1975), Block and Block (1984), Hindelang and Davis (1977), Johnson and Wasielewski (1982), O'Brien (1983), and Reiss (1986).

6 Federal and state criminal justice reporting systems use the term "Part One Crimes" to refer to a class of felonies that include homicide, rape, robbery, aggravated assault, burglary, larceny (theft), and grand theft auto.

7 Exceptional means is used in the *Uniform Crime Reports* to refer to crimes that are cleared from police records for some reason other than arrest of the accused. Included within this category are situations in which the police lack jurisdiction over a crime because, for example, the accused is a juvenile.

8 Locus of control can be either internal or external. A person with an internal locus of control believes that s/he is able to control events through his/her abilities or behaviors. A person with an external locus of control believes that s/he is unable to control events and that the environment (e.g., other people, social institutions, fate, etc.) determine what happens to her/him. See chapter 4 and Rotter (1966) for further discussion of locus of control as a construct.

3 Men Who Rape

1 Koss and Leonard (1984), Knight, Rosenberg, and Schneider (1985), and Rada (1978) provide good reviews of the findings from such research studies.
2 A major concern in all scale construction and measurement, but of particular concern in the development of new measures or indices, is the extent to which a measure converges or overlaps with another measure of a similar concept. In developing a measure of depression, for example, we are concerned with differentiating depression from anxiety. In selecting a measure of social status we must concern ourselves with the high intercorrelations traditionally found in the United States between education, income, and occupation, and thus with overlap between the three variables. Are the three included in our study because they are hypothesized to measure different concepts or are the three variables included because each is hypothesized to contribute to a larger concept called socioeconomic status? To decide whether constructs should be considered independent of each other or interdependent, inter-item correlation matrices are examined and manipulated to decide whether one or more constructs is being measured. To the extent that two or more clusters of items can be identified where the items within a cluster have high correlations with each other but low correlations with the items in the other cluster(s), the clustered items are independent of each other and measure two or more constructs. See McKennel (1977) and Nunnally (1967) for further discussion.

4 Individual Definitions of Rape

1 See LaFree (1980) for a summary of this area of research.
2 Cognitive dissonance refers to a situation in which a person's behavior contradicts an important attitude or value, the feelings that result from that occurrence, and the process by which the person resolves or justifies the discrepancy between the behavior and his/her values or attitudes. See Festinger (1957) for further discussion of cognitive dissonance.
3 See Burt (1983), Hindelang (1976), Tyler (1984), and Wortman (1983) for overviews of the victimization literature, and note 2 in chapter 2 for a brief description of victim precipitation.
4 Modifications of the vignettes originally presented in Jones and Aronson (1973) are found in Prytula, Whiteside, and Davidson (1975), Luginbuhl

and Mullin (1974), Feldman-Summers and Lindner (1976), Calhoun, Selby, and Warring (1976), Scroggs (1976), Smith, Keating, Hester, and Mitchell (1976), Joe, McGee, and Dazey (1977), Rumsey and Rumsey (1977), Seligman, Brickman, and Koulack (1977), Selby, Calhoun, and Brock (1977), Krulewitz and Payne (1978), Paulsen (1979), Juhnke, Vought, Pyszczynski, Dane, Losure, and Wrightsman (1979), Acock and Ireland (1983), Alexander (1980), L'Armand and Pepitone (1982).

5 Appendix 2 demonstrates how minor changes in the design of vignettes can affect the data obtained. The changes made by later researchers in Jones and Aronson's (1973) original vignettes may explain the discrepancies in findings across the various studies.

6 Analysis of variance is a statistical technique for finding out whether two or more groups differ from each other and from the larger population. To compute analysis of variance, one must be able to compute a meaningful mean and variance for the dependent variable. See Dunn and Clark (1974) for a complete discussion of analysis of variance.

7 Problems associated with operationalizing concepts such as "respectability" are discussed in appendix 2 in more detail as part of a broader discussion of vignette methodologies. For the moment it is sufficient to note the appeal that a simulated rape has for the testing of attribution theory.

8 Problems of cultural comparability exist, however, between studies conducted in India (Kanekar, Kolsawalla, and colleagues) and those conducted in the United States.

9 As is discussed at length in chapter 6, three research groups have used vignettes similar to those used in attribution studies in community surveys while two other research groups have incorporated freestanding, uncrossed vignettes in community studies. Freestanding, uncrossed vignettes are ones in which none of the information is systematically varied between the vignettes; for example, varying the force used so that a weapon is referenced in half of the vignettes and verbal threats are referenced in the other half of the vignettes. The objective is to see whether the kind of force portrayed affects the respondent's judgment that a rape was committed.

5 Institutional Definitions of Rape

1 Statutory law refers to regulations or laws that are proposed by a legislator, passed by a legislature, and signed by a chief executive. "An act of the legislature declaring, commanding, or prohibiting something; a particular law enacted and established by the will of the legislative department of government . . ." (Black, 1979, p. 1264).

Case law refers to the body of legal interpretations and precedents that arises during the processing and trial of specific cases. Actions of judges, prosecutors, and defense attorneys create the basis of case law. In contrast to statutory law, case law is unwritten. "The aggregate of reported cases as forming a body of jurisprudence, or the law of a particular subject as evidenced or formed by the adjudged cases, in distinction to statutes and other sources of law" (Black, 1979, p. 196).

2 Substantive statutes define the crime and what constitutes proof of the crime. According to Black (1979), substantive law is ". . . [t]he basic law of rights and duties (contract law, criminal law, tort law, law of wills, etc.) as opposed to procedural law (law of pleading, law of evidence, law of jurisdiction, etc.)" (p. 1281).

In contrast, evidentiary statutes are part of procedural law. Evidentiary laws specify what can be put into evidence and how it is done. "Rules which govern the admissibility of evidence at hearings and trials. . . . In certain states evidence rules are codified (e.g., California Evidence Code) or otherwise set forth in statutes (e.g., state statutes commonly govern admissibility of confidential communications)" (Black, 1979, p. 500).

3 See Bienen (1976), Greenberg (1984), Hanawalt (1982), Kittel (1982), and Lindemann (1984) for discussion of how the crime of rape developed within English Common Law.

4 See Edwards (1982) and Tong (1984) for detailed discussions of women, sexuality, and the law.

5 A case is declared "unfounded" if after investigation of the available evidence, police or the district attorney's office decides that there is not enough evidence to bring charges or conduct a trial. A brief description of the "unfounding" of Part One Crimes is found in O'Brien (1985, pp. 19–21), and in a Comment in the *University of Pennsylvania Law Review* (1968).

6 As used by Caringella-MacDonald, nolle dismissal apparently refers to the term *nolle prosequi*, which in this context means ". . . a formal entry on the record by the prosecuting officer by which he declares that he will not prosecute the case further. . . . Commonly called 'nol pros' " (Black, 1979, p. 945).

7 In this context, authorization apparently means a prosecutorial decision not to charge the accused or, after formal charge, a prosecutorial decision to reduce the charge to a lesser offense, possibly as a result of plea bargaining; c.f., "To empower; to give a right or authority to act . . ." (Black, 1979, p. 122).

8 My discussion of character evidence relies heavily on two extensive presentations by Galvin (1986) and Davis (1984) of the legal view of character evidence as it relates to rape trials.

9 Simpson (1986), in contrast to prior writers, presents Hale as generally sympathetic to rape victims and, if anything, less bigoted than most men of his time as regards women. He also suggests that contemporary legal perceptions of rape originated in England during the eighteenth century rather than in the writings of either Hale or Wigmore.

10 Most of the articles dealt with one or more of the following issues: rape by subterfuge, rape as it relates to marriage, the duplicity of women who charge rape and the difficulties of defending against it, and whether drugged or unconscious women could be raped. Titles included "The Charge of Rape" (*Law Times*, 1866), "The Law of Rape—Chloroform in Rape Cases" (*Monthly Western Jurist*, 1874), "Rape Followed By Marriage" (*Irish Law Times*, 1877), "Unconsciousness in Rape" (*Weekly Law Bulletin*, 1883), "Concurrence of Rape and Adultery or Incest" (*Albany Law Journal*, 1882), "Observations on the Law of Rape in Ohio" (*Weekly Law Bulletin*, 1883), "Consent Given by Error—What Constitutes Rape" (*Legal News*, 1884), "Rape—Consent Obtained by Personation of Husband, The Queen v. Dee" (*Criminal Law Magazine*, 1885), "Consent To Carnal Connexion Conduced By Fraud on Female" (*Irish Law Times*, 1885), "Evidence in Prosecutions For Rape" (*Irish Law Times*, 1887), "Evidence As To Complaint Made By Prosecutrix" (*Irish Law Times*, 1888), and the only signed article, "Declarations in Rape Cases-Ohio Law" by Frances B. James in *Weekly Law Bulletin*, June 2, 1890. No articles were listed in volumes covering the years from 1898 through 1910, and the UCLA library holds no volumes that cover the years 1911–15.

11 When the author(s) is identified, 41 percent or 156 of the articles published after 1980 have one or more female author. Prior to 1973 almost all legal comments and notes related to rape were written by men. (I say "almost all" because in numerous instances the author of the note or comment is not listed; consequently his or her sex is unknown.)

12 Rape shield provisions prohibit or limit the use of evidence about the woman victim's prior sexual conduct. They are discussed in detail later in this chapter.

13 The sixth amendment to the U.S. Constitution was written in 1791 as part of the Bill of Rights. It ". . . includes such rights as the right to [a] speedy and public trial by an impartial jury, [the] right to be informed of the nature of the accusation, the right to confront witnesses, the right to assistance of counsel and compulsory process" (Black, 1979, p. 1244). The exact wording of the amendment follows.

> In all criminal prosecutions the accused shall enjoy the right to a speedy and public trial, by an impartial jury of the State and district wherein the crime shall have been committed, which district shall have been previously ascertained by law, and to be informed of the nature and cause of the accusation; to be confronted with the witnesses against him; to have compulsory process for obtaining witnesses in his favor, and to have the Assistance of Counsel for his defense (Black, 1979, pp. 1498–99).

14 As generally used, "[a] case is said to be heard *in camera* either when the hearing is had before the judge in his private chambers or when all spectators are excluded from the courtroom" (Black, 1979, p. 684).

15 Earlier I noted that between 1970 and 1980 seven of the articles listed in the *Index to Legal Periodicals* focused on marital rape and the spousal exemption; this contrasts with only four articles written before 1970 and 34 between 1980 and 1986. Clearly, interest is increasing in the problems posed by rapes occurring within marriage (e.g., Stecich, 1977; Jeffords, 1984).

16 "Clearance rate" is a term used by the Federal Bureau of Investigation in the *Uniform Crime Reports* to refer to crimes closed by the police either because of arrest or exceptional means. See note 7, chapter 2, for a definition of exceptional means.

17 Earlier jury simulations were not conducted within the context of attribution theory; they include studies by James (1959), Rose and Prell (1955), and Strodtbeck, James, and Hawkins (1957).

18 Chapter 4, chapter 6, and appendix 2 contain more extended discussions of vignette design and methodology and examples of their use.

19 Voir dire occurs during selection of a jury. Each potential juror is questioned by the judge, prosecuting attorney, and defense attorney in an effort to determine whether there is reason to consider that person biased. A French term, *voir dire* translates as "To speak the truth. This phrase denotes the preliminary examination which the court may make of one presented as a witness or juror, where his competency, interest, etc., is objected to" (Black, 1979, p. 1412).

20 See chapter 6 for a more detailed discussion of the vignettes used and the study conducted by Feild and Bienen (1980).

6 Community Definitions of Rape

1 For Ageton, "integrated theory of delinquency" refers to a model for explaining sexual assault that is derived by integrating social-control, strain, and social-learning theories. From this perspective, sexual assault is one of a number of delinquent and illegal acts in which the adolescent engages. It is implied that the sexual assault behavior is learned, is characteristic of the behaviors and values of the peer group with which the adolescent associates, and that this group represents a subculture of all adolescents. Derived from some of the ideas discussed in chapter 2, Ageton's contrasting theoretical model, feminist conflict theory, predicts that women are socialized to be victims, men are socialized to be offenders, and that men and women are in conflict.

2 Developed by Leslie Kish (1949), Kish tables randomly determine which person in a multiperson household is to be interviewed after all persons who meet the study criteria have been listed in a prescribed order.

3 Originally developed by Duncan (1961), Duncan scores are a measure of socioeconomic status that is determined by a person's occupation and educa-

tion. Scores range from 0, lowest socioeconomic status, to 100, highest socioeconomic status.

4 Item analyses examine the correlations between a single question or item of information and all the other questions being considered for inclusion in an index. Both inter-item and item-sum correlations are examined as part of item analyses.

Ranging from 0 to 1.0, Cronbach's alpha (1951) assesses the homogeneity and internal consistency of a set of questions (or other indicators) that are being tested for their ability to be combined into a single measure, idea, dimension, or construct. In order to conclude that the questions can be appropriately combined into an index, a Cronbach's alpha greater than or equal to 0.7 should be obtained.

5 Factor analysis is an analytical procedure that manipulates the inter-item correlation matrix. It is often used to evaluate whether a set of questions or other indicators measure a single underlying idea or construct or multiple underlying dimensions or constructs.

7 Los Angeles Study

1 Some readers may consider data collected in 1979 outdated. In evaluating the timeliness of the Los Angeles study, three points should be considered. First, data for all community surveys in which information about attitudes toward rape has been collected were collected at about the same time, namely 1976–80 (see chapter 6). No later community surveys have been reported. Secondly, the other community studies were either done in areas of the country that are assumed to be substantially more politically and sexually conservative than Los Angeles (e.g., Alabama, Minnesota, South Carolina, Texas) or, like the Los Angeles study, had restricted samples (e.g., age in Goodchilds et al., 1979; sex in Klemmacks, 1976), or were forced to restrict data collection in some way (e.g., Feild and Bienen, 1981, in South Carolina). Thus, not only is there something to be learned from the Los Angeles study itself, but its findings can be compared to other community surveys conducted elsewhere in the United States during the same time period. Moreover, while no community surveys have yet been conducted in the 1980s, data collected within the context of other research suggest that in spite of changes in legal statutes and expansion of treatment options for rape victims, attitudes about rape, and possibly even community residents' awareness of rape, have not changed appreciably over the last ten years. To evaluate the timeliness of the Los Angeles study and the extent to which it represents current attitudes of both California and non-California residents, recent studies by Neil Malamuth, Diana Russell, Gary LaFree, Susan Sorenson, Robert Borgida, and Mary Koss may be consulted.

2 The Los Angeles sample was restricted to blacks and non-Hispanic whites for two reasons. The first and predominant reason was that the original objective of the study was methodological. It was designed to be a preliminary test of the feasibility of designing vignettes about rape that could be administered in a community survey. Thus, the sample needed to be constructed to maximize internal variability while minimizing costs associated with administering the survey. Secondly, we were concerned about both the process and cost of translating data collection instruments. Los Angeles is heavily multiethnic, with approximately a third of the population Hispanic and significant proportions of Asian immigrants. Translating vignettes into multiple Asian languages would have been prohibitively expensive and available expertise would have been difficult to locate. Interviewing Hispanics, particularly those over the age of forty, would have necessitated translation into Spanish. Because the original focus of the study was on the vignette methodology, and we suspected that the Hispanic culture differed significantly in its perceptions of rape and sexuality, we chose not to attempt such a Spanish translation. At the time when these data were collected, no systematic information on the prevalence of reported rapes in Hispanic communities or on Hispanic attitudes and perceptions relevant to its prevalence was available. The *Uniform Crime Reports* and the National Crime Survey did not identify Hispanic victims or perpetrators. Joyce Williams and Karen Holmes (1981) were in the field in San Antonio, Texas, and the Epidemiological Catchment Area study (Sorenson et al., 1987) was only in the design stage.

3 The sample's representativeness was checked by comparing it to census data and to samples drawn for other studies conducted by the UCLA Institute for Social Science Research. Demographic characteristics of black and white respondents did not differ significantly from those of black and white respondents interviewed in a study of depression conducted in 1979 (Frerichs, Aneshensel, and Clark, 1981). Other analytical comparisons are reported in Rita Engelhardt, 1978.

The disproportionate stratified sample design poses no problems unless population estimates are desired. When ethnic groups are combined for population estimates, a weighting factor must be incorporated into the analyses. Respondents from the white primary sampling units (PSUS), which contain both blacks and whites, need a weight of 6.5/3.7. Respondents from black PSUS need a weight of 1.0/3.7. Derivation of the weights is diagrammed in the following table where the average raw weight is derived as follows

$$\text{Average raw weight} = (128 + 123(6.5))/251$$
$$= 3.7$$

Distribution of respondents by race and identity of PSU

Predominant race of PSU	Race of respondent Black	White	Total	Raw weight for PSU
Black	122	6	128	1.0
White	3	120	123	6.5
Total	125	126	251	3.7

4 The strength of the vignette technique is its ability to manipulate a range of hypothetically possible characteristics that combine to describe an event while at the same time creating each dimension independently. Statistically infrequent but theoretically interesting combinations of characteristics, as well as those combinations frequently associated with the event under study, can be adequately investigated using vignettes.

A difficulty in studying problems such as the conceptions of and responses to rape stems from the interrelations between various relevant domains and factors. Vignettes allow us to conceptualize the full range of content within each of the domains, and then to use a systematic, computerized sampling procedure to generate vignettes to which various groups of persons can respond. By systematically sampling a proportion of the total set of possible permutations we can evaluate the influence of each of the dimensions, and the content within them, on an individual's conception of dynamic link processes.

Whereas dimensions often are confounded in real life, the vignette technique allows each dimension to be treated as orthogonal. For example, knowledge of an individual's race increases our ability to successfully predict an individual's social class. As a result, when both race and social class are included in an analysis, it is often difficult to separate out the contribution of each when predicting a third variable. Vignettes allow us to assess the independent impact of each dimension or variable. For example, in the present study we can evaluate the extent to which the race of the victim rather than her marital status independently contributes to defining an event as rape.

As noted in appendix 2, vignettes have been successfully used with a wide variety of populations. Although systematic studies of respondents' reactions to vignettes have not been done, past studies suggest that most persons are able to respond to them and that meaningful, stable associations are established between vignettes and their dimensions, and other characteristics of respondents, behaviors, and groups.

5 As discussed in more detail in appendix 2, fractional replication assigns balanced sets of vignettes to each respondent. During analysis, balance insures that linear functions have the same number of combinations in each level of

each variable. However, administration of only a fraction of the universe of vignettes to a respondent results in some linear functions being equivalent during analysis. These equivalences, called aliases, are set by the researcher. In the present study, each respondent received thirty-two vignettes which comprised an eighth replicate of a 28 factorial design. This fractional replication was designed by aliasing the following seven, higher-order interactions with replicate:

a. ethnicity of male, occupation of male, location, and marital status of female;
b. occupation of male, ethnicity of female, force, and location;
c. ethnicity of male, ethnicity of female, force, and marital status of female;
d. ethnicity of male, occupation of male, acquaintanceship, resistance, and ethnicity of female;
e. acquaintanceship, ethnicity of female, location, and resistance;
f. ethnicity of male, acquaintanceship, resistance, force, and location; and
g. occupation of male, acquaintanceship, resistance, force, and marital status of the female.

6 The National Institute for Mental Health (NIMH) grant that funded data collection stipulated that no data about respondents' actual victimization experiences could be collected. Items on perceived vulnerability to crime were adapted from Tyler (1978) to serve as a surrogate for information on actual victimization.

7 The following questions are included in the nine-item vulnerability index:

a. To what extent are you *afraid* of being robbed, or having somebody take or try to take something from you by force when you are *outside your home and in your neighborhood*?
b. How much do you *worry* about being robbed while *you are in your home*?
c. How much are you *afraid* of being assaulted or physically attacked when you are *in your neighborhood but not in your home*?
d. How much are you *afraid* about being assaulted or physically attacked *in your home*?
e. How *likely* do you think it is that you will be robbed or assaulted *in your neighborhood*—but not in your home—in the coming year?
f. How *likely* do you think it is that you will be robbed or assaulted *in your own home* in the coming year?
g. How *afraid* are you of someone burglarizing or breaking into your (home/apartment)?

  h. How *likely* do you think that it is that your (home/apartment) will be burglarized or broken into *at night* when you are away during the next year?

  i. How *likely* do you think that it is that your home would be broken into *during the day*?

8 Statistics for Part One Crimes were obtained from the Los Angeles Police Department (LAPD), the Los Angeles County Sheriff's Department, and individual police departments not covered under LAPD or Sheriff's jurisdictions (e.g., Alhambra, Azusa, Beverly Hills, Pasadena, etc.). Crime rates for each area were computed for a base of 10,000 persons. The median rates for the county as a whole for the seven Part One Crimes at the time of the study were: homicide, 1.3; rape, 4.2; robbery, 33.0; assault, 36.9; burglary, 209.1; larceny (or theft), 261.9; and grand theft auto, 85.0. Since multiple respondents from the same locale could be assigned identical crime scores, the measure presents problems associated with ecological fallacy (Hammond, 1973), which may bias estimates of associations.

9 The formula used in creating the composite standardized crime score for each respondent was

$$F = b_{ij} \, ((x_{ij}-x_i)/s_i)$$
$$= b_{1j} \, ((x_{1j}-x_1)/s_1) + b_{2j} \, ((x_{2j}-x_2)/s_2)$$
$$+ \, b_{3j} \, ((x_{3j}-x_3)/s_3)$$

where i = 3 crime scores, j = 251 respondents
  F = composite crime rate
  b_{1j} = factor score coefficient for rape = .35
  b_{2j} = factor score coefficient for robbery = .36
  b_{3j} = factor score coefficient for burglary = .34
  x_{1j} = rape statistics assigned to individual respondent
  x_{2j} = robbery statistics assigned to individual respondent
  x_{3j} = burglary statistics assigned to individual respondent
  x_1 = mean score for rape = 10.7
  x_2 = mean score for robbery = 69.5
  x_3 = mean score for burglary = 265.7
  s_1 = standard deviation for rape = 7.3
  s_2 = standard deviation for robbery = 43.8
  s_3 = standard deviation for burglary = 80.2

To create nonstandardized scores delete x_1, x_2, x_3, s_1, s_2, and s_3 from the equation.

10 Regressions using the vignette as the unit of analysis were computed using the following formula (Nock and Rossi, 1978, p. 572).

$$R_i = f[(V_i) + (I_{ij}) + (IV_{ij}) + (VV_{ik,ik+1})] + e$$

where R_i = rating given to vignette i

V_i = coded characteristics of information of vignette i

I_{ij} = characteristics of respondent j who rated vignette i

IV_{ij} = interaction of characteristics of respondent j and characteristics of vignette i

$VV_{ik,ik+1}$ = interaction of vignette characteristic k and vignette characteristic k + 1, etc., and

e = random error

R_i can represent either the respondent's rating or the Z score or standardized rating computed using the formula

$$Z = (R_{ij} - R_j)/{}^sR_j$$

where Z = the standardized rating

R_{ij} = rating given to vignette by respondent j

R_j = respondent j's mean rating

${}^sR_j$ = the standardized deviation of respondent j's ratings

11 Both multiple regression and multiple discriminant analyses are used to summarize the effect of two or more independent variables on a dependent variable. Both analytical techniques assume that the independent variables are naturally interval measures or can be transformed into interval measures for which means and variance can be computed. In regression analysis the dependent variable also is assumed to be an interval measure and the objective of the analysis is to determine the set of independent variables that best predicts the dependent variable given the hypotheses being tested and the theory under consideration. In contrast, in discriminant analysis the dependent variable is assumed to be nominal, categorical, or discrete. The object of the analysis is to ascertain the combination of independent variables that best differentiates between the various categories of the dependent variable. Numerous variants of regression and discriminant analysis exist, and each variant makes certain assumptions about the data being analyzed. See Afifi and Clark (1984) for further discussion of the two procedures.

8 When a Sexual Encounter Becomes a Rape

1 Within the eight-way analysis of variance, 2 significant main effects, 1 marginally significant main effect, and 14 significant interactions were found. Of the fourteen significant interactions, two were the three-way interactions discussed and presented in figures 8.3 and 8.4, five were four-way interactions, one was a six-way interaction, and one was a seven-way interaction.

9 Ethnic, Gender, and Social-Class Differences in Perceptions of Rape

1 Numerous arguments can be made regarding which set of regression equations most accurately represents the data set while simultaneously being easy to understand and present. My decision to present the reduced equations using the vignette as the unit of analysis in the text reflects two observations. First, equations using the vignette as the unit of analysis are more adequate when "adequacy" is determined by the difference between the R^2 and the adjusted R^2. The greater adequacy of the vignette equations is largely a statistical artifact that results from two characteristics of the vignette data file: the much larger N (8,032) in the vignette file than in the respondent file (251 cases) and the necessity of adding identical respondent information to all 32 vignettes rated by a respondent. Second, vignette information is more easily added to the vignette equations than to the respondent equations. Whereas in the respondent equations dummy variable combinations have to be manipulated, in the vignette equations, the actual information presented in the vignette rated by the respondent can be added to the equations.

2 Ibid.

3 Given the restricted variance available in some of the decision groups and the lack of comparability of variance across the six groups, generalizations and interpretations of these analyses are limited.

10 Actors, Causes, and Solutions

1 Answers that referenced force were separated from the first category because the word "forced" was used in the vignettes and we wanted to see whether its presence in the vignettes influenced respondents' answers to this set of questions.

12 Rape in Los Angeles

1 The three members who gave a consistently low or ambivalent rating are probably more appropriately considered to have conservative attitudes about rape and, thus, are excluded from this discussion. Other information available about them suggests that they are more appropriately considered members of either the nonnormative or resistance-only groups which is where they were assigned in the discriminant analyses conducted and reported in chapter 9.

Appendix 2

1 Respondents in the pilot study were 120 persons approached in four different shopping centers on a September Saturday and Sunday in 1978.

2 Some investigators suggest that the vignettes used in many studies are too far removed from actual encounters to be considered authentic by a respondent (e.g., Burt, 1979; Borgida, personal communication, 1979). Others have suggested that respondents presented with multiple, simple vignettes will be bored by the lack of variety available within a set of vignettes and that this boredom will affect respondents' interest in rating vignettes. In contrast, it can be argued that every piece of information presented has a potential impact on the ratings and, therefore, properly should be assumed to be an independent variable. In particular, the location, content, and length of contextual material relative to the variables under investigation may significantly influence respondents' perception of the activity portrayed in the vignette.

3 At the beginning of the group administration the following instructions were read to respondents.

> Each card describes a possible rape. The six envelopes on this board are numbered 1 to 6. If you feel that a rape definitely was not committed, rate it "1." If you feel a rape definitely was committed, rate it "6." Use envelopes 2, 3, 4, or 5 to rate cards that you are less sure about. After you have rated a card, put it in the envelope with the number that matches your rating.

The same instructions were repeated on the first IBM card in the set of vignette cards assigned to each respondent.

Bibliography

Abel, G. G., and E. B. Blanchard (1974). "The role of fantasy in the treatment of sexual deviation." *Archives of General Psychiatry* 30:467–75.

———. (1976). "The measurement and generation of sexual arousal in male sexual deviates." In *Progress in Behavior Modification*, vol. 2, ed. M. Hersen, P. M. Miller, and R. M. Eisler, pp. 99–136. New York: Academic Press.

Abel, G. G., D. H. Barlow, E. B. Blanchard, and D. Guild (1977). "The components of rapists' sexual arousal." *Archives of General Psychiatry* 34:895–903.

Abel, G. G., E. B. Blanchard, and J. V. Becker (1978). "An integrated treatment program for rapists." In *Clinical Aspects of the Rapist*, ed. R. T. Rada, pp. 161–214. New York: Grune and Stratton.

Abelson, R. P. (1968). "Simulation of social behavior." In *Handbook of Social Psychology*, vol. 2, ed. G. Lindzey and E. Aronson, pp. 274–356. Menlo Park: Addison Wesley Publishing Company.

———. (1976). "Social psychology's rational man." In *Rationality and the social sciences*, ed. S. Benn and G. Mortimore, pp. 58–89. Boston: Routledge and Kegan Paul.

Acock, A. C., and N. K. Ireland (1983). "Attribution of blame in rape cases: the impact of norm violation, gender, and sex-role attitude." *Sex Roles* 9:179–93.

Afifi, A. A., and V. A. Clark (1984). *Computer-aided multivariate analysis.* Belmont: Lifetime Learning Publications.

Ageton, S. S. (1983). *Sexual Assault among Adolescents.* Lexington, Mass.: D. C. Heath and Company.

Albany Law Journal (1882). "Concurrence of rape and adultery or incest." *Albany Law Journal* 25:484–85.

Albin, R. S. (1977). "Psychological studies of rape." *Signs: Journal of Women in Culture and Society* 3:423–35.

Alder, C. (1985). "An exploration of self-reported sexually aggressive behavior." *Crime and Delinquency* 31:306–31.

Alexander, C. S. (1980). "The responsible victim: Nurses' perceptions of victims of rape." *Journal of Health and Social Behavior* 21:22–33.

Alexander, C. S., and H. J. Becker (1978). "The use of vignettes in survey research." *Public Opinion Quarterly* 42:93–104.

Allgeier, E. R. (1986). "Coercive versus consensual sexual interactions." G. Stanley Hall Lecture, American Psychological Association, Washington, D.C.

Alves, W. M., and P. H. Rossi (1978). "Who should get what? Fairness judgments of the distribution of earnings." *American Journal of Sociology* 84:541–64.

Alwin, D. F., and R. M. Hauser (1975). "The decomposition of effects in path analysis." *American Sociological Review* 40:37–47.

American Psychiatric Association (1980). *Diagnostic and Statistical Manual of Mental Disorders*. Washington, D.C.: American Psychiatric Association.

Amir, M. (1971). *Patterns in Forcible Rape*. Chicago: University of Chicago Press.

Aneshensel, C. S., E. P. Fielder, and R. Becerra (1989). "Fertility and fertility-related behavior among Mexican-American and non-Hispanic white adolescent females." *Journal of Health and Social Behavior* 30.

Arax, M. (1986). "Judge says law doesn't protect prostitutes, drops rape count." *Los Angeles Times*, April 24 and May 11.

Argana, M. G. (1975). "Development of a national victimization survey." In *Victimology: A new focus*, ed. I. Drapkin and E. Viano, pp. 171–79. Lexington, Mass.: D. C. Heath and Company.

Aronson, E., and J. M. Carlsmith (1968). "Experimentation in social psychology." In *Handbook of Social Psychology*, ed. G. Lindzey and E. Aronson, vol. 2, pp. 1–79. Menlo Park, Calif.: Addison-Wesley Publishing Company.

Ashworth, C. D., and S. Feldman-Summers (1978). "Perceptions of the effectiveness of the criminal justice system: The female victim's perspective." *Criminal Justice and Behavior* 5:227–40.

Back, K. W. (1972). "Psychologism, structuralism, and interactionism." Presidential Address to the American Sociological Association: Section on Methodology.

Barnett, N. J., and H. S. Feild (1978). "Character of the defendant and length of sentence in rape and burglary crimes." *Journal of Social Psychology* 104:271–77.

Barr, A. J., J. Goodnight, J. Sall, and J. Hellwig (1976). *A User's Guide to SAS*. Raleigh: SAS Institute.

Bart, P. B. (1975). "Rape doesn't end with a kiss." *Viva*, June.

———. (1981). "A study of women who both were raped and avoided rape." *Journal of Social Issues* 37:123–37.

Bart, P. B., and P. H. O'Brien (1985). *Stopping Rape, Successful Survival Strategies*. New York: Pergamon Press.

Becker, J. V., L. J. Skinner, G. G. Abel, J. Howell, and K. Bruce (1982). "The effects of sexual assault on rape and attempted rape victims." *Victimology: An International Journal* 7:106–13.

Belcastro, P. A. (1982). "A comparison of latent sexual behavior patterns between raped and never-raped females." *Victimology: An International Journal* 7:224–30.

Berger, V. (1977). "Man's trial, woman's tribulation: rape cases in the courtroom." *Columbia Law Review* 77:1–103.

Bermant, G., M. McGuire, W. McKinley, and C. Salo (1974). "The logic of simulation in jury research." *Criminal Justice and Behavior* 1:224–33.

Biderman, A. D. (1975). "Victimology and victimization surveys." In *Victimology: A New Focus*, vol. 3, ed. I. Drapkin and E. Viano, pp. 153–69. Lexington, Mass.: D. C. Heath and Company.

Bienen, L. (1976). "Rape I." *Women's Rights Law Reporter* 3:45–57.

———. (1977). "Rape II." *Women's Rights Law Reporter* 3:90–137.

———. (1980). "Rape III: National developments in rape reform legislation." *Women's Rights Law Reporter* 6:170–213.

Black, H. C. (1979). *Black's law dictionary, definitions of the terms and phrases of American and English jurisprudence, ancient and modern*. 5th ed. St. Paul: West Publishing Company.

Block, C. R., and R. L. Block (1984). "Crime definition, crime measurement, and victim surveys." *Journal of Social Issues* 40:137–60.

Bohmer, C. (1977). "Judicial attitudes toward rape victims." In *Forcible rape: The crime, the victim, and the offender,* ed. D. Chappell, R. Geis, and G. Geis, pp. 303–7. New York: Columbia University Press.

Bolt, M., and J. Caswell (1981). "Attribution of responsibility to a rape victim." *Journal of Social Psychology* 114:137–38.

Borgida, E. (1980). "Evidentiary reform of rape laws: a psycholegal approach." In *New Directions in Psycholegal Research*, ed. P. D. Lipsett and B. D. Sales, pp. 57–75. New York: Van Nostrand Reinhold.

———. (1981). "Legal reform of rape laws." In *Applied Social Psychology Annual,* ed. L. Bickman, pp. 211–41. Beverly Hills: Sage Publications.

Borgida, E., and N. Brekke (1985). "Psycholegal research on rape trials." In *Rape and Sexual Assault,* ed. A. W. Burgess, pp. 313–42. New York: Garland Publishing, Inc.

Borgida, E., and P. White (1978). "Social perception of rape victims: the impact of legal reform." *Law and Human Behavior* 2:339–51.

Bourque, L. B. (1978). "Preliminary analysis of vignettes used in part one, 'Expressed attitudes about rape: a preliminary study.'" Unpublished manuscript.

————. (1978). "Description of findings on non-vignette rape items in part one of 'Expressed attitudes toward rape: a preliminary study' and comparison with Williams categories." Unpublished manuscript.

————. (1980). "Reliability of vignettes in measuring attitudes." Paper presented at the annual meeting of the American Sociological Association, New York.

Bourque, L. B., and R. Engelhardt (1978). "Design and methodological findings from preliminary and formal pretests using vignettes to measure expressed attitudes toward rape." Unpublished manuscript.

————. (1979). "Measuring attitudes using vignettes." Paper presented at the annual meeting of the American Sociological Association, Boston.

————. (1980). "Issues to consider in designing vignettes." Unpublished manuscript.

Brickman, J., and J. Briere (1984). "Incidence of rape and sexual assault in an urban Canadian population." *International Journal of Women's Studies* 7:195–206.

Brookover, W. B., and E. L. Erickson (1975). *Sociology of Education.* Homewood: The Dorsey Press.

Brown, R. (1962). "Models of attitude change." In *New Directions in Psychology*, vol. 1, ed. R. Brown, E. Galanter, E. H. Hess, and G. Mandler, pp. 1–85. New York: Holt, Rinehart, and Winston.

Brown, V. B., L. Garnets, and B. Levy (1981). *Consensus and controversy in sexual assault prevention and intervention: A delphi study.* Research Monograph. Culver City: Southern California Rape Prevention Study Center, Didi Hirsch Community Mental Health Center.

Brownmiller, S. (1975). *Against our will: Men, women and rape.* New York: Simon and Schuster.

Brunswick, E. (1956). *Perception and the Representative Design of Psychological Experiments.* Berkeley: University of California Press.

Bureau of Justice Statistics (1980). *Criminal Victimization in the United States, 1978.* A National Crime Survey Report, NCS-N-17, NCJ-66480. Washington, D.C.: U.S. Department of Justice.

————. (1981). *Criminal Victimization in the United States, 1979.* A National Crime Survey Report, NCJ-76710, NCS-N-19. Washington, D.C.: U.S. Department of Justice.

————. (1982). *Criminal Victimization in the United States, 1980.* A National Crime Survey Report, NCJ-84015. Washington, D.C.: U.S. Department of Justice.

————. (1983). *Criminal Victimization in the United States, 1981.* A National Crime Survey Report, NCJ-90208. Washington, D.C.: U.S. Department of Justice.

————. (1984). *Criminal Victimization in the United States, 1982*. A National Crime Survey Report, NCJ-92820. Washington, D.C.: U.S. Department of Justice.

————. (1985). *Criminal Victimization 1984*. Washington, D.C.: U.S. Department of Justice.

————. (1985). *Criminal Victimization in the United States, 1983*. A National Crime Survey Report, NCJ-96459. Washington, D.C.: U.S. Department of Justice.

————. (1985). *United States Department of Justice Bulletin 1*: The Crime of Rape. Washington, D.C: U.S. Department of Justice.

————. (1986). *Criminal Victimization 1985*. Washington, D.C.: U.S. Department of Justice.

Burgess, A. W., ed. (1985). *Rape and sexual assault*. New York: Garland Publishing, Inc.

————. (1988). *Rape and sexual assault II*. New York: Garland Publishing, Inc.

Burgess, A. W., and L. L. Holmstrom (1974). *Rape: Victims of Crisis*. Bowie, Mass.: Robert J. Brady & Co.

————. (1985). "Rape trauma syndrome and post-traumatic stress response." In *Rape and Sexual Assault*, ed. A. W. Burgess, pp. 46–60. New York: Garland Publishing, Inc.

Burnett, R. C., D. I. Templer, and P. C. Barker (1985). "Personality variables and circumstances of sexual assault predictive of a woman's resistance." *Archives of Sexual Behavior* 14:2:183–88.

Burstein, K., E. B. Doughtie, and A. Raphaeli (1980). "Contrastive vignette technique: an indirect methodology designed to address reactive social attitude measurement." *Journal of Applied Social Psychology* 10:147–65.

Burt, M. R. (1979). *Attitudes supportive of rape in American culture*. Final Report to National Institute of Mental Health. National Center for the Prevention and Control of Rape. Grant Number RO1 MH29023.

————. (1980). "Cultural myths and supports for rape." *Journal of Personality and Social Psychology* 38:217–30.

————. (1983). "Justifying personal violence: A comparison of rapists and the general public." *Victimology: An International Journal* 8:131–50.

Burt, M. R., and R. Albin (1981). "Rape myths, rape definitions and probability of conviction." *Journal of Applied Social Psychology* 11:212–30.

Burt, M. R., and B. L. Katz (1985). "Rape, robbery, and burglary: Responses to actual and feared criminal victimization, with special focus on women and the elderly." *Victimology: An International Journal* 10:325–58.

Calhoun, L. G., J. W. Selby, and L. J. Warring (1976). "Social perception of the victim's causal role in rape: An exploratory examination of four factors." *Human Relations* 29:517–26.

Calhoun, L. G., A. Cann, J. W. Selby, and D. L. Magee (1981). "Victim emotional response: Effects on social reaction to victims of rape." *British Journal of Social Psychology* 20:17–21.

Calhoun, L. G., J. W. Selby, A. Cann, and G. T. Keller (1978). "The effects of victim physical attractiveness and sex of respondent on social reactions to victims of rape." *British Journal of Social and Clinical Psychology* 17:191–92.

Calhoun, L. G., J. W. Selby, G. T. Long, and S. Laney (1980). "Reactions to the rape victim as a function of victim age." *Journal of Community Psychology* 8:172–75.

Cann, A., L. G. Calhoun, and J. W. Selby (1979). "Attributing responsibility to the victim of rape: Influence of information regarding past sexual experience." *Human Relations* 32:57–67.

Caringella-MacDonald, S. (1985). "The comparability in sexual and nonsexual assault case treatment: Did statute change meet the objective?" *Crime and Delinquency* 31:206–22.

Carmen, E. H., P. P. Rieker, and T. Mills (1988). "Victims of violence and psychiatric illness." In *Sexual Assault II*, ed. A. W. Burgess, pp. 27–60. New York: Garland Publishing, Inc.

Carter, D. L., R. A. Prentky, and A. W. Burgess (1988). "Victim response strategies." In *Sexual Assault II*, ed. A. W. Burgess, pp. 105–32. New York: Garland Publishing, Inc.

Chaikin, A. L., and J. M. Darley (1973). "Victim or perpetrator? Defensive attribution of responsibility and the need for order and justice." *Journal of Personality and Social Psychology* 25:268–75.

Chappell, D., and S. Singer (1977). "Rape in New York City: A study of material in the police files and its meaning." In *Forcible Rape: The crime, the victim, and the offender*, ed. D. Chappell, R. Geis, and G. Geis. New York: Columbia University Press.

Clark, L. G., and D. J. Lewis (1977). *Rape: The Price of Coercive Sexuality*. Toronto: The Canadian Women's Educational Press.

Cloward, R. A. (1959). "Illegitimate means, anomie, and deviant behavior." *American Sociological Review* 24:164–76.

Cluss, P. A., J. Boughton, E. Frank, B. D. Stewart, and D. West (1983). "The rape victim, psychological correlates of participation in the legal process." *Criminal Justice and Behavior* 10:342–57.

Coates, D., C. B. Wortman, and A. Abbey (1979). "Reactions to victims." In *New approaches to social problems*, ed. I. H. Frieze, D. Bar-Tal, and J. S. Carroll, pp. 21–52. San Francisco: Jossey-Bass Publishers.

Cochran, W. G., and G. M. Cox (1957). *Experimental Designs*. New York: Wiley.

Cohen, A. K. (1955). *Delinquent Boys: The Culture of the Gang*. New York: The Free Press.

Cohen, M. L., R. F. Garafolo, R. Boucher, and T. Segham (1971). "The psychology of rapists." *Seminars in Psychiatry* 3:307–27.

Cohen, P. B. (1984). "Resistance during sexual assaults: Avoiding rape and injury." *Victimology: An International Journal* 9:120–29.

Converse, J., and S. Presser (1986). *Survey questions, hand-crafting the standardized questionnaire*. Beverly Hills: Sage Publications.

Cook, J. A., and M. M. Fonow (1986). "Knowledge and women's interests: Issues of epistemology and methodology in feminist sociological research." *Sociological Inquiry* 56:2–29.

Criminal Law Magazine (1885). "Rape—Consent obtained by personation of husband." *Criminal Law Magazine* 6:220–45.

Cronbach, L. J. (1951). "Coefficient alpha and the internal structure of tests." *Psychometrika* 16:297–334.

Cronkite, R. C. (1980). "Social psychological simulations: An alternative to experiments?" *Social Psychology Quarterly* 43:199–216.

Curtis, L. A. (1976). "Rape, race, and culture: some speculation in search of a theory." In *Sexual Assault,* ed. M. J. Walker and S. L. Brodsky, pp. 117–34. Lexington, Mass.: D. C. Heath and Company.

Davidson, P. R., and P. B. Malcolm (1985). "The reliability of the rape index: a rapist sample." *Behavioral Assessment* 7:283–92.

Davis, E. M. (1984). "Rape shield statutes: legislative responses to probative dangers." *Journal of Urban and Contemporary Law* 27:271–94.

Deitz, S. R., and L. E. Byrnes (1981). "Attribution of responsibility for sexual assault: the influence of observer empathy and defendant occupation and attractiveness." *The Journal of Psychology* 108:17–29.

Deming, M. B., and A. Eppy (1984). "The sociology of rape." *Sociology and Social Research* 65:357–80.

Deming, M. B., P. H. Landry, and D. D. McFarland (1984). "Rape case processing in California: The impact of a rape shield law." Paper presented at the annual meeting of the American Sociological Association, San Antonio.

Denzin, N. K. (1970). *The research act: a theoretical introduction to sociological methods*. Chicago: Aldine.

Dietz, P. E. (1978). "Social factors in rapist behavior." In *Clinical aspects of the rapist,* ed. R. T. Rada, pp. 59–115. New York: Grune and Stratton.

DiVasto, P. V., A. Kaufman, L. Rosner, R. Jackson, J. Christy, S. Pearson, and T. Burgett (1984). "The prevalence of sexually stressful events among females in the general population." *Archives of Sexual Behavior* 13:59–67.

Duncan, O. D. (1961). "A socioeconomic index for all occupations." In *Occupations and social status,* ed. A. J. Reiss, pp. 109–38. New York: Free Press of Glencoe.

Dunn, O. J., and V. A. Clark (1974). *Applied statistics: Analysis of variance and regression*. New York: John Wiley and Sons.

Durkheim, E. (1964). *The rules of sociological method*. New York: Free Press.

Edwards, S. (1982). "Sexuality, sexual offenses and conceptions of victims in the criminal justice process." *Victimology: An International Journal* 7:113–30.

Ellis, E. M., B. M. Atkeson, and K. S. Calhoun (1982). "An examination of differences between multiple- and single-incident victims of sexual assault." *Journal of Abnormal Psychology* 91:221–24.

Engelhardt, R. (1978). "Profile of LAMAS samples." Unpublished paper, Institute of Social Science Research, University of California.

Essock-Vitale, S. M., and M. T. McGuire (1985). "Women's lives viewed from an evolutionary perspective. I. Sexual histories, reproductive success, and demographic characteristics of a random sample of American women." *Ethology and Sociobiology* 6:137–54.

Estrich, S. (1987). *Real rape*. Cambridge: Harvard University Press.

Farganis, S. (1986). "Social theory and feminist theory: The need for dialogue." *Sociological Inquiry* 56:50–68.

Featherman, D. L., M. Sobel, and D. Dickens (1975). *A manual for coding occupations and industries into detailed 1970 categories and a listing of 1970-basis Duncan socioeconomic and NORC prestige scores*. University of Wisconsin-Madison, Center for Demography and Ecology. Working paper No. 75-1.

Feild, H. S. (1978a). "Juror background characteristics and attitudes toward rape." *Law and Human Behavior* 2:73–93.

———. (1978b). "Attitudes toward rape: A comparative analysis of police, rapists, crisis counselors, and citizens." *Journal of Personality and Social Psychology* 36:156–79.

———. (1979). "Rape trials and jurors' decisions: A psycholegal analysis of the effects of victim, defendant, and case characteristics." *Law and Human Behavior* 3:261–84.

Feild, H. S., and N. J. Barnett (1977). "Forcible rape: An updated bibliography." *Journal of Criminal Law and Criminology* 68:146–59.

———. (1978). "Simulated jury trials: Students vs. 'real' people as jurors." *Journal of Social Psychology* 104:287–93.

Feild, H. S., and L. B. Bienen (1980). *Jurors and Rape*. Lexington, Mass.: Lexington Books.

Feldman-Summers, S. (1976). "Conceptual and empirical issues associated with rape." In *Victims and society*, ed. E. Viano, pp. 91–104. Washington, D.C.: Visage Press.

Feldman-Summers, S., and C. D. Ashworth (1981). "Factors related to intentions to report a rape." *Journal of Social Issues* 37:53–70.

Feldman-Summers, S., and K. Lindner (1976). "Perceptions of victims and defendants in criminal assault cases." *Criminal Justice and Behavior* 3:135–50.

Feldman-Summers, S., and J. Norris (1984). "Differences between rape victims who report and those who do not report to a public agency." *Journal of Applied Social Psychology* 14:562–73.

Festinger, L. (1957). *A theory of cognitive dissonance*. Stanford: Stanford University Press.

Fine, M. (1985). "Reflections on a feminist psychology of women: Paradoxes and prospects." *Psychology of Women Quarterly* 9:167–83.

Fischer, G. J. (1986a). "College student attitudes toward forcible date rape: Changes after taking a human sexuality course." *Journal of Sex Education and Therapy* 12:42–46.

———. (1986b). "College student attitudes toward forcible date rape: I. Cognitive predictors." *Archives of Sexual Behavior* 15:457–66.

Fishbein, M., and I. Ajzen (1973). "Attribution of responsibility: A theoretical note." *Journal of Experimental Social Psychology* 9:148–53.

Flannagan, T. J., and M. McLeod (1983). *Sourcebook of Criminal Justice Statistics-1982*, ed. T. J. Flannagan and M. McLeod. Washington, D.C.: U.S. Department of Justice, Bureau of Justice Statistics.

Foa, U. G. (1965). "New developments in facet design and analysis." *Psychology Review* 72:262–74.

Fogarty, F. A. (1977). "A selective bibliography." In *Forcible Rape*, ed. D. Chappell, and R. Geis, G. Geis. New York: Columbia University Press.

Forman, B. D. (1982). "Reported male rape." *Victimology: An International Journal* 7:235–36.

Forman, B. D., and J. C. Wadsworth (1983). "Delivery of rape-related services in CMHCs: an initial study." *Journal of Community Psychology* 11:236–40.

Formby, W. A., and R. T. Sigler (1982). "Crime and victim characteristics on college campuses: A research report." *Victimology: An International Journal* 7:218–23.

Forward, J., R. Canter, and N. Kirsch (1976). "Role enactment and deception methodologies." *American Psychologist* 31:595–604.

Foss, R. D. (1976). "Group decision processes in the simulated trial jury." *Sociometry* 39:305–16.

Freedman, J. L. (1969). "Role-playing: Psychology by consensus." *Journal of Personality and Social Psychology* 13:107–14.

Frerichs, R., C. Aneshensel, and V. Clark (1981). "Prevalence of depression in Los Angeles." *American Journal of Epidemiology* 113:691–99.

Friedan, B. (1963). *The feminine mystique*. New York: Dell Publishing Co.

Frieze, I. H., and D. Bar-Tal (1979). "Attribution theory: past and present." In *New Approaches to Social Problems*, ed. I. H. Frieze, D. Bar-Tal, and J. S. Carroll, pp. 1–20. San Francisco: Jossey-Bass Publishers.

Furby, L., and B. Fischhoff (1986 forthcoming). "Rape self-defense strategies: A review of their effectiveness." *Victimology: An International Journal*.

Galvin, H. R. (1986). "Shielding rape victims in the state and federal courts: A proposal for the second decade." *Minnesota Law Review* 70:763–916.

Galvin, J., and K. Polk (1983). "Attrition in case processing: Is rape unique?" *Journal of Research in Crime and Delinquency* 20:126–56.

Garofalo, J. (1986). "Lifestyles and victimization: an update." In *From crime policy to victim policy,* ed. E. Z. Fattah, pp. 135–55. London: Macmillan Press, Ltd.

Garrett, K. (1982). "Child abuse: problems of definition." In *Measuring social judgments, the factorial survey approach,* ed. P. H. Rossi and S. L. Nock, pp. 177–203. Beverly Hills: Sage Publications.

Gebhard, P. H., J. H. Gagnon, W. B. Pomeroy, and C. V. Christenson (1965). *Sex offenders: An analysis of types.* New York: Harper and Row.

Geis, G. (1977). "Forcible rape: An introduction." In *Forcible Rape: The crime, the victim and the offender,* ed. D. Chappell, R. Geis, and G. Geis, pp. 1–44. New York: Columbia University Press.

George, L. K., and I. Winfield-Laird (1986). *Sexual assault: prevalence and mental health consequences.* Final report submitted to NIMH for supplemental funding to the Duke University Epidemiologic Catchment Area Program.

Giarrusso, R., P. B. Johnson, J. D. Goodchilds, and G. L. Zellman (1979). "Adolescents' cues and signals: sex and assault." Paper presented at the Western Psychological Association Meeting, San Diego.

Gibbons, D. C. (1973). *Society, crime, and criminal careers,* 2nd ed. Englewood Cliffs, N.J.: Prentice-Hall.

Giovannoni, J. M., and R. M. Becerra (1979). *Defining child abuse.* New York: Free Press.

Goodchilds, J. D., and G. L. Zellman (1984). "Sexual signaling and sexual aggression in adolescent relationships." In *Pornography and sexual aggression,* ed. N. M. Malamuth and E. Donnerstein. Orlando: Academic Press.

Goodchilds, J. D., G. L. Zellman, P. B. Johnson, and R. Giarrusso (1979). "Adolescent perceptions of responsibility for 'dating' outcomes." Paper presented as part of the symposium, "The use of power within close relationships," Eastern Psychological Association, Philadelphia.

Goodchilds, J. D., G. L. Zellman, P. B. Johnson, and R. Giarrusso (1988). "Adolescents and their perceptions of sexual interactions." In *Sexual assault II,* ed. A. W. Burgess, pp. 245–70. New York: Garland Publishing, Inc.

Gottesman, S. (1977). "Police attitudes toward rape before and after a training program." *JPN and Mental Health Services,* December, pp. 14–18.

Green, A. W. (1941). "The 'cult of personality' and sexual relations." *Psychiatry* 4:343–48.

Greenberg, J. (1984). "The victim in historical perspective: Some aspects of the English experience." *Journal of Social Issues* 40(1):77–102.

Griffin, B. S., and C. T. Griffin (1981). "Victims in rape confrontation."

Victimology: An International Journal 6:59–75.

Griffin, S. (1977). "Rape: The All-American crime." In *Forcible Rape: The crime, the victim and the offender,* ed. D. Chappell, R. Geis, and G. Geis. New York: Columbia University Press.

Groth, A. N., and H. J. Birnbaum (1985). *Men who rape, the psychology of the offender.* New York: Plenum Press.

Guttmacher, M. S. (1951). *Sex offenses: the problem, causes, and prevention.* New York: W. W. Norton & Co.

Hale, I. M (1778). *The history of the pleas to the crown.* London: Edition published by S. Emlyn, p. 629.

Hall, E. R., and P. J. Flannery (1984). "Prevalence and correlates of sexual assault experiences in adolescents." *Victimology: An International Journal* 9:398–406.

Hammond, J. L. (1973). "Two sources of error in ecological correlations." *American Sociological Review* 38:764–77.

Hanawalt, B. A. (1982). "Women before the law: Females as felons and prey in fourteenth-century England." In *Women and the law, a social historical perspective.* Vol. 1, "Women and the criminal law," ed. D. K. Weisberg. Cambridge, Mass.: Schenkman Publishing Co., Inc.

Hanks, M., and L. Zimet (1984). "Liability for rape." In *Women and the law,* ed. C. H. Lefcourt. New York: Clark Boardman and Company, Ltd.

Hans, V. P., and N. Vidmar (1986). *Judging the jury.* New York: Plenum Publishing.

Hansen, R. D., and V. E. O'Leary (1985). "Sex-determined attributions." In *Women, gender, and social psychology,* ed. V. E. O'Leary, R. K. Unger, and B. S. Wallston. Hillsdale, N.J.: Lawrence Erlbaum Associates, Publishers.

Harris, L. R. (1976). "Toward a consent standard in the law of rape." *University of Chicago Law Review* 43:613–45.

Hauser, R. M., and D. L. Featherman (1977). *The process of stratification.* Orlando: Academic Press.

Heider, F. (1958). *The psychology of interpersonal relations.* New York: Wiley.

Heilbrun, A. B., Jr. (1980). "Presumed motive in the male and female perceptions of rape." *Criminal Justice and Behavior* 7:257–74.

Herman, L. (1977). "What's wrong with the rape reform laws?" *Victimology: An International Journal* 2:8–21.

Herold, E. S., D. Mantle, and O. Zemitis (1979). "A study of sexual offenses against females." *Adolescence* 14:65–72.

Hibey, R. A. (1975). "The trial of a rape case: an advocate's analysis of corroboration, consent, and character." In *Rape victimology,* ed. L. G. Schultz. Springfield, Mass.: Charles C. Thomas.

Hindelang, M. J. (1976). *Criminal victimization in eight American cities: a descriptive analysis of common theft and assault.* Cambridge, Mass.: Ballinger Publishing Company.

———. (1978). "Race and involvement in common law personal crimes." *American Sociological Review* 43:93–109.

———. (1981). "Variations in sex-race-age-specific incidence rates of offending." *American Sociological Review* 46:461–74.

Hindelang, M. J., and B. J. Davis (1977). "Forcible rape in the United States: A statistical profile." In *Forcible rape: The crime, the victim and the offender,* ed. D. Chappell, R. Geis, and G. Geis, pp. 87–114. New York: Columbia University Press.

Hindelang, M. J., and C. Dunn (1974). *Sourcebook of criminal justice statistics.* U.S. Department of Justice, Law, and Enforcement Assistance Administration, National Criminal Information and Statistics Service.

Hochschild, A. R. (1973). "A review of sex role research." In *Changing women in a changing society,* ed. J. Huber, 249–67. Chicago: University of Chicago Press.

Hodge, R. W., P. M. Siegel, and P. H. Rossi (1964). "Occupational prestige in the United States, 1925–63." *American Journal of Sociology* 70:286–302.

Holmes, K. A., and J. E. Williams (1979). "Problems and pitfalls of rape victim research: an analysis of selected methodological, ethical and pragmatic concerns." *Victimology: An International Journal* 4:17–28.

House, J. S. (1977). "The three faces of social psychology." *Sociometry* 40:161–77.

Howitt, D. (1977). "Situational and victims' characteristics in simulated penal judgments." *Psychological Reports* 40:55–58.

Huber, J., ed. (1973). *Changing women in a changing society.* Chicago: University of Chicago Press.

Irish Law Times (1877). "Rape followed by marriage." *Irish Law Times* 11:242.

———. (1885). "Consent to carnal connexion conduced by fraud on female." *Irish Law Times* 19:14–15.

———. (1887). "Evidence in prosecutions for rape." *Irish Law Times* 21:1.

———. (1888). "Evidence as to complaint made by prosecutrix." *Irish Law Times* 22:504–5.

Izzett, R. R., and W. Leginski (1974). "Group discussion and the influence of defendant characteristics in a simulated jury setting." *Journal of Social Psychology* 93:271–79.

Jackson, M. (1966). "Conformity and reference groups in Metropolitan Los Angeles." Ph.D. dissertation, Department of Sociology, University of California, Los Angeles.

Jacobson, M. B. (1981). "Effects of victim's and defendant's physical attractiveness on subject's judgments in a rape case." *Sex Roles* 7:247–55.

Jacobson, M. B., and P. M. Popovich (1983). "Victim attractiveness and perceptions of responsibility in an ambiguous rape case." *Psychology of Women Quarterly* 8:100–104.

James, F. B. (1890). "Declarations in rape cases—Ohio law." *Weekly Law*

Bulletin 23:388–90.

James, R. M. (1959). "Status and competence of jurors." *American Journal of Sociology* 64:563–70.

Janoff-Bulman, R. (1979). "Characterological versus behavioral self-blame: inquiries into depression and rape." *Journal of Personality and Social Psychology* 37:1798–1809.

Janoff-Bulman, R., and I. H. Frieze (1983). "A theoretical perspective for understanding reactions to victimization." *Journal of Social Issues* 39:1–17.

Jasso, G., and P. H. Rossi (1977). "Distributive justice and earned income." *American Sociological Review* 42:639–51.

Jeffords, C. R. (1984). "Prosecutorial discretion in cases of marital rape." *Victimology: An International Journal* 9:415–25.

Jensen, I. W., and B. A. Gutek (1982). "Attributions and assignment of responsibility for sexual harassment." *Journal of Social Issues* 38:121–36.

Joe, V. C., S. J. McGee, and D. Dazey (1977). "Religiousness and devaluation of a rape victim." *Journal of Clinical Psychology* 33:64.

Johnson, A. G. (1980). "On the prevalence of rape in the United States." *Signs: Journal of Women in Culture and Society* 6:136–46.

Johnson, K. A., and P. L. Wasielewski (1982). "A commentary on victimization research and the importance of meaning structures." *Criminology* 20:205–22.

Jones, C., and E. Aronson (1973). "Attribution of fault to a rape victim as a function of respectability of the victim." *Journal of Personality and Social Psychology* 26:415–19.

Jones, E., D. E. Kanouse, H. H. Kelley, R. E. Nisbett, S. Valins, and B. Weiner (1972). *Attribution: perceiving the causes of behavior.* Morristown, N.J.: General Learning Press.

Juhnke, R., C. Vought, T. A. Pyszczynski, F. C. Dane, B. D. Losure, and L. S. Wrightsman (1979). "Effects of presentation mode upon mock jurors' reactions to a trial." *Personality and Social Psychology Bulletin* 5:36–39.

Kahn, A., L. A. Gilbert, R. M. Latta, C. Deutsch, R. Hagen, M. Hill, T. McGaughey, A. H. Ryen, and D. W. Wilson (1977). "Attribution of fault to a rape victim as a function of respectability of the victim: A failure to replicate or extend." *Representative Research in Social Psychology* 8:98–107.

Kahn, A. S., and W. P. Gaeddert (1985). "From theories of equity to theories of justice: the liberating consequences of studying women." In *Women, gender, and social psychology,* ed. V. E. O'Leary, R. K. Unger, and B. S. Wallston. Hillsdale, N.J.: Lawrence Erlbaum Associates, Publishers.

Kalven, H., and H. Zeisel (1966). *The American jury.* Boston: Little Brown.

Kanekar, S., and M. B. Kolsawalla (1980). "Responsibility of a rape victim in relation to her respectability, attractiveness, and provocativeness." *Journal of Social Psychology* 112:153–54.

———. (1981). "Factors affecting responsibility attributed to a rape victim."

Journal of Social Psychology 113:285–86.

Kanekar, S., M. B. Kolsawalla, and A. D'Souza (1981). "Attribution of responsibility to a victim of rape." *British Journal of Social Psychology* 20:165–70.

Kanekar, S., and R. B. Ahluwalia (1981). "Perception of an aggressor as a function of the victim's strength and retaliation." *European Journal of Social Psychology* 7:505–7.

Kanin, E. J. (1957). "Male aggression in dating-courtship relations." *American Journal of Sociology* 63:197–204.

———. (1982). "Female rape fantasies: a victimization study." *Victimology: An International Journal* 7:114–21.

———. (1984). "Date rape: Unofficial criminals and victims." *Victimology: An International Journal* 9:95–108.

———. (1985). "Date rapists: Differential sexual socialization and relative deprivation." *Archives of Sexual Behavior* 14:219–31.

Kanin, E. J., and S. R. Parcell (1977). "Sexual aggression: A second look at the offended female." *Archives of Sexual Behavior* 6:67–76.

Kanouse, D. (1972). "Language, labeling, and attribution." In *Attribution: Perceiving the causes of behavior,* ed. E. E. Jones et al., pp. 121–34. Morristown, N.J.: General Learning Press.

Kaplan, M. F., and L. E. Miller (1978). "Effects of jurors' identification with the victim depend on likelihood of victimization." *Law and Human Behavior* 2:353–61.

Katz, B. L., and M. R. Burt (1988). "Self-blame in recovery from rape." In *Rape and sexual assault II,* ed. A. W. Burgess, 151–68. New York: Garland Publishing, Inc.

Kelley, H. (1972). "Attribution in social interaction." In *Attribution: perceiving the causes of behavior,* ed. E. E. Jones et al., pp. 1–26. Morristown, N.J.: General Learning Press.

———. (1973). "The processes of causal attribution." *American Psychologist* 28:107–28.

Kelman, H. C. (1974). Panel discussion on "New approaches to role-playing as a research methodology." Presented at the American Psychological Association Convention, New Orleans.

Keltner, A. A., and C. L. Doyle (1986). "Alcohol-state-dependent penile tumescence measurements in the assessment of a sexually aggressive man." *Criminal Justice and Behavior* 13:223–36.

Kerr, N. L., and S. T. Kurtz (1977). "Effects of a victim's suffering and respectability on mock juror judgments: further evidence on the just world theory." *Representative Research in Social Psychology* 8:42–56.

Kidd, R. F., and E. F. Chayet (1984). "Why do victims fail to report? The psychology of criminal victimization." *Journal of Social Issues* 40:39–50.

Kidder, L. H., and E. S. Cohn (1979). "Public views of crime and crime prevention." In *New approaches to social problems,* ed. I. H. Frieze, D. Bar-Tal, and J. S. Carroll, pp. 237–64. San Francisco: Jossey-Bass Publishers.

Kilpatrick, D. G., L. J. Veronen, and C. L. Best (1985). "Factors predicting psychological distress among rape victims." In *Trauma and its wake,* ed. C. R. Figley. New York: Brunner/Mazel.

Kilpatrick, D. G., L. J. Veronen, and P. A. Resick (1982). "Psychological sequelae to rape: assessment and treatment strategies." In *Behavioral medicine: assessment and treatment strategies,* ed. D. M. Doleys, R. L. Meredith, and A. R. Ciminero, 473–97. New York: Plenum.

Kilpatrick, D. G., C. L. Best., L. J. Veronen, A. E. Amick, L. A. Villeponteaux, and G. A. Ruft (1985). "Mental health correlates of criminal victimization: a random community survey." *Journal of Consulting and Clinical Psychology* 53:866–73.

Kilpatrick, D. G., P. A. Resick, and L. J. Veronen (1981). "Effects of a rape experience: a longitudinal study." *Journal of Social Issues* 37:105–22.

Kirkpatrick, C., and E. J. Kanin (1957). "Male sexual aggression on a university campus." *American Sociological Review* 22:52–58.

———. (1985). "The hidden rape victim: personality, attitudinal, and situational characteristics." *Psychology of Women Quarterly* 9:193–212.

Kish, L. A. (1949). "A procedure for objective respondent selection within the household." *Journal of the American Statistical Association* 44:380–87.

Kittel, R. (1982). "Rape in thirteenth-century England: a study of the common-law courts." In *Women and the Law, a Social Historical Perspective.* Volume II: *Property, Family and the Legal Profession,* ed. D. K. Weisberg, pp. 101–15. Cambridge, Mass.: Schenkman Publishing Company.

Klein, D. (1981). "Violence against women: some considerations regarding its causes and its elimination." *Crime and Delinquency* 27:64–80.

Klemmack, S. H., and D. L. Klemmack (1976). "The social definition of rape." In *Sexual assault,* ed. M. J. Walker and S. L. Brodsky, pp. 135–47. Lexington, Mass.: D. C. Heath and Co.

Knight, R. A., R. Rosenberg, and B. Schneider (1985). "Classification of sexual offenders: Perspectives, methods and validation." In *Rape and sexual assault,* ed. A. W. Burgess, pp. 222–93. New York: Garland Publishing, Inc.

Kopp, S. P. (1962). "The character structure of sex offenders." *American Journal of Psychotherapy* 16:64–70.

Koss, M. P. (1983). "The scope of rape: implications for the clinical treatment of victims." *The Clinical Psychologist* 36(4):88–91.

———. (1988). "Hidden rape: sexual aggression and victimization in a national sample in higher education." In *Rape and sexual assault II,* ed. A. W. Burgess, pp. 3–25. New York: Garland Publishing, Inc.

Koss, M. P., and C. J. Oros (1982). "Sexual experiences survey: a research instrument investigating sexual aggression and victimization." *Journal of Consulting and Clinical Psychology* 50:455–57.

Koss, M. P., and C. A. Gidycz (1985). "Sexual experiences survey: reliability and validity." *Journal of Consulting and Clinical Psychology* 53:422–23.

Koss, M. P., C. A. Gidycz, and N. Wisniewski (1987). "The scope of rape: incidence and prevalence of sexual aggression and victimization in a national sample of higher education students." *Journal of Consulting and Clinical Psychology* 55:162–70.

Koss, M. P., and K. E. Leonard (1984). "Sexually aggressive men: empirical findings and theoretical implications." In *Pornography and sexual aggression,* ed. N. M. Malamuth and E. Donnerstein. Orlando: Academic Press, Inc.

Koss, M. P., K. E. Leonard, D. A. Beezley, and C. J. Oros (1985). "Nonstranger sexual aggression: A discriminant analysis of the psychological characteristics of undetected offenders." *Sex Roles* 12:981–92.

Krulewitz, J. E. (1981). "Sex differences in evaluations of female and male victims' responses to assault." *Journal of Applied Social Psychology* 11:460–74.

Krulewitz, J. E., and E. J. Payne (1978). "Attributions about rape: effects of rapist force, observer sex and sex role attitudes." *Journal of Applied Social Psychology* 8:291–305.

Krulewitz, J. E., and J. E. Nash (1979). "Effects of rape victim resistance, assault outcome, and sex of observer on attributions about rape." *Journal of Personality and Social Psychology* 47:557–74.

LaFree, G. D. (1980). "The effect of sexual stratification by race on official reactions to rape." *American Sociological Review* 45:842–54.

———. (1982). "Male power and female victimization: toward a theory of interracial rape." *American Journal of Sociology* 88:311–28.

LaFree, G. D., B. F. Reskin, and C. A. Visher (1985). "Jurors' responses to victims' behavior and legal issues in sexual assault trials." *Social Problems* 32:389–407.

Landers, Ann (1987). *Los Angeles Times*, April 13 and July 2.

Landy, D., and E. Aronson (1969). "The influence of the character of the criminal and his victim on the decisions of simulated jurors." *Journal of Experimental Social Psychology* 5:141–52.

Largen, M. A. (1976). "History of women's movement. Changing attitudes, laws, and treatment toward rape victims." In *Sexual assault,* ed. M. J. Walker and S. L. Brodsky, pp. 69–73. Lexington, Mass.: D. C. Heath and Company.

———. (1985). "The anti-rape movement: past and present." In *Rape and sexual assault,* ed. A. W. Burgess, pp. 1–13. New York: Garland Publishing, Inc.

L'Armand, K., and A. Pepitone (1982). "Judgments of rape: a study of victim-rapist relationship and victim sexual history." *Personality and Social Psychology Bulletin* 8:134–39.

Laws, J. L., and P. Schwartz (1977). *Sexual scripts: the social construction of female sexuality.* Hinsdale, Ill.: Dryden.

Law Times (1866). "The charge of rape." *Law Times,* August 4, p. 693.

LeDoux, J. C., and R. R. Hazelwood (1985). "Police attitudes and beliefs toward rape." *Journal of Police Science and Administration* 13:211–20.

Ledray, L. E. (1988). "Responding to the needs of rape victims, research findings." In *Rape and sexual assault II,* ed. A. W. Burgess, pp. 169–90. New York: Garland Publishing, Inc.

Legal News (1884). "Consent given by error—what constitutes rape." *Legal News* 8:29–30.

LeGrand, C. E. (1973). "Rape and rape laws: sexism in society and law." *California Law Review* 61:919–41.

LeGrand, C. E., and F. Leonard (1979). "Civil suits for sexual assault: compensating rape victims." *Women's Law Forum* 8:479–513.

Lenehan, C. E., and P. O'Neal (1981). "Reactance as determinants of a judgment in a mock jury experiment." *Journal of Applied Social Psychology* 11:231–39.

Lerner, M. J. (1965). "Evaluation of a performance as a function of performer's reward and attractiveness." *Journal of Personality and Social Psychology* 1:355–60.

Letwin, L. (1980). "'Unchaste character,' ideology, and the California rape evidence laws." *Southern California Law Review* 54:35–89.

Levine, R. A. (1959). "Gusii sex offenses: a study in social control." *American Anthropologist* 61:965–90.

Lindemann, B. S. (1984). "To ravish and carnally know: rape in eighteenth-century Massachusetts." *Signs: Journal of Women in Culture and Society* 10:63–81.

Lizotte, A. J. (1985). "The uniqueness of rape: reporting assaultive violence to the police." *Crime and Delinquency* 31:169–90.

Loh, W. D. (1981). "What has reform of rape legislation wrought?" *The Journal of Social Issues* 37:28–52.

Luginbuhl, J., and C. Mullin (1981). "Rape and responsibility: How and how much is the victim blamed?" *Sex Roles* 7:547–59.

Lystad, M. H. (1985). "The National Center for the Prevention and Control of Rape." In *Rape and sexual assault,* ed. A. W. Burgess, 14–34. New York: Garland Publishing, Inc.

Malamuth, N. M. (1983). "Factors associated with rape as predictors of laboratory aggression against women." *Journal of Personality and Social Psychology* 45:432–42.

———. (1985). "The mass media and aggression against women: Research findings and prevention." In *Rape and sexual assault,* ed. A. W. Burgess, pp. 392–412. New York: Garland Publishing, Inc.

———. (1986). "Predictors of naturalistic sexual aggression." *Journal of Personality and Social Psychology* 50:5–20.

Malamuth, N. M., and J. V. P. Check (1980a). "Penile tumescence and perceptual responses to rape as a function of victim's perceived reaction." *Journal of Applied Social Psychology* 10:528–47.

———. (1980b). "Sexual arousal to rape and consenting depictions: the importance of the woman's arousal." *Journal of Abnormal Psychology* 89:763–6.

———. (1981). "The effects of mass media exposure on acceptance of violence against women: a field experiment." *Journal of Research in Personality* 15:436–46.

———. (1983). "Sexual arousal to rape depictions: individual differences." *Journal of Abnormal Psychology* 92:55–67.

———. (1985). "The effects of aggressive pornography on beliefs in rape myths: individual differences." *Journal of Research in Personality* 19:299–320.

Malamuth, N. M., J. V. P. Check, and J. Briere (1986). "Sexual arousal in response to aggression: Ideological, aggressive, and sexual correlates." *Journal of Personality and Social Psychology* 50:330–40.

Malamuth, N. M., and E. Donnerstein (1984). *Pornography and sexual aggression*. Orlando: Academic Press, Inc.

Manis, M., and M. B. Platt (1979). "Order effects in the integration of verbal descriptions." *Personality and Social Psychology Bulletin* 5:57–60.

Marsh, J. C., A. Geist, and N. Caplan (1982). *Rape and the limits of law reform*. Boston: Auburn House.

McArthur, L. A. (1972). "The how and what of why: some determinants and consequences of causal attribution." *Journal of Personality and Social Psychology* 22:171–93.

McGillis, D. (1979). "Biases and jury decision making." In *New approaches to social problems*, ed. I. H. Frieze, D. Bar-Tal, and J. S. Carroll, pp. 265–84. San Francisco: Jossey-Bass Publishers.

McKennel, A. C. (1977). "Attitude scale construction." In *Exploring data structure—the analysis of survey data*, vol. 1, ed. C. A. O'Muircheataugh and C. Payne. Somerset, N.J.: John Wiley and Sons.

Mellinger, G. D., C. L. Huffine, and M. B. Balter (1982). "Assessing comprehension in a survey of public reactions to complex issues." *Public Opinion Quarterly* 46:97–109.

Merton, R. K. (1968). *Social theory and social structure*. New York: The Free Press.

Miller, A. G. (1972). "Role-playing: an alternative to deception? A review of the evidence." *American Psychologist* 27:623–36.

Millett, K. (1970). *Sexual Politics*. New York: Doubleday.

Mixon, D. (1971). "Behavior analysis: Treating subjects as actors rather than organisms." *Journal for Theory of Social Behavior* 1:19–31.

Monthly Western Jurist (1874). "The law of rape—chloroform in rape cases." *Monthly Western Jurist* 1:291–309.

Muehlenhard, C. L. (1988). "Misinterpreted dating behaviors and the risk of date rape." *Journal of Social and Clinical Psychology*, 6:20–37.

Muehlenhard, C. L., D. E. Friedman, and C. M. Thomas (1985). "Is date rape justifiable? The effects of dating activity, who initiated, who paid, and men's attitudes toward women." *Psychology of Women Quarterly* 9:297–310.

Muehlenhard, C. L., and M. A. Linton (1987). "Date rape and sexual aggression in dating situations: incidence and risk factors." *Journal of Counseling Psychology* 34:186–96.

Muehlenhard, C. L., and T. J. Scardino (1985). "What will he think? Men's impressions of women who initiate dates and achieve academically." *Journal of Counseling Psychology* 32:560–69.

Murphy, K. (1986). "Action taken against judge in rape case." *Los Angeles Times,* October 30.

Myers, M. A. (1980). "Social contexts and attributions of criminal responsibility." *Social Psychology Quarterly* 43:405–19.

Myers, M. A., and G. D. LaFree (1982). "Sexual assault and its prosecution: a comparison with other crimes." *Journal of Criminal Law and Criminology* 73:1282–1305.

Myers, M. B., D. I. Templer, and R. Brown (1984). "Coping ability of women who become victims of rape." *Journal of Consulting and Clinical Psychology* 52:73–78.

National Crime Panel Surveys (1975). *Criminal victimization surveys in 13 American cities.* Washington, D.C.: U.S. Department of Justice, Law Enforcement Assistance Administration.

National Institute of Law Enforcement and Criminal Justice (1977). *Forcible rape, medical and legal information.* Washington, D.C.: U.S. Department of Justice, Law Enforcement Assistance Administration.

———. (1977). *Forcible rape, a national survey of the response by police. Police volume I.* Washington, D.C.: U.S. Department of Justice, Law Enforcement Assistance Administration.

———. (1977). *Forcible rape, a national survey of the response by prosecutors. Prosecutors' volume I.* Washington, D.C.: U.S. Department of Justice, Law Enforcement Assistance Administration.

———. (1978). *Forcible rape, final project report.* Washington, D.C.: U.S. Department of Justice, Law Enforcement Assistance Administration.

———. (1978). *Forcible rape, final report.* Washington, D.C.: U.S. Department of Justice, Law Enforcement Assistance Administration.

———. (1978). *Forcible rape, a manual for filing and trial prosecutors. Prosecutors' volume II.* Washington, D.C.: U.S. Department of Justice, Law Enforcement Assistance Administration.

———. (1978). *Forcible rape, a manual for patrol officers. Police volume II.* Washington, D.C.: U.S. Department of Justice, Law Enforcement Assistance Administration.

———. (1978). *Forcible rape, a manual for sex crime investigators. Police volume III.* Washington, D.C.: U.S. Department of Justice, Law Enforcement

Assistance Administration.

———. (1978). *Forcible rape, police administrative and policy issues. Police volume IV*. Washington, D.C.: U.S. Department of Justice, Law Enforcement Assistance Administration.

———. (1978). *Forcible rape, prosecutor administrative and policy issues. Prosecutors' volume III*. Washington, D.C.: U.S. Department of Justice, Law Enforcement Assistance Administration.

Nemeth, C. P. (1984). "Legal emancipation for the victim of rape." *Human Rights* 11:30–35.

Newcomb, T. M. (1966). Foreword to *Role theory: concepts and research*, ed. B. J. Biddle and E. G. Thomas, p. vi. New York: John Wiley and Sons.

Nisbett, R. E., C. Caputo, P. Legant, and J. Marecek (1973). "Behavior as seen by the actor and as seen by the observer." *Journal of Personality and Social Psychology* 27:154–64.

Nock, S. L., and P. H. Rossi (1978). "Ascription versus achievement in the attribution of family social status." *American Journal of Sociology* 84:565–90.

Nunnally, J. C. (1967). *Psychometric theory*. New York: McGraw-Hill.

O'Brien, R. M. (1983). *Crime and Victimization Data*. Beverly Hills: Sage Publications.

O'Leary, V. E., R. K. Unger, and B. S. Wallston, eds. (1985). *Women, gender and social psychology*. Hillsdale, N.J.: Lawrence Erlbaum Associates, Publishers.

Oppenheimer, V. K. (1968). "The sex-labeling of jobs." *Industrial Relations* 7:219–34.

Oros, C. J., and D. Elman (1979). "Impact of judge's instructions upon jurors' decisions: the 'cautionary charge' in rape trials." *Representative Research in Social Psychology* 10:28–36.

Partington, D. H. (1965). "The incidence of the death penalty for rape in Virginia." *Washington and Lee Law Review* 22:43–75.

Paulsen, K. (1979). "Attribution of fault to a rape victim as a function of locus of control." *Journal of Social Psychology* 107:131–32.

Pawloski, B. M. (1983). "Forcible rape: an updated bibliography." *The Journal of Criminal Law and Criminology* 74:601–25.

Peterson, C., and M. E. P. Seligman (1983). "Learned helplessness and victimization." *Journal of Social Issues* 2:103–16.

Polk, K. (1985). "Rape reform and criminal justice processing." *Crime and Delinquency* 31:191–205.

Popiel, D. A., and E. C. Susskind (1985). "The impact of rape: social support as a moderator of stress." *American Journal of Community Psychology* 13:645–76.

Prentky, R. A., and R. A. Knight (1986). "Impulsivity in the lifestyle and criminal behavior of sexual offenders." *Criminal Justice and Behavior* 13:141–64.

Prytula, R. E., H. D. Whiteside, and P. L. Davidson (1975). "Police experience and attribution of personal responsibility." *Psychological Reports* 37:1346.

Pugh, M. D. (1983). "Contributory fault and rape convictions: loglinear models for blaming the victim." *Social Psychology Quarterly* 46:233–42.

Quinsey, V. L., and D. Upfold (1985). "Rape completion and victim injury as a function of female resistance strategy." *Canadian Journal of Behavioral Science* 17:40–50.

Quinsey, V. L., T. C. Chaplin, and D. Upfold (1984). "Sexual arousal to nonsexual violence and sadomasochistic themes among rapist and non-sex-offenders." *Journal of Consulting and Clinical Psychology* 52:651–57.

Rabkin, J. G. (1979). "The epidemiology of forcible rape." *American Journal of Orthopsychiatry* 49:634–47.

Rada, R. T., ed. (1978). *Clinical aspects of the rapist.* New York: Grune and Stratton.

Rasch, R. L. (1974). "A paper-and-pencil simulation study of the impact of the complex political-military context on the operation of third area deterrence." Ph.D. dissertation, University of California, Los Angeles.

Reed, D., and M. S. Weinberg (1984). "Premarital coitus: developing and established sexual scripts." *Social Psychology Quarterly* 47:129–38.

Reilly, T., S. Carpenter, V. Dull, and K. Bartlett (1982). "The factorial survey technique: An approach to defining sexual harassment on campus." *Journal of Social Issues* 38:99–110.

Reiss, A. J., Jr. (1986a). "Policy implications of crime victim surveys." In *From crime policy to victim policy,* ed. E. Z. Fattah, pp. 246–60. London: Macmillan Press Ltd.

———. (1986b). "Official and survey crime statistics." In *From crime policy to victim policy,* ed. E. Z. Fattah, 53–79. London: Macmillan Press Ltd.

Reynolds, P. D., and D. A. Blyth (1975). "Sources of variation affecting relationship between police and survey-based estimates of crime rates." In *Victimology: A new focus, crimes, victims, and justice, vol.* 3, ed. I. Drapkin and E. Viano, pp. 201–25. Lexington, Mass.: D. C. Heath and Company.

Rose, A. M., and A. E. Prell (1955). "Does the punishment fit the crime? A study in social valuation." *American Journal of Sociology* 61:247–59.

Rose, V. M. (1977). "Rape as a social problem: a by-product of the feminist movement." *Social Problems* 25:75–89.

Rosenblum, K. E. (1986). "The conflict between and within genders: an appraisal of contemporary American femininity and masculinity." *Sociological Inquiry* 56:93–104.

Rossi, P. H., W. A. Sampson, C. E. Bose, G. Jasso, and J. Passell (1974). "Measuring household social standing." *Social Science Research* 3:169–90.

Rossi, P. H., E. Waite, C. E. Bose, and R. E. Berk (1974). "The seriousness of crimes: normative structure and individual differences." *American Sociological Review* 39:224–37.

Rossi, P. H., and S. L. Nock, eds. (1982). *Measuring Social Judgments*. Beverly Hills: Sage Publications.

Rotter, J. B. (1966). "Generalized expectancies for internal versus external control of reinforcement." *Psychological Monographs* 80 (1) (whole number 609).

Ruch, L. O., S. M. Chandler, and R. A. Harter (1980). "Life change and rape impact." *Journal of Health and Social Behavior* 21:248–60.

Ruch, L. O., and S. M. Chandler (1983). "Sexual assault trauma during the acute phase: An exploratory model and multivariate analysis." *Journal of Health and Social Behavior* 24:174–85.

Ruch, L. O., and M. Hennessy (1982). "Sexual assault: victim and attack dimensions." *Victimology: An International Journal* 7:94–105.

Rumsey, M. G. (1976). "Effects of defendant background and remorse on sentencing judgments." *Journal of Applied Social Psychology* 6:64–68.

Rumsey, M. G., and J. M. Rumsey (1977). "A case of rape: sentencing judgments of males and females." *Psychological Reports* 41:459–65.

Russell, D. E. H. (1975). *The politics of rape: the victims' perspective*. New York: Stein and Day Publishers.

———. (1982). "The prevalence and incidence of forcible rape and attempted rape of females." *Victimology: An International Journal* 7:81–93.

———. (1984). *Sexual exploitation: rape, child sexual abuse, and workplace harassment*. Beverly Hills: Sage Publications.

Russell, D. E. H., and N. Howell (1983). "The prevalence of rape in the United States revisited." *Signs: Journal of Women in Culture and Society* 8:688–95.

Sales, E., M. Baum, and B. Shore (1984). "Victim readjustment following assault." *Journal of Social Issues* 40:117–36.

Sampson, W., and P. H. Rossi (1976). "Race and family social standing." *American Sociological Review* 40:201–14.

Sanday, P. R. (1981). "The socio-cultural context of rape: a cross-cultural study." *Journal of Social Issues* 37:5–27.

Sanders, W. (1980). *Rape and woman's identity*. Beverly Hills: Sage Publications.

Sanford, J., L. Cryer, B. L. Cristensen, and K. L. Mattox (1979). "Patterns of reported rape in a tri-ethnic population: Houston, Texas, 1974–75." *American Journal of Public Health* 69:480–84.

Sasko, H., and D. Sesek (1975). "Rape reform legislation: is it the solution?" *Cleveland State Law Review* 24:463–503.

Scheffe, H. (1959). "The effects of departures from the underlying assumptions." In *The analysis of variance*, pp. 331–69. New York: John Wiley and Sons.

Schwartz, J., H. Williams, and F. Pepitone-Rockwell (1981). "Construction of a rape awareness scale." *Victimology: An International Journal* 6:110–19.

Schwendinger, J. R., and H. Schwendinger (1983). *Rape and inequality*. Beverly Hills: Sage Publications.

Scott, W. A. (1968). "Attitude measurement." In *The handbook of social psychology,* 2nd ed., ed. G. Lindsey and E. Aronson, pp. 204–66.

Scroggs, J. R. (1976). "Penalties for rape as a function of victim provocativeness, damage, and resistance." *Journal of Applied Social Psychology* 6:360–68.

Scully, D., and J. Marolla (1984). "Convicted rapists' vocabulary of motive: excuses and justifications." *Social Problems* 31:530–44.

——. (1985). "'Riding the Bull at Gilley's': convicted rapists describe the rewards of rape." *Social Problems* 32:251–63.

Scully, D., and P. Bart (1973). "A funny thing happened on the way to the orifice: women in gynecology textbooks." In *Changing women in a changing society,* ed. J. Huber, pp. 283–88. Chicago: University of Chicago Press.

Selby, J., L. Calhoun, and T. A. Brock (1977). "Sex differences in the social perception of rape victims." *Personality and Social Psychology Bulletin* 3:412–15.

Seligman, C., J. Brickman, and D. Koulack (1977). "Rape and physical attractiveness: assigning responsibility to victims." *Journal of Personality* 45:554–63.

Selkin, J. (1978). "Protecting personal space: victim and resister reactions to assaultive rape." *Journal of Community Psychology* 6:263–68.

Shotland, R. L., and L. Goodstein (1983). "Just because she doesn't want to doesn't mean it's rape: An experimentally based causal model of perception of rape in a dating situation." *Social Psychology Quarterly* 46:220–32.

Siegel, P., and R. Hodge (1975). *The prestige of occupations.* New York: Academic Press.

Sigelman, C. K., C. J. Berry, and K. A. Wiles (1984). "Violence in college students' dating relationships." *Journal of Applied Social Psychology* 14:530–48.

Simpson, A. E. (1986). "The 'Blackmail Myth' and the prosecution of rape and its attempt in eighteenth-century London: the creation of a legal tradition." *Journal of Criminal Law and Criminology* 77:101–50.

Skogan, W. G. (1986). "Methodological issues in the study of victimization." In *From crime policy to victim policy,* ed. E. Z. Fattah, pp. 80–116. London: Macmillan Press Ltd.

Smith, M. D., and N. Bennett (1985). "Poverty, inequality, and theories of forcible rape." *Crime and Delinquency* 31:295–305.

Smith, R. E., J. P. Keating, R. K. Hester, and H. E. Mitchell (1976). "Role and justice considerations in the attribution of responsibility to a rape victim." *Journal of Research in Personality* 10:346–57.

Smithyman, S. D. (1979). "Characteristics of 'undetected' rapists." In *Perspectives on Victimology,* ed. W. H. Parsonage, pp. 99–120. Beverly Hills: Sage Publications.

Sorenson, S. B., J. A. Stein, J. M. Siegel, J. M. Golding, and M. A. Burnam (1987). "The prevalence of adult sexual assault: The Los Angeles Epidemiologic Catchment Area Project." *American Journal of Epidemiology*

126:1154–64.

Spence, J. T., and L. L. Sawin (1985). "Images of masculinity and femininity: a reconceptualization." In *Women, gender, and social psychology,* eds. V. E. O'Leary, R. K. Unger, and B. S. Wallston. Hillsdale, N.J.: Lawrence Erlbaum Associates, Publishers.

Spence, J. T., and R. L. Helmreich (1978). *Masculinity and femininity: their psychological dimensions, correlates, and antecedents.* Austin: University of Texas Press.

Star, S. A. (1952). "Confidential forecast of the results of the survey: Popular thinking in the field of mental health." In *Contemporary attitudes toward mental illness,* survey no. 272, eds. G. Crocetti, H. Spiro, and I. Siassi. Chicago: National Opinion Research Center, University of Chicago.

———. (1952). "What the public thinks about mental health and mental illness." Paper presented at the annual meeting of the National Association for Mental Health.

———. (1955). *The public's ideas about mental illness.* Chicago: National Opinion Research Center, University of Chicago.

———. (1957). "The place of psychiatry in popular thinking." Paper presented at the Annual Association for the Advancement of Public Opinion Research Meeting, Washington, D.C.

———. (n.d.) "Popular views of psychiatry." Unpublished.

Storms, M. D. (1973). "Videotape and the attribution process: reversing actors' and observers' points of view." *Journal of Personality and Social Psychology* 27:165–75.

Strodtbeck, F. L., R. M. James, and C. Hawkins (1957). "Social status in jury deliberations." *American Sociological Review* 22:713–19.

Stryker, S. (1977). "Developments in 'two social psychologies': toward an appreciation of mutual relevance." *Sociometry* 40:145–60.

———. (1980). *Symbolic Interactionism: a social structural version.* Menlo Park: Benjamin/Cummings.

———. (1987). "The vitalization of symbolic interactionism." *Social Psychology Quarterly* 50:83–94.

Svalastoga, K. (1962). "Rape and social structure." *Pacific Sociological Review* Spring:48–53.

Tanford, J. A., and A. J. Bocchino (1980). "Rape victim shield laws and the sixth amendment." *University of Pennsylvania Law Review* 128:544–602.

Thornton, B. (1977). "Effect of rape victim's attractiveness in a jury simulation." *Personality and Social Psychology Bulletin* 3:666–69.

Thornton, B., and R. M. Ryckman (1983). "The influence of a rape victim's physical attractiveness on observers' attributions of responsibility." *Human Relations* 36:549–62.

Tieger, T. (1981). "Self-rated likelihood of raping and the social perception of rape." *Journal of Research in Personality* 15:147–58.

Tong, R. (1984). *Women, sex and the law*. Totowa: Roman and Allanheld.

Tsegaye-Spates, C. R. (1985). "The mental health needs of victims." In *Rape and sexual assault*, ed. A. W. Burgess, pp. 35–45. New York: Garland Publishing, Inc.

Turner, R. H. (1976). "The real self: from institution to impulse." *American Journal of Sociology* 81:989–1016.

———. (1978). "The role and the person." *American Journal of Sociology* 84:1–23.

Turner, R. H., and N. Shosid (1976). "Ambiguity and interchangeability in role attribution: the effect of alter's response." *American Sociological Review* 41:993–1006.

Tyler, T. R. (1978). "Drawing inferences from experience: The effects of crime victimization experiences upon crime-related attitudes and behaviors." Ph.D. dissertation, Department of Psychology, University of California, Los Angeles.

———. (1984). "Assessing the risk of crime victimization: the integration of personal victimization experience and socially transmitted information." *Journal of Social Issues* 40:27–38.

Ugweugbu, D. (1979). "Racial and evidential factors in juror attribution of legal responsibility." *Journal of Experimental Social Psychology* 15:133–46.

United States Department of Justice (1979a). *How to protect yourself against sexual assault*. Washington, D.C.: Office of Justice Assistance, Research and Statistics.

———. (1979b). *Uniform Crime Reports for the United States*. Washington, D.C.: U.S. Dept. of Justice.

———. (1980). *Uniform Crime Reports for the United States*. Washington, D.C.: U.S. Dept. of Justice.

———. (1981a). *Report to the nation on crime and justice. The data*. Washington, D.C.: Bureau of Justice Statistics.

———. (1981b). *Uniform Crime Reports for the United States*. Washington, D.C.: U.S. Dept. of Justice.

———. (1982a). *Report to the nation on crime and justice. The data*. Washington, D.C.: Bureau of Justice Statistics.

———. (1982b). *Uniform Crime Reports for the United States*. Washington, D.C.: U.S. Dept. of Justice.

———. (1983a). *Report to the nation on crime and justice. The data*. Washington, D.C.: Bureau of Justice Statistics.

———. (1983b). *Uniform Crime Reports for the United States*. Washington, D.C.: U.S. Dept. of Justice.

———. (1984a). *Report to the nation on crime and justice. The data*. Bureau of Justice Statistics.

———. (1984b). *Uniform Crime Reports for the United States*. Washington, D.C.: U.S. Dept. of Justice.

University of Pennsylvania Law Review (1968). "Police discretion and the judgment that a crime has been committed—rape in Philadelphia." *University of Pennsylvania Law Review* 117:277–322.

———. (1970). "The corroboration rule and crimes accompanying a rape." *University of Pennsylvania Law Review* 118:458–72.

Valparaiso University Law Review (1976). "If she consented once, she consented again—a legal fallacy in forcible rape cases." *Valparaiso University Law Review* 10:127–67.

Veronen, L. J., and D. G. Kilpatrick (1983). "Stress management for rape victims." In *Stress reduction and prevention,* ed. D. Meichenbaum and M. E. Jaremko, pp. 341–74. New York: Plenum Press.

Veronen, L. J., D. G. Kilpatrick, and P. A. Resick (1979). "Treating fear and anxiety in rape victims: Implications for the criminal justice system." In *Perspectives on victimology,* ed. W. H. Parsonage, pp. 148–59. Beverly Hills: Sage Publications.

Wallston, B. S., and K. E. Grady (1985). "Integrating the feminist critique and the crisis in social psychology: another look at research methods." In *Women, Gender, and Social Psychology,* ed. V. E. O'Leary, R. K. Unger, and B. S. Wallston. Hillsdale, N.J.: Lawrence Erlbaum Associates, Publishers.

Walster, E. (1966). "Assignment of responsibility for an accident." *Journal of Personality and Social Psychology* 3:73–79.

Webb, E. J., D. T. Campbell, R. D. Schwartz, and L. Sechrest (1966). *Unobtrusive measures: nonreactive research in the social sciences*. Chicago: Rand McNally and Company.

Weber-Burdin, E., and P. H. Rossi (1982). "Defining sexual harassment on campus: A replication and extension." *Journal of Social Issues* 38:111–20.

Weekly Law Bulletin (1883). "Observations on the law of rape in Ohio." *Weekly Law Bulletin* 10:222–24.

———. (1883). "Unconsciousness in rape." *Weekly Law Bulletin* 10:317–19.

Weinberg, M. S., and C. J. Williams (1980). "Sexual embourgeoisment? Social class and sexual activity: 1938–70." *American Sociological Review* 45:33–48.

Weiner, B., I. Frieze, A. Kukla, L. Reed, S. Rest, and R. M. Rosenbaum (1972). "Perceiving the causes of success and failure." In *Attribution: perceiving the causes of behavior,* ed. E. E. Jones et al., pp. 95–120. Morristown, N.J.: General Learning Press.

Weis, K., and S. Borges (1973). "Victimology and rape: the case of the legitimate victim." *Issues in Criminology* 8:71–115.

Western Jurist (1874). "The law of rape—chloroform in rape cases." *The Monthly Western Jurist* 1:289–309.

West's California Codes (1983). Compact edition. St. Paul: West Publishing Company.

White, W. S. (1976). "Disproportionality and the death penalty: death as a punishment for rape." *University of Pittsburgh Law Review* 38:145–84.

Whyte, W. F. (1943). "A slum sex code." *American Journal of Sociology* 49:24–31.

Williams, J. E., and K. A. Holmes (1978). *Questionnaire used in public attitude survey*. Department of Sociology, Trinity University, San Antonio.

———. (1979). *Rape: The public view—the personal experience*. Final Project, Report for Grant No. ROIMH 27928, National Institute of Mental Health.

———. (1981). *The second assault: rape and public attitudes*. Westport, Conn.: Greenwood Press.

Williams, L. S. (1984). "The classic rape: when do victims report?" *Social Problems* 31:459–67.

Wolfgang, M. E., and F. Ferracuti (1967). *The subculture of violence: towards an integrated theory in criminology*. London: Tavistock-Social Science Paperbacks.

Wolfgang, M. E., and M. Riedel (1975). "Race, rape, and the death penalty in Georgia." *American Journal of Orthopsychiatry* 45:658–68.

Wortman, C. B. (1983). "Coping with victimization: conclusions and implications for future research." *Journal of Social Issues* 39:195–221.

Wyatt, G. E. (1985). "The sexual abuse of Afro-American and White-American women in childhood." *Child Abuse and Neglect* 9:507–19.

Wyatt, G. E., and S. D. Peters (1986). "Issues in the definition of child sexual abuse." *Prevalence Research* 10:231–40.

Yarmey, A. D. (1985a). "Attitudes and sentencing for sexual assault as a function of age and sex of subjects." *Canadian Journal on Aging* 4:20–28.

———. (1985b). "Older and younger adults' attributions of responsibility toward rape victims and rapists." *Canadian Journal of Behavioral Science* 17:327–38.

Yinger, M. (1960). "Contraculture and subculture." *American Sociological Review* 25:625–35.

Yllo, K., and D. Finkelhor (1985). "Marital rape." In *Rape and Sexual Assault*, ed. A. W. Burgess, pp. 146–58. New York: Garland Publishing, Inc.

Younger, I. (1971). "The requirement of corroboration in prosecutions for sex offenses in New York." *Fordham Law Review* 40:263–78.

Zellman, G. L., J. D. Goodchilds, P. B. Johnson, and R. Giarrusso (1981). "Teenagers' application of the label 'rape' to nonconsensual sex between acquaintances." Paper presented at the meeting of the American Psychological Association, Los Angeles.

Zellman, G. L., P. B. Johnson, R. Giarrusso, and J. D. Goodchilds (1979). "Expectations for dating relationships: consensus and conflict between the sexes." Paper presented at the meeting of the American Psychological Association, New York.

Index

3/8/90

Linda Brookover Bourque is Professor of Public Health at the University of California, Los Angeles, and previously taught in the Department of Sociology at California State University, Los Angeles. She received her B.A. in history from Indiana University and her M.A. and Ph.D. in sociology from Duke University. Dr. Bourque is the author of numerous papers in sociology and public health.

DATE		

Baldwin Public Library

Baldwin, L.I., New York

Telephone: BA 3-6228

14
DAY
BOOK

This book may be kept
for 14 days only
It cannot be renewed

BA